W9-ACD-087

TALES OF HONOR

"ON BASILISK STATION"

Based on the novels written and created by David Weber.

EVERGREEN
STUDIOS

published by
Top Cow Productions, Inc.
Los Angeles

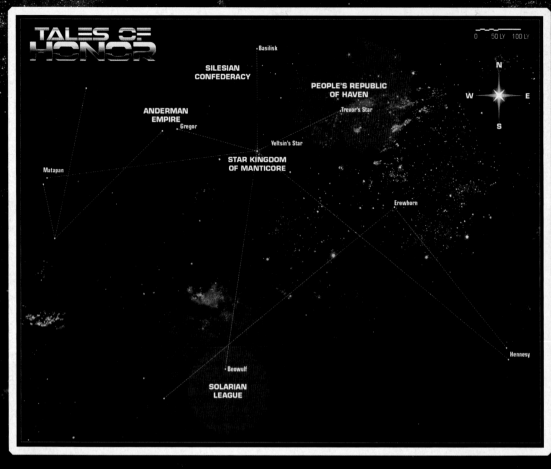

TALES OF HONOR

0   50 LY   100 LY

- Basilisk

SILESIAN
CONFEDERACY

PEOPLE'S REPUBLIC
OF HAVEN

· Trevor's Star

ANDERMAN
EMPIRE
· Gregor

Yeltsin's Star

· STAR KINGDOM
OF MANTICORE ·

Matapan

Erewhorn

· Beowulf

SOLARIAN
LEAGUE

Hennesy

"ON BASILISK STATION"

MATT HAWKINS WRITER

JUNG-GEUN YOON & SANG-IL JEONG ARTISTS

TROY PETERI LETTERER

Special Thanks to **Linda Sejic** for Art Assists

Cover art by: **Jung-Geun Yoon & Sang-Il Jeong**
Original editions edited by: **Betsy Gonia**
For this edition book design and layout by: **Addison Duke**

For Top Cow Productions, Inc.

Marc Silvestri - *CEO* • Matt Hawkins - *President and COO* • Betsy Gonia - *Managing Editor*
Elena Salcedo - *Operations Manager* • Ryan Cady - *Editorial Assistant* • Vincent Valentine - *Production Assistan*

www.topcow.com

IMAGE COMICS, INC.
Robert Kirkman – Chief Operating Officer
Erik Larsen – Chief Financial Officer
Todd McFarlane – President
Marc Silvestri – Chief Executive Officer
Jim Valentino – Vice-President

Eric Stephenson – Publisher
Ron Richards – Director of Business Development
Jennifer de Guzman – Director of Trade Book Sales
Kat Salazar – Director of PR & Marketing
Corey Murphy – Director of Retail Sales
Jeremy Sullivan – Director of Digital Sales
Emilio Bautista – Sales Assistant
Branwyn Bigglestone – Senior Accounts Manager
Emily Miller – Accounts Manager
Jessica Ambriz – Administrative Assistant
Tyler Shainline – Events Coordinator
David Brothers – Content Manager
Jonathan Chan – Production Manager
Drew Gill – Art Director
Meredith Wallace – Print Manager
Monica Garcia – Senior Production Artist
Addison Duke – Production Artist
Tricia Ramos – Production Assistant
IMAGECOMICS.COM

Tales of Honor On Basilisk Station Volume 1 Trade Paperback.
NOVEMBER 2014. FIRST PRINTING. ISBN: 978-1-63215-020-2, $19.99 U.S.D.

Published by Image Comics Inc. Office of Publication: 2001 Center Street, 6th Floor, Berkeley, CA 90704. Origin
published in single magazine form as TALES OF HONOR ON BASILISK STATION 1-5. Tales of Honor© 2014 Fear
Productions, LLC. All rights reserved. "Tales of Honor," Tales of Honor logos, and the likenesses of all featu
characters (human or otherwise) featured herein are copyrights of Fearless Productions, LLC. Image Comics
the Image Comics logo are trademarks of Image Comics Inc. The characters, events, and stories in this publica
are entirely fictional. Any resemblance to actual persons (living or dead), events, institutions, or locales, with
satiric intent, is coincidental. No portion of this publication may be reproduced or transmitted, in any form o
any means, without the express written permission of Top Cow Productions, Inc. Printed in the United States.
information regarding the CPSIA on this printed material call: 203-595-3636 and provide reference RICH-5920

image

nce this is the first volume of *Tales of Honor*, I thought I'd write a little something about how exciting is entire project is for the author of the novels upon which it's based. This is only the first stage of cross-media project. Evergreen Studios intends to produce the graphic novels, mobile games, and nematic release movies, and this is the very beginning of that process, the starting point. We invite mments as it evolves, grows, and changes, and we hope you'll come along for the entire trip.

oout twenty years ago, my publisher, Baen Books, asked me to propose the concept for a series of ience fiction novels, and I did, but neither Jim Baen nor I anticipated what that proposal was going to unch. No author can predict a series will take off the way the novels about Honor Harrington did; he n only be thankful after the fact for the many, many fans which made it happen.

hen I began thinking about the series which eventually became the Honorverse, I was building on a elong interest in history — diplomatic and military, especially naval — and on my fascination with the emes of personal responsibility, integrity, and the willingness to sacrifice for the things in which one elieves. In addition, I've always been attracted to strong, competent people, including the many strong, mpetent women I've known, and the fact that Honor Harrington is exactly the sort of woman who nbodies those qualities of character, integrity, obligation, and sacrifice also allowed me to play with ender roles, which was icing on the cake from my perspective. And, of course, if the books turned out to rousing good novels with lots of action, so much the better!

ıd thus the Honorverse was born all those years ago. I confess that I didn't expect to still be writing vels, both as solo works and as collaborations, in the same series twenty years later. I think that ngevity is a testimony to the life the characters in the books have taken on in the hearts and minds of air fans, and I think those themes of responsibility-taking and sacrifice have resonated very strongly th my readers over the years. It's been a privilege to be the creator of stories which have generated ch strong loyalty among their readers, and I've spent so much time in the Star Kingdom of Manticore, e People's Republic of Haven, the Silesian Confederacy, and on a planet named Grayson over the last o decades that they've taken on a life and a texture for me which is far deeper than I ever expected d which I have tried to share with my readers.

w Honor and I are moving into entirely new media, and I feel confident Evergreen and Top Cow will roduce Honor and her friends — and enemies — to an even larger audience, with a few new, exciting inkles of their own as my literary creations are given a strong graphic look and the characters are ought to life on the screen.

eally like the art of Jung-Geun Yoon and Sang-Il Jeong who bring a stunning, painterly style to rtraying all of the Honorverse's complexity, and Matt Hawkins has done a remarkable job of staying thful to the original story and the science while adding his own unique perspective to it. I don't think at should surprise anyone, given Matt's works like *Think Tank* and *Aphrodite IX*, both of which explore ries with real grounding in scientific fact in thoughtful, yet highly entertaining ways. In the case of *les of Honor*, his decision to create a story in which Honor reflects on her past creates a focused rspective on these characters and stories which should be exciting for new readers while offering ıgstanding fans fresh insights into stories they may have read long ago.

r those of you who are first-time visitors to the Honorverse, I think this is a very good introduction it. The characters, the star nations, the politics, and the conflicts which drive the novels are fully presented here. I hope you'll enjoy your visit, and that you'll be a repeat offender and join us in future ues as they, too, are released.

r those of you who are longtime fans of the Honorverse, and who will inevitably encounter aspects of *les of Honor*, which don't mesh smoothly with your vision of the books, I invite you to look at them from lifferent, possibly expanded perspective. By their very nature, comic books are highly collaborative rks. The artist, the writer, and (in this case) the original author all have to combine their efforts into final product, and along the way that opens the opportunity for fresh viewpoints and angles. The real k in adapting an existing story to a new format is to find ways to make it stronger without sacrificing critical elements — especially the characters — which made the original work. While some of the aracters may not look exactly the way I've always visualized them, they are all the people they were in original novels, and I'm very, very happy with the outcome so far.

you're invited to join us for a brand new ride though the Honorverse. We're excited about all the new ff we've got to show you . . . and we won't be brokenhearted if you have a good time along the way.

anks,
vid Weber, Creator of the Honorverse

TALES OF HONOR

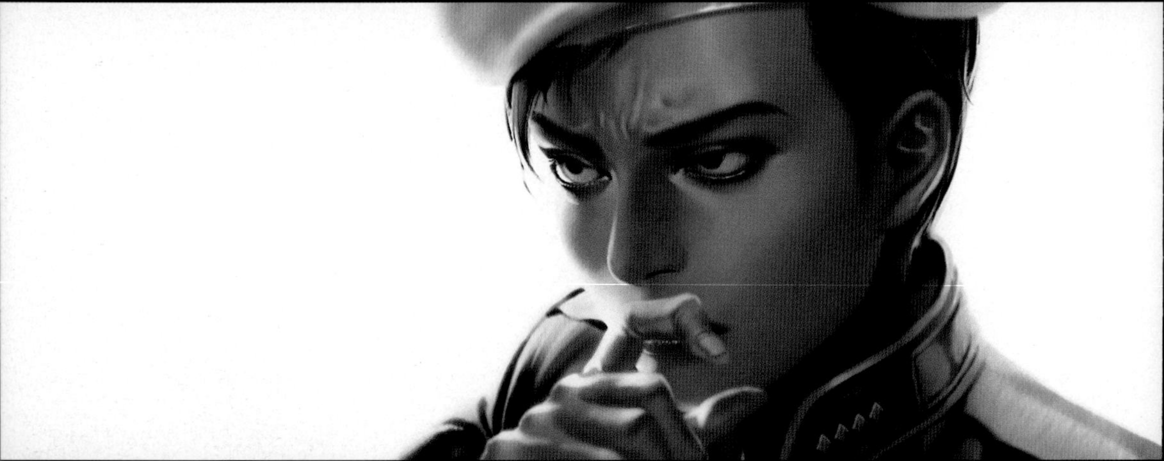

CHAPTER ONE

In the year 2130, a colony ship left Old Earth with the mission of interstellar colonization, launching the largest diaspora in the history of mankind. A new calendar system was born that year with 1 PD commemorating the "post-diaspora" era.

Sublight colonization allowed like-minded individuals to populate and govern new Star Nations however they deemed appropriate. Theocracies, monarchies, communist states, democracies and fringe groups all flourished. Initially a source of great peace, technological advances in transit speed and further expansion shrunk the distances between star systems, bringing about an inevitable clash of ideologies.

One of these Star Nations, The People's Republic of Haven, is on the surface a democracy, but in practicality a central party controlled dictatorship. Wasted economically by its welfare state, Haven embraced an expansionist policy of military conquest to sustain its bloated system.

Conquering system after system, Haven finally set its sights on the Star Kingdom of Manticore, home to our hero Honor Harrington...

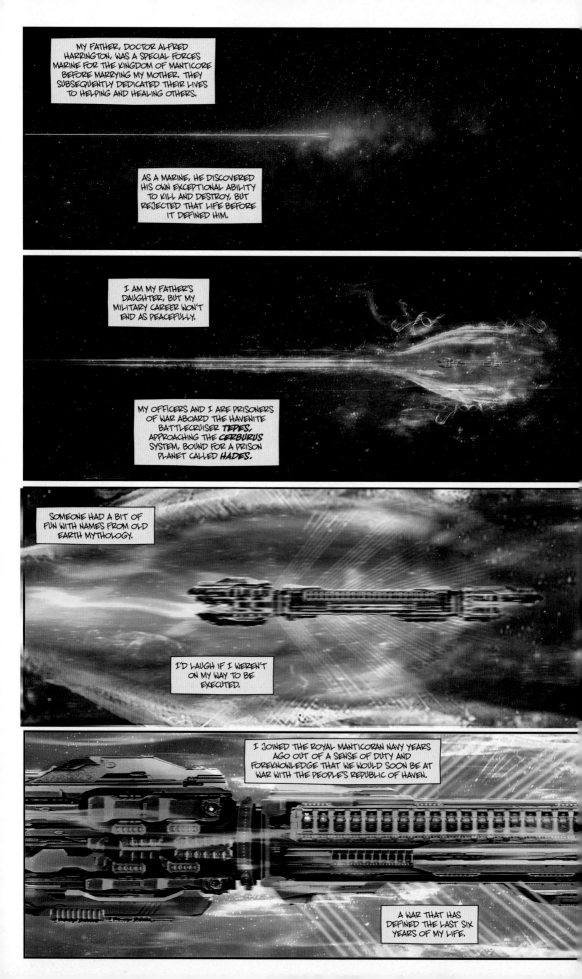

MY FATHER, DOCTOR ALFRED HARRINGTON, WAS A SPECIAL FORCES MARINE FOR THE KINGDOM OF MANTICORE BEFORE MARRYING MY MOTHER. THEY SUBSEQUENTLY DEDICATED THEIR LIVES TO HELPING AND HEALING OTHERS.

AS A MARINE, HE DISCOVERED HIS OWN EXCEPTIONAL ABILITY TO KILL AND DESTROY, BUT REJECTED THAT LIFE BEFORE IT DEFINED HIM.

I AM MY FATHER'S DAUGHTER, BUT MY MILITARY CAREER WON'T END AS PEACEFULLY.

MY OFFICERS AND I ARE PRISONERS OF WAR ABOARD THE HAVENITE BATTLECRUISER *TEPES*, APPROACHING THE *CERBURUS* SYSTEM, BOUND FOR A PRISON PLANET CALLED *HADES*.

SOMEONE HAD A BIT OF FUN WITH NAMES FROM OLD EARTH MYTHOLOGY.

I'D LAUGH IF I WEREN'T ON MY WAY TO BE EXECUTED.

I JOINED THE ROYAL MANTICORAN NAVY YEARS AGO OUT OF A SENSE OF DUTY AND FOREKNOWLEDGE THAT WE WOULD SOON BE AT WAR WITH THE PEOPLE'S REPUBLIC OF HAVEN.

A WAR THAT HAS DEFINED THE LAST SIX YEARS OF MY LIFE.

CALL IT ALTRUISM OR THE BRAVADO OF YOUTH, BUT I WANTED TO DO MY PART. I STILL DO...WITH WHAT LITTLE TIME I MAY HAVE LEFT.

I'M PAST THE POINT OF CARING WHAT THEY DO TO ME. MY REAL CONCERN IS FOR MY CREW AND MY TREECAT *NIMITZ*, ALSO IMPRISONED ON BOARD THIS SHIP.

SO THE GREAT COMMODORE HONOR HARRINGTON...I EXPECTED MORE.

THIS WOMAN, *CORDELIA RANSOM*, IS THE HAVENITE SECRETARY OF PUBLIC INFORMATION; ONE OF THE THREE MOST POWERFUL PEOPLE IN THEIR POST-COUP GOVERNMENT.

DISAPPOINTING, REALLY.

IT'S ALWAYS AMAZED ME HOW MANY IN OUR FLEET ARE TERRIFIED OF YOU, LIKE YOU'RE SOME DEMIGOD ALWAYS OVERCOMING INSURMOUNTABLE ODDS AND DEFYING DEATH.

SPINNING LIES INTO TRUTHS, SHE'S A PROPAGANDIST OF THE WORST KIND. HER BIGOTRY IS ALL THE MORE FRIGHTENING BECAUSE SHE REALLY BELIEVES IN IT.

STILL NOTHING TO SAY?

WHEN YOUR NECK SNAPS IN THE GALLOWS, THEY'LL SEE YOU'RE MERELY HUMAN AFTER ALL.

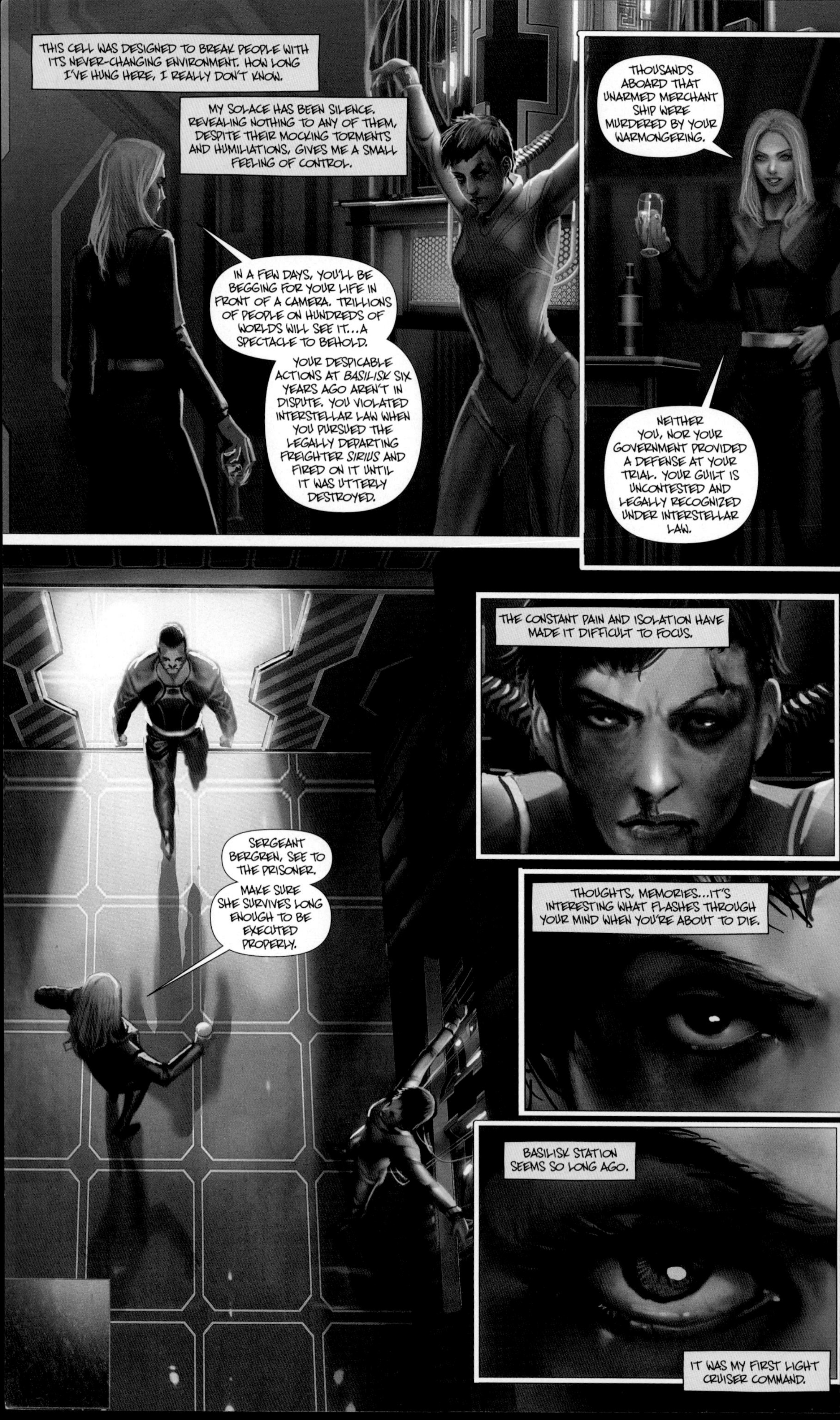
THIS CELL WAS DESIGNED TO BREAK PEOPLE WITH ITS NEVER-CHANGING ENVIRONMENT. HOW LONG I'VE HUNG HERE, I REALLY DON'T KNOW.
MY SOLACE HAS BEEN SILENCE. REVEALING NOTHING TO ANY OF THEM, DESPITE THEIR MOCKING TORMENTS AND HUMILIATIONS, GIVES ME A SMALL FEELING OF CONTROL.
IN A FEW DAYS, YOU'LL BE BEGGING FOR YOUR LIFE IN FRONT OF A CAMERA. TRILLIONS OF PEOPLE ON HUNDREDS OF WORLDS WILL SEE IT...A SPECTACLE TO BEHOLD.
YOUR DESPICABLE ACTIONS AT BASILISK SIX YEARS AGO AREN'T IN DISPUTE. YOU VIOLATED INTERSTELLAR LAW WHEN YOU PURSUED THE LEGALLY DEPARTING FREIGHTER SIRIUS AND FIRED ON IT UNTIL IT WAS UTTERLY DESTROYED.
THOUSANDS ABOARD THAT UNARMED MERCHANT SHIP WERE MURDERED BY YOUR WARMONGERING.
NEITHER YOU, NOR YOUR GOVERNMENT PROVIDED A DEFENSE AT YOUR TRIAL. YOUR GUILT IS UNCONTESTED AND LEGALLY RECOGNIZED UNDER INTERSTELLAR LAW.
SERGEANT BERGREN, SEE TO THE PRISONER.
MAKE SURE SHE SURVIVES LONG ENOUGH TO BE EXECUTED PROPERLY.
THE CONSTANT PAIN AND ISOLATION HAVE MADE IT DIFFICULT TO FOCUS.
THOUGHTS, MEMORIES...IT'S INTERESTING WHAT FLASHES THROUGH YOUR MIND WHEN YOU'RE ABOUT TO DIE.
BASILISK STATION SEEMS SO LONG AGO.
IT WAS MY FIRST LIGHT CRUISER COMMAND.

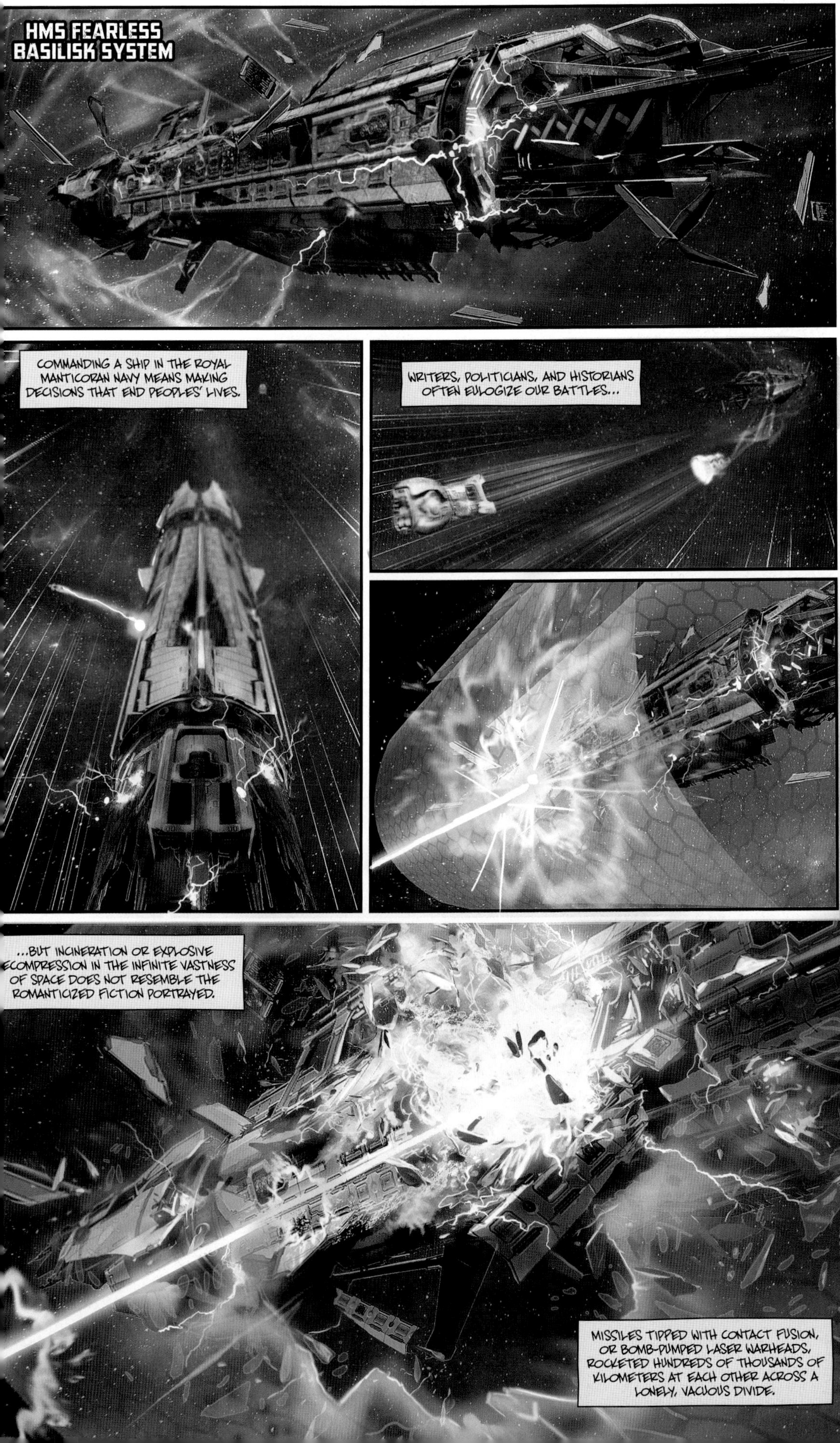
HMS FEARLESS
BASILISK SYSTEM
COMMANDING A SHIP IN THE ROYAL MANTICORAN NAVY MEANS MAKING DECISIONS THAT END PEOPLES' LIVES.
WRITERS, POLITICIANS, AND HISTORIANS OFTEN EULOGIZE OUR BATTLES...
...BUT INCINERATION OR EXPLOSIVE DECOMPRESSION IN THE INFINITE VASTNESS OF SPACE DOES NOT RESEMBLE THE ROMANTICIZED FICTION PORTRAYED.
MISSILES TIPPED WITH CONTACT FUSION, OR BOMB-PUMPED LASER WARHEADS, ROCKETED HUNDREDS OF THOUSANDS OF KILOMETERS AT EACH OTHER ACROSS A LONELY, VACUOUS DIVIDE.

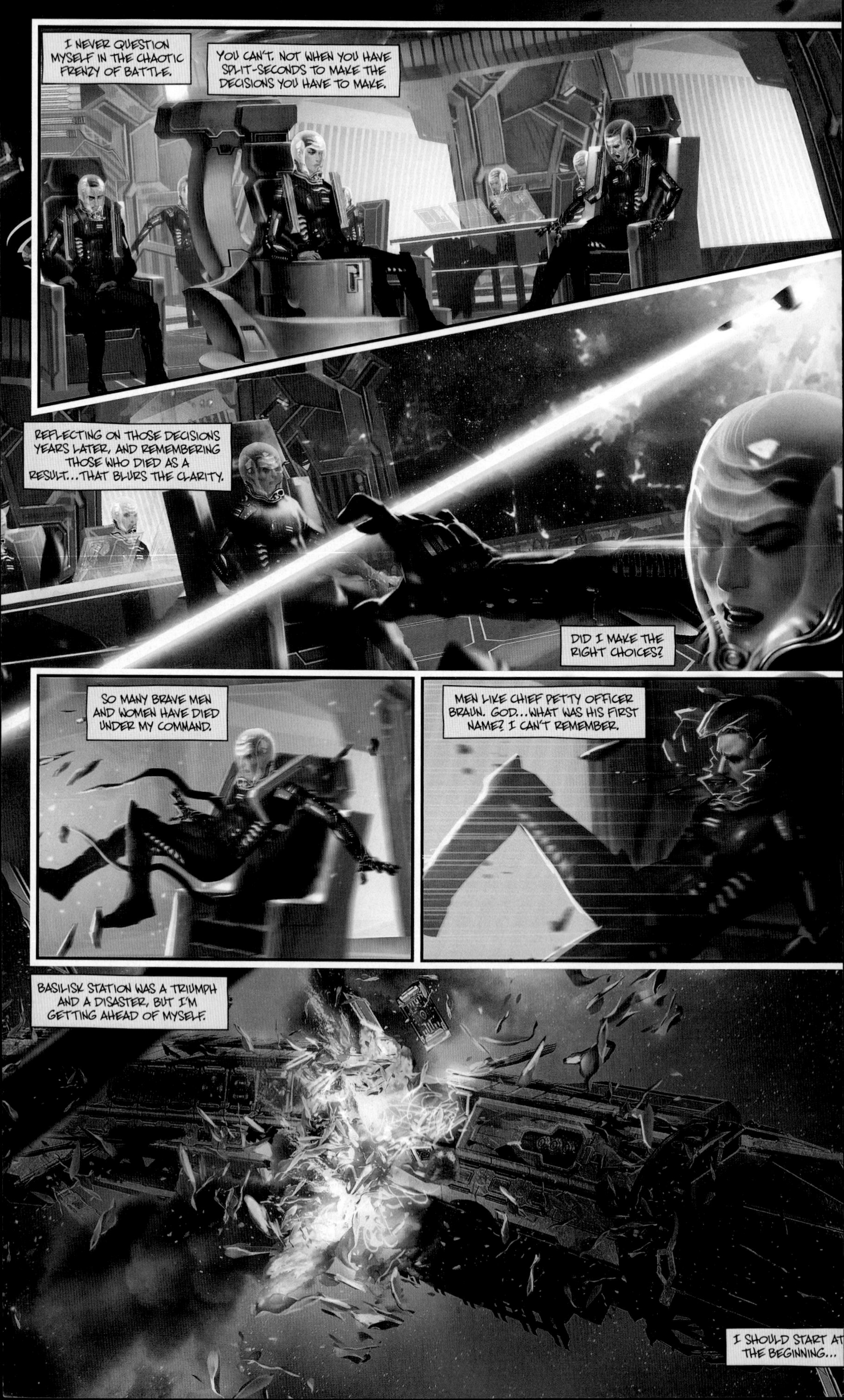
I NEVER QUESTION MYSELF IN THE CHAOTIC FRENZY OF BATTLE.
YOU CAN'T. NOT WHEN YOU HAVE SPLIT-SECONDS TO MAKE THE DECISIONS YOU HAVE TO MAKE.
REFLECTING ON THOSE DECISIONS YEARS LATER, AND REMEMBERING THOSE WHO DIED AS A RESULT...THAT BLURS THE CLARITY.
DID I MAKE THE RIGHT CHOICES?
SO MANY BRAVE MEN AND WOMEN HAVE DIED UNDER MY COMMAND.
MEN LIKE CHIEF PETTY OFFICER BRAUN. GOD...WHAT WAS HIS FIRST NAME? I CAN'T REMEMBER.
BASILISK STATION WAS A TRIUMPH AND A DISASTER, BUT I'M GETTING AHEAD OF MYSELF.
I SHOULD START AT THE BEGINNING...

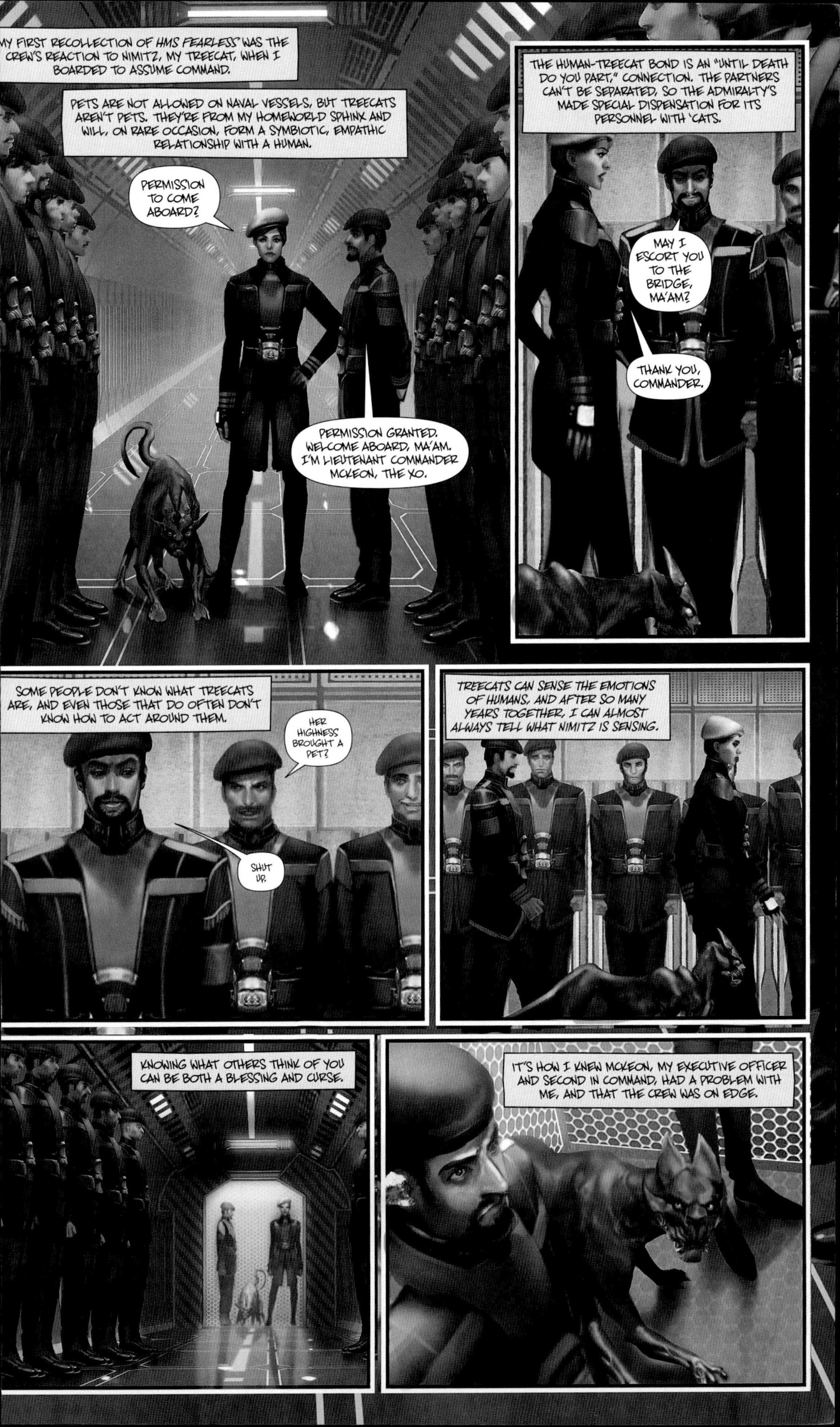
MY FIRST RECOLLECTION OF HMS FEARLESS WAS THE CREW'S REACTION TO NIMITZ, MY TREECAT, WHEN I BOARDED TO ASSUME COMMAND.
PETS ARE NOT ALLOWED ON NAVAL VESSELS, BUT TREECATS AREN'T PETS. THEY'RE FROM MY HOMEWORLD SPHINX AND WILL, ON RARE OCCASION, FORM A SYMBIOTIC, EMPATHIC RELATIONSHIP WITH A HUMAN.
PERMISSION TO COME ABOARD?
PERMISSION GRANTED. WELCOME ABOARD, MA'AM. I'M LIEUTENANT COMMANDER MCKEON, THE XO.
THE HUMAN-TREECAT BOND IS AN "UNTIL DEATH DO YOU PART," CONNECTION. THE PARTNERS CAN'T BE SEPARATED, SO THE ADMIRALTY'S MADE SPECIAL DISPENSATION FOR ITS PERSONNEL WITH 'CATS.
MAY I ESCORT YOU TO THE BRIDGE, MA'AM?
THANK YOU, COMMANDER.
SOME PEOPLE DON'T KNOW WHAT TREECATS ARE, AND EVEN THOSE THAT DO OFTEN DON'T KNOW HOW TO ACT AROUND THEM.
HER HIGHNESS BROUGHT A PET?
SHUT UP.
TREECATS CAN SENSE THE EMOTIONS OF HUMANS, AND AFTER SO MANY YEARS TOGETHER, I CAN ALMOST ALWAYS TELL WHAT NIMITZ IS SENSING.
KNOWING WHAT OTHERS THINK OF YOU CAN BE BOTH A BLESSING AND CURSE.
IT'S HOW I KNEW MCKEON, MY EXECUTIVE OFFICER AND SECOND IN COMMAND, HAD A PROBLEM WITH ME, AND THAT THE CREW WAS ON EDGE.

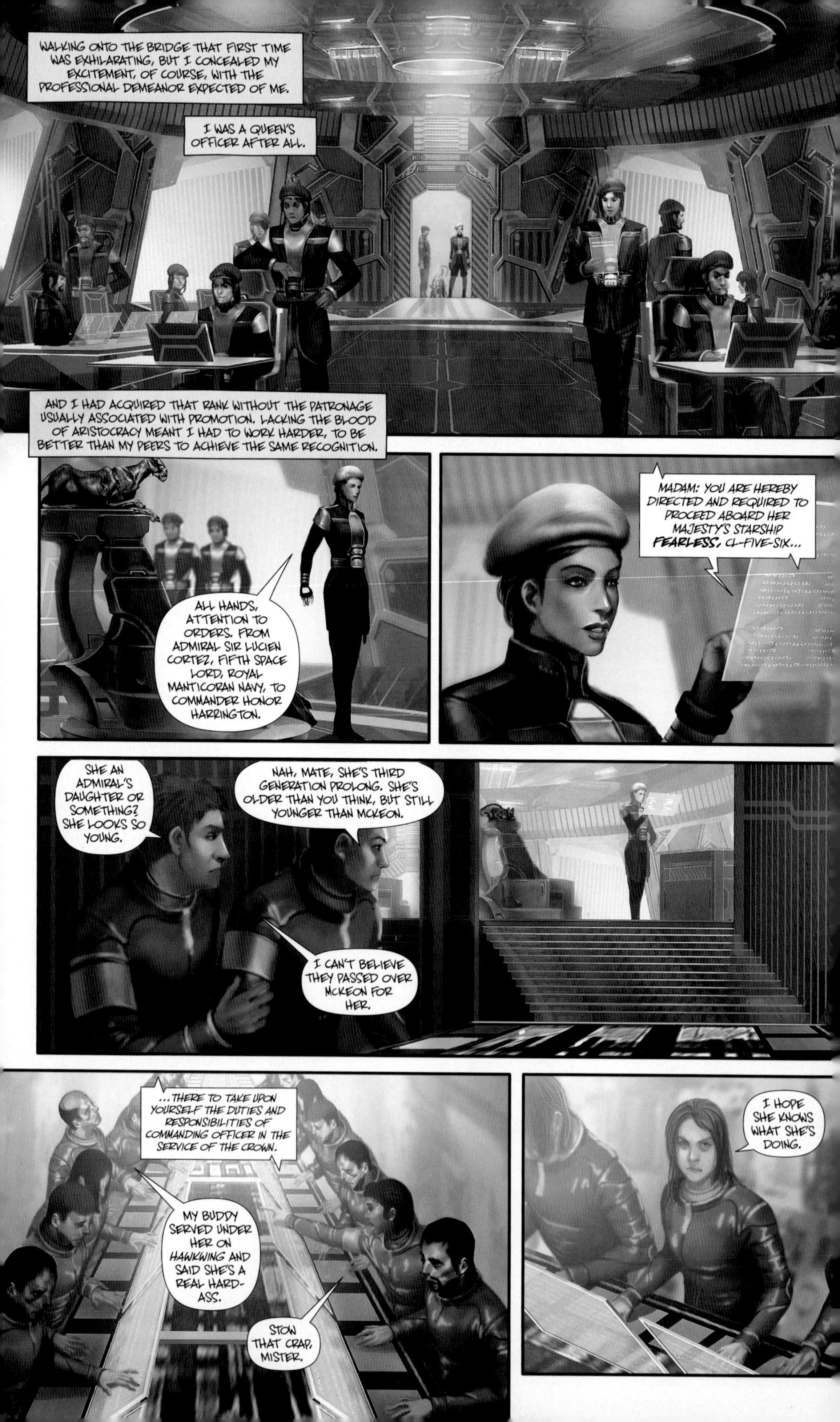
WALKING ONTO THE BRIDGE THAT FIRST TIME WAS EXHILARATING, BUT I CONCEALED MY EXCITEMENT, OF COURSE, WITH THE PROFESSIONAL DEMEANOR EXPECTED OF ME.
I WAS A QUEEN'S OFFICER AFTER ALL.
AND I HAD ACQUIRED THAT RANK WITHOUT THE PATRONAGE USUALLY ASSOCIATED WITH PROMOTION. LACKING THE BLOOD OF ARISTOCRACY MEANT I HAD TO WORK HARDER, TO BE BETTER THAN MY PEERS TO ACHIEVE THE SAME RECOGNITION.
ALL HANDS, ATTENTION TO ORDERS. FROM ADMIRAL SIR LUCIEN CORTEZ, FIFTH SPACE LORD, ROYAL MANTICORAN NAVY, TO COMMANDER HONOR HARRINGTON.
MADAM: YOU ARE HEREBY DIRECTED AND REQUIRED TO PROCEED ABOARD HER MAJESTY'S STARSHIP **FEARLESS**, CL-FIVE-SIX...
SHE AN ADMIRAL'S DAUGHTER OR SOMETHING? SHE LOOKS SO YOUNG.
NAH, MATE, SHE'S THIRD GENERATION PROLONG. SHE'S OLDER THAN YOU THINK, BUT STILL YOUNGER THAN MCKEON.
I CAN'T BELIEVE THEY PASSED OVER MCKEON FOR HER.
...THERE TO TAKE UPON YOURSELF THE DUTIES AND RESPONSIBILITIES OF COMMANDING OFFICER IN THE SERVICE OF THE CROWN.
MY BUDDY SERVED UNDER HER ON HAWKWING AND SAID SHE'S A REAL HARD-ASS.
STOW THAT CRAP, MISTER.
I HOPE SHE KNOWS WHAT SHE'S DOING.

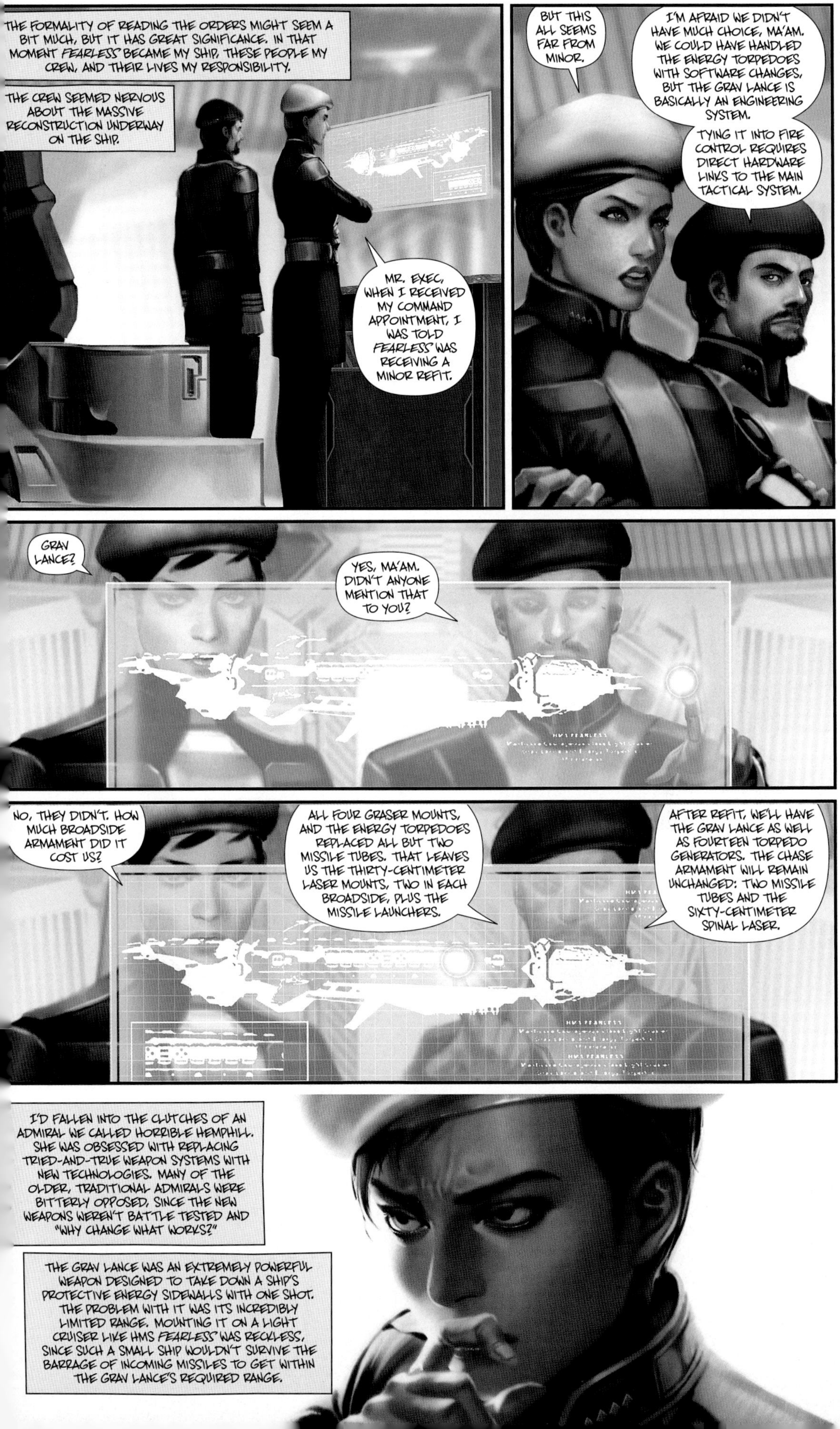

THE FORMALITY OF READING THE ORDERS MIGHT SEEM A BIT MUCH, BUT IT HAS GREAT SIGNIFICANCE. IN THAT MOMENT *FEARLESS* BECAME MY SHIP, THESE PEOPLE MY CREW, AND THEIR LIVES MY RESPONSIBILITY.
THE CREW SEEMED NERVOUS ABOUT THE MASSIVE RECONSTRUCTION UNDERWAY ON THE SHIP.
MR. EXEC, WHEN I RECEIVED MY COMMAND APPOINTMENT, I WAS TOLD *FEARLESS* WAS RECEIVING A MINOR REFIT.
BUT THIS ALL SEEMS FAR FROM MINOR.
I'M AFRAID WE DIDN'T HAVE MUCH CHOICE, MA'AM. WE COULD HAVE HANDLED THE ENERGY TORPEDOES WITH SOFTWARE CHANGES, BUT THE GRAV LANCE IS BASICALLY AN ENGINEERING SYSTEM.
TYING IT INTO FIRE CONTROL REQUIRES DIRECT HARDWARE LINKS TO THE MAIN TACTICAL SYSTEM.
GRAV LANCE?
YES, MA'AM. DIDN'T ANYONE MENTION THAT TO YOU?
NO, THEY DIDN'T. HOW MUCH BROADSIDE ARMAMENT DID IT COST US?
ALL FOUR GRASER MOUNTS, AND THE ENERGY TORPEDOES REPLACED ALL BUT TWO MISSILE TUBES. THAT LEAVES US THE THIRTY-CENTIMETER LASER MOUNTS, TWO IN EACH BROADSIDE, PLUS THE MISSILE LAUNCHERS.
AFTER REFIT, WE'LL HAVE THE GRAV LANCE AS WELL AS FOURTEEN TORPEDO GENERATORS. THE CHASE ARMAMENT WILL REMAIN UNCHANGED: TWO MISSILE TUBES AND THE SIXTY-CENTIMETER SPINAL LASER.
I'D FALLEN INTO THE CLUTCHES OF AN ADMIRAL WE CALLED HORRIBLE HEMPHILL. SHE WAS OBSESSED WITH REPLACING TRIED-AND-TRUE WEAPON SYSTEMS WITH NEW TECHNOLOGIES. MANY OF THE OLDER, TRADITIONAL ADMIRALS WERE BITTERLY OPPOSED, SINCE THE NEW WEAPONS WEREN'T BATTLE TESTED AND "WHY CHANGE WHAT WORKS?"
THE GRAV LANCE WAS AN EXTREMELY POWERFUL WEAPON DESIGNED TO TAKE DOWN A SHIP'S PROTECTIVE ENERGY SIDEWALLS WITH ONE SHOT. THE PROBLEM WITH IT WAS ITS INCREDIBLY LIMITED RANGE. MOUNTING IT ON A LIGHT CRUISER LIKE HMS *FEARLESS* WAS RECKLESS, SINCE SUCH A SMALL SHIP WOULDN'T SURVIVE THE BARRAGE OF INCOMING MISSILES TO GET WITHIN THE GRAV LANCE'S REQUIRED RANGE.

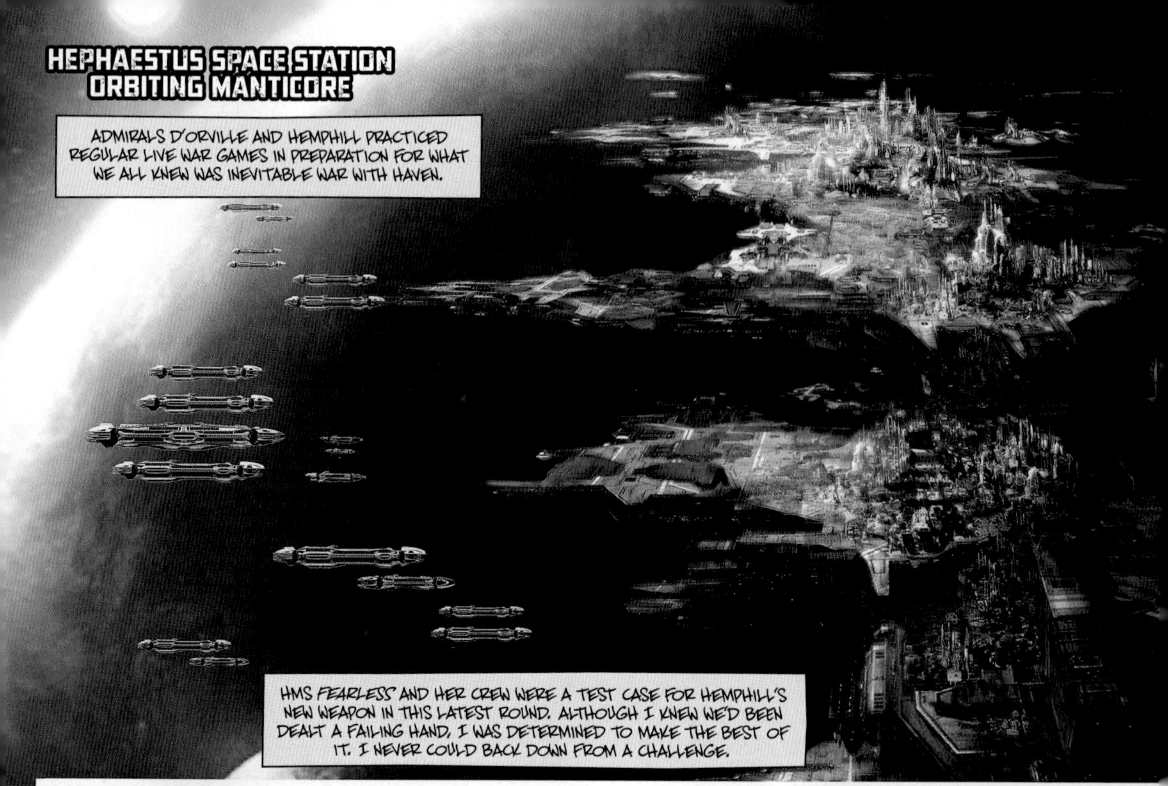
HEPHAESTUS SPACE STATION
ORBITING MANTICORE
ADMIRALS D'ORVILLE AND HEMPHILL PRACTICED REGULAR LIVE WAR GAMES IN PREPARATION FOR WHAT WE ALL KNEW WAS INEVITABLE WAR WITH HAVEN.
HMS *FEARLESS* AND HER CREW WERE A TEST CASE FOR HEMPHILL'S NEW WEAPON IN THIS LATEST ROUND. ALTHOUGH I KNEW WE'D BEEN DEALT A FAILING HAND, I WAS DETERMINED TO MAKE THE BEST OF IT. I NEVER COULD BACK DOWN FROM A CHALLENGE.

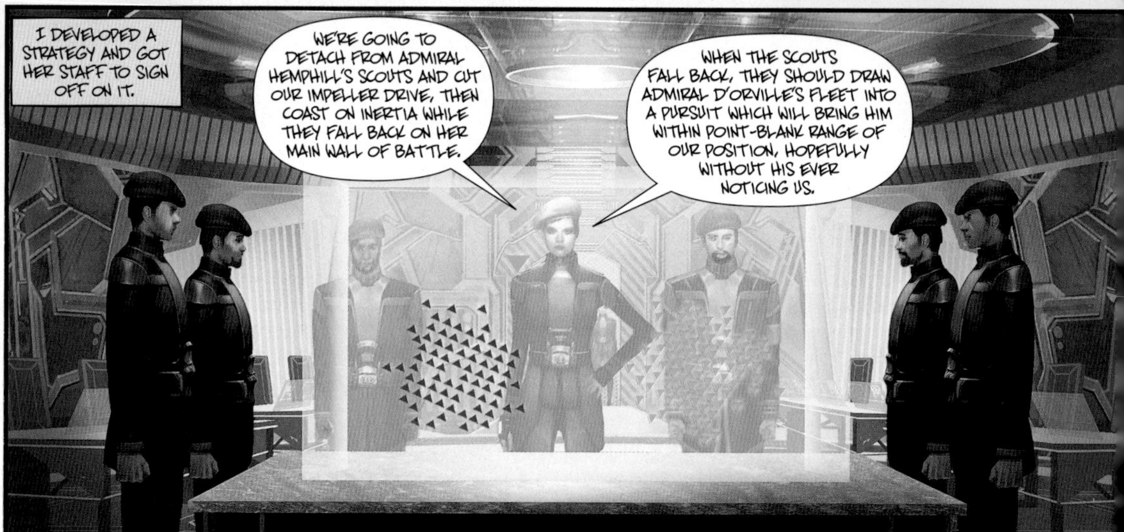
I DEVELOPED A STRATEGY AND GOT HER STAFF TO SIGN OFF ON IT.
WE'RE GOING TO DETACH FROM ADMIRAL HEMPHILL'S SCOUTS AND CUT OUR IMPELLER DRIVE, THEN COAST ON INERTIA WHILE THEY FALL BACK ON HER MAIN WALL OF BATTLE.
WHEN THE SCOUTS FALL BACK, THEY SHOULD DRAW ADMIRAL D'ORVILLE'S FLEET INTO A PURSUIT WHICH WILL BRING HIM WITHIN POINT-BLANK RANGE OF OUR POSITION, HOPEFULLY WITHOUT HIS EVER NOTICING US.

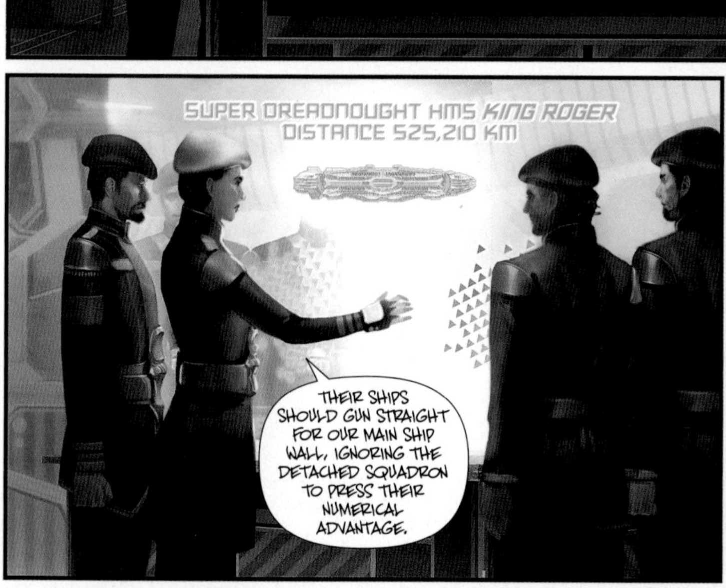
SUPER DREADNOUGHT HMS *KING ROGER*
DISTANCE 525,210 KM
THEIR SHIPS SHOULD GUN STRAIGHT FOR OUR MAIN SHIP WALL, IGNORING THE DETACHED SQUADRON TO PRESS THEIR NUMERICAL ADVANTAGE.

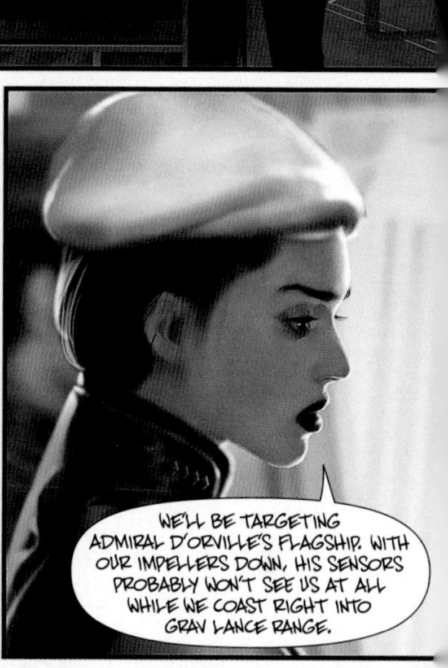
WE'LL BE TARGETING ADMIRAL D'ORVILLE'S FLAGSHIP. WITH OUR IMPELLERS DOWN, HIS SENSORS PROBABLY WON'T SEE US AT ALL WHILE WE COAST RIGHT INTO GRAV LANCE RANGE.

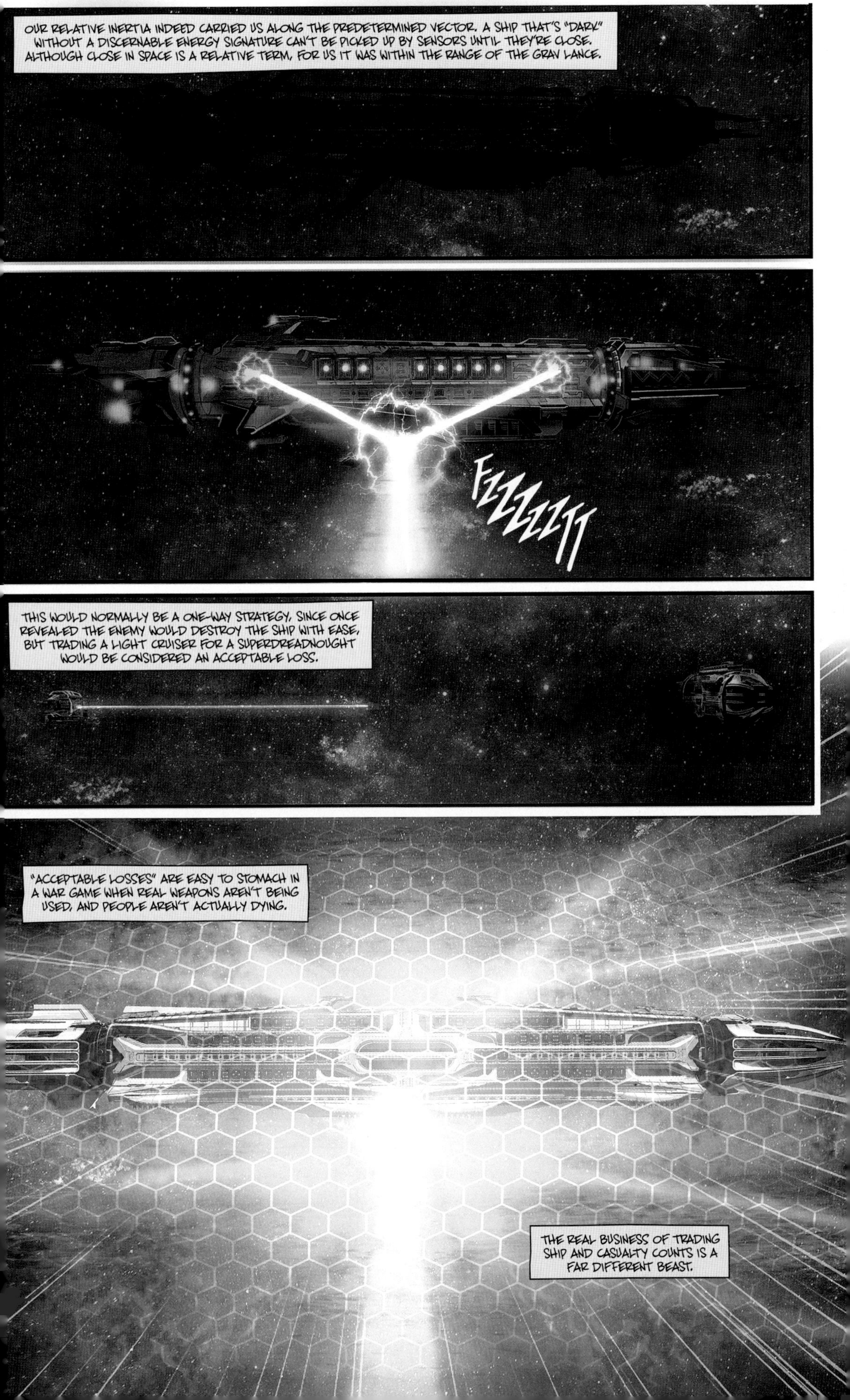
OUR RELATIVE INERTIA INDEED CARRIED US ALONG THE PREDETERMINED VECTOR. A SHIP THAT'S "DARK" WITHOUT A DISCERNABLE ENERGY SIGNATURE CAN'T BE PICKED UP BY SENSORS UNTIL THEY'RE CLOSE. ALTHOUGH CLOSE IN SPACE IS A RELATIVE TERM, FOR US IT WAS WITHIN THE RANGE OF THE GRAV LANCE.
FZZZZZTT
THIS WOULD NORMALLY BE A ONE-WAY STRATEGY, SINCE ONCE REVEALED THE ENEMY WOULD DESTROY THE SHIP WITH EASE, BUT TRADING A LIGHT CRUISER FOR A SUPERDREADNOUGHT WOULD BE CONSIDERED AN ACCEPTABLE LOSS.
"ACCEPTABLE LOSSES" ARE EASY TO STOMACH IN A WAR GAME WHEN REAL WEAPONS AREN'T BEING USED, AND PEOPLE AREN'T ACTUALLY DYING.
THE REAL BUSINESS OF TRADING SHIP AND CASUALTY COUNTS IS A FAR DIFFERENT BEAST.

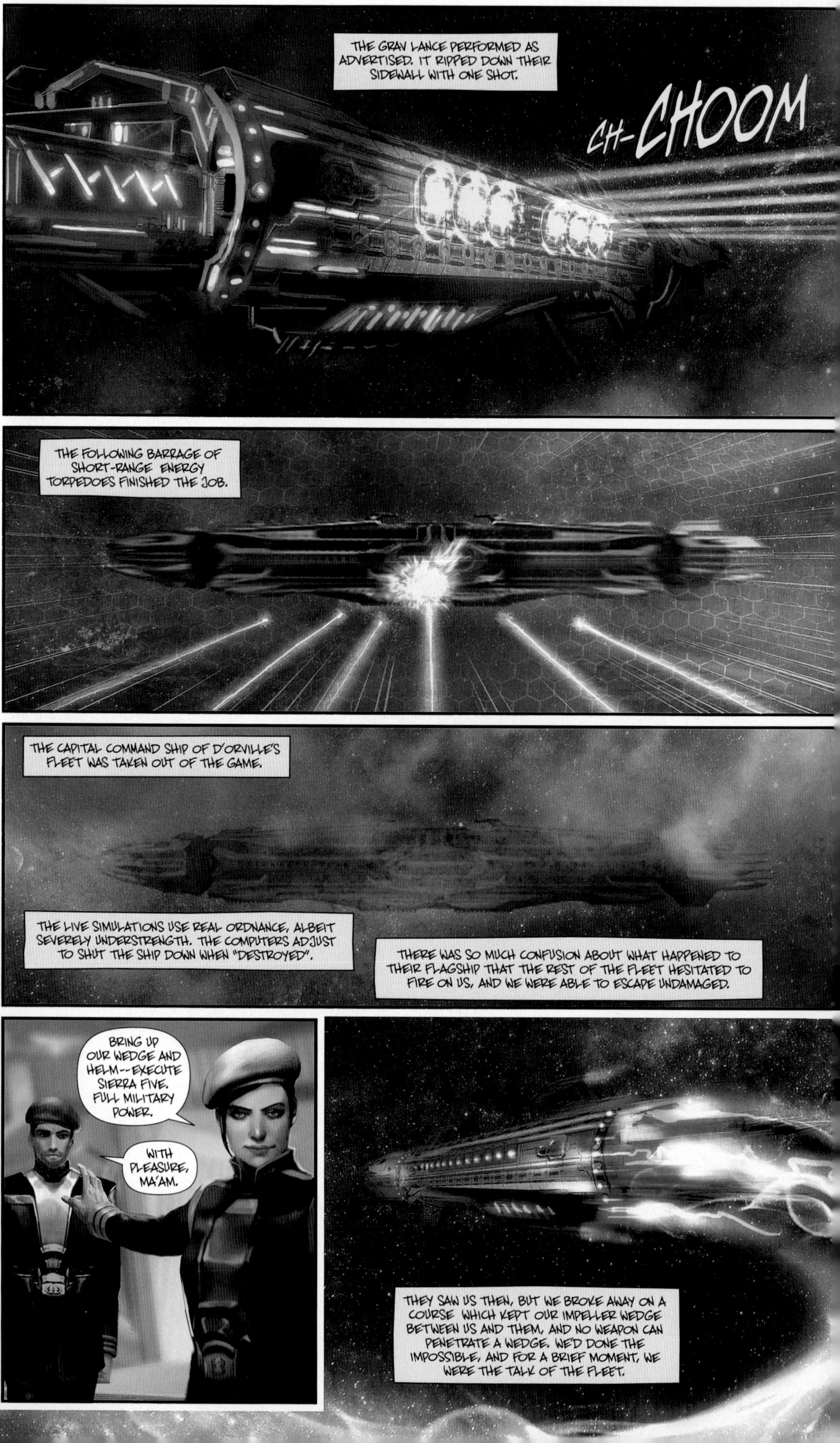
THE GRAV LANCE PERFORMED AS ADVERTISED. IT RIPPED DOWN THEIR SIDEWALL WITH ONE SHOT.
CH-CHOOM
THE FOLLOWING BARRAGE OF SHORT-RANGE ENERGY TORPEDOES FINISHED THE JOB.
THE CAPITAL COMMAND SHIP OF D'ORVILLE'S FLEET WAS TAKEN OUT OF THE GAME.
THE LIVE SIMULATIONS USE REAL ORDNANCE, ALBEIT SEVERELY UNDERSTRENGTH. THE COMPUTERS ADJUST TO SHUT THE SHIP DOWN WHEN "DESTROYED".
THERE WAS SO MUCH CONFUSION ABOUT WHAT HAPPENED TO THEIR FLAGSHIP THAT THE REST OF THE FLEET HESITATED TO FIRE ON US, AND WE WERE ABLE TO ESCAPE UNDAMAGED.
BRING UP OUR WEDGE AND HELM--EXECUTE SIERRA FIVE. FULL MILITARY POWER.
WITH PLEASURE, MA'AM.
THEY SAW US THEN, BUT WE BROKE AWAY ON A COURSE WHICH KEPT OUR IMPELLER WEDGE BETWEEN US AND THEM, AND NO WEAPON CAN PENETRATE A WEDGE. WE'D DONE THE IMPOSSIBLE, AND FOR A BRIEF MOMENT, WE WERE THE TALK OF THE FLEET.

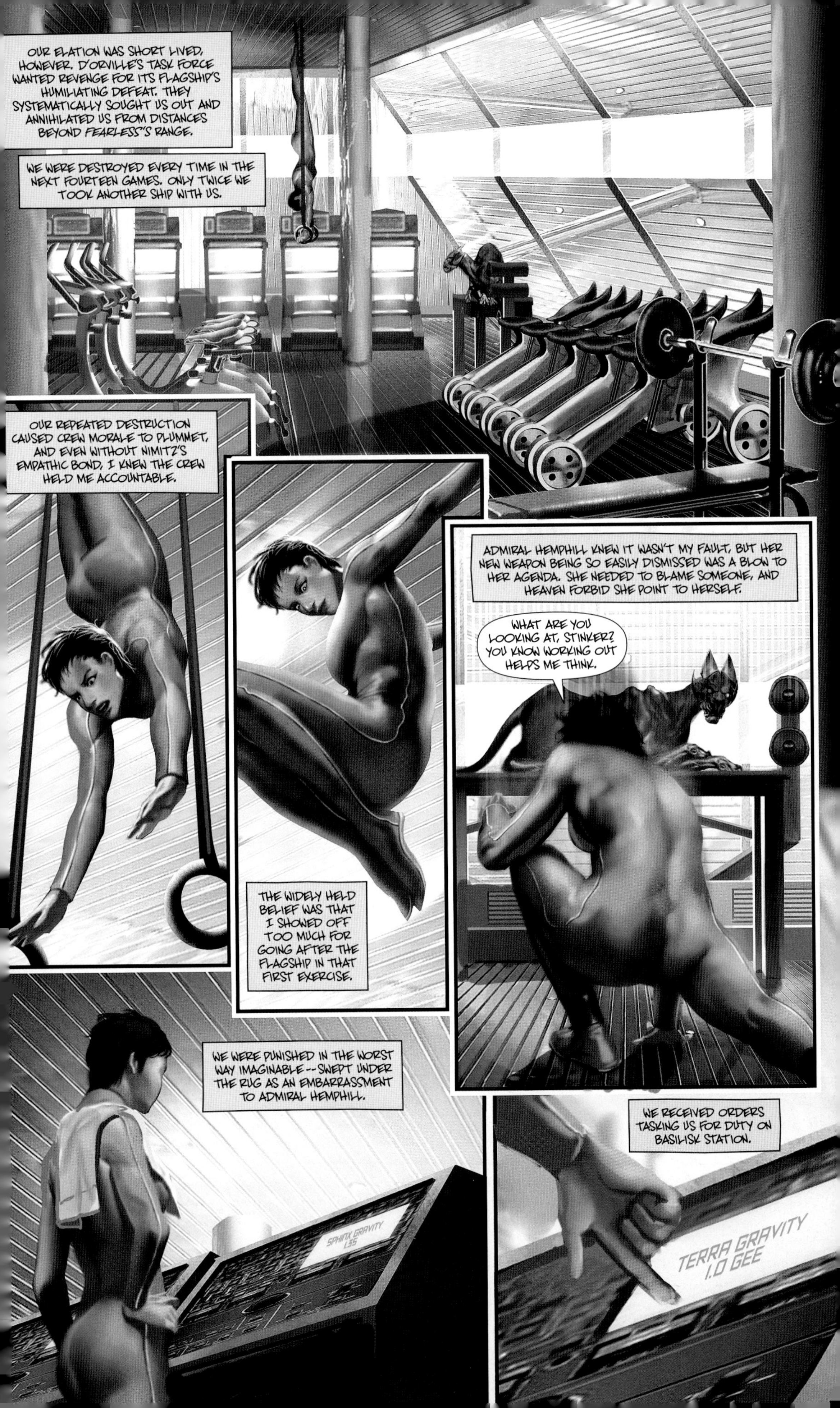

OUR ELATION WAS SHORT LIVED, HOWEVER. D'ORVILLE'S TASK FORCE WANTED REVENGE FOR ITS FLAGSHIP'S HUMILIATING DEFEAT. THEY SYSTEMATICALLY SOUGHT US OUT AND ANNIHILATED US FROM DISTANCES BEYOND FEARLESS'S RANGE.
WE WERE DESTROYED EVERY TIME IN THE NEXT FOURTEEN GAMES. ONLY TWICE WE TOOK ANOTHER SHIP WITH US.
OUR REPEATED DESTRUCTION CAUSED CREW MORALE TO PLUMMET, AND EVEN WITHOUT NIMITZ'S EMPATHIC BOND, I KNEW THE CREW HELD ME ACCOUNTABLE.
THE WIDELY HELD BELIEF WAS THAT I SHOWED OFF TOO MUCH FOR GOING AFTER THE FLAGSHIP IN THAT FIRST EXERCISE.
ADMIRAL HEMPHILL KNEW IT WASN'T MY FAULT, BUT HER NEW WEAPON BEING SO EASILY DISMISSED WAS A BLOW TO HER AGENDA. SHE NEEDED TO BLAME SOMEONE, AND HEAVEN FORBID SHE POINT TO HERSELF.
WHAT ARE YOU LOOKING AT, STINKER? YOU KNOW WORKING OUT HELPS ME THINK.
WE WERE PUNISHED IN THE WORST WAY IMAGINABLE--SWEPT UNDER THE RUG AS AN EMBARRASSMENT TO ADMIRAL HEMPHILL.
SPHINX GRAVITY 1.35
WE RECEIVED ORDERS TASKING US FOR DUTY ON BASILISK STATION.
TERRA GRAVITY 1.0 GEE

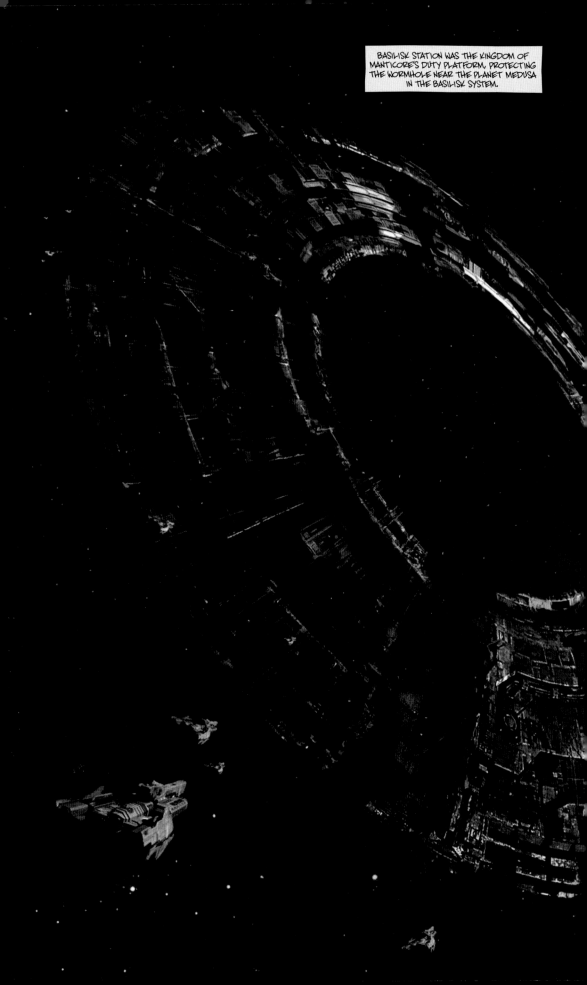

BASILISK STATION WAS THE KINGDOM OF MANTICORE'S DUTY PLATFORM, PROTECTING THE WORMHOLE NEAR THE PLANET MEDUSA IN THE BASILISK SYSTEM.

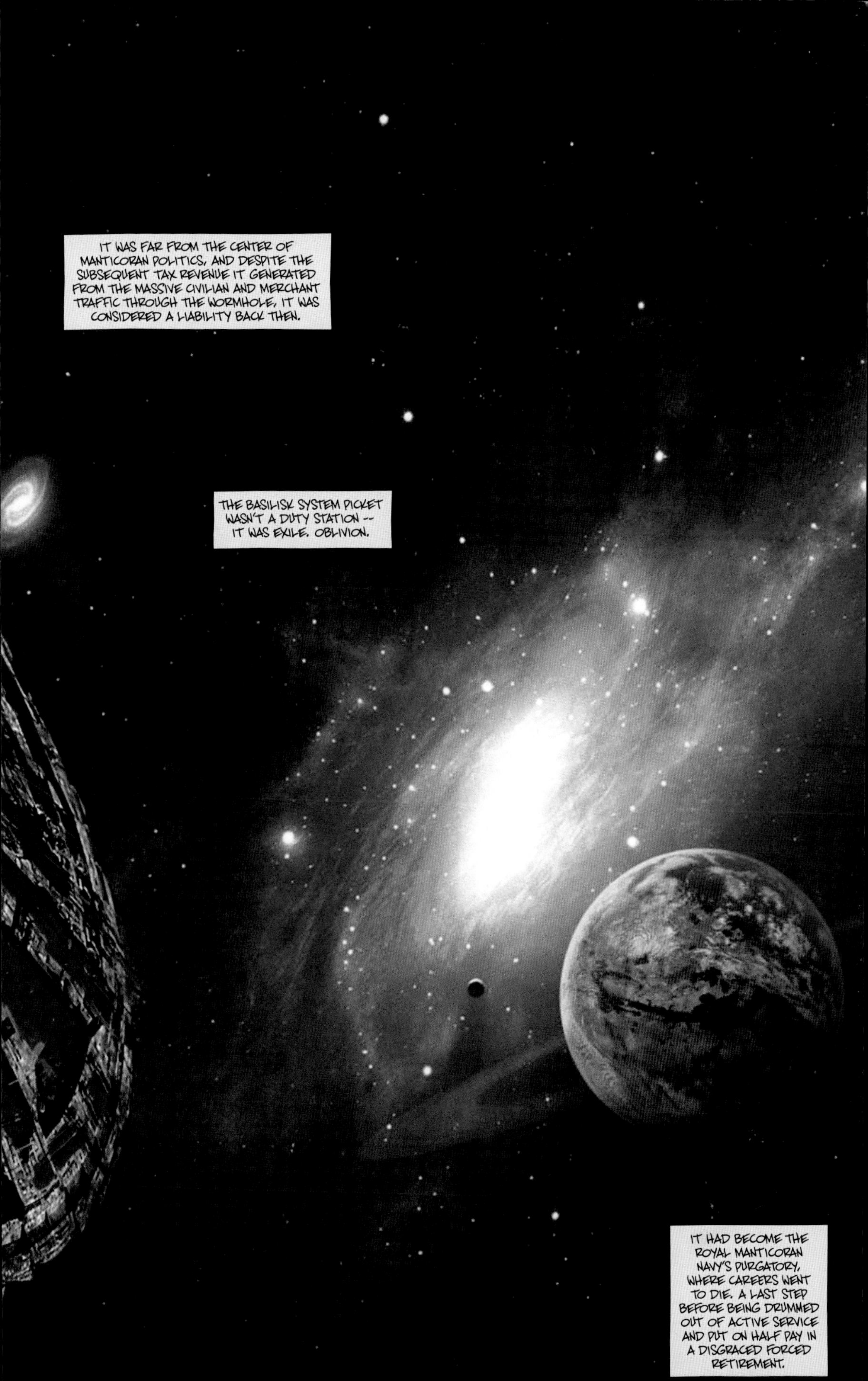
IT WAS FAR FROM THE CENTER OF MANTICORAN POLITICS, AND DESPITE THE SUBSEQUENT TAX REVENUE IT GENERATED FROM THE MASSIVE CIVILIAN AND MERCHANT TRAFFIC THROUGH THE WORMHOLE, IT WAS CONSIDERED A LIABILITY BACK THEN.
THE BASILISK SYSTEM PICKET WASN'T A DUTY STATION -- IT WAS EXILE. OBLIVION.
IT HAD BECOME THE ROYAL MANTICORAN NAVY'S PURGATORY, WHERE CAREERS WENT TO DIE. A LAST STEP BEFORE BEING DRUMMED OUT OF ACTIVE SERVICE AND PUT ON HALF PAY IN A DISGRACED FORCED RETIREMENT.

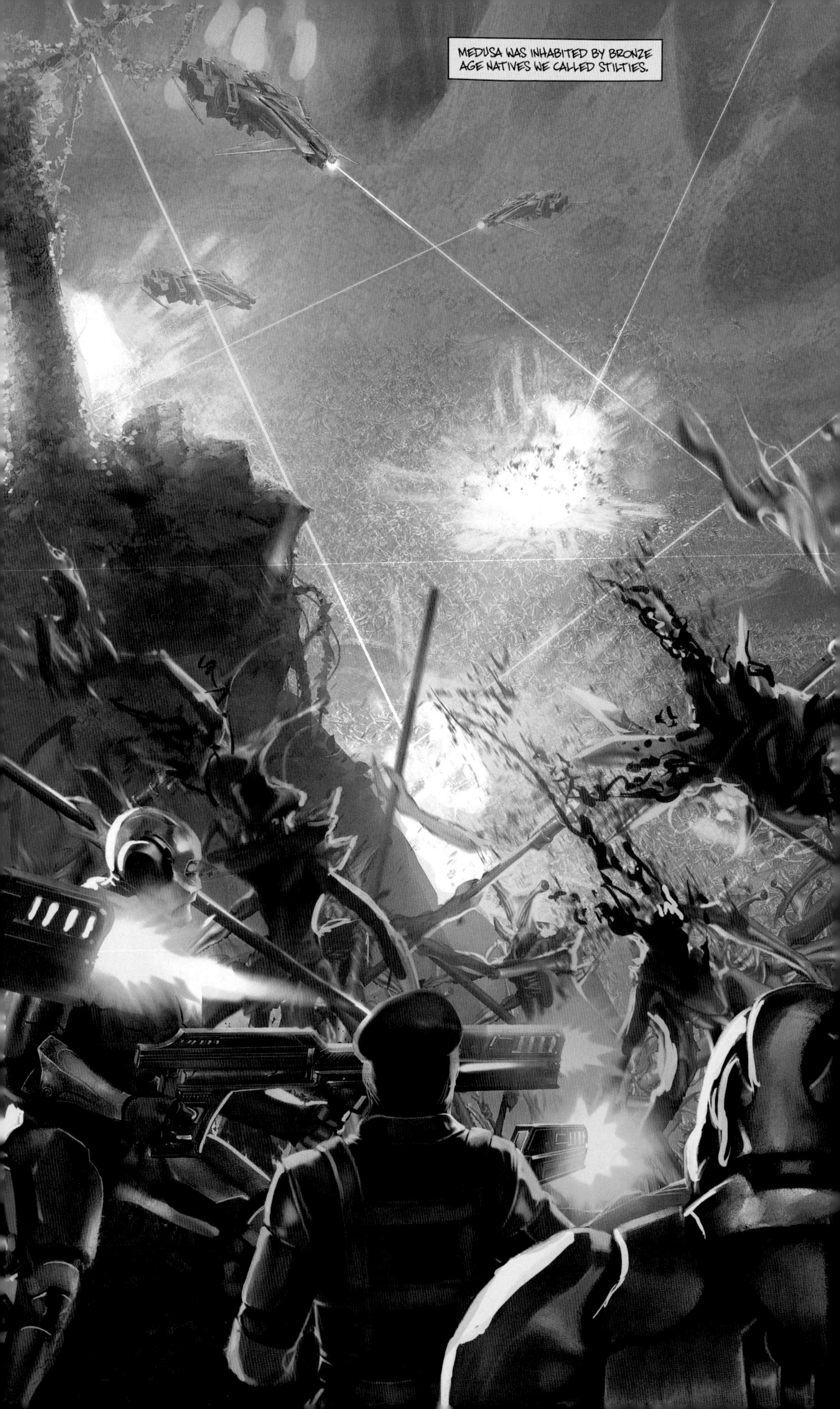
MEDUSA WAS INHABITED BY BRONZE AGE NATIVES WE CALLED STILTIES.

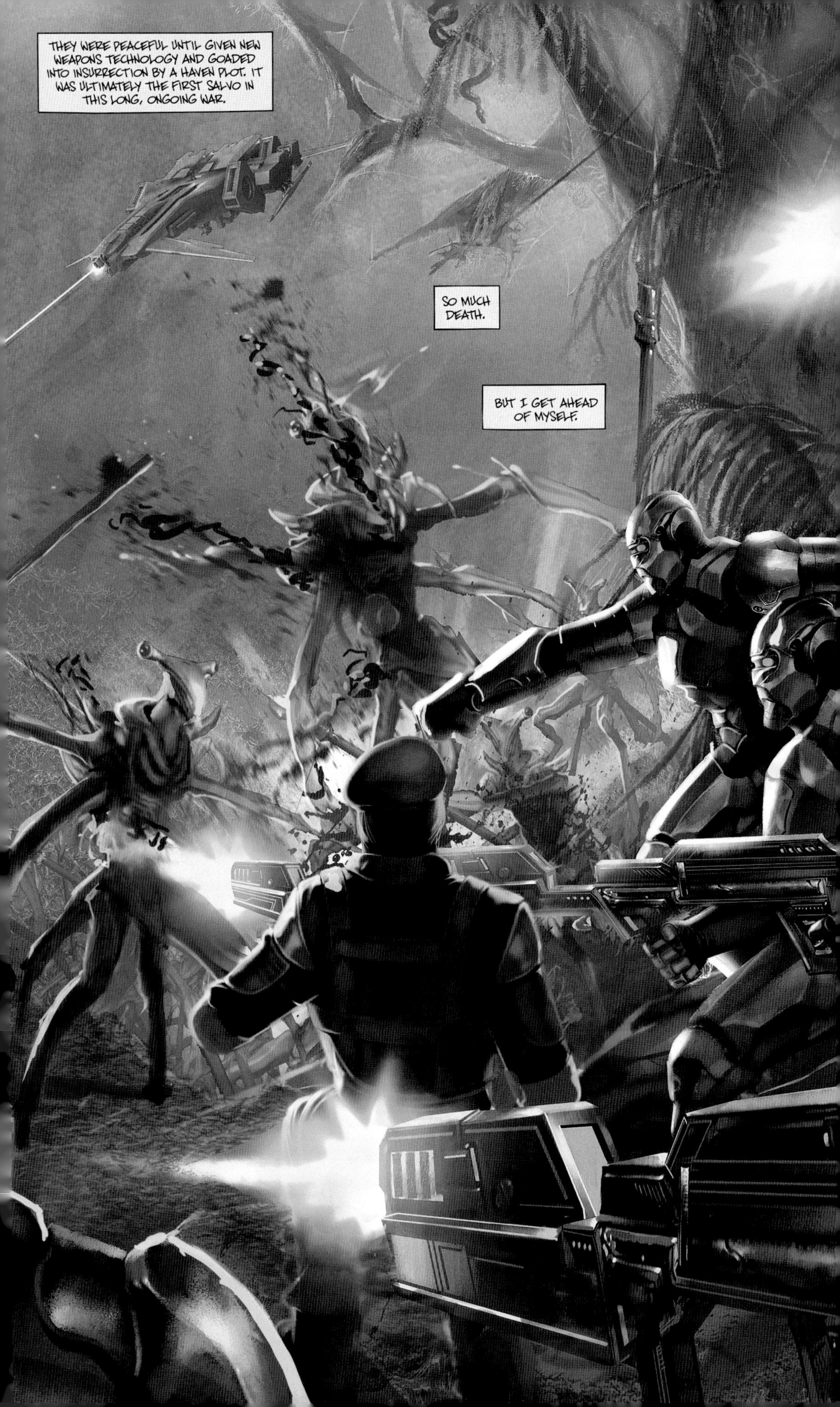
THEY WERE PEACEFUL UNTIL GIVEN NEW WEAPONS TECHNOLOGY AND GOADED INTO INSURRECTION BY A HAVEN PLOT. IT WAS ULTIMATELY THE FIRST SALVO IN THIS LONG, ONGOING WAR.
SO MUCH DEATH.
BUT I GET AHEAD OF MYSELF.

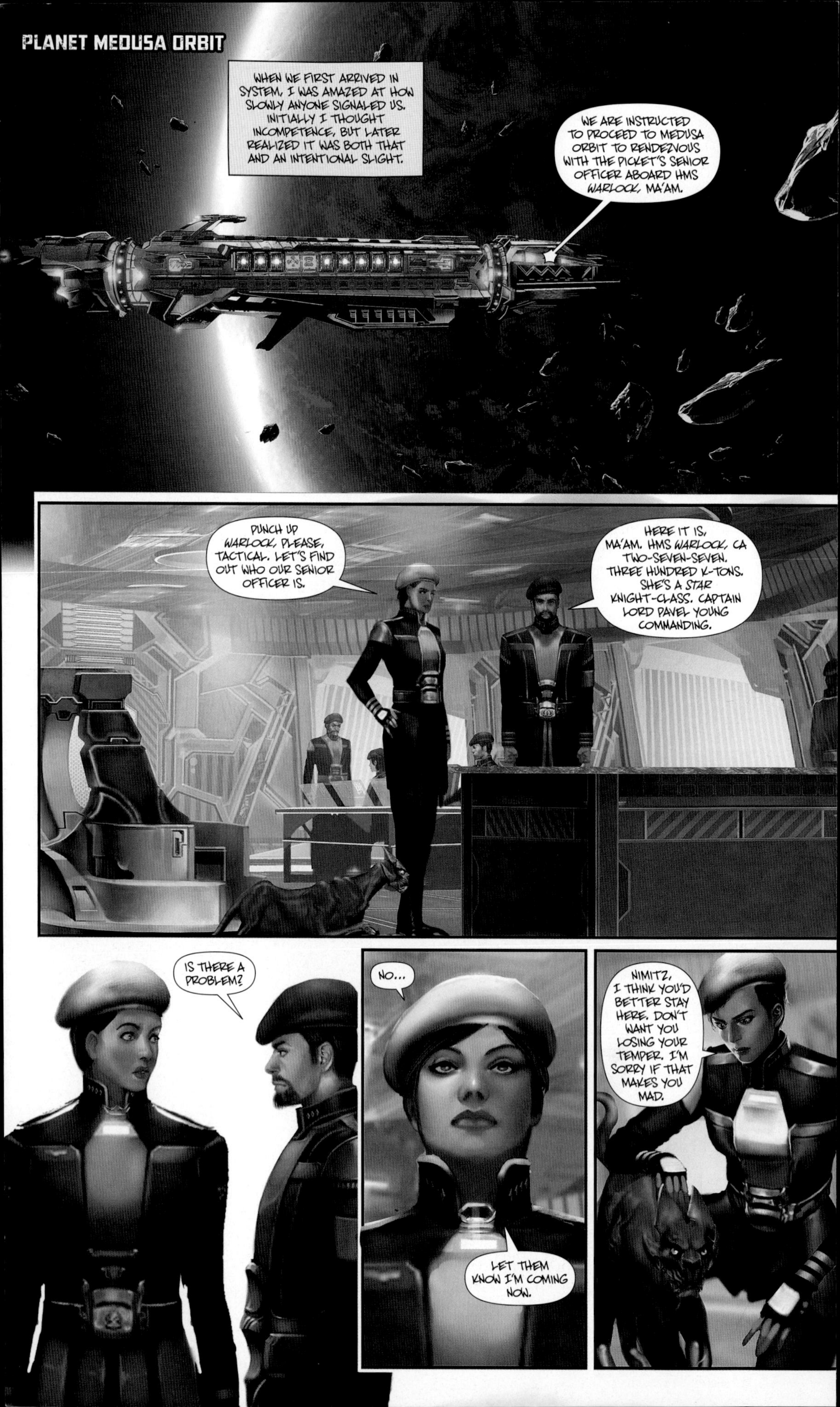
PLANET MEDUSA ORBIT
WHEN WE FIRST ARRIVED IN SYSTEM, I WAS AMAZED AT HOW SLOWLY ANYONE SIGNALED US. INITIALLY I THOUGHT INCOMPETENCE, BUT LATER REALIZED IT WAS BOTH THAT AND AN INTENTIONAL SLIGHT.
WE ARE INSTRUCTED TO PROCEED TO MEDUSA ORBIT TO RENDEZVOUS WITH THE PICKET'S SENIOR OFFICER ABOARD HMS WARLOCK, MA'AM.
PUNCH UP WARLOCK, PLEASE, TACTICAL. LET'S FIND OUT WHO OUR SENIOR OFFICER IS.
HERE IT IS, MA'AM. HMS WARLOCK, CA TWO-SEVEN-SEVEN. THREE HUNDRED K-TONS. SHE'S A STAR KNIGHT-CLASS. CAPTAIN LORD PAVEL YOUNG COMMANDING.
IS THERE A PROBLEM?
NO...
LET THEM KNOW I'M COMING NOW.
NIMITZ, I THINK YOU'D BETTER STAY HERE. DON'T WANT YOU LOSING YOUR TEMPER. I'M SORRY IF THAT MAKES YOU MAD.

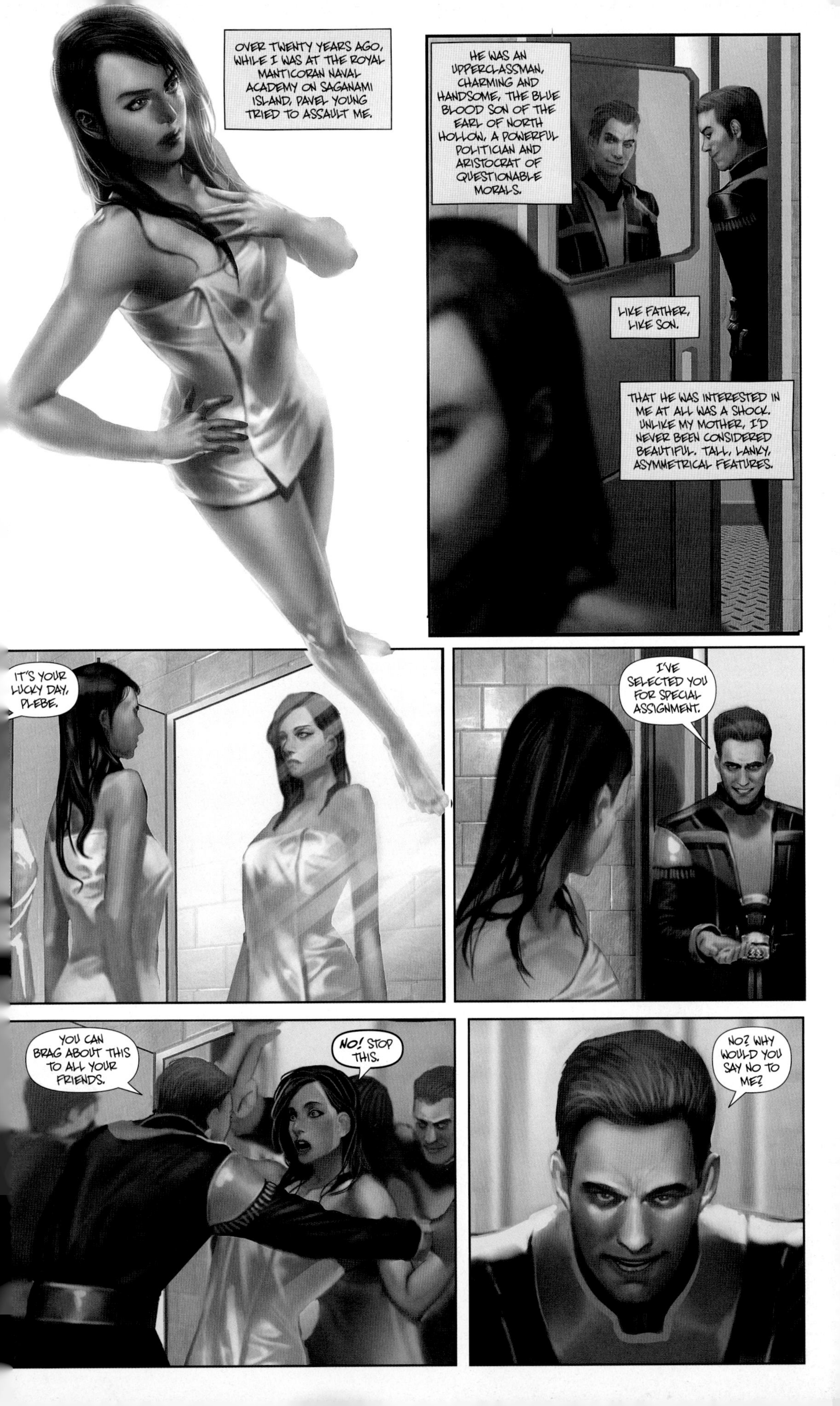
OVER TWENTY YEARS AGO, WHILE I WAS AT THE ROYAL MANTICORAN NAVAL ACADEMY ON SAGANAMI ISLAND, PAVEL YOUNG TRIED TO ASSAULT ME.
HE WAS AN UPPERCLASSMAN, CHARMING AND HANDSOME, THE BLUE BLOOD SON OF THE EARL OF NORTH HOLLOW, A POWERFUL POLITICIAN AND ARISTOCRAT OF QUESTIONABLE MORALS.
LIKE FATHER, LIKE SON.
THAT HE WAS INTERESTED IN ME AT ALL WAS A SHOCK. UNLIKE MY MOTHER, I'D NEVER BEEN CONSIDERED BEAUTIFUL. TALL, LANKY, ASYMMETRICAL FEATURES.
IT'S YOUR LUCKY DAY, PLEBE.
I'VE SELECTED YOU FOR SPECIAL ASSIGNMENT.
YOU CAN BRAG ABOUT THIS TO ALL YOUR FRIENDS.
NO! STOP THIS.
NO? WHY WOULD YOU SAY NO TO ME?

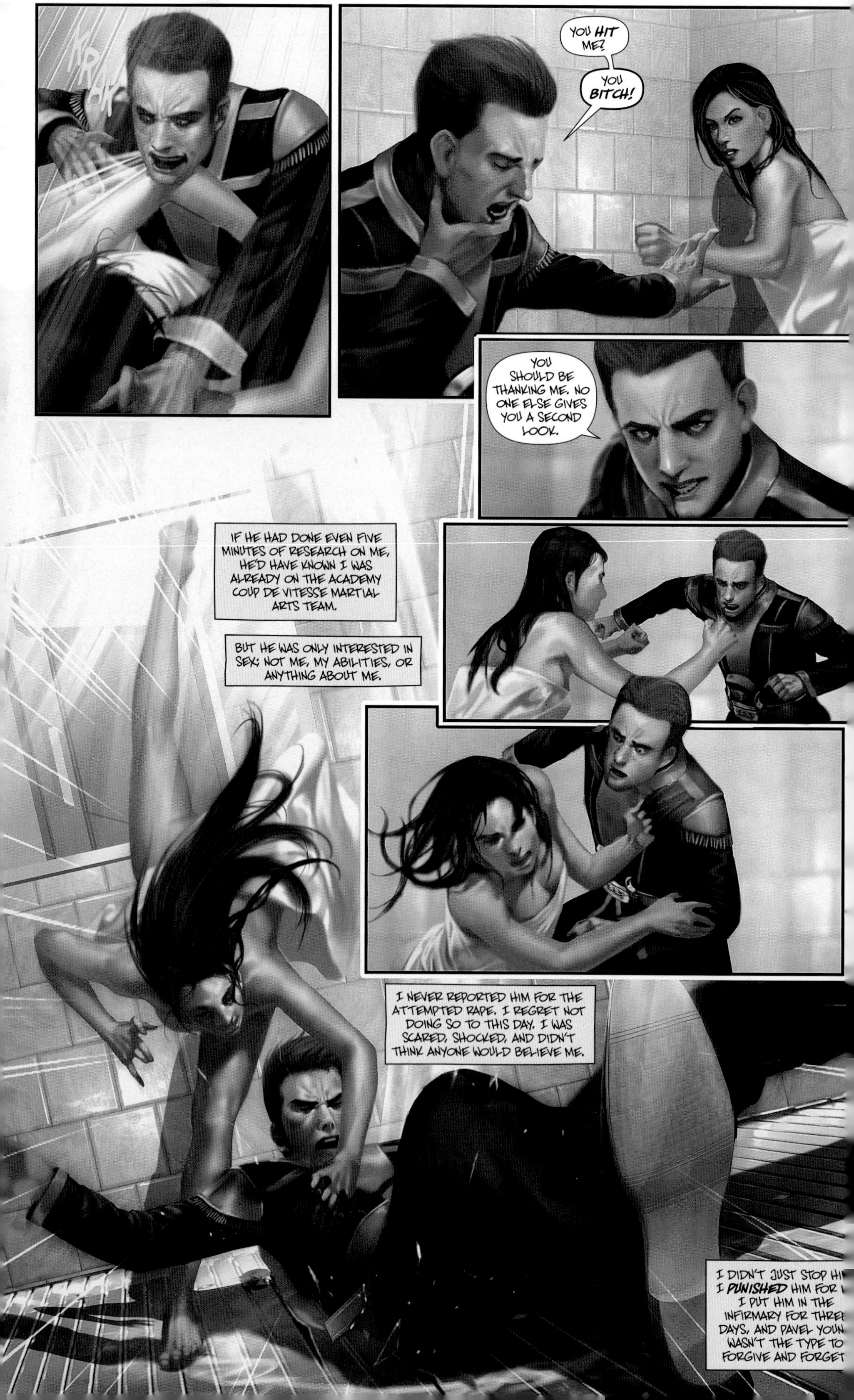
KRAK
YOU HIT ME?
YOU BITCH!
YOU SHOULD BE THANKING ME. NO ONE ELSE GIVES YOU A SECOND LOOK.
IF HE HAD DONE EVEN FIVE MINUTES OF RESEARCH ON ME, HE'D HAVE KNOWN I WAS ALREADY ON THE ACADEMY COUP DE VITESSE MARTIAL ARTS TEAM.
BUT HE WAS ONLY INTERESTED IN SEX; NOT ME, MY ABILITIES, OR ANYTHING ABOUT ME.
I NEVER REPORTED HIM FOR THE ATTEMPTED RAPE. I REGRET NOT DOING SO TO THIS DAY. I WAS SCARED, SHOCKED, AND DIDN'T THINK ANYONE WOULD BELIEVE ME.
I DIDN'T JUST STOP HI I PUNISHED HIM FOR I PUT HIM IN THE INFIRMARY FOR THRE DAYS, AND PAVEL YOUN WASN'T THE TYPE TO FORGIVE AND FORGET

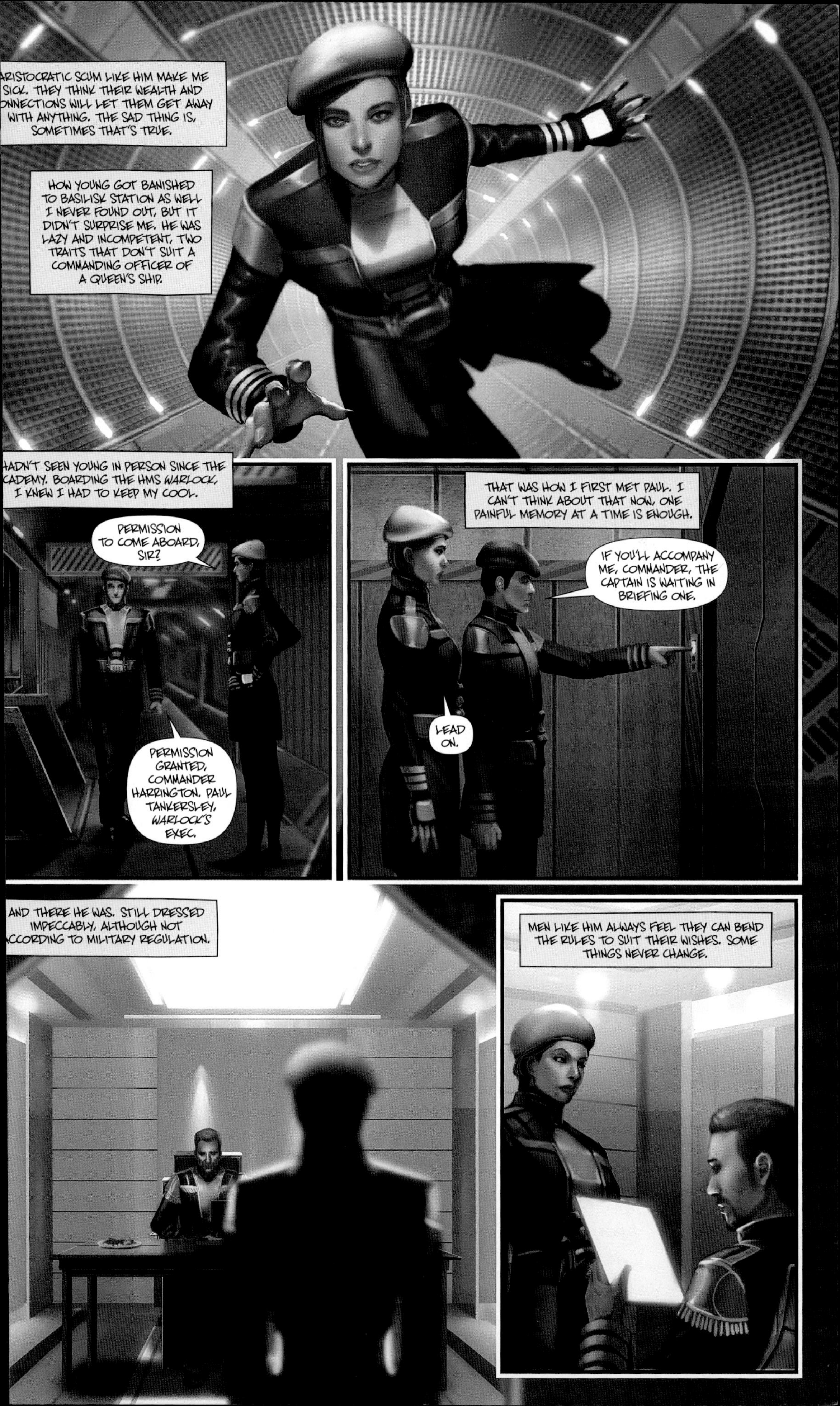
ARISTOCRATIC SCUM LIKE HIM MAKE ME SICK. THEY THINK THEIR WEALTH AND ONNECTIONS WILL LET THEM GET AWAY WITH ANYTHING. THE SAD THING IS, SOMETIMES THAT'S TRUE.
HOW YOUNG GOT BANISHED TO BASILISK STATION AS WELL I NEVER FOUND OUT, BUT IT DIDN'T SURPRISE ME. HE WAS LAZY AND INCOMPETENT, TWO TRAITS THAT DON'T SUIT A COMMANDING OFFICER OF A QUEEN'S SHIP.
HADN'T SEEN YOUNG IN PERSON SINCE THE CADEMY. BOARDING THE HMS WARLOCK, I KNEW I HAD TO KEEP MY COOL.
PERMISSION TO COME ABOARD, SIR?
PERMISSION GRANTED, COMMANDER HARRINGTON. PAUL TANKERSLEY, WARLOCK'S EXEC.
THAT WAS HOW I FIRST MET PAUL. I CAN'T THINK ABOUT THAT NOW, ONE PAINFUL MEMORY AT A TIME IS ENOUGH.
IF YOU'LL ACCOMPANY ME, COMMANDER, THE CAPTAIN IS WAITING IN BRIEFING ONE.
LEAD ON.
AND THERE HE WAS. STILL DRESSED IMPECCABLY, ALTHOUGH NOT CCORDING TO MILITARY REGULATION.
MEN LIKE HIM ALWAYS FEEL THEY CAN BEND THE RULES TO SUIT THEIR WISHES. SOME THINGS NEVER CHANGE.

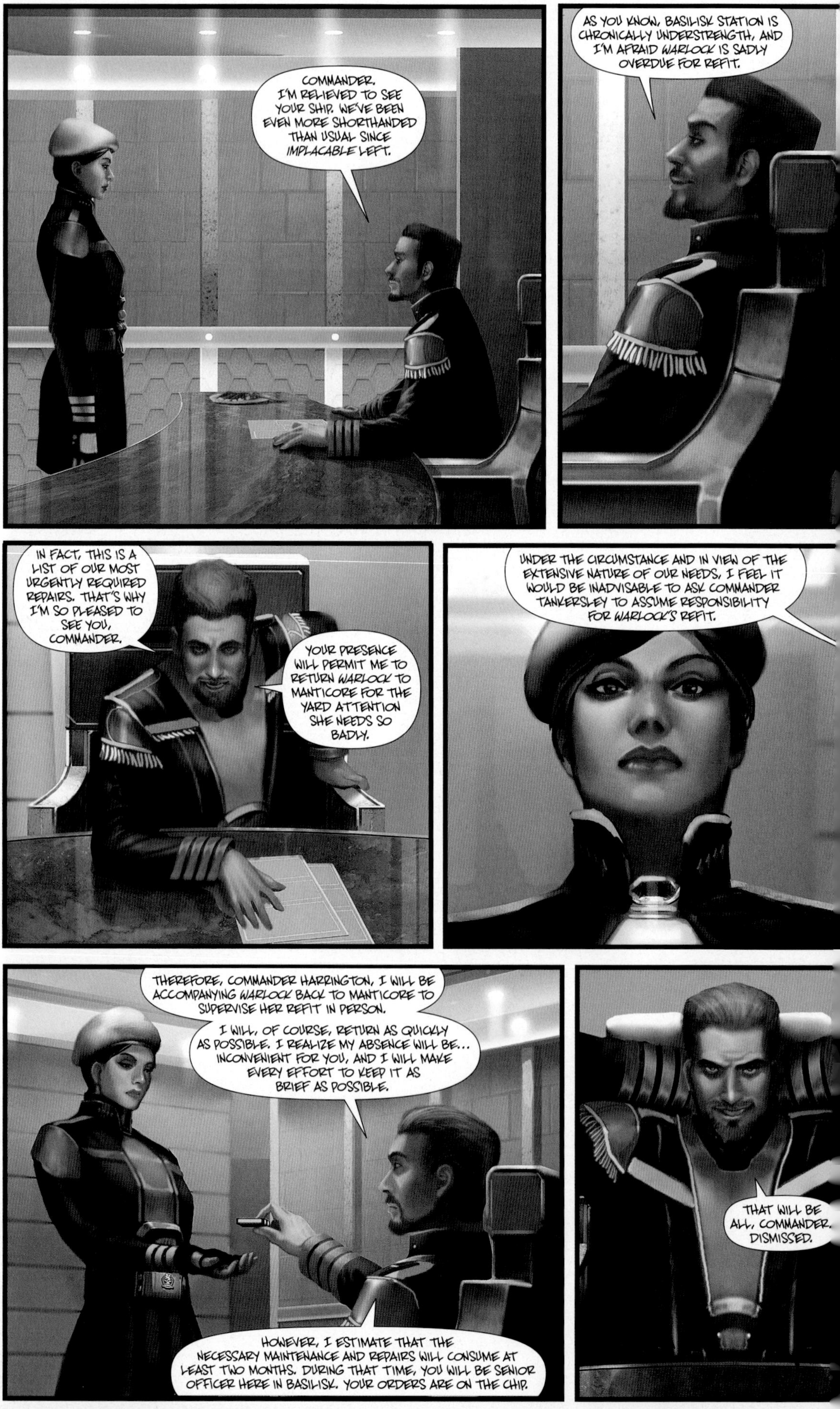

COMMANDER. I'M RELIEVED TO SEE YOUR SHIP. WE'VE BEEN EVEN MORE SHORTHANDED THAN USUAL SINCE *IMPLACABLE* LEFT.
AS YOU KNOW, BASILISK STATION IS CHRONICALLY UNDERSTRENGTH, AND I'M AFRAID *WARLOCK* IS SADLY OVERDUE FOR REFIT.
IN FACT, THIS IS A LIST OF OUR MOST URGENTLY REQUIRED REPAIRS. THAT'S WHY I'M SO PLEASED TO SEE YOU, COMMANDER.
YOUR PRESENCE WILL PERMIT ME TO RETURN *WARLOCK* TO MANTICORE FOR THE YARD ATTENTION SHE NEEDS SO BADLY.
UNDER THE CIRCUMSTANCE AND IN VIEW OF THE EXTENSIVE NATURE OF OUR NEEDS, I FEEL IT WOULD BE INADVISABLE TO ASK COMMANDER TANKERSLEY TO ASSUME RESPONSIBILITY FOR *WARLOCK'S* REFIT.
THEREFORE, COMMANDER HARRINGTON, I WILL BE ACCOMPANYING *WARLOCK* BACK TO MANTICORE TO SUPERVISE HER REFIT IN PERSON.
I WILL, OF COURSE, RETURN AS QUICKLY AS POSSIBLE. I REALIZE MY ABSENCE WILL BE... INCONVENIENT FOR YOU, AND I WILL MAKE EVERY EFFORT TO KEEP IT AS BRIEF AS POSSIBLE.
HOWEVER, I ESTIMATE THAT THE NECESSARY MAINTENANCE AND REPAIRS WILL CONSUME AT LEAST TWO MONTHS. DURING THAT TIME, YOU WILL BE SENIOR OFFICER HERE IN BASILISK. YOUR ORDERS ARE ON THE CHIP.
THAT WILL BE ALL, COMMANDER. DISMISSED.

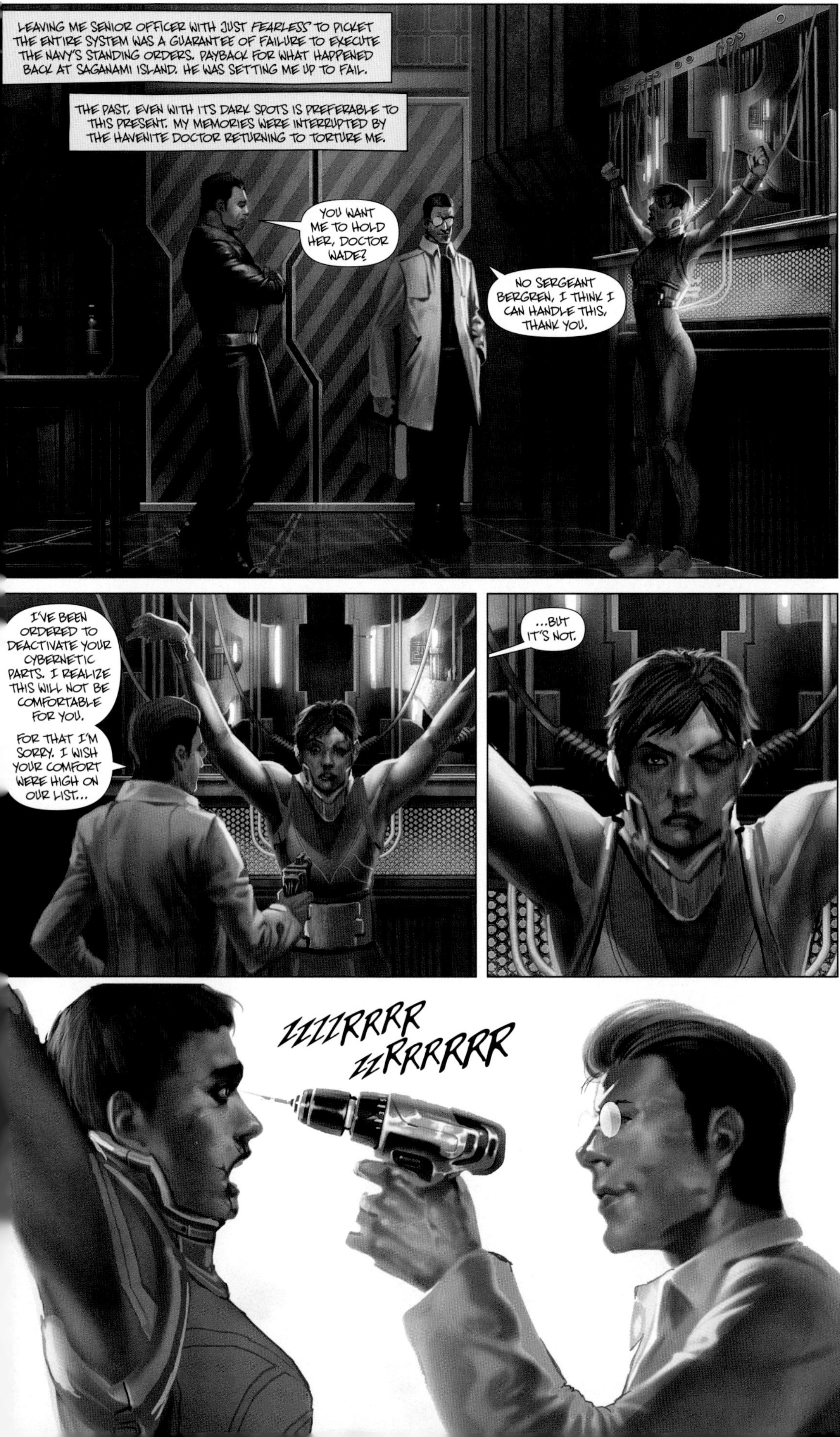
LEAVING ME SENIOR OFFICER WITH JUST FEARLESS TO PICKET THE ENTIRE SYSTEM WAS A GUARANTEE OF FAILURE TO EXECUTE THE NAVY'S STANDING ORDERS. PAYBACK FOR WHAT HAPPENED BACK AT SAGANAMI ISLAND. HE WAS SETTING ME UP TO FAIL.
THE PAST, EVEN WITH ITS DARK SPOTS IS PREFERABLE TO THIS PRESENT. MY MEMORIES WERE INTERRUPTED BY THE HAVENITE DOCTOR RETURNING TO TORTURE ME.
YOU WANT ME TO HOLD HER, DOCTOR WADE?
NO SERGEANT BERGREN, I THINK I CAN HANDLE THIS, THANK YOU.
I'VE BEEN ORDERED TO DEACTIVATE YOUR CYBERNETIC PARTS. I REALIZE THIS WILL NOT BE COMFORTABLE FOR YOU.
FOR THAT I'M SORRY. I WISH YOUR COMFORT WERE HIGH ON OUR LIST...
...BUT IT'S NOT.
ZZZZRRRR ZZRRRRRR

TALES OF HONOR

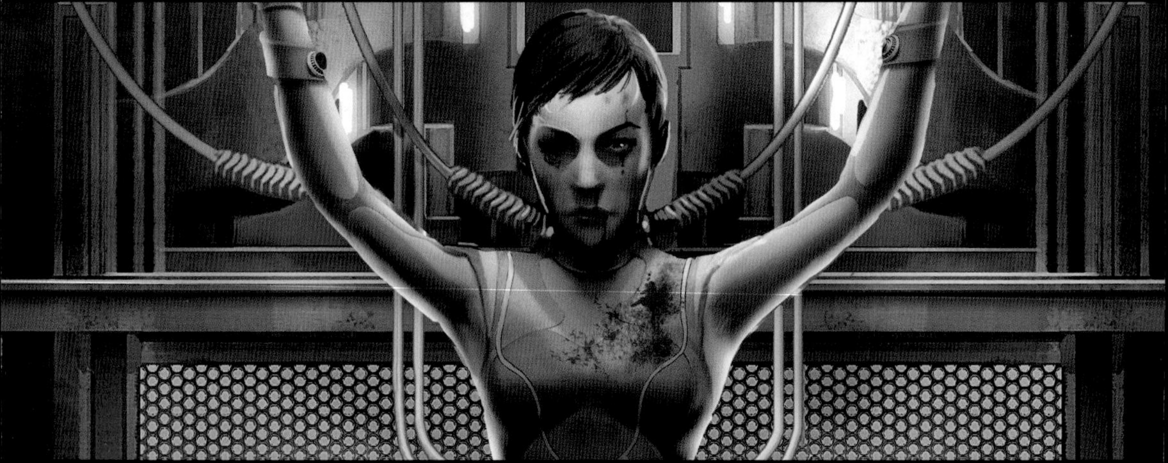

CHAPTER TWO

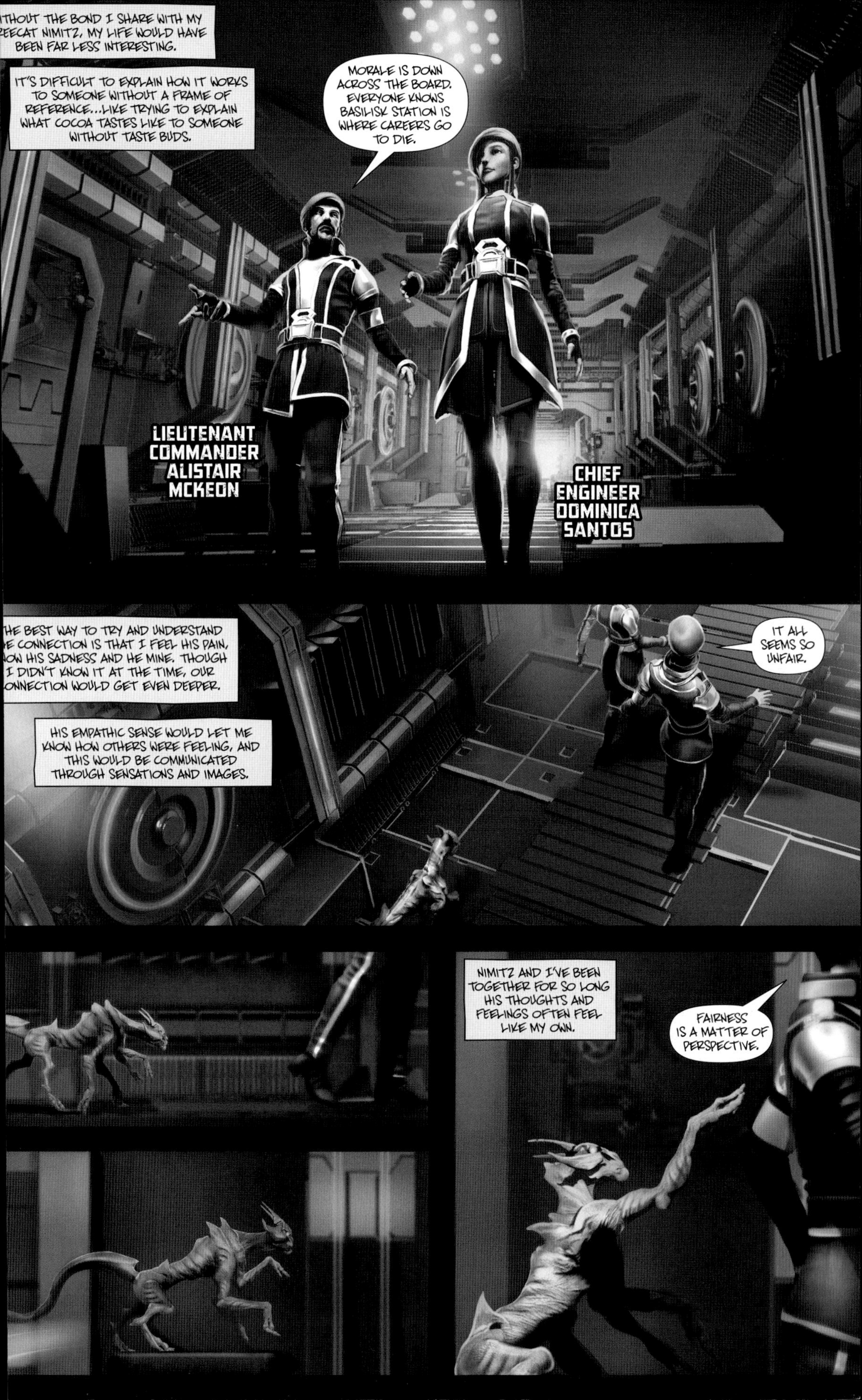
ITHOUT THE BOND I SHARE WITH MY EECAT NIMITZ, MY LIFE WOULD HAVE BEEN FAR LESS INTERESTING.
IT'S DIFFICULT TO EXPLAIN HOW IT WORKS TO SOMEONE WITHOUT A FRAME OF REFERENCE...LIKE TRYING TO EXPLAIN WHAT COCOA TASTES LIKE TO SOMEONE WITHOUT TASTE BUDS.
MORALE IS DOWN ACROSS THE BOARD. EVERYONE KNOWS BASILISK STATION IS WHERE CAREERS GO TO DIE.
LIEUTENANT COMMANDER ALISTAIR MCKEON
CHIEF ENGINEER DOMINICA SANTOS
HE BEST WAY TO TRY AND UNDERSTAND E CONNECTION IS THAT I FEEL HIS PAIN, NOW HIS SADNESS AND HE MINE. THOUGH I DIDN'T KNOW IT AT THE TIME, OUR ONNECTION WOULD GET EVEN DEEPER.
HIS EMPATHIC SENSE WOULD LET ME KNOW HOW OTHERS WERE FEELING, AND THIS WOULD BE COMMUNICATED THROUGH SENSATIONS AND IMAGES.
IT ALL SEEMS SO UNFAIR.
NIMITZ AND I'VE BEEN TOGETHER FOR SO LONG HIS THOUGHTS AND FEELINGS OFTEN FEEL LIKE MY OWN.
FAIRNESS IS A MATTER OF PERSPECTIVE.

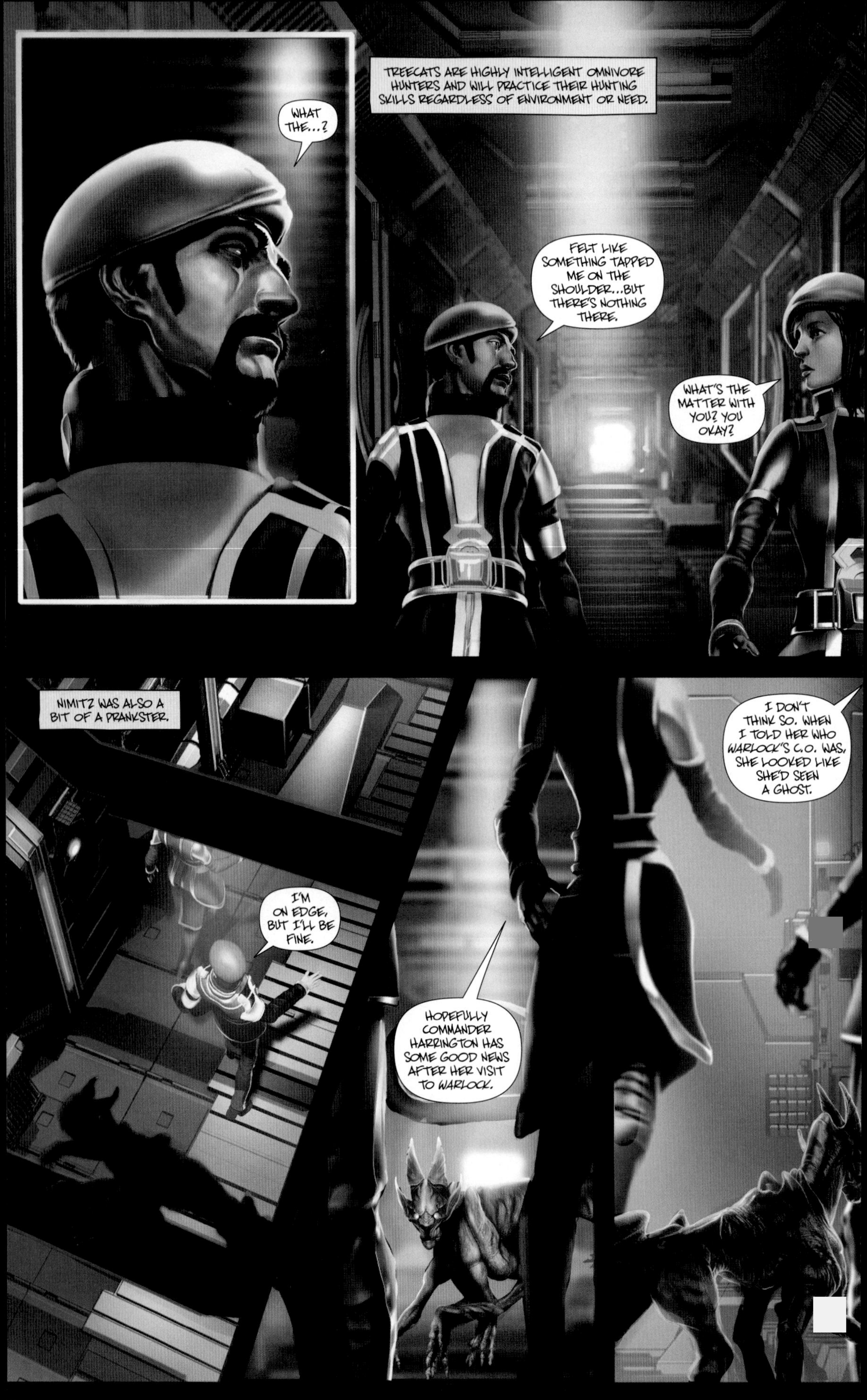
WHAT THE...?
TREECATS ARE HIGHLY INTELLIGENT OMNIVORE HUNTERS AND WILL PRACTICE THEIR HUNTING SKILLS REGARDLESS OF ENVIRONMENT OR NEED.
FELT LIKE SOMETHING TAPPED ME ON THE SHOULDER...BUT THERE'S NOTHING THERE.
WHAT'S THE MATTER WITH YOU? YOU OKAY?
NIMITZ WAS ALSO A BIT OF A PRANKSTER.
I'M ON EDGE, BUT I'LL BE FINE.
HOPEFULLY COMMANDER HARRINGTON HAS SOME GOOD NEWS AFTER HER VISIT TO WARLOCK.
I DON'T THINK SO. WHEN I TOLD HER WHO WARLOCK'S C.O. WAS, SHE LOOKED LIKE SHE'D SEEN A GHOST.

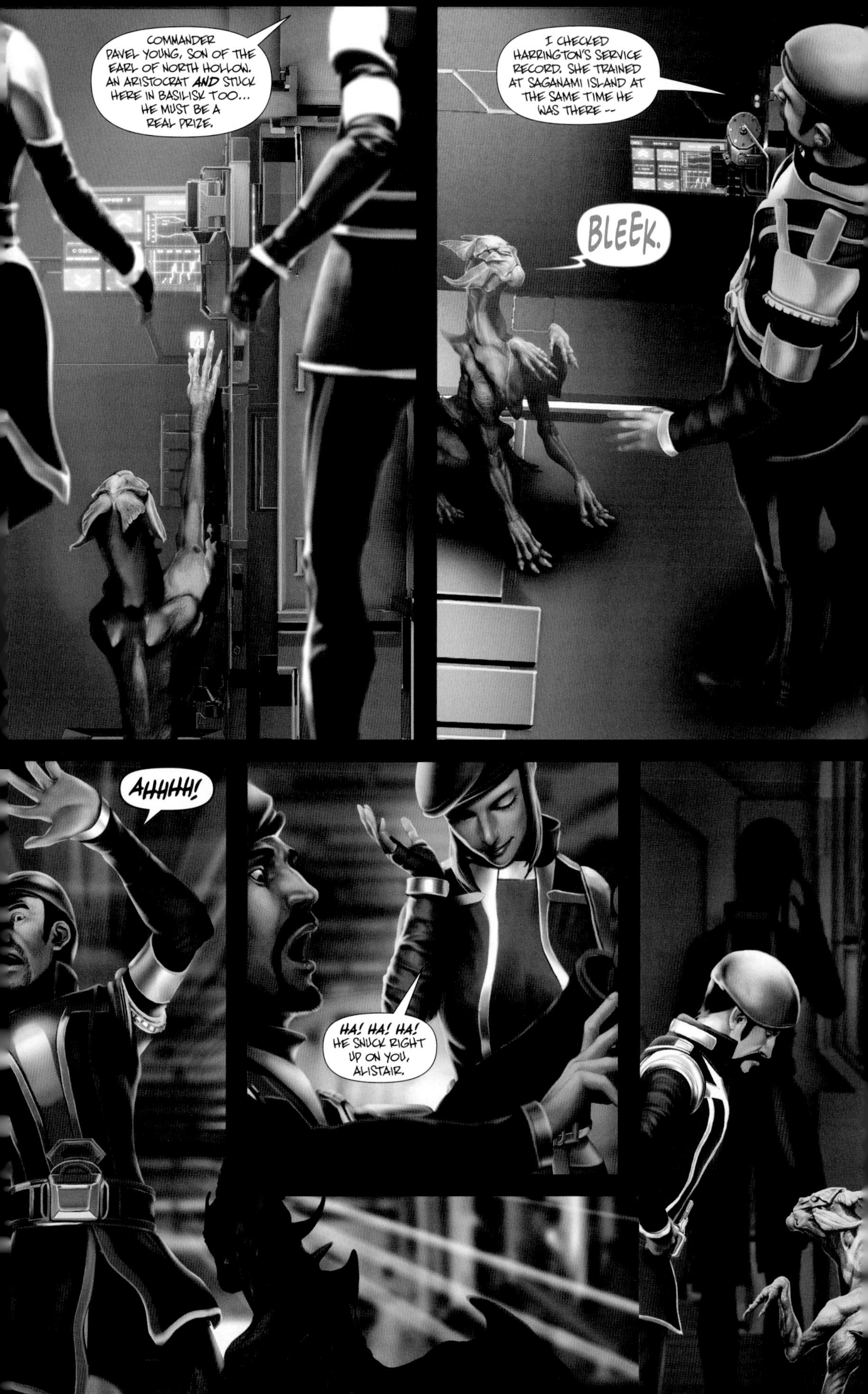
COMMANDER PAVEL YOUNG, SON OF THE EARL OF NORTH HOLLOW. AN ARISTOCRAT **AND** STUCK HERE IN BASILISK TOO... HE MUST BE A REAL PRIZE.
I CHECKED HARRINGTON'S SERVICE RECORD. SHE TRAINED AT SAGANAMI ISLAND AT THE SAME TIME HE WAS THERE --
BLEEK.
AHHHH!
HA! HA! HA! HE SNUCK RIGHT UP ON YOU, ALISTAIR.

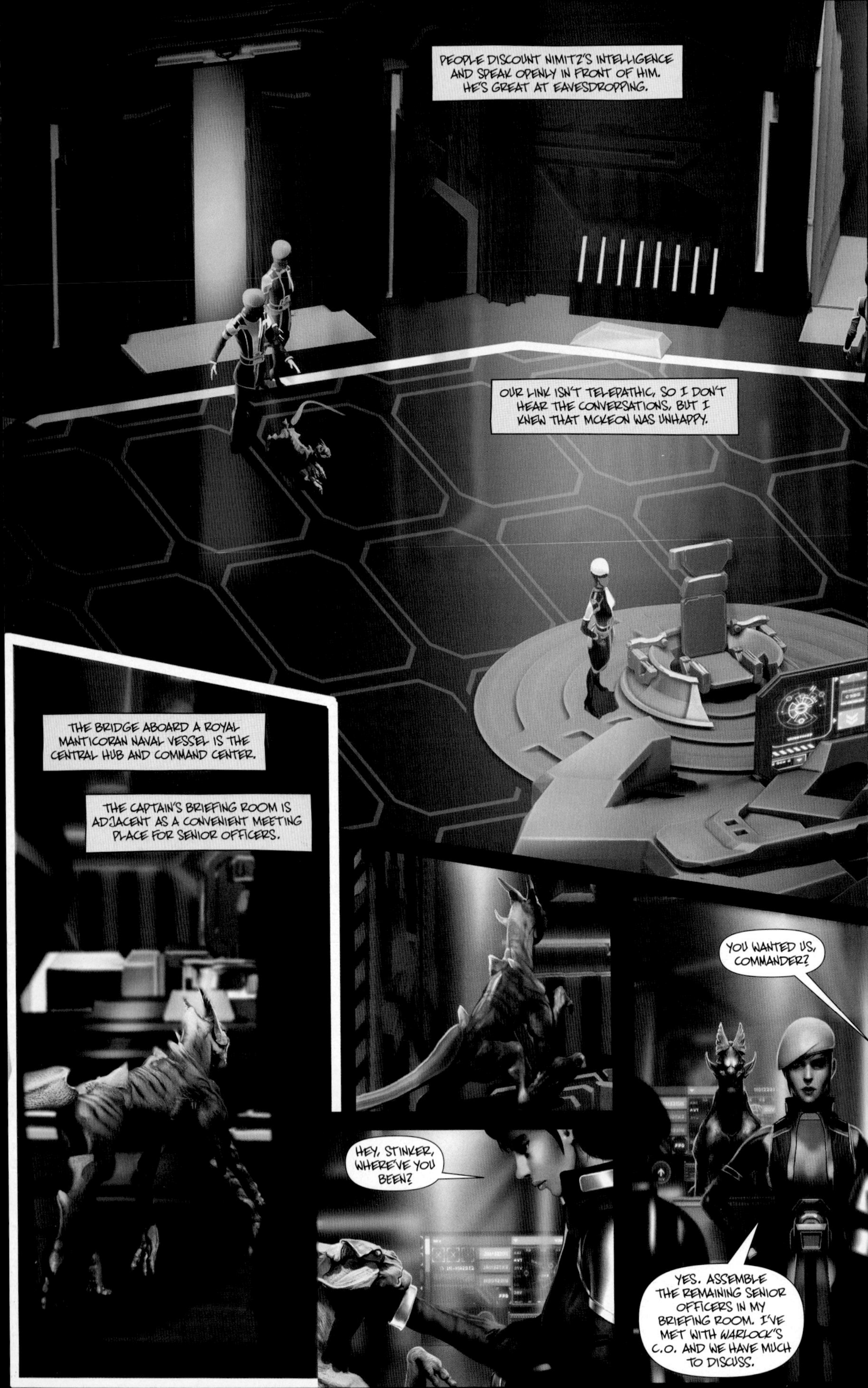
PEOPLE DISCOUNT NIMITZ'S INTELLIGENCE AND SPEAK OPENLY IN FRONT OF HIM. HE'S GREAT AT EAVESDROPPING.
OUR LINK ISN'T TELEPATHIC, SO I DON'T HEAR THE CONVERSATIONS, BUT I KNEW THAT MCKEON WAS UNHAPPY.
THE BRIDGE ABOARD A ROYAL MANTICORAN NAVAL VESSEL IS THE CENTRAL HUB AND COMMAND CENTER.
THE CAPTAIN'S BRIEFING ROOM IS ADJACENT AS A CONVENIENT MEETING PLACE FOR SENIOR OFFICERS.
HEY, STINKER, WHERE'VE YOU BEEN?
YOU WANTED US, COMMANDER?
YES. ASSEMBLE THE REMAINING SENIOR OFFICERS IN MY BRIEFING ROOM. I'VE MET WITH WARLOCK'S C.O. AND WE HAVE MUCH TO DISCUSS.

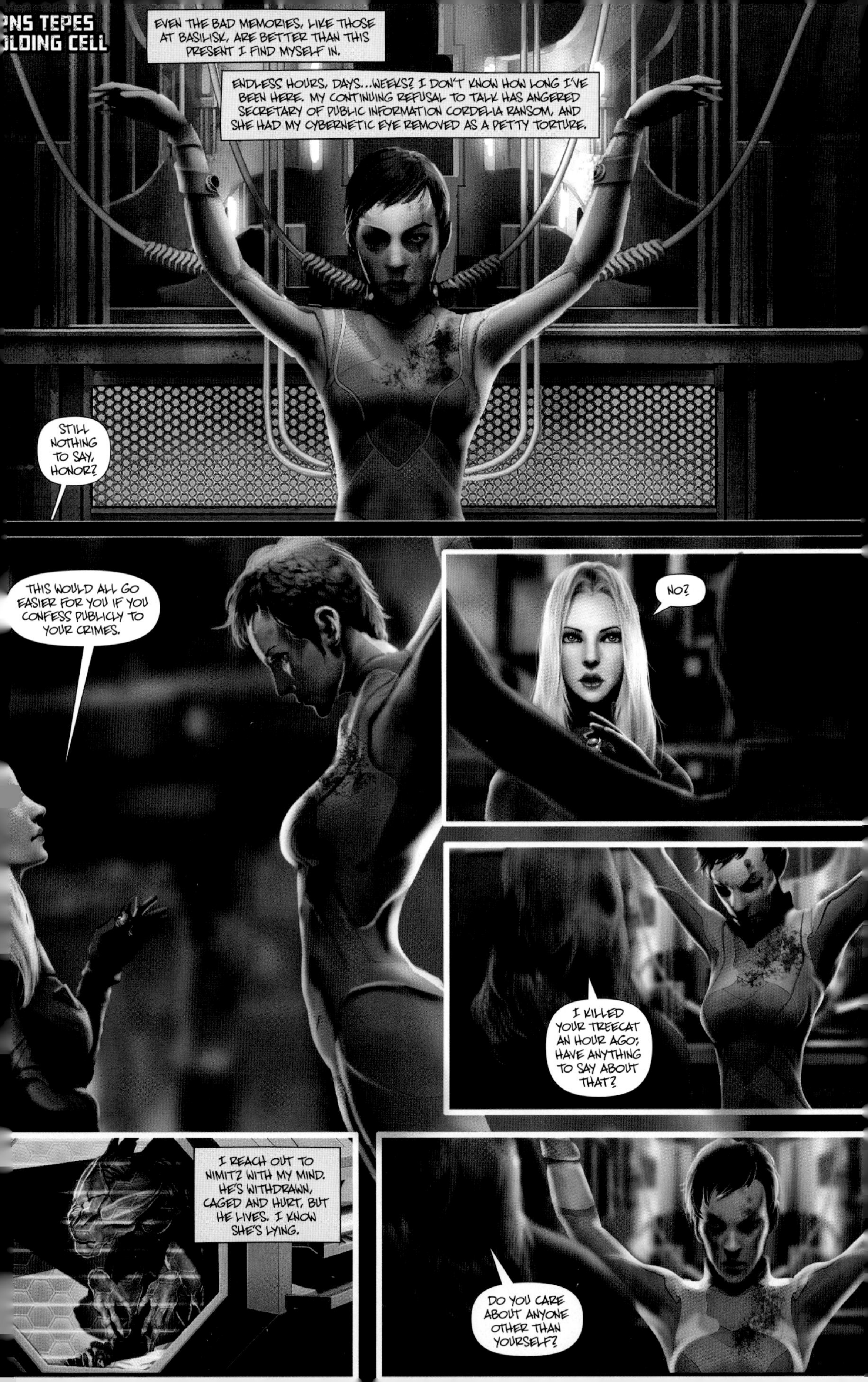
PNS TEPES
OLDING CELL
EVEN THE BAD MEMORIES, LIKE THOSE AT BASILISK, ARE BETTER THAN THIS PRESENT I FIND MYSELF IN.
ENDLESS HOURS, DAYS...WEEKS? I DON'T KNOW HOW LONG I'VE BEEN HERE. MY CONTINUING REFUSAL TO TALK HAS ANGERED SECRETARY OF PUBLIC INFORMATION CORDELIA RANSOM, AND SHE HAD MY CYBERNETIC EYE REMOVED AS A PETTY TORTURE.
STILL NOTHING TO SAY, HONOR?
THIS WOULD ALL GO EASIER FOR YOU IF YOU CONFESS PUBLICLY TO YOUR CRIMES.
NO?
I KILLED YOUR TREECAT AN HOUR AGO; HAVE ANYTHING TO SAY ABOUT THAT?
I REACH OUT TO NIMITZ WITH MY MIND. HE'S WITHDRAWN, CAGED AND HURT, BUT HE LIVES. I KNOW SHE'S LYING.
DO YOU CARE ABOUT ANYONE OTHER THAN YOURSELF?

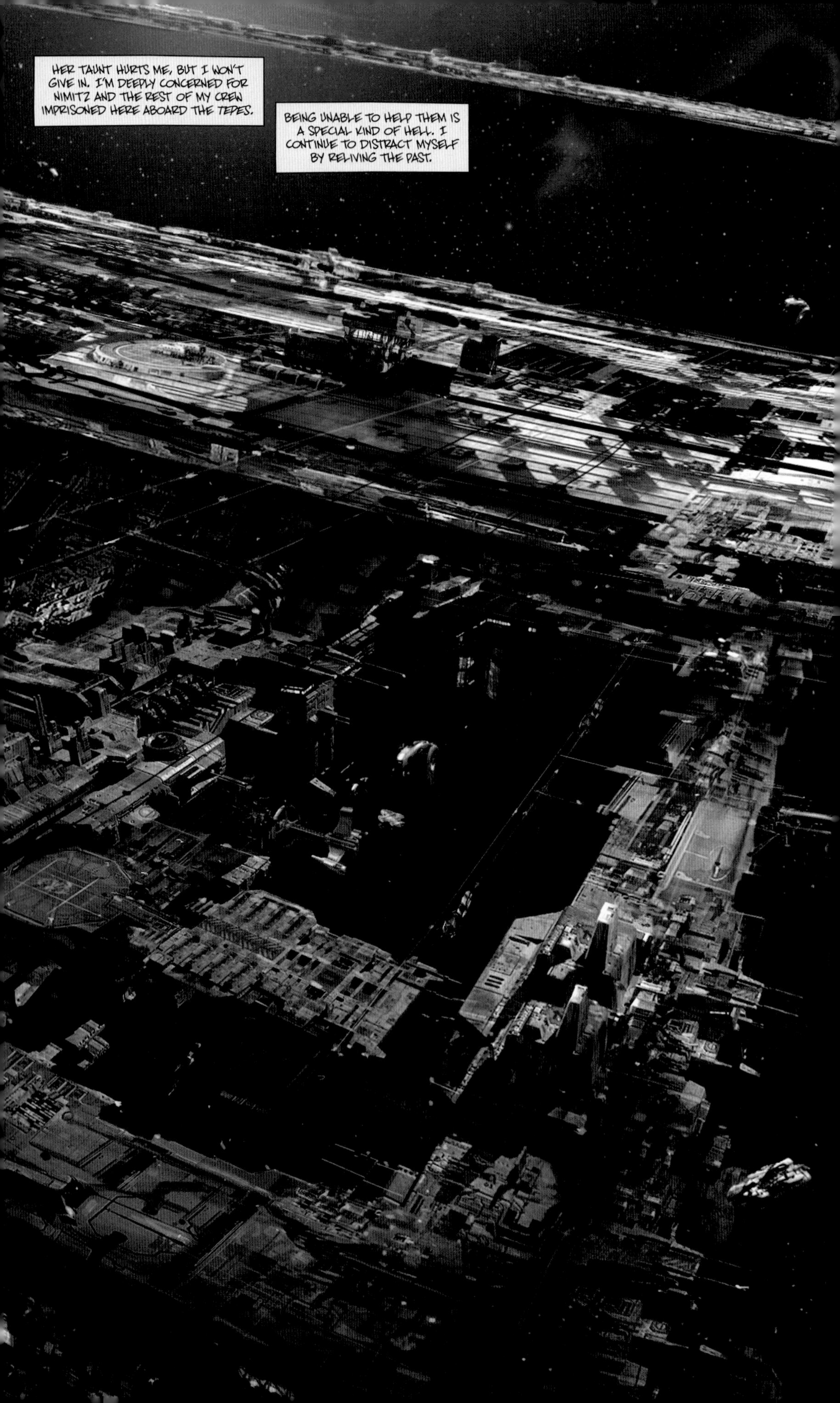
HER TAUNT HURTS ME, BUT I WON'T GIVE IN. I'M DEEPLY CONCERNED FOR NIMITZ AND THE REST OF MY CREW IMPRISONED HERE ABOARD THE TEPES.
BEING UNABLE TO HELP THEM IS A SPECIAL KIND OF HELL. I CONTINUE TO DISTRACT MYSELF BY RELIVING THE PAST.

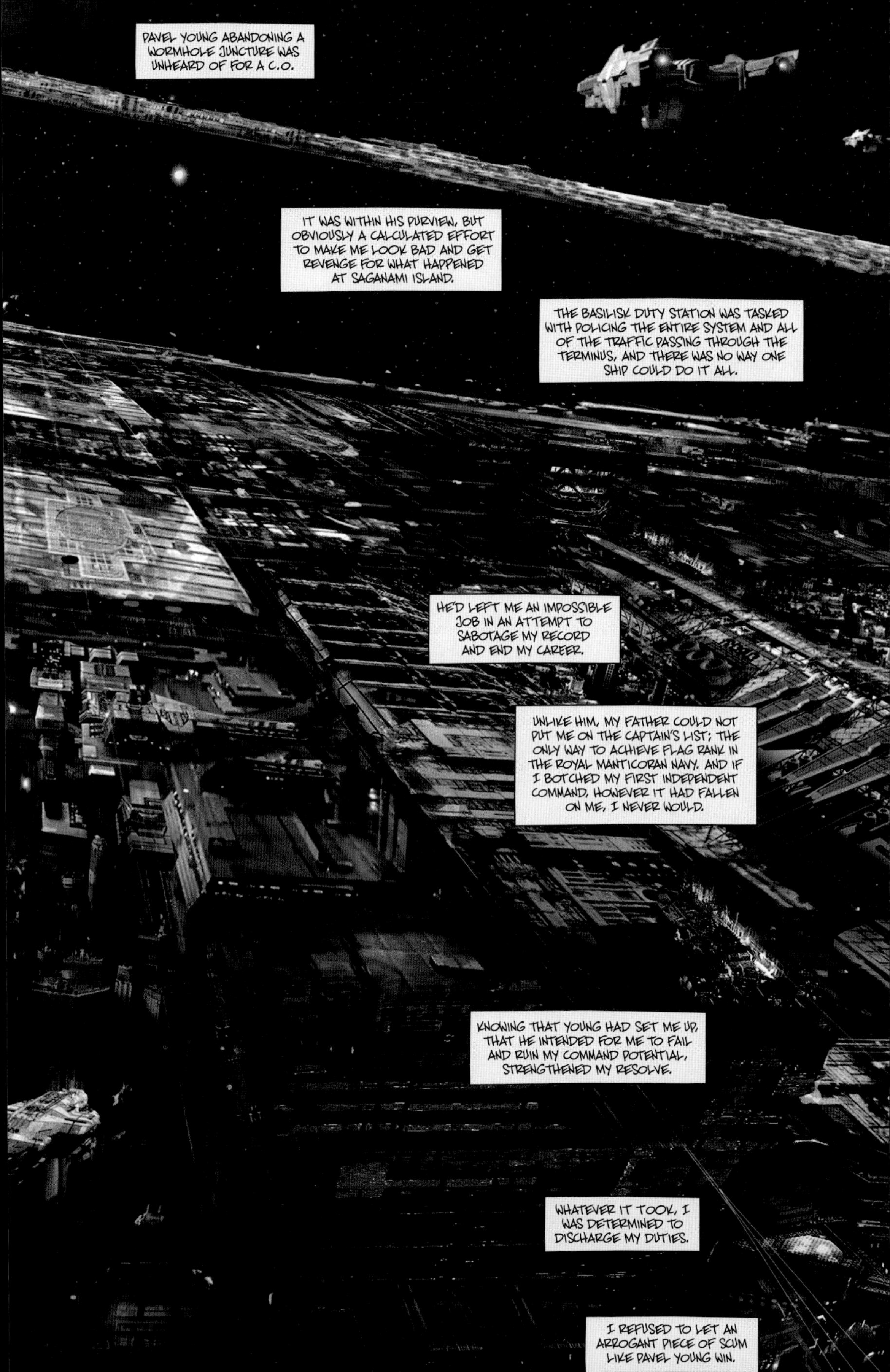
PAVEL YOUNG ABANDONING A WORMHOLE JUNCTURE WAS UNHEARD OF FOR A C.O.
IT WAS WITHIN HIS PURVIEW, BUT OBVIOUSLY A CALCULATED EFFORT TO MAKE ME LOOK BAD AND GET REVENGE FOR WHAT HAPPENED AT SAGANAMI ISLAND.
THE BASILISK DUTY STATION WAS TASKED WITH POLICING THE ENTIRE SYSTEM AND ALL OF THE TRAFFIC PASSING THROUGH THE TERMINUS, AND THERE WAS NO WAY ONE SHIP COULD DO IT ALL.
HE'D LEFT ME AN IMPOSSIBLE JOB IN AN ATTEMPT TO SABOTAGE MY RECORD AND END MY CAREER.
UNLIKE HIM, MY FATHER COULD NOT PUT ME ON THE CAPTAIN'S LIST; THE ONLY WAY TO ACHIEVE FLAG RANK IN THE ROYAL MANTICORAN NAVY. AND IF I BOTCHED MY FIRST INDEPENDENT COMMAND, HOWEVER IT HAD FALLEN ON ME, I NEVER WOULD.
KNOWING THAT YOUNG HAD SET ME UP, THAT HE INTENDED FOR ME TO FAIL AND RUIN MY COMMAND POTENTIAL, STRENGTHENED MY RESOLVE.
WHATEVER IT TOOK, I WAS DETERMINED TO DISCHARGE MY DUTIES.
I REFUSED TO LET AN ARROGANT PIECE OF SCUM LIKE PAVEL YOUNG WIN.

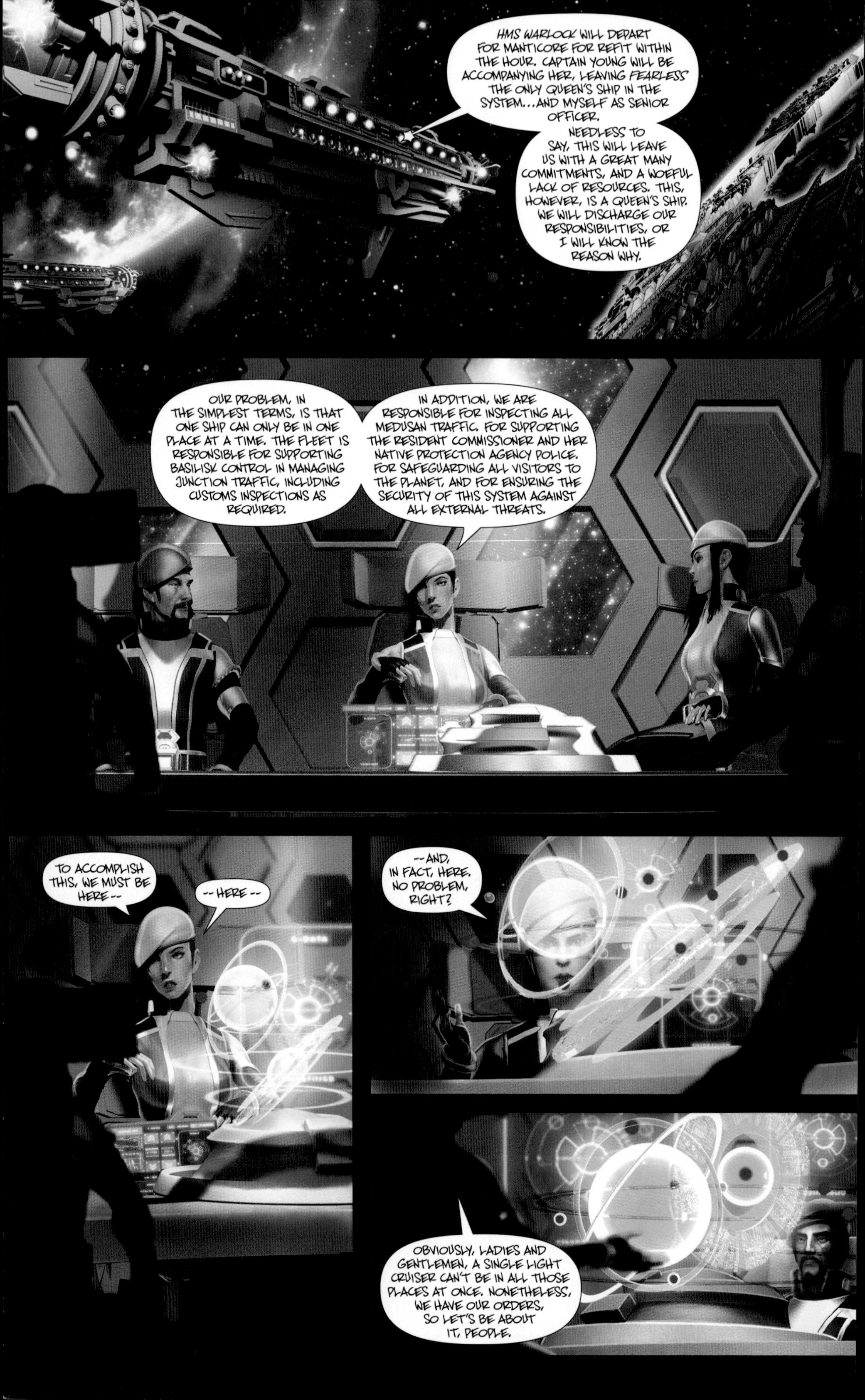
HMS WARLOCK WILL DEPART FOR MANTICORE FOR REFIT WITHIN THE HOUR. CAPTAIN YOUNG WILL BE ACCOMPANYING HER, LEAVING FEARLESS THE ONLY QUEEN'S SHIP IN THE SYSTEM...AND MYSELF AS SENIOR OFFICER.
NEEDLESS TO SAY, THIS WILL LEAVE US WITH A GREAT MANY COMMITMENTS, AND A WOEFUL LACK OF RESOURCES. THIS, HOWEVER, IS A QUEEN'S SHIP. WE WILL DISCHARGE OUR RESPONSIBILITIES, OR I WILL KNOW THE REASON WHY.
OUR PROBLEM, IN THE SIMPLEST TERMS, IS THAT ONE SHIP CAN ONLY BE IN ONE PLACE AT A TIME. THE FLEET IS RESPONSIBLE FOR SUPPORTING BASILISK CONTROL IN MANAGING JUNCTION TRAFFIC, INCLUDING CUSTOMS INSPECTIONS AS REQUIRED.
IN ADDITION, WE ARE RESPONSIBLE FOR INSPECTING ALL MEDUSAN TRAFFIC. FOR SUPPORTING THE RESIDENT COMMISSIONER AND HER NATIVE PROTECTION AGENCY POLICE. FOR SAFEGUARDING ALL VISITORS TO THE PLANET, AND FOR ENSURING THE SECURITY OF THIS SYSTEM AGAINST ALL EXTERNAL THREATS.
TO ACCOMPLISH THIS, WE MUST BE HERE--
--HERE--
--AND, IN FACT, HERE. NO PROBLEM, RIGHT?
OBVIOUSLY, LADIES AND GENTLEMEN, A SINGLE LIGHT CRUISER CAN'T BE IN ALL THOSE PLACES AT ONCE. NONETHELESS, WE HAVE OUR ORDERS, SO LET'S BE ABOUT IT, PEOPLE.

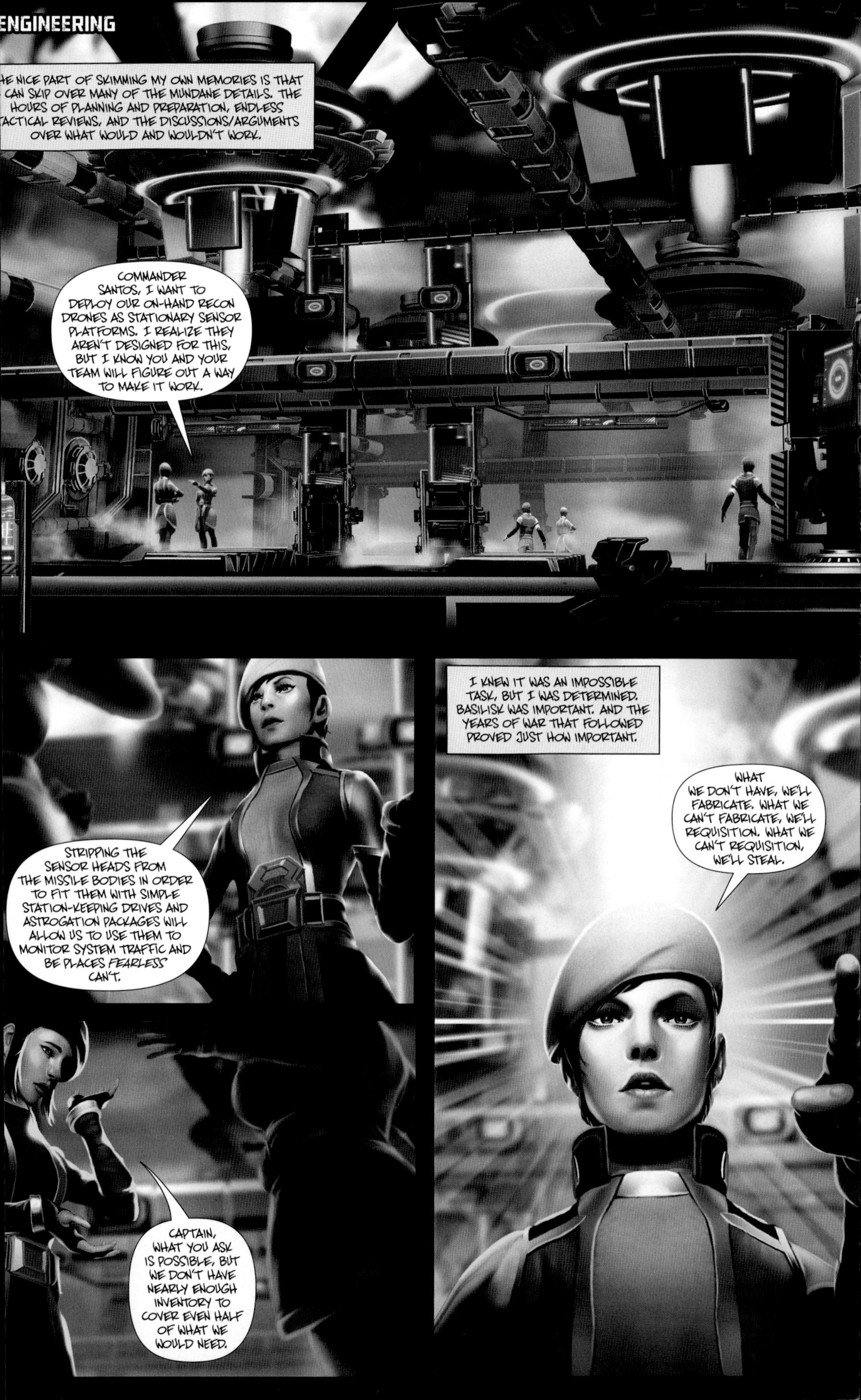
HE NICE PART OF SKIMMING MY OWN MEMORIES IS THAT CAN SKIP OVER MANY OF THE MUNDANE DETAILS. THE HOURS OF PLANNING AND PREPARATION, ENDLESS TACTICAL REVIEWS, AND THE DISCUSSIONS/ARGUMENTS OVER WHAT WOULD AND WOULDN'T WORK.
COMMANDER SANTOS, I WANT TO DEPLOY OUR ON-HAND RECON DRONES AS STATIONARY SENSOR PLATFORMS. I REALIZE THEY AREN'T DESIGNED FOR THIS, BUT I KNOW YOU AND YOUR TEAM WILL FIGURE OUT A WAY TO MAKE IT WORK.
STRIPPING THE SENSOR HEADS FROM THE MISSILE BODIES IN ORDER TO FIT THEM WITH SIMPLE STATION-KEEPING DRIVES AND ASTROGATION PACKAGES WILL ALLOW US TO USE THEM TO MONITOR SYSTEM TRAFFIC AND BE PLACES *FEARLESS* CAN'T.
CAPTAIN, WHAT YOU ASK IS POSSIBLE, BUT WE DON'T HAVE NEARLY ENOUGH INVENTORY TO COVER EVEN HALF OF WHAT WE WOULD NEED.
I KNEW IT WAS AN IMPOSSIBLE TASK, BUT I WAS DETERMINED. BASILISK WAS IMPORTANT. AND THE YEARS OF WAR THAT FOLLOWED PROVED JUST HOW IMPORTANT.
WHAT WE DON'T HAVE, WE'LL FABRICATE. WHAT WE CAN'T FABRICATE, WE'LL REQUISITION. WHAT WE CAN'T REQUISITION, WE'LL STEAL.

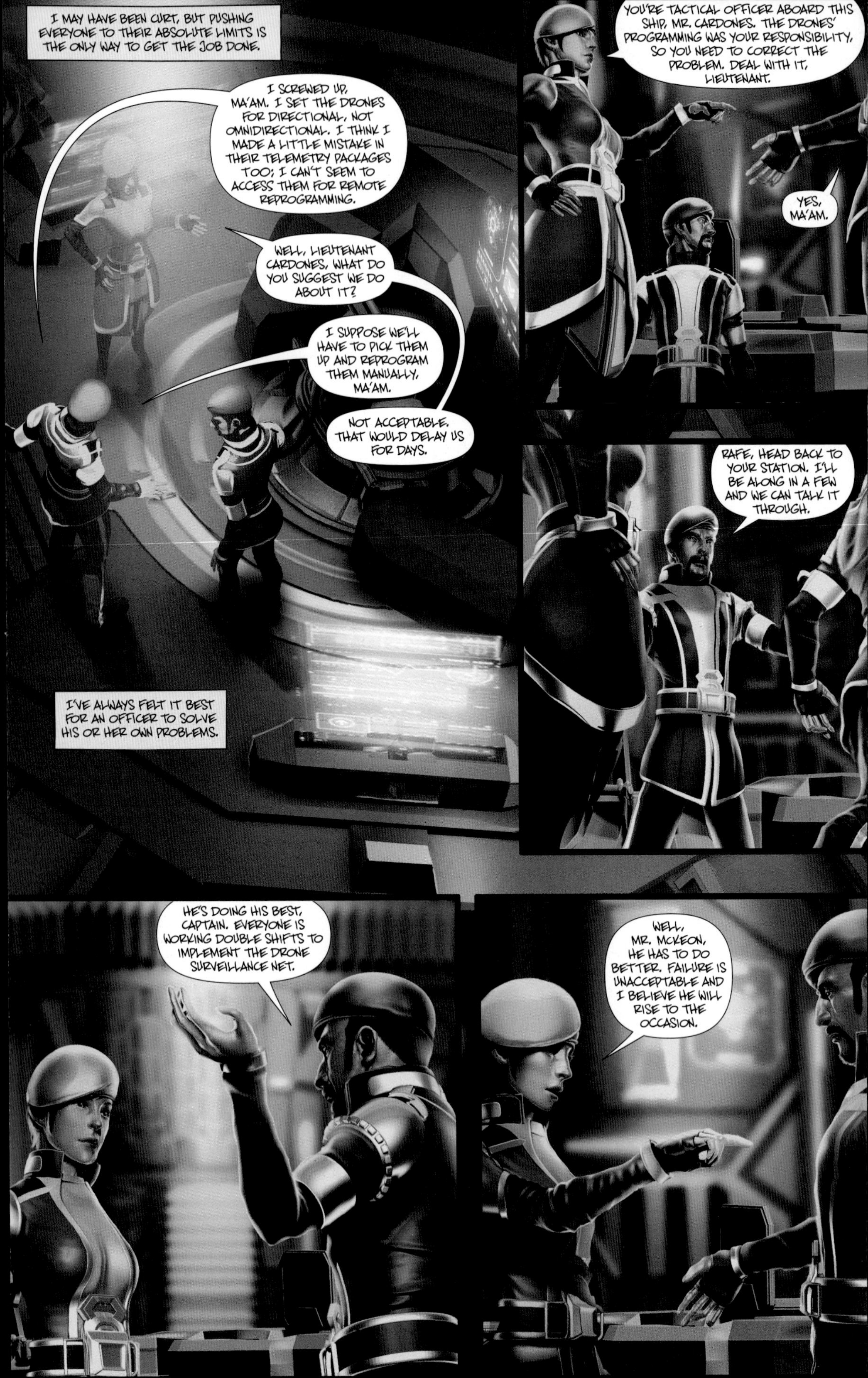
I MAY HAVE BEEN CURT, BUT PUSHING EVERYONE TO THEIR ABSOLUTE LIMITS IS THE ONLY WAY TO GET THE JOB DONE.
I SCREWED UP, MA'AM. I SET THE DRONES FOR DIRECTIONAL, NOT OMNIDIRECTIONAL. I THINK I MADE A LITTLE MISTAKE IN THEIR TELEMETRY PACKAGES TOO; I CAN'T SEEM TO ACCESS THEM FOR REMOTE REPROGRAMMING.
WELL, LIEUTENANT CARDONES, WHAT DO YOU SUGGEST WE DO ABOUT IT?
I SUPPOSE WE'LL HAVE TO PICK THEM UP AND REPROGRAM THEM MANUALLY, MA'AM.
NOT ACCEPTABLE. THAT WOULD DELAY US FOR DAYS.
I'VE ALWAYS FELT IT BEST FOR AN OFFICER TO SOLVE HIS OR HER OWN PROBLEMS.
YOU'RE TACTICAL OFFICER ABOARD THIS SHIP, MR. CARDONES. THE DRONES' PROGRAMMING WAS YOUR RESPONSIBILITY, SO YOU NEED TO CORRECT THE PROBLEM. DEAL WITH IT, LIEUTENANT.
YES, MA'AM.
RAFE, HEAD BACK TO YOUR STATION. I'LL BE ALONG IN A FEW AND WE CAN TALK IT THROUGH.
HE'S DOING HIS BEST, CAPTAIN. EVERYONE IS WORKING DOUBLE SHIFTS TO IMPLEMENT THE DRONE SURVEILLANCE NET.
WELL, MR. MCKEON, HE HAS TO DO BETTER. FAILURE IS UNACCEPTABLE AND I BELIEVE HE WILL RISE TO THE OCCASION.

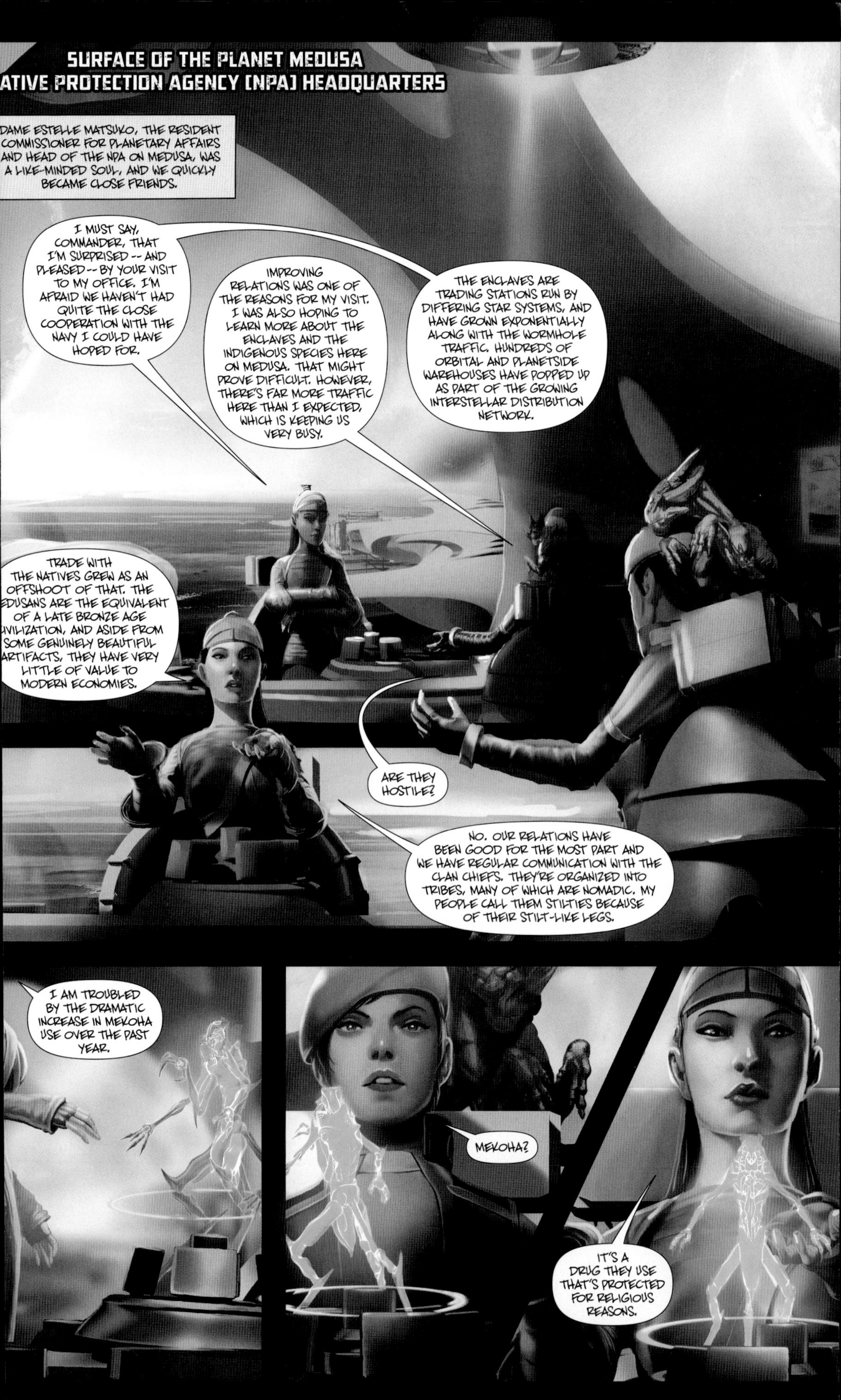
SURFACE OF THE PLANET MEDUSA
ATIVE PROTECTION AGENCY [NPA] HEADQUARTERS
DAME ESTELLE MATSUKO, THE RESIDENT COMMISSIONER FOR PLANETARY AFFAIRS AND HEAD OF THE NPA ON MEDUSA, WAS A LIKE-MINDED SOUL, AND WE QUICKLY BECAME CLOSE FRIENDS.
I MUST SAY, COMMANDER, THAT I'M SURPRISED -- AND PLEASED -- BY YOUR VISIT TO MY OFFICE. I'M AFRAID WE HAVEN'T HAD QUITE THE CLOSE COOPERATION WITH THE NAVY I COULD HAVE HOPED FOR.
IMPROVING RELATIONS WAS ONE OF THE REASONS FOR MY VISIT. I WAS ALSO HOPING TO LEARN MORE ABOUT THE ENCLAVES AND THE INDIGENOUS SPECIES HERE ON MEDUSA. THAT MIGHT PROVE DIFFICULT. HOWEVER, THERE'S FAR MORE TRAFFIC HERE THAN I EXPECTED, WHICH IS KEEPING US VERY BUSY.
THE ENCLAVES ARE TRADING STATIONS RUN BY DIFFERING STAR SYSTEMS, AND HAVE GROWN EXPONENTIALLY ALONG WITH THE WORMHOLE TRAFFIC. HUNDREDS OF ORBITAL AND PLANETSIDE WAREHOUSES HAVE POPPED UP AS PART OF THE GROWING INTERSTELLAR DISTRIBUTION NETWORK.
TRADE WITH THE NATIVES GREW AS AN OFFSHOOT OF THAT. THE EDUSANS ARE THE EQUIVALENT OF A LATE BRONZE AGE IVILIZATION, AND ASIDE FROM SOME GENUINELY BEAUTIFUL ARTIFACTS, THEY HAVE VERY LITTLE OF VALUE TO MODERN ECONOMIES.
ARE THEY HOSTILE?
NO. OUR RELATIONS HAVE BEEN GOOD FOR THE MOST PART AND WE HAVE REGULAR COMMUNICATION WITH THE CLAN CHIEFS. THEY'RE ORGANIZED INTO TRIBES, MANY OF WHICH ARE NOMADIC. MY PEOPLE CALL THEM STILTIES BECAUSE OF THEIR STILT-LIKE LEGS.
I AM TROUBLED BY THE DRAMATIC INCREASE IN MEKOHA USE OVER THE PAST YEAR.
MEKOHA?
IT'S A DRUG THEY USE THAT'S PROTECTED FOR RELIGIOUS REASONS.

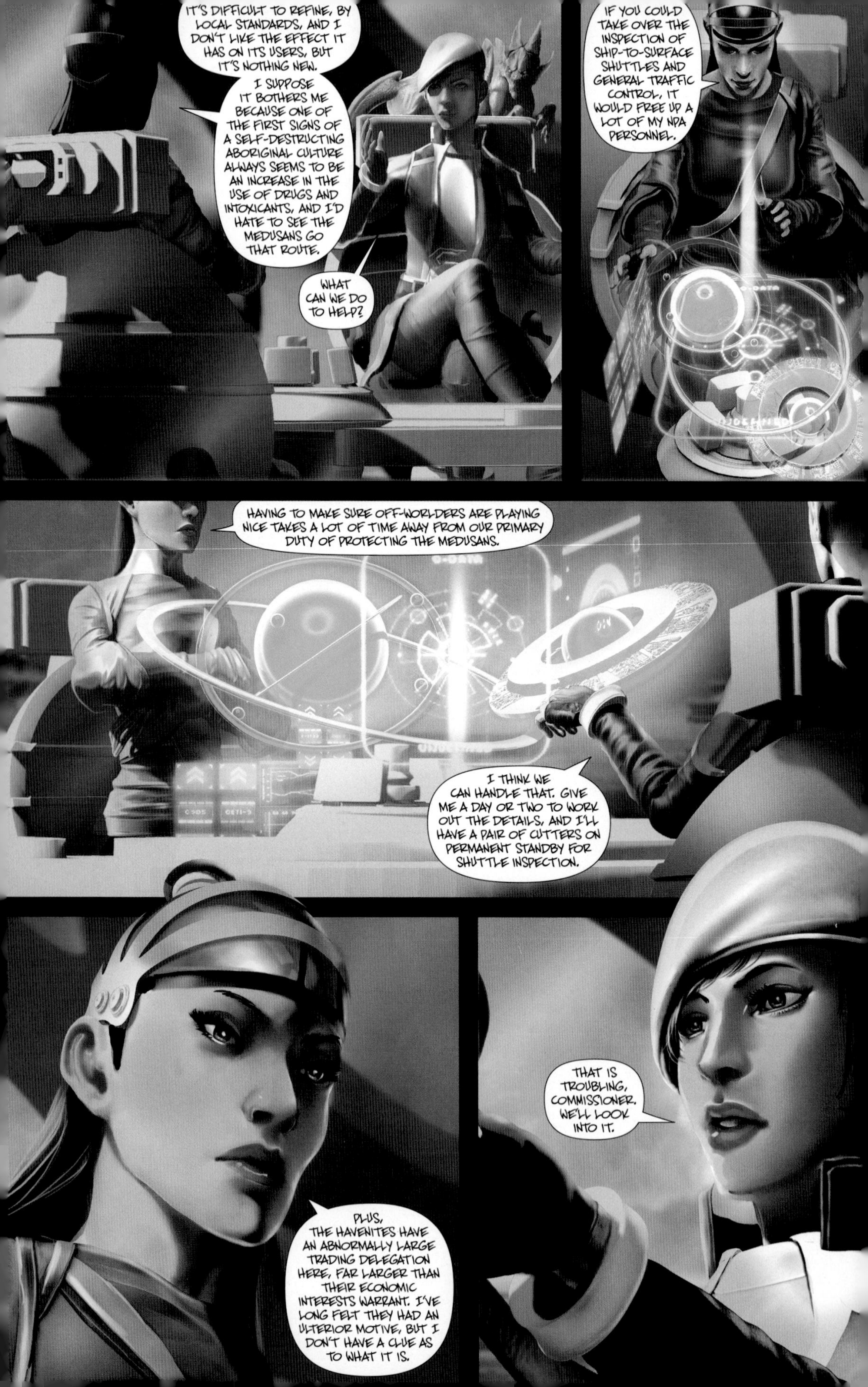
IT'S DIFFICULT TO REFINE, BY LOCAL STANDARDS, AND I DON'T LIKE THE EFFECT IT HAS ON ITS USERS, BUT IT'S NOTHING NEW.
I SUPPOSE IT BOTHERS ME BECAUSE ONE OF THE FIRST SIGNS OF A SELF-DESTRUCTING ABORIGINAL CULTURE ALWAYS SEEMS TO BE AN INCREASE IN THE USE OF DRUGS AND INTOXICANTS, AND I'D HATE TO SEE THE MEDUSANS GO THAT ROUTE.
WHAT CAN WE DO TO HELP?
IF YOU COULD TAKE OVER THE INSPECTION OF SHIP-TO-SURFACE SHUTTLES AND GENERAL TRAFFIC CONTROL, IT WOULD FREE UP A LOT OF MY NPA PERSONNEL.
HAVING TO MAKE SURE OFF-WORLDERS ARE PLAYING NICE TAKES A LOT OF TIME AWAY FROM OUR PRIMARY DUTY OF PROTECTING THE MEDUSANS.
I THINK WE CAN HANDLE THAT. GIVE ME A DAY OR TWO TO WORK OUT THE DETAILS, AND I'LL HAVE A PAIR OF CUTTERS ON PERMANENT STANDBY FOR SHUTTLE INSPECTION.
PLUS, THE HAVENITES HAVE AN ABNORMALLY LARGE TRADING DELEGATION HERE, FAR LARGER THAN THEIR ECONOMIC INTERESTS WARRANT. I'VE LONG FELT THEY HAD AN ULTERIOR MOTIVE, BUT I DON'T HAVE A CLUE AS TO WHAT IT IS.
THAT IS TROUBLING, COMMISSIONER. WE'LL LOOK INTO IT.

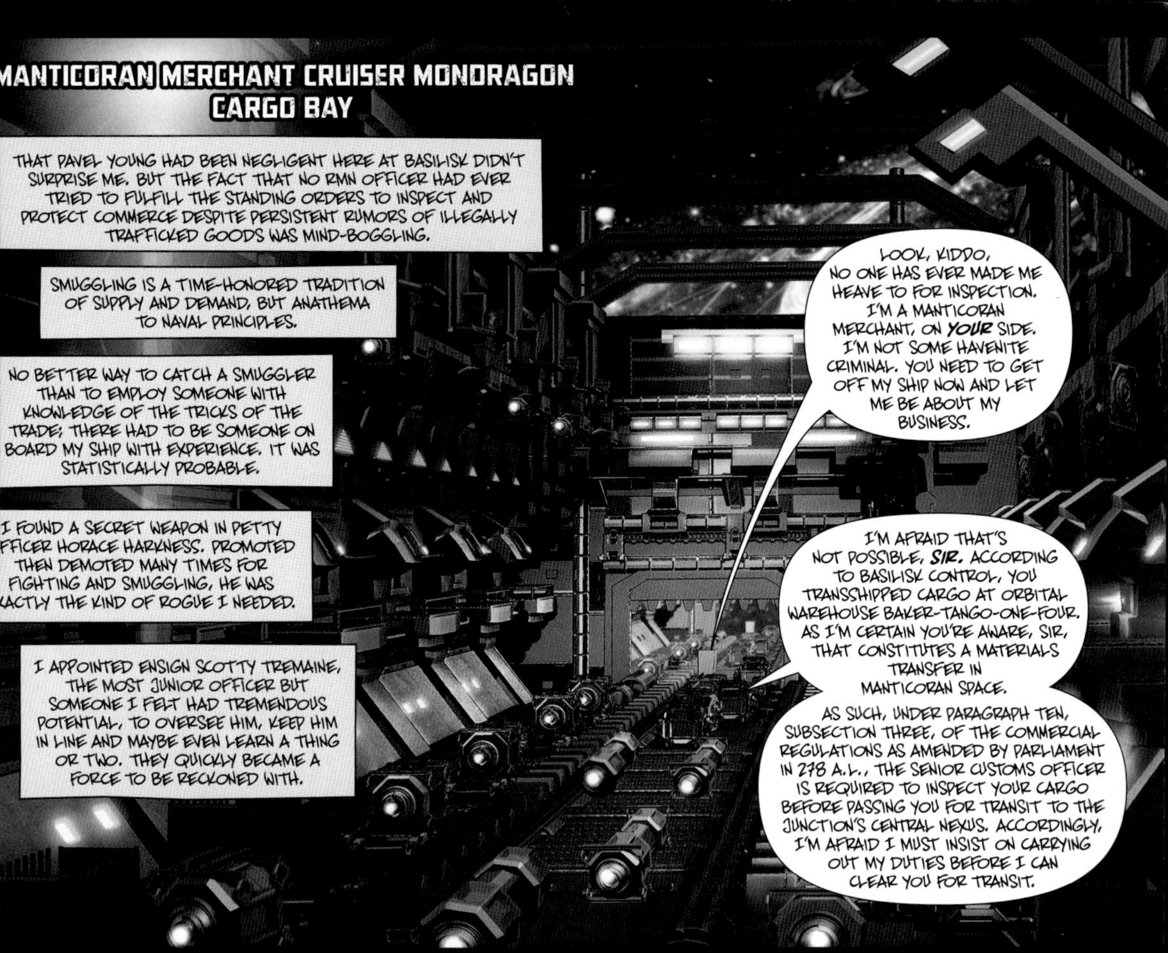
MANTICORAN MERCHANT CRUISER MONDRAGON
CARGO BAY
THAT PAVEL YOUNG HAD BEEN NEGLIGENT HERE AT BASILISK DIDN'T SURPRISE ME. BUT THE FACT THAT NO RMN OFFICER HAD EVER TRIED TO FULFILL THE STANDING ORDERS TO INSPECT AND PROTECT COMMERCE DESPITE PERSISTENT RUMORS OF ILLEGALLY TRAFFICKED GOODS WAS MIND-BOGGLING.
SMUGGLING IS A TIME-HONORED TRADITION OF SUPPLY AND DEMAND, BUT ANATHEMA TO NAVAL PRINCIPLES.
NO BETTER WAY TO CATCH A SMUGGLER THAN TO EMPLOY SOMEONE WITH KNOWLEDGE OF THE TRICKS OF THE TRADE; THERE HAD TO BE SOMEONE ON BOARD MY SHIP WITH EXPERIENCE. IT WAS STATISTICALLY PROBABLE.
I FOUND A SECRET WEAPON IN PETTY OFFICER HORACE HARKNESS. PROMOTED THEN DEMOTED MANY TIMES FOR FIGHTING AND SMUGGLING, HE WAS EXACTLY THE KIND OF ROGUE I NEEDED.
I APPOINTED ENSIGN SCOTTY TREMAINE, THE MOST JUNIOR OFFICER BUT SOMEONE I FELT HAD TREMENDOUS POTENTIAL, TO OVERSEE HIM, KEEP HIM IN LINE AND MAYBE EVEN LEARN A THING OR TWO. THEY QUICKLY BECAME A FORCE TO BE RECKONED WITH.
LOOK, KIDDO, NO ONE HAS EVER MADE ME HEAVE TO FOR INSPECTION. I'M A MANTICORAN MERCHANT, ON ***YOUR*** SIDE. I'M NOT SOME HAVENITE CRIMINAL. YOU NEED TO GET OFF MY SHIP NOW AND LET ME BE ABOUT MY BUSINESS.
I'M AFRAID THAT'S NOT POSSIBLE, ***SIR.*** ACCORDING TO BASILISK CONTROL, YOU TRANSSHIPPED CARGO AT ORBITAL WAREHOUSE BAKER-TANGO-ONE-FOUR. AS I'M CERTAIN YOU'RE AWARE, SIR, THAT CONSTITUTES A MATERIALS TRANSFER IN MANTICORAN SPACE.
AS SUCH, UNDER PARAGRAPH TEN, SUBSECTION THREE, OF THE COMMERCIAL REGULATIONS AS AMENDED BY PARLIAMENT IN 278 A.L., THE SENIOR CUSTOMS OFFICER IS REQUIRED TO INSPECT YOUR CARGO BEFORE PASSING YOU FOR TRANSIT TO THE JUNCTION'S CENTRAL NEXUS. ACCORDINGLY, I'M AFRAID I MUST INSIST ON CARRYING OUT MY DUTIES BEFORE I CAN CLEAR YOU FOR TRANSIT.

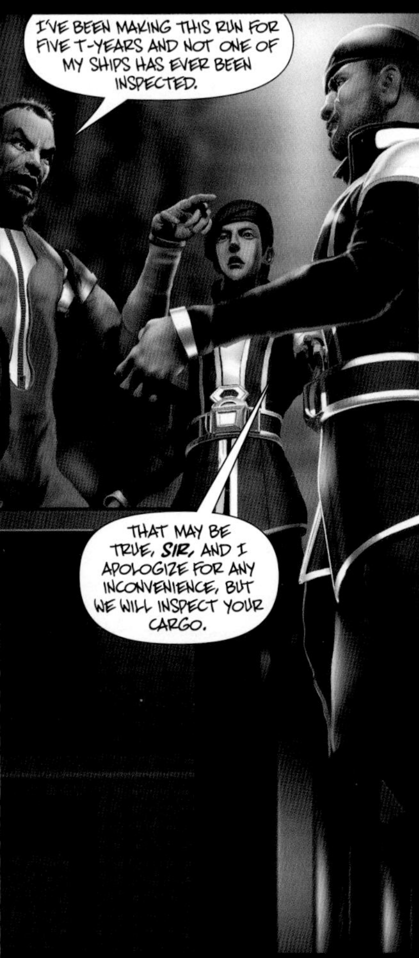
I'VE BEEN MAKING THIS RUN FOR FIVE T-YEARS AND NOT ONE OF MY SHIPS HAS EVER BEEN INSPECTED.
THAT MAY BE TRUE, ***SIR,*** AND I APOLOGIZE FOR ANY INCONVENIENCE, BUT WE WILL INSPECT YOUR CARGO.

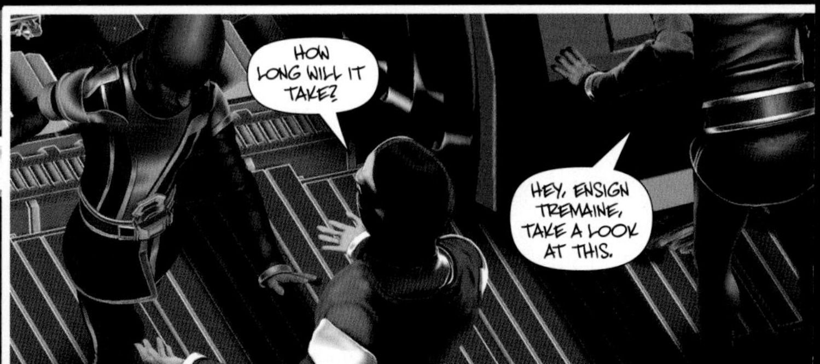
HOW LONG WILL IT TAKE?
HEY, ENSIGN TREMAINE, TAKE A LOOK AT THIS.

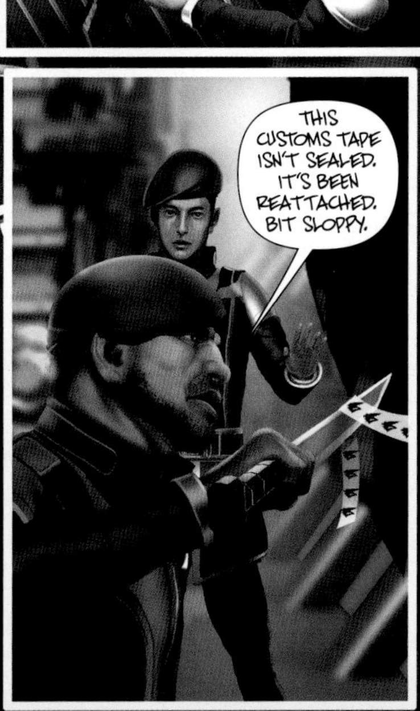
THIS CUSTOMS TAPE ISN'T SEALED. IT'S BEEN REATTACHED. BIT SLOPPY.

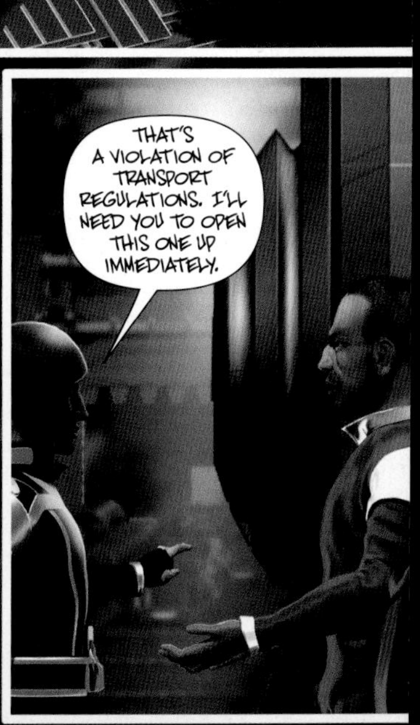
THAT'S A VIOLATION OF TRANSPORT REGULATIONS. I'LL NEED YOU TO OPEN THIS ONE UP IMMEDIATELY.

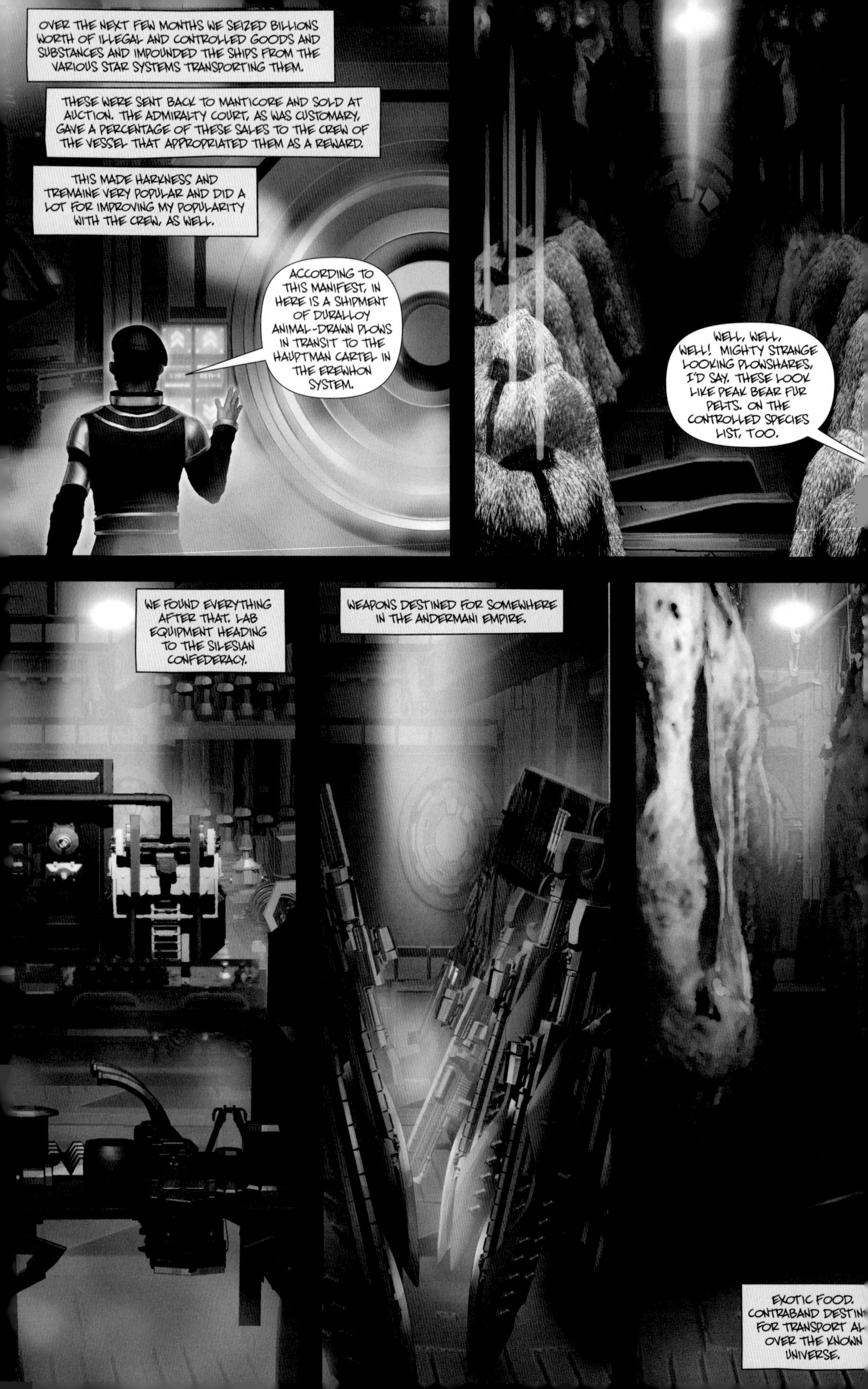
OVER THE NEXT FEW MONTHS WE SEIZED BILLIONS WORTH OF ILLEGAL AND CONTROLLED GOODS AND SUBSTANCES AND IMPOUNDED THE SHIPS FROM THE VARIOUS STAR SYSTEMS TRANSPORTING THEM.
THESE WERE SENT BACK TO MANTICORE AND SOLD AT AUCTION. THE ADMIRALTY COURT, AS WAS CUSTOMARY, GAVE A PERCENTAGE OF THESE SALES TO THE CREW OF THE VESSEL THAT APPROPRIATED THEM AS A REWARD.
THIS MADE HARKNESS AND TREMAINE VERY POPULAR AND DID A LOT FOR IMPROVING MY POPULARITY WITH THE CREW, AS WELL.
ACCORDING TO THIS MANIFEST, IN HERE IS A SHIPMENT OF DURALLOY ANIMAL-DRAWN PLOWS IN TRANSIT TO THE HAUPTMAN CARTEL IN THE EREWHON SYSTEM.
WELL, WELL, WELL! MIGHTY STRANGE LOOKING PLOWSHARES, I'D SAY. THESE LOOK LIKE PEAK BEAR FUR PELTS. ON THE CONTROLLED SPECIES LIST, TOO.
WE FOUND EVERYTHING AFTER THAT. LAB EQUIPMENT HEADING TO THE SILESIAN CONFEDERACY.
WEAPONS DESTINED FOR SOMEWHERE IN THE ANDERMANI EMPIRE.
EXOTIC FOOD. CONTRABAND DESTIN FOR TRANSPORT AL OVER THE KNOWN UNIVERSE.

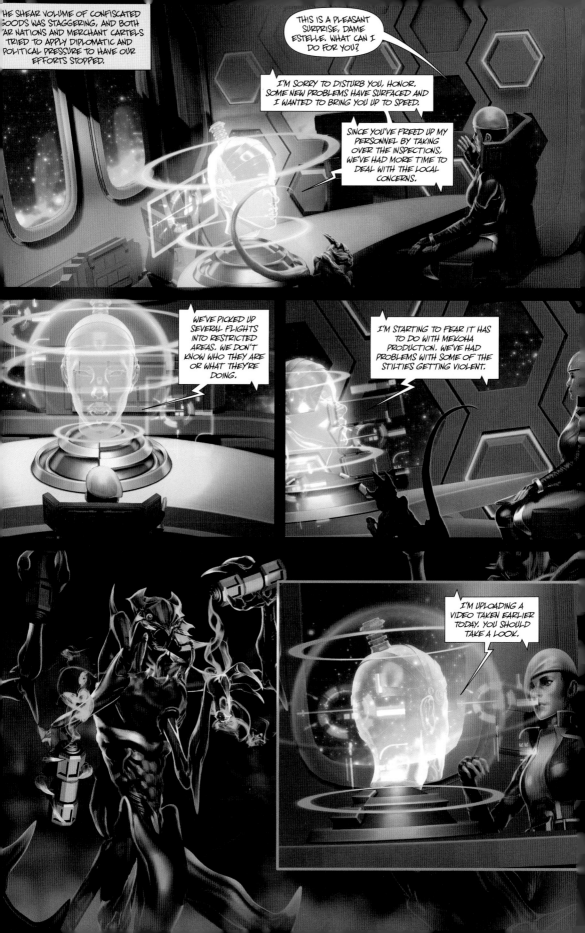

THE SHEAR VOLUME OF CONFISCATED GOODS WAS STAGGERING, AND BOTH STAR NATIONS AND MERCHANT CARTELS TRIED TO APPLY DIPLOMATIC AND POLITICAL PRESSURE TO HAVE OUR EFFORTS STOPPED.

THIS IS A PLEASANT SURPRISE, DAME ESTELLE. WHAT CAN I DO FOR YOU?

I'M SORRY TO DISTURB YOU, HONOR. SOME NEW PROBLEMS HAVE SURFACED AND I WANTED TO BRING YOU UP TO SPEED.

SINCE YOU'VE FREED UP MY PERSONNEL BY TAKING OVER THE INSPECTIONS, WE'VE HAD MORE TIME TO DEAL WITH THE LOCAL CONCERNS.

WE'VE PICKED UP SEVERAL FLIGHTS INTO RESTRICTED AREAS. WE DON'T KNOW WHO THEY ARE OR WHAT THEY'RE DOING.

I'M STARTING TO FEAR IT HAS TO DO WITH MEKOHA PRODUCTION. WE'VE HAD PROBLEMS WITH SOME OF THE STILTIES GETTING VIOLENT.

I'M UPLOADING A VIDEO TAKEN EARLIER TODAY. YOU SHOULD TAKE A LOOK.

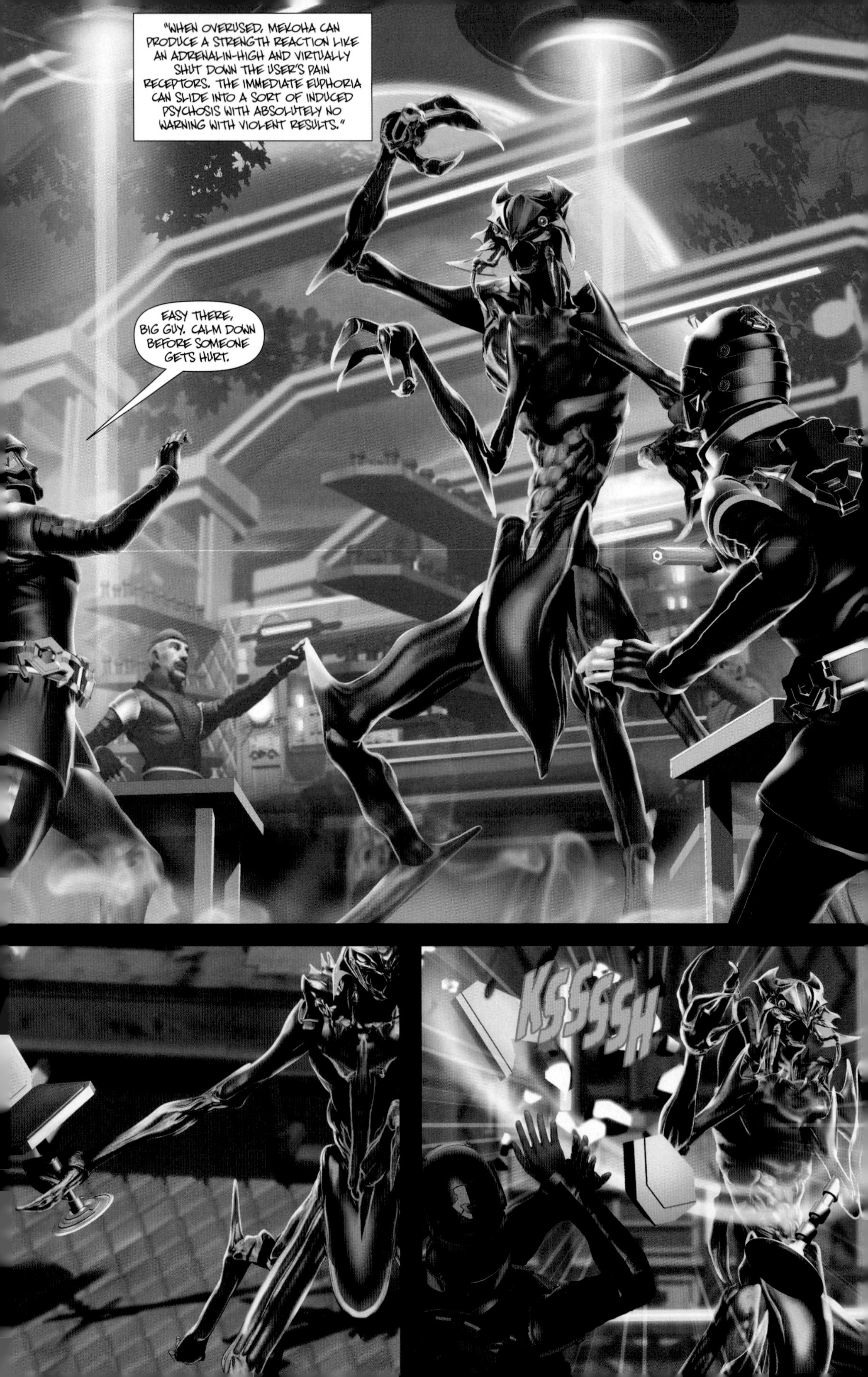
"WHEN OVERUSED, MEKOHA CAN PRODUCE A STRENGTH REACTION LIKE AN ADRENALIN-HIGH AND VIRTUALLY SHUT DOWN THE USER'S PAIN RECEPTORS. THE IMMEDIATE EUPHORIA CAN SLIDE INTO A SORT OF INDUCED PSYCHOSIS WITH ABSOLUTELY NO WARNING WITH VIOLENT RESULTS."
EASY THERE, BIG GUY. CALM DOWN BEFORE SOMEONE GETS HURT.
KSSSSH

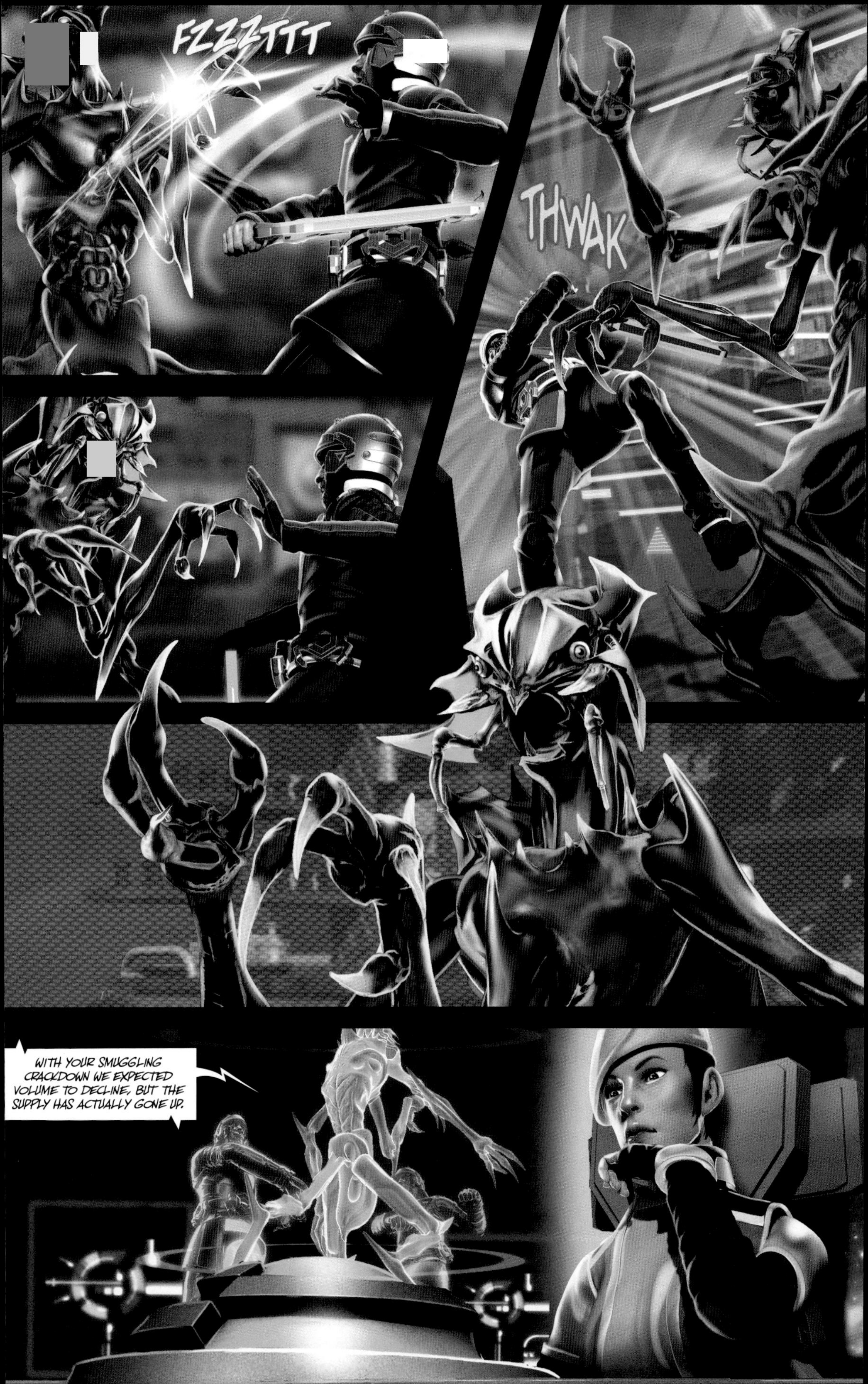
FZZZTTT
THWAK
WITH YOUR SMUGGLING CRACKDOWN WE EXPECTED VOLUME TO DECLINE, BUT THE SUPPLY HAS ACTUALLY GONE UP.

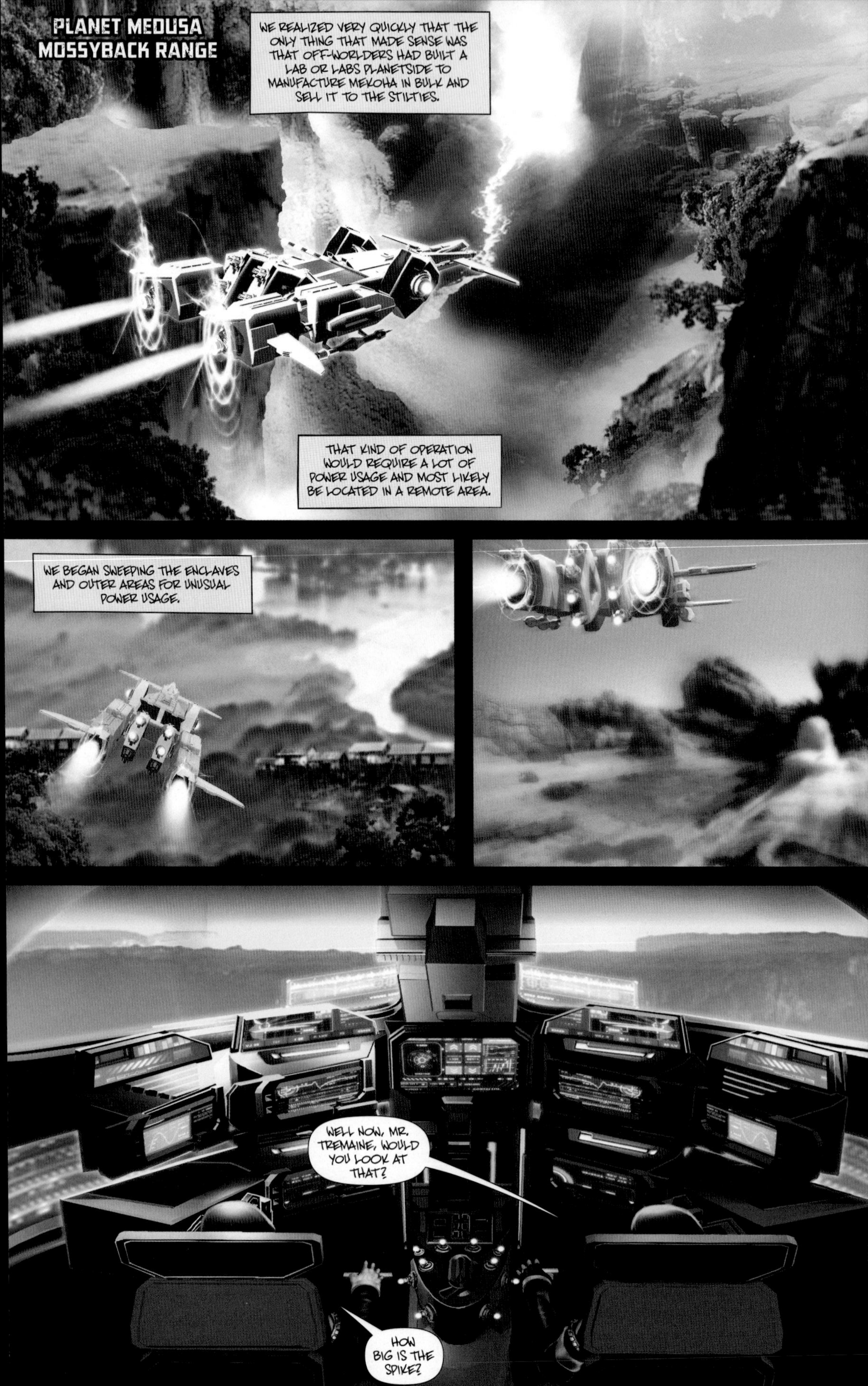
PLANET MEDUSA
MOSSYBACK RANGE
WE REALIZED VERY QUICKLY THAT THE ONLY THING THAT MADE SENSE WAS THAT OFF-WORLDERS HAD BUILT A LAB OR LABS PLANETSIDE TO MANUFACTURE MEKOHA IN BULK AND SELL IT TO THE STILTIES.
THAT KIND OF OPERATION WOULD REQUIRE A LOT OF POWER USAGE AND MOST LIKELY BE LOCATED IN A REMOTE AREA.
WE BEGAN SWEEPING THE ENCLAVES AND OUTER AREAS FOR UNUSUAL POWER USAGE.
WELL NOW, MR. TREMAINE, WOULD YOU LOOK AT THAT?
HOW BIG IS THE SPIKE?

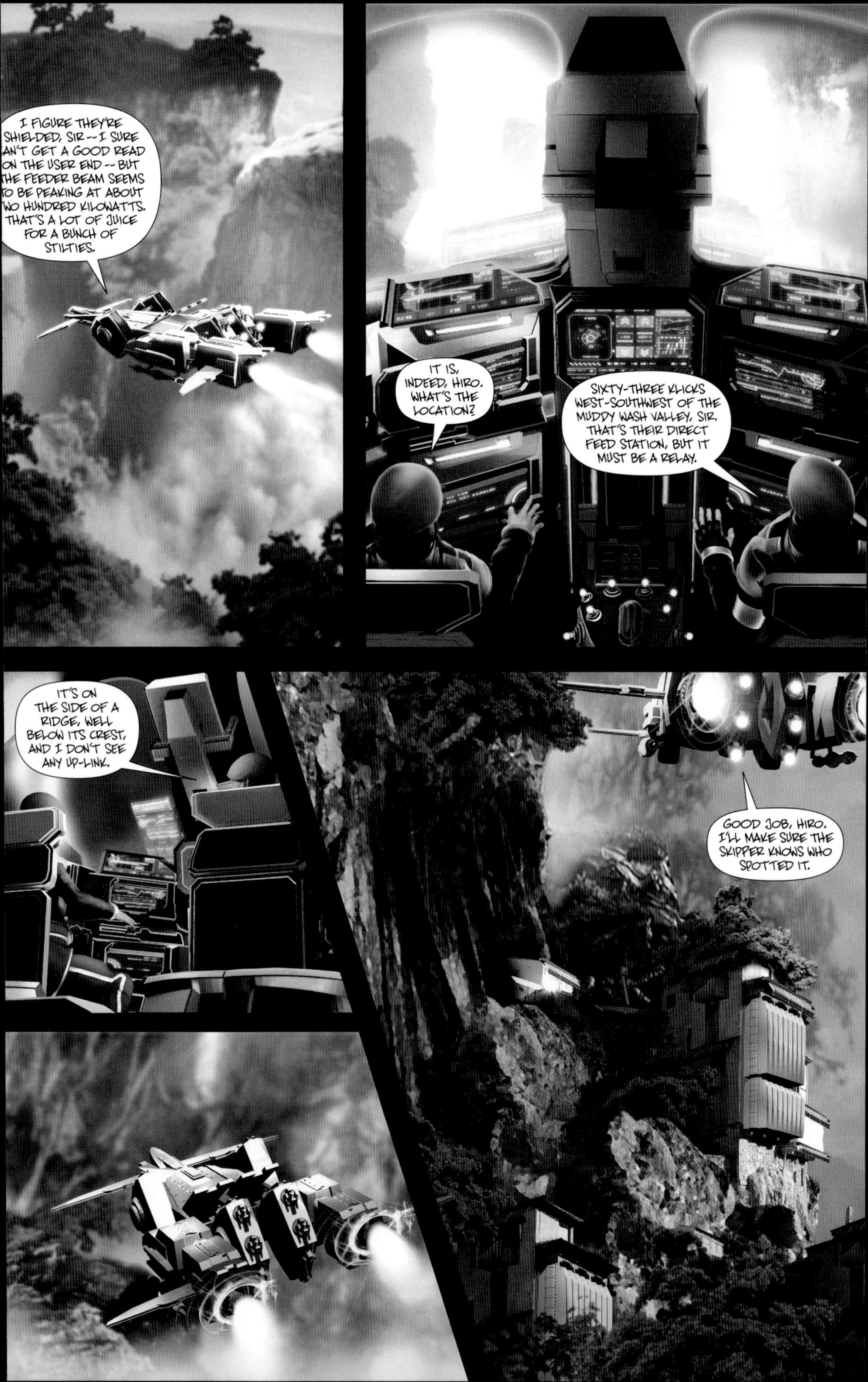
I FIGURE THEY'RE SHIELDED, SIR--I SURE AN'T GET A GOOD READ ON THE USER END--BUT HE FEEDER BEAM SEEMS O BE PEAKING AT ABOUT WO HUNDRED KILOWATTS. THAT'S A LOT OF JUICE FOR A BUNCH OF STILTIES.
IT IS, INDEED, HIRO. WHAT'S THE LOCATION?
SIXTY-THREE KLICKS WEST-SOUTHWEST OF THE MUDDY WASH VALLEY, SIR. THAT'S THEIR DIRECT FEED STATION, BUT IT MUST BE A RELAY.
IT'S ON THE SIDE OF A RIDGE, WELL BELOW ITS CREST, AND I DON'T SEE ANY UP-LINK.
GOOD JOB, HIRO. I'LL MAKE SURE THE SKIPPER KNOWS WHO SPOTTED IT.

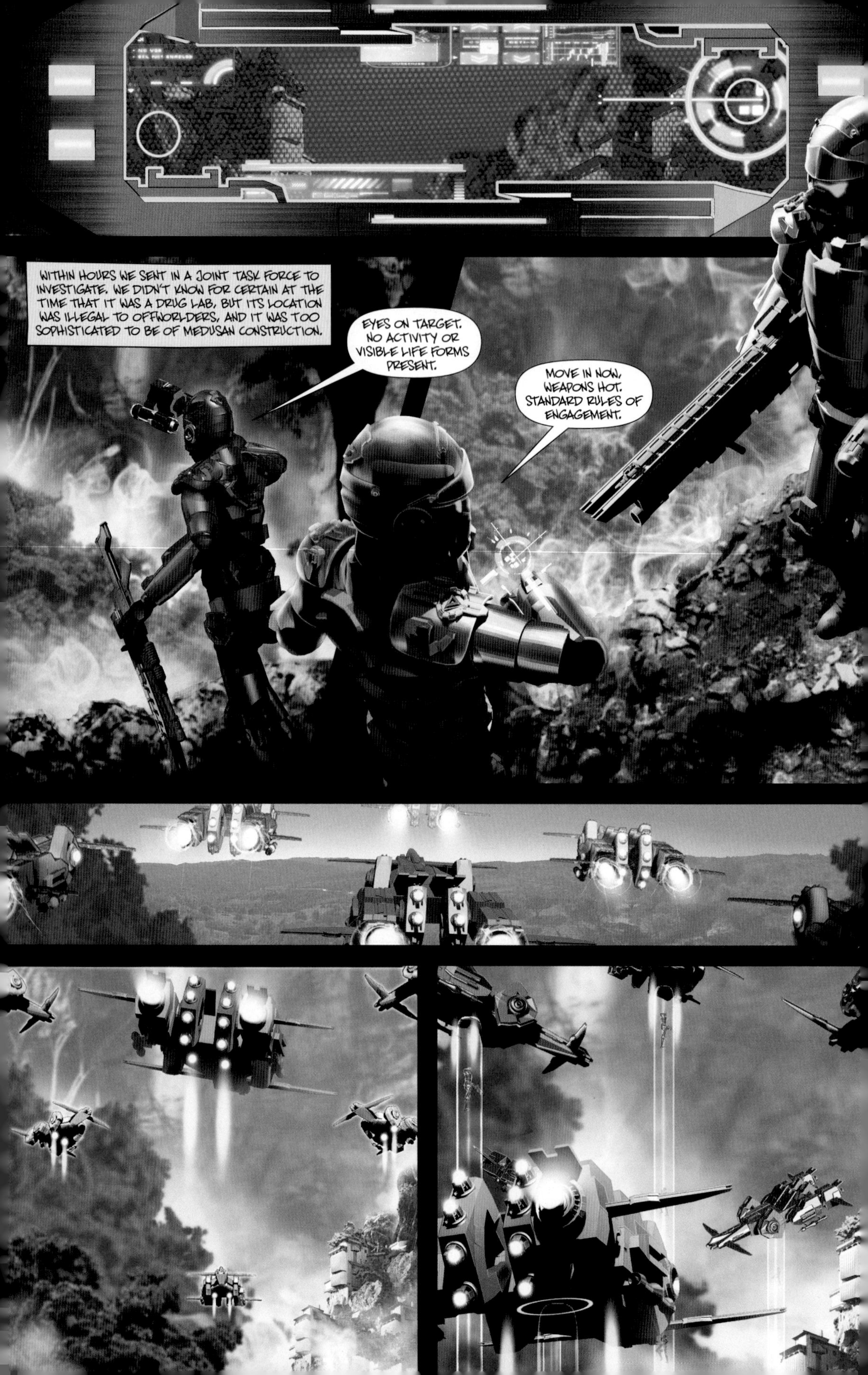
WITHIN HOURS WE SENT IN A JOINT TASK FORCE TO INVESTIGATE. WE DIDN'T KNOW FOR CERTAIN AT THE TIME THAT IT WAS A DRUG LAB, BUT ITS LOCATION WAS ILLEGAL TO OFFWORLDERS, AND IT WAS TOO SOPHISTICATED TO BE OF MEDUSAN CONSTRUCTION.
EYES ON TARGET. NO ACTIVITY OR VISIBLE LIFE FORMS PRESENT.
MOVE IN NOW, WEAPONS HOT. STANDARD RULES OF ENGAGEMENT.

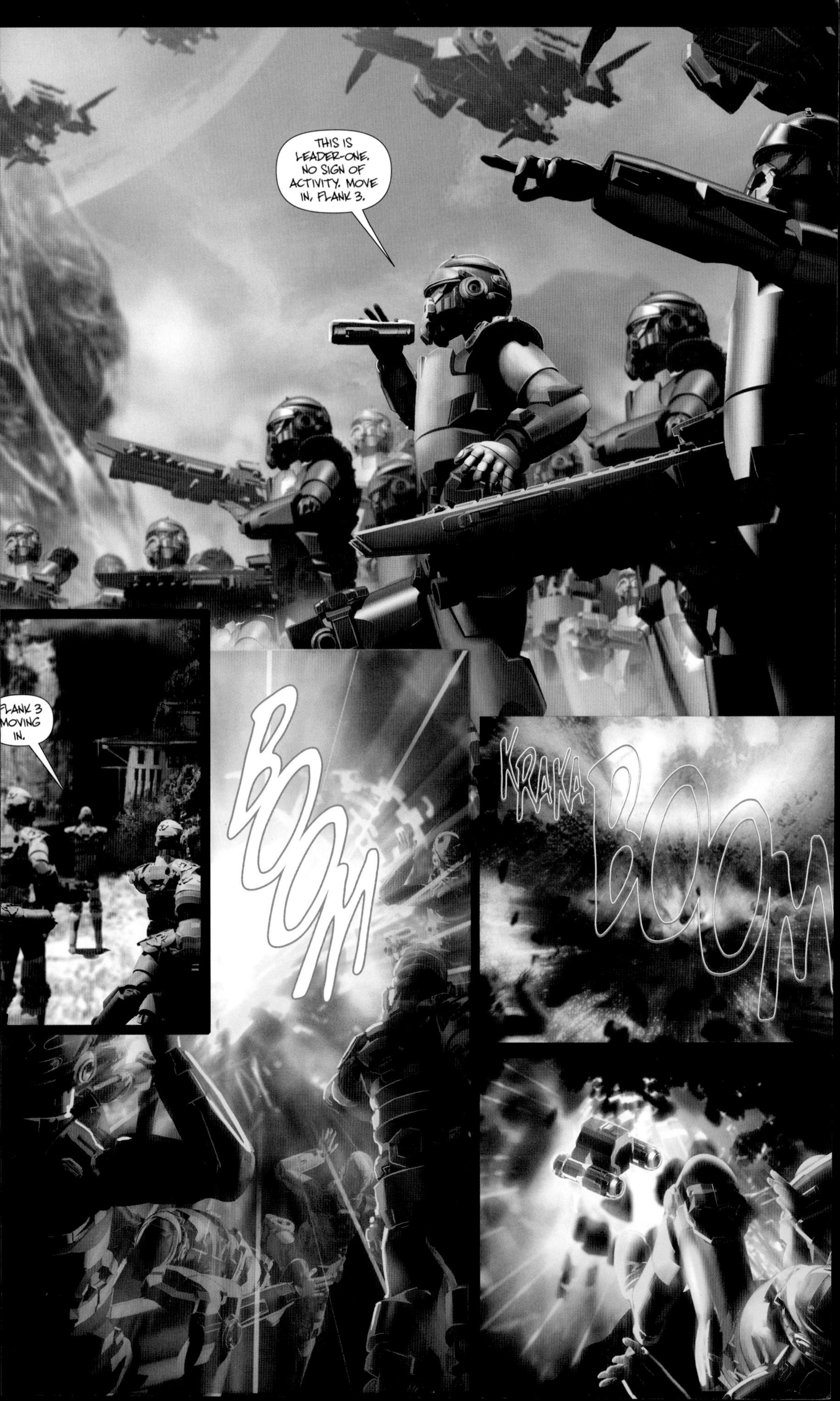
THIS IS LEADER-ONE. NO SIGN OF ACTIVITY. MOVE IN, FLANK 3.
FLANK 3 MOVING IN.
BOOM
KRAKA BOOM

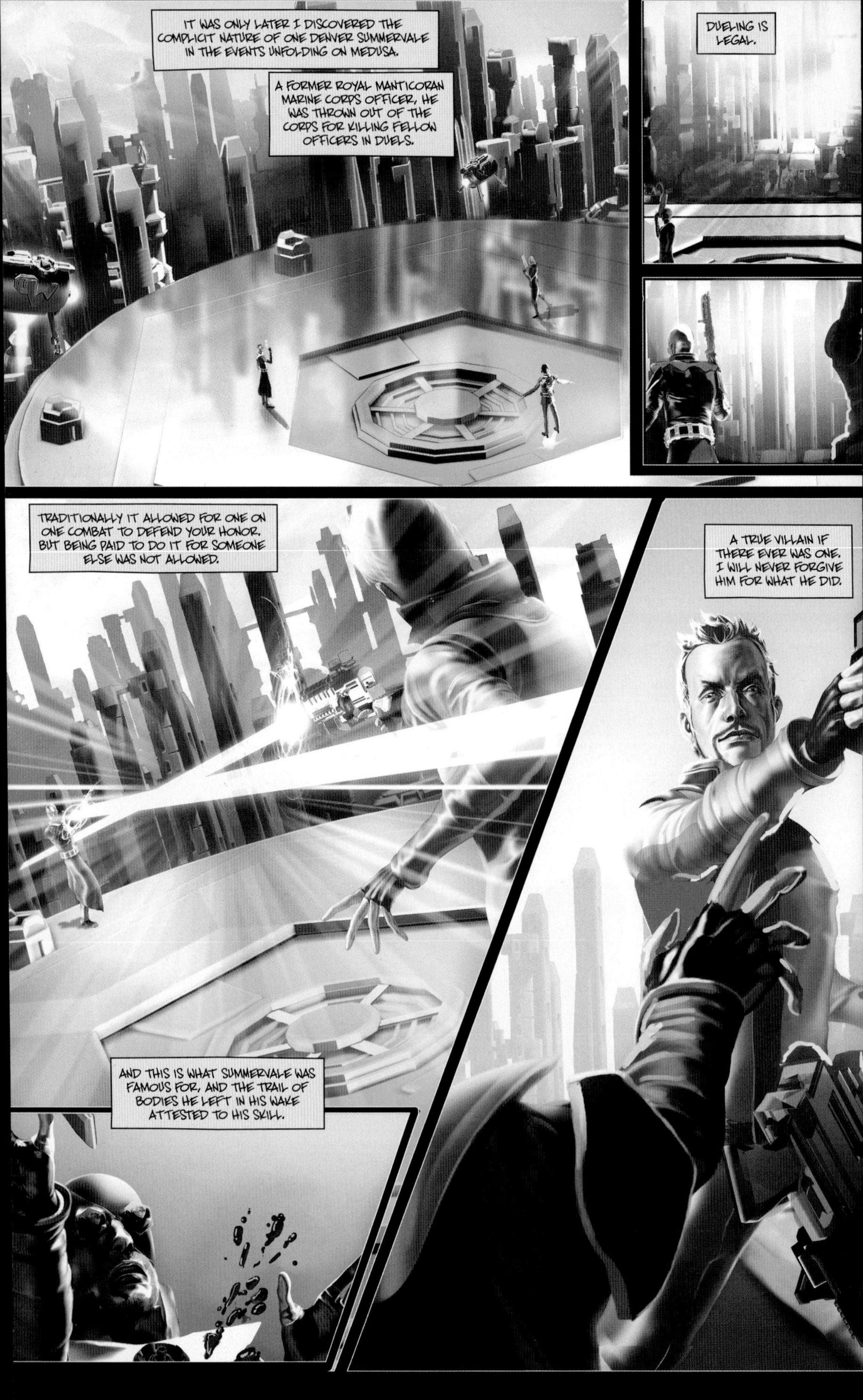
IT WAS ONLY LATER I DISCOVERED THE COMPLICIT NATURE OF ONE DENVER SUMMERVALE IN THE EVENTS UNFOLDING ON MEDUSA.
A FORMER ROYAL MANTICORAN MARINE CORPS OFFICER, HE WAS THROWN OUT OF THE CORPS FOR KILLING FELLOW OFFICERS IN DUELS.
DUELING IS LEGAL.
TRADITIONALLY IT ALLOWED FOR ONE ON ONE COMBAT TO DEFEND YOUR HONOR. BUT BEING PAID TO DO IT FOR SOMEONE ELSE WAS NOT ALLOWED.
AND THIS IS WHAT SUMMERVALE WAS FAMOUS FOR, AND THE TRAIL OF BODIES HE LEFT IN HIS WAKE ATTESTED TO HIS SKILL.
A TRUE VILLAIN IF THERE EVER WAS ONE. I WILL NEVER FORGIVE HIM FOR WHAT HE DID.

TALES OF HONOR

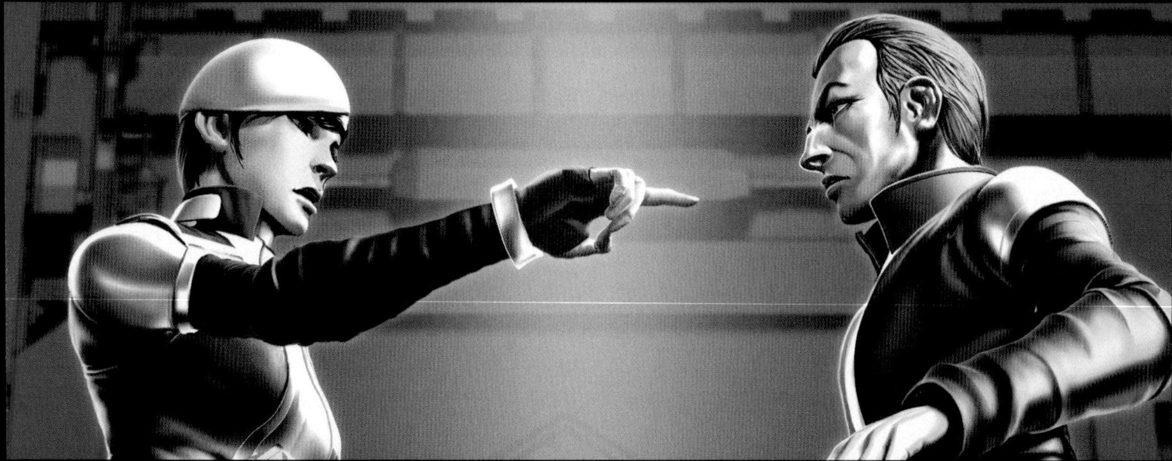

CHAPTER THREE

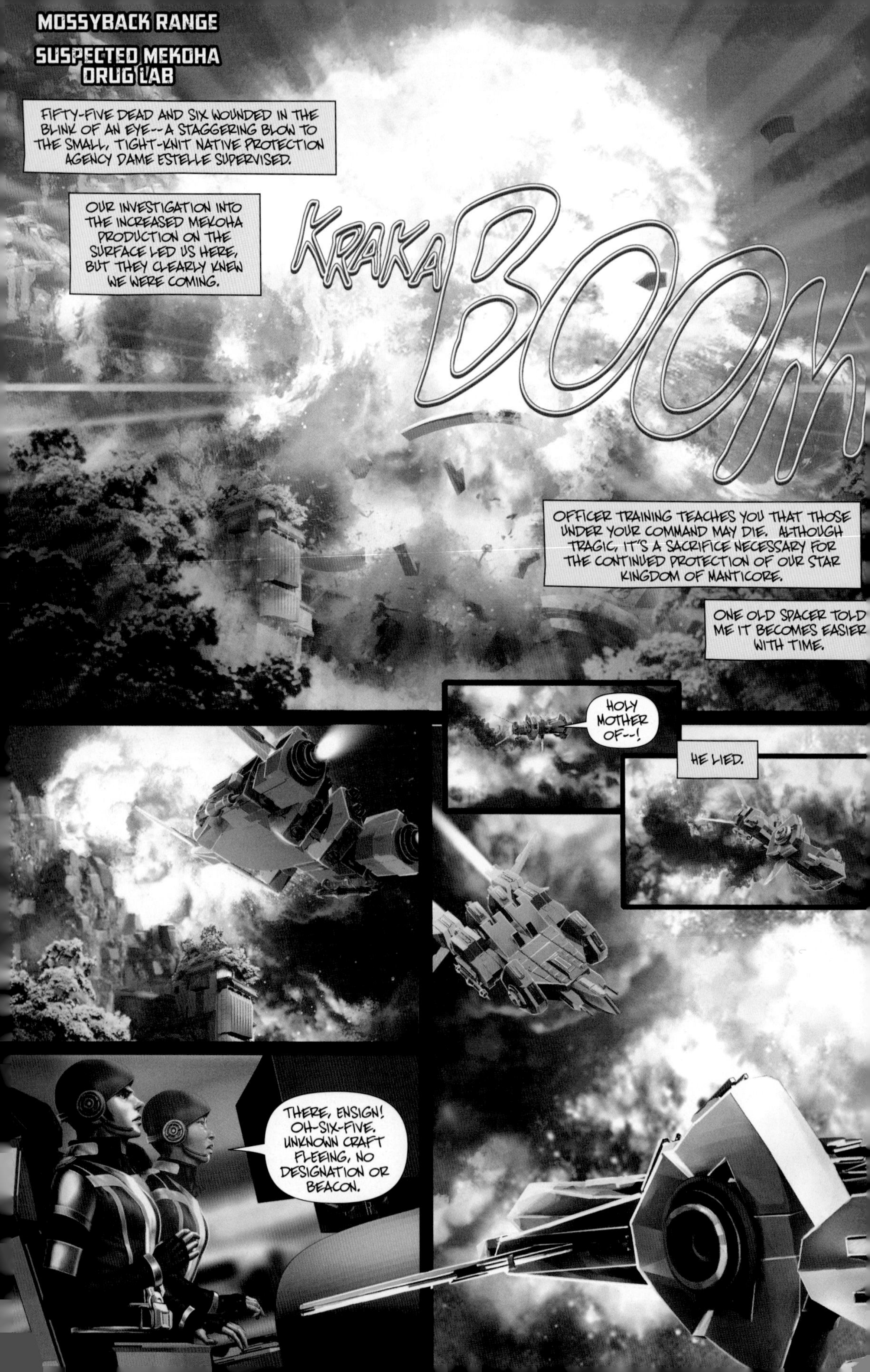
MOSSYBACK RANGE
SUSPECTED MEKOHA DRUG LAB
FIFTY-FIVE DEAD AND SIX WOUNDED IN THE BLINK OF AN EYE--A STAGGERING BLOW TO THE SMALL, TIGHT-KNIT NATIVE PROTECTION AGENCY DAME ESTELLE SUPERVISED.
OUR INVESTIGATION INTO THE INCREASED MEKOHA PRODUCTION ON THE SURFACE LED US HERE, BUT THEY CLEARLY KNEW WE WERE COMING.
KRAKABOOM
OFFICER TRAINING TEACHES YOU THAT THOSE UNDER YOUR COMMAND MAY DIE. ALTHOUGH TRAGIC, IT'S A SACRIFICE NECESSARY FOR THE CONTINUED PROTECTION OF OUR STAR KINGDOM OF MANTICORE.
ONE OLD SPACER TOLD ME IT BECOMES EASIER WITH TIME.
HOLY MOTHER OF--!
HE LIED.
THERE, ENSIGN! OH-SIX-FIVE. UNKNOWN CRAFT FLEEING, NO DESIGNATION OR BEACON.

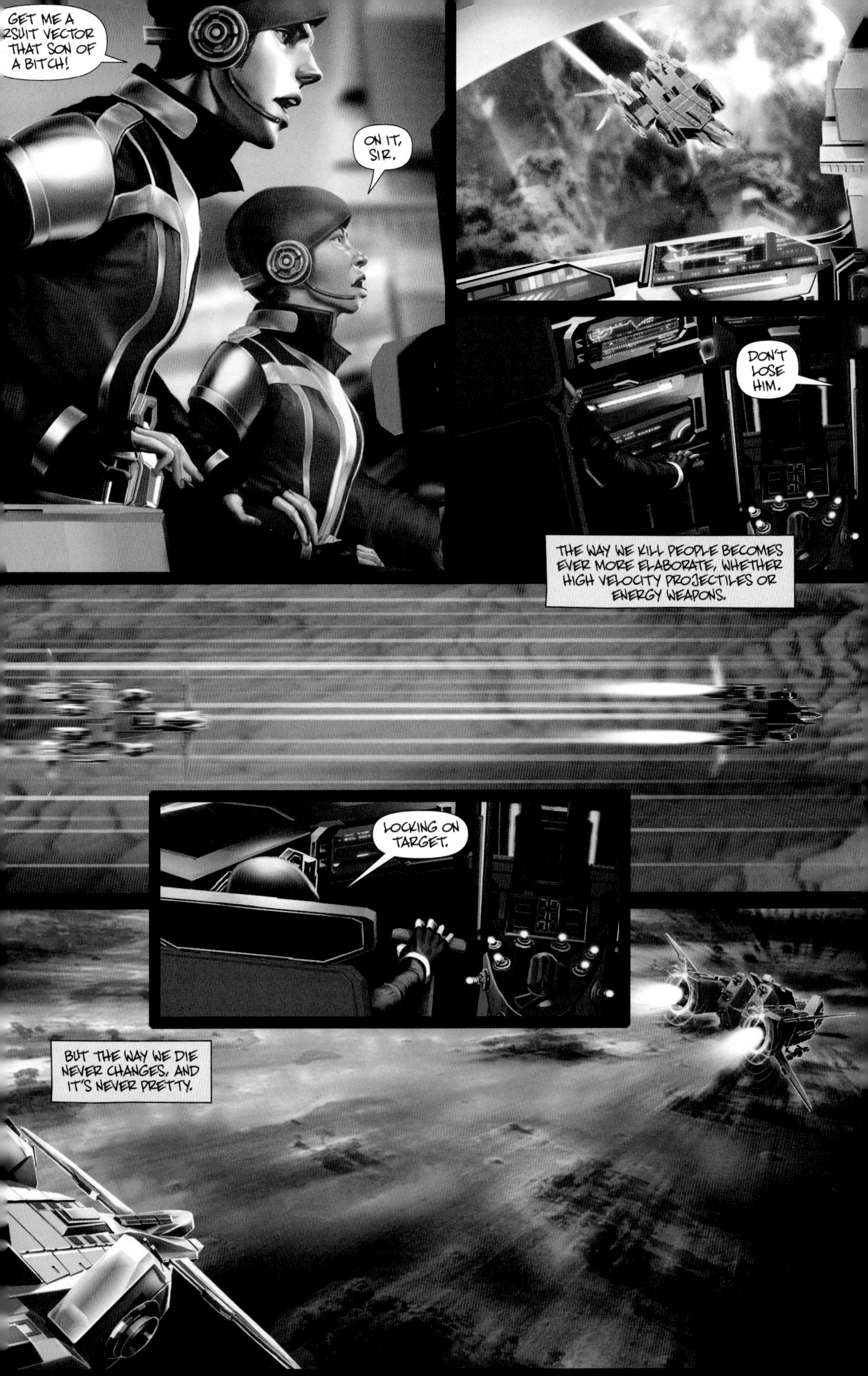

GET ME A RSUIT VECTOR THAT SON OF A BITCH!
ON IT, SIR.
DON'T LOSE HIM.
THE WAY WE KILL PEOPLE BECOMES EVER MORE ELABORATE, WHETHER HIGH VELOCITY PROJECTILES OR ENERGY WEAPONS.
LOCKING ON TARGET.
BUT THE WAY WE DIE NEVER CHANGES, AND IT'S NEVER PRETTY.

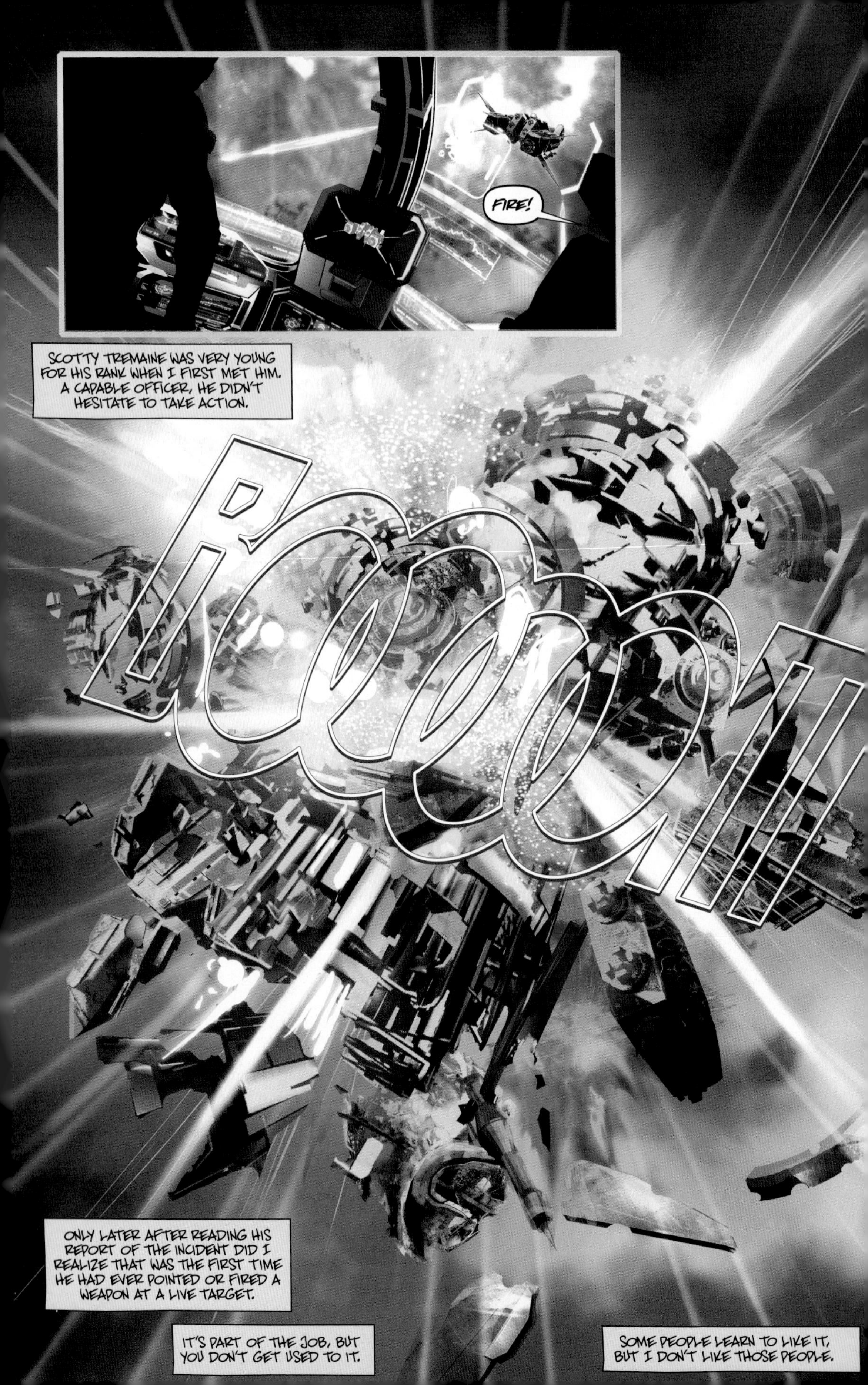
FIRE!
SCOTTY TREMAINE WAS VERY YOUNG FOR HIS RANK WHEN I FIRST MET HIM. A CAPABLE OFFICER, HE DIDN'T HESITATE TO TAKE ACTION.
BOOOOM!!!
ONLY LATER AFTER READING HIS REPORT OF THE INCIDENT DID I REALIZE THAT WAS THE FIRST TIME HE HAD EVER POINTED OR FIRED A WEAPON AT A LIVE TARGET.
IT'S PART OF THE JOB, BUT YOU DON'T GET USED TO IT.
SOME PEOPLE LEARN TO LIKE IT, BUT I DON'T LIKE THOSE PEOPLE.

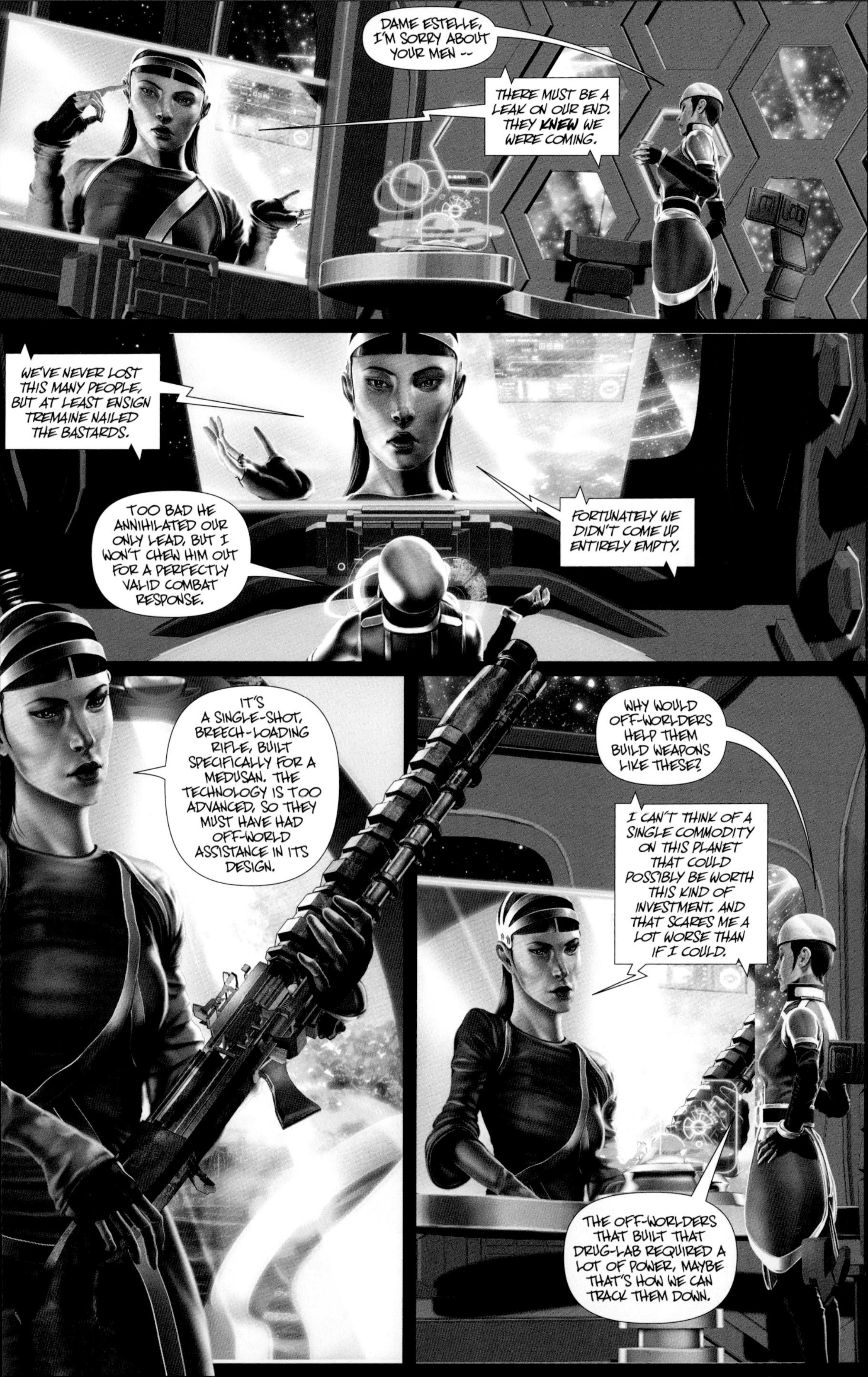
DAME ESTELLE, I'M SORRY ABOUT YOUR MEN --
THERE MUST BE A LEAK ON OUR END. THEY **KNEW** WE WERE COMING.
WE'VE NEVER LOST THIS MANY PEOPLE, BUT AT LEAST ENSIGN TREMAINE NAILED THE BASTARDS.
TOO BAD HE ANNIHILATED OUR ONLY LEAD, BUT I WON'T CHEW HIM OUT FOR A PERFECTLY VALID COMBAT RESPONSE.
FORTUNATELY WE DIDN'T COME UP ENTIRELY EMPTY.
IT'S A SINGLE-SHOT, BREECH-LOADING RIFLE, BUILT SPECIFICALLY FOR A MEDUSAN. THE TECHNOLOGY IS TOO ADVANCED, SO THEY MUST HAVE HAD OFF-WORLD ASSISTANCE IN ITS DESIGN.
WHY WOULD OFF-WORLDERS HELP THEM BUILD WEAPONS LIKE THESE?
I CAN'T THINK OF A SINGLE COMMODITY ON THIS PLANET THAT COULD POSSIBLY BE WORTH THIS KIND OF INVESTMENT. AND THAT SCARES ME A LOT WORSE THAN IF I COULD.
THE OFF-WORLDERS THAT BUILT THAT DRUG-LAB REQUIRED A LOT OF POWER, MAYBE THAT'S HOW WE CAN TRACK THEM DOWN.

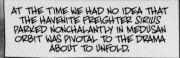

AT THE TIME WE HAD NO IDEA THAT THE HAVENITE FREIGHTER *SIRIUS* PARKED NONCHALANTLY IN MEDUSAN ORBIT WAS PIVOTAL TO THE DRAMA ABOUT TO UNFOLD.

WE WEREN'T AT WAR THEN, AND NO ONE WANTED TO BELIEVE HAVEN WOULD RISK STARTING ONE HERE.

BUT THESE THREE PLAYERS WERE ABOUT TO MAKE THEMSELVES KNOWN AS THEIR PLAN WAS ALREADY IN MOTION.

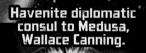

Havenite diplomatic consul to Medusa, Wallace Canning.

Sirius Merchant Captain, Johan Coglin.

Former Manticoran Marine Captain, Denver Summervale.

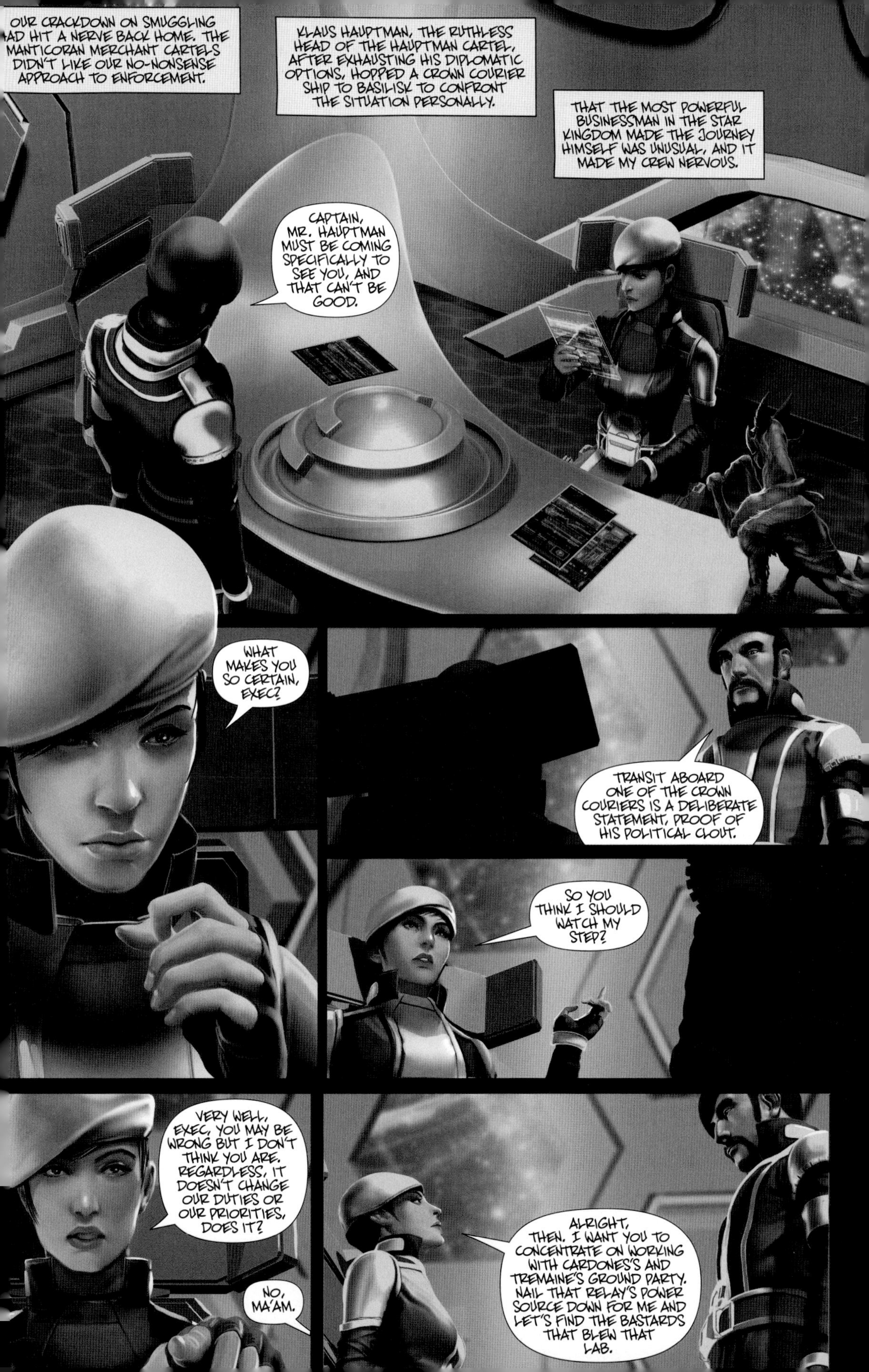
OUR CRACKDOWN ON SMUGGLING HAD HIT A NERVE BACK HOME. THE MANTICORAN MERCHANT CARTELS DIDN'T LIKE OUR NO-NONSENSE APPROACH TO ENFORCEMENT.
KLAUS HAUPTMAN, THE RUTHLESS HEAD OF THE HAUPTMAN CARTEL, AFTER EXHAUSTING HIS DIPLOMATIC OPTIONS, HOPPED A CROWN COURIER SHIP TO BASILISK TO CONFRONT THE SITUATION PERSONALLY.
THAT THE MOST POWERFUL BUSINESSMAN IN THE STAR KINGDOM MADE THE JOURNEY HIMSELF WAS UNUSUAL, AND IT MADE MY CREW NERVOUS.
CAPTAIN, MR. HAUPTMAN MUST BE COMING SPECIFICALLY TO SEE YOU, AND THAT CAN'T BE GOOD.
WHAT MAKES YOU SO CERTAIN, EXEC?
TRANSIT ABOARD ONE OF THE CROWN COURIERS IS A DELIBERATE STATEMENT, PROOF OF HIS POLITICAL CLOUT.
SO YOU THINK I SHOULD WATCH MY STEP?
VERY WELL, EXEC, YOU MAY BE WRONG BUT I DON'T THINK YOU ARE. REGARDLESS, IT DOESN'T CHANGE OUR DUTIES OR OUR PRIORITIES, DOES IT?
NO, MA'AM.
ALRIGHT, THEN. I WANT YOU TO CONCENTRATE ON WORKING WITH CARDONES'S AND TREMAINE'S GROUND PARTY. NAIL THAT RELAY'S POWER SOURCE DOWN FOR ME AND LET'S FIND THE BASTARDS THAT BLEW THAT LAB.

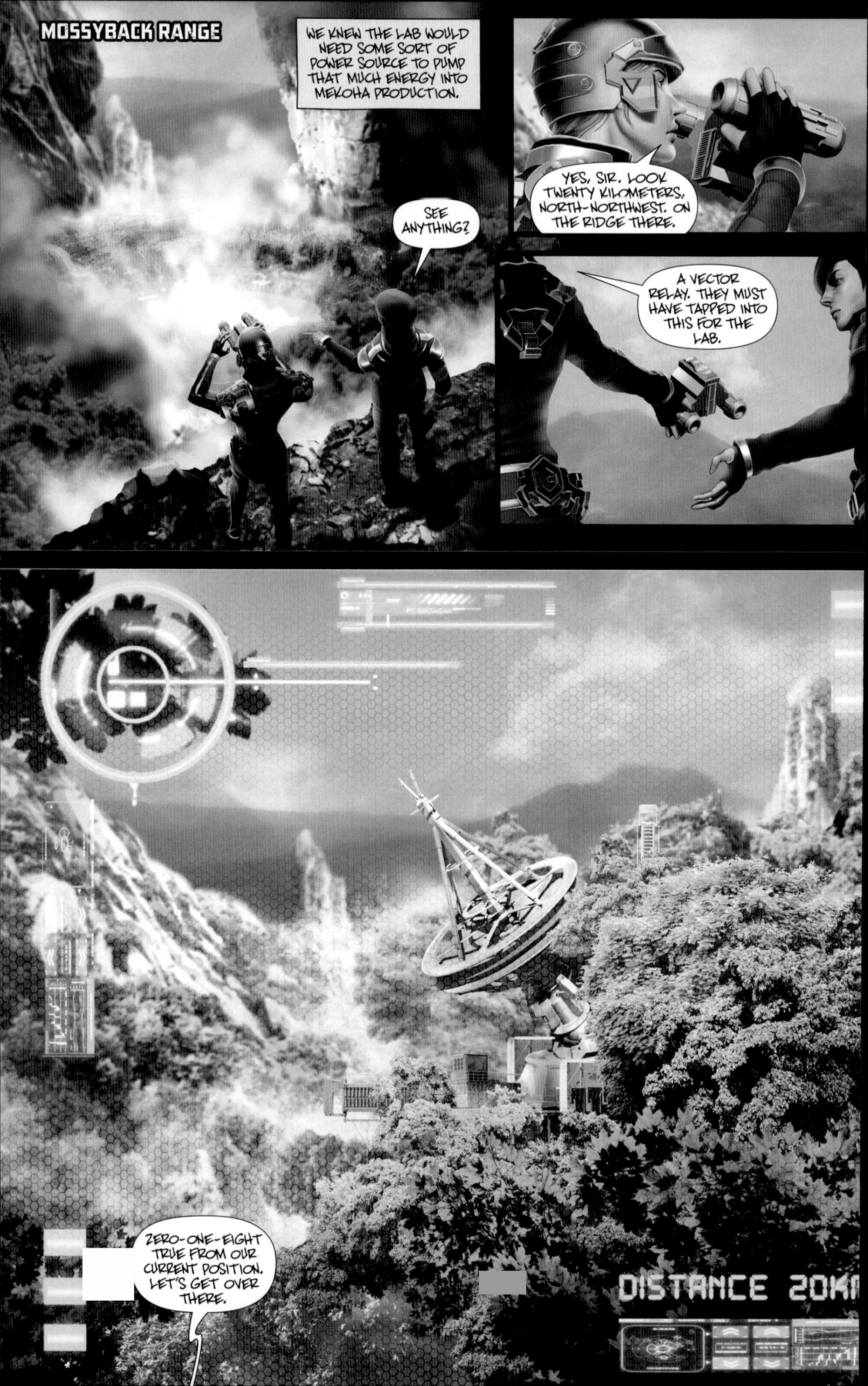
MOSSYBACK RANGE
WE KNEW THE LAB WOULD NEED SOME SORT OF POWER SOURCE TO PUMP THAT MUCH ENERGY INTO MEKOHA PRODUCTION.
SEE ANYTHING?
YES, SIR. LOOK TWENTY KILOMETERS, NORTH-NORTHWEST. ON THE RIDGE THERE.
A VECTOR RELAY. THEY MUST HAVE TAPPED INTO THIS FOR THE LAB.
ZERO-ONE-EIGHT TRUE FROM OUR CURRENT POSITION. LET'S GET OVER THERE.
DISTANCE 20K

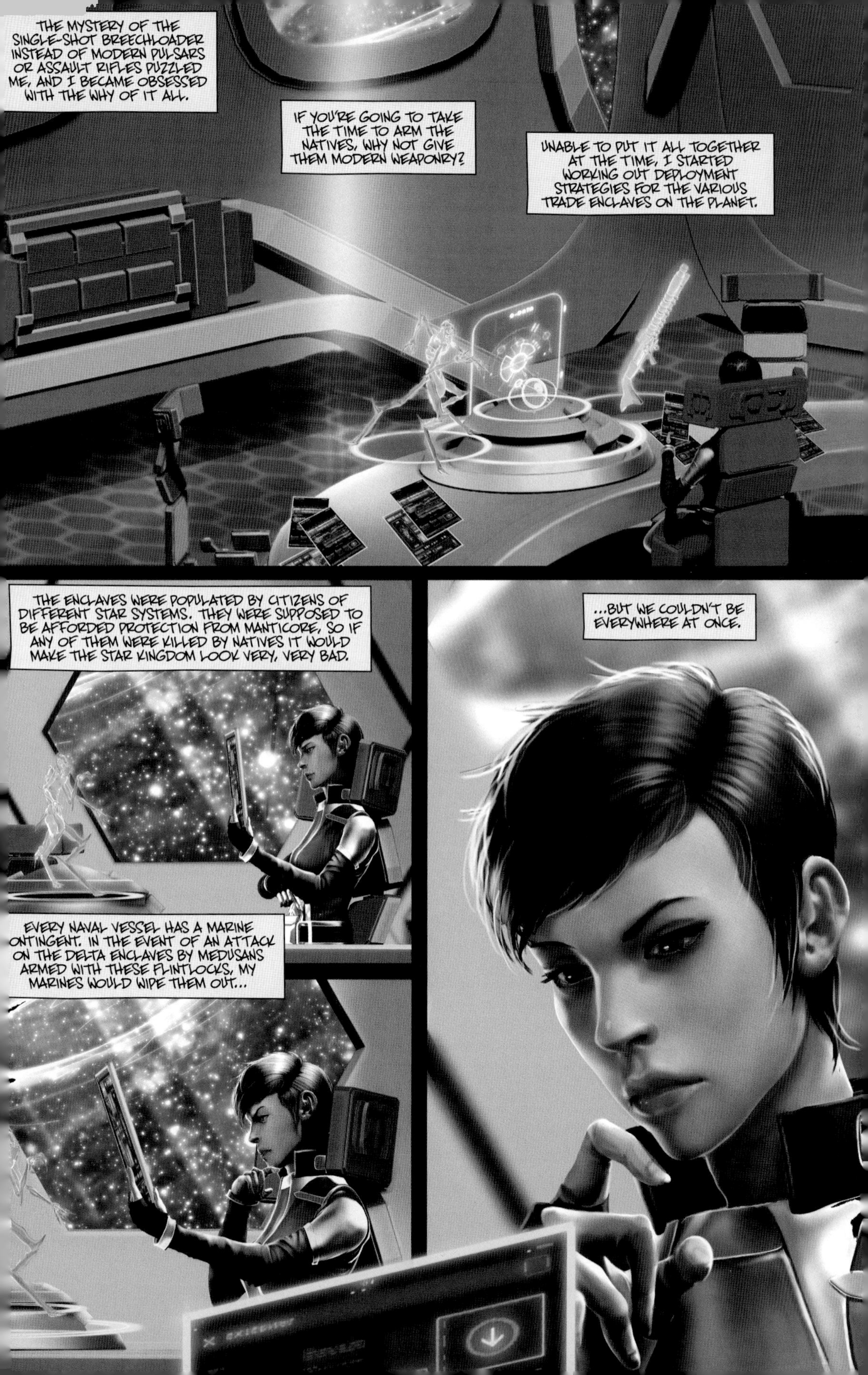
THE MYSTERY OF THE SINGLE-SHOT BREECHLOADER INSTEAD OF MODERN PULSARS OR ASSAULT RIFLES PUZZLED ME, AND I BECAME OBSESSED WITH THE WHY OF IT ALL.
IF YOU'RE GOING TO TAKE THE TIME TO ARM THE NATIVES, WHY NOT GIVE THEM MODERN WEAPONRY?
UNABLE TO PUT IT ALL TOGETHER AT THE TIME, I STARTED WORKING OUT DEPLOYMENT STRATEGIES FOR THE VARIOUS TRADE ENCLAVES ON THE PLANET.
THE ENCLAVES WERE POPULATED BY CITIZENS OF DIFFERENT STAR SYSTEMS. THEY WERE SUPPOSED TO BE AFFORDED PROTECTION FROM MANTICORE, SO IF ANY OF THEM WERE KILLED BY NATIVES IT WOULD MAKE THE STAR KINGDOM LOOK VERY, VERY BAD.
EVERY NAVAL VESSEL HAS A MARINE ONTINGENT. IN THE EVENT OF AN ATTACK ON THE DELTA ENCLAVES BY MEDUSANS ARMED WITH THESE FLINTLOCKS, MY MARINES WOULD WIPE THEM OUT...
...BUT WE COULDN'T BE EVERYWHERE AT ONCE.

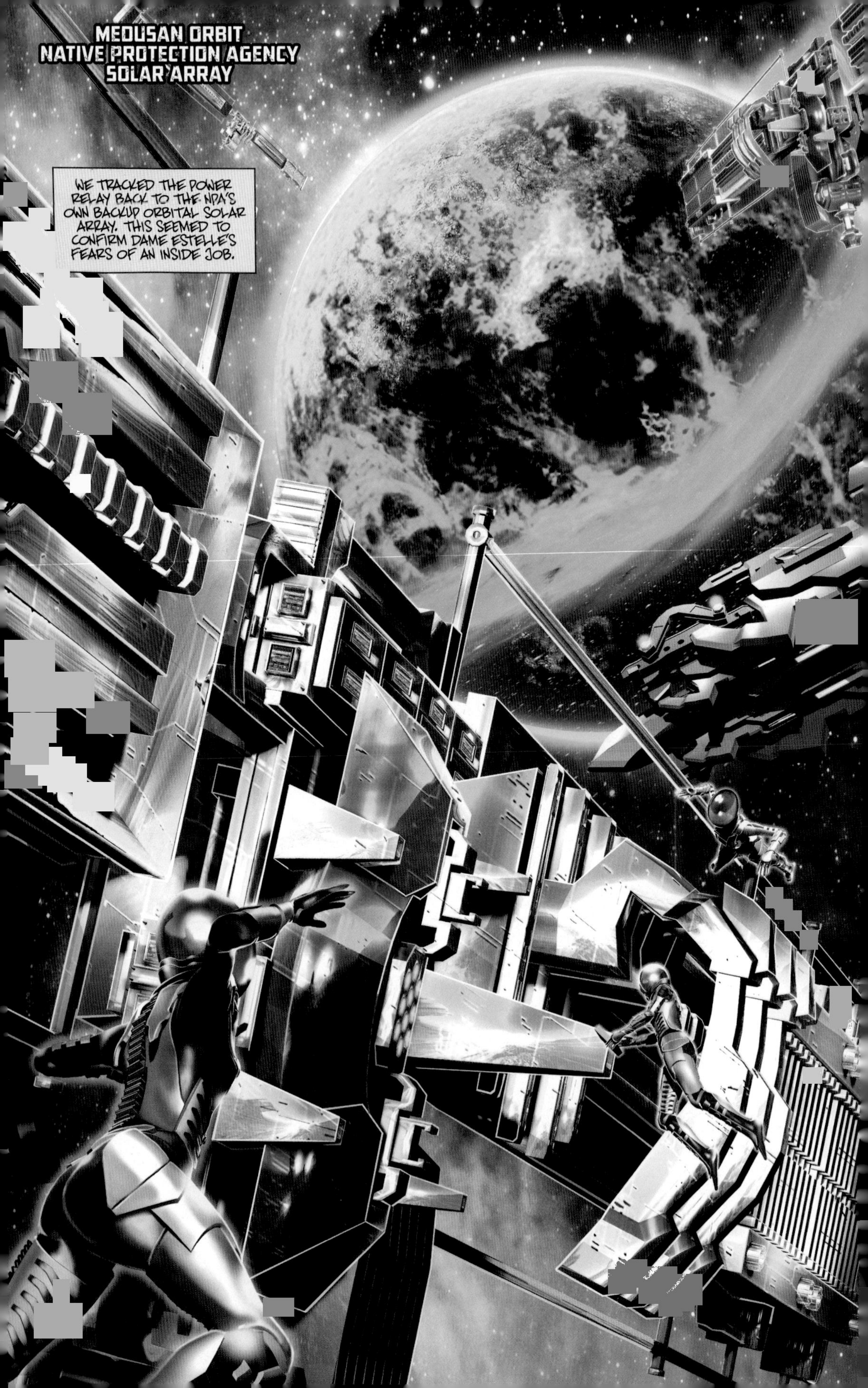
MEDUSAN ORBIT
NATIVE PROTECTION AGENCY
SOLAR ARRAY
WE TRACKED THE POWER RELAY BACK TO THE NPA'S OWN BACKUP ORBITAL SOLAR ARRAY. THIS SEEMED TO CONFIRM DAME ESTELLE'S FEARS OF AN INSIDE JOB.

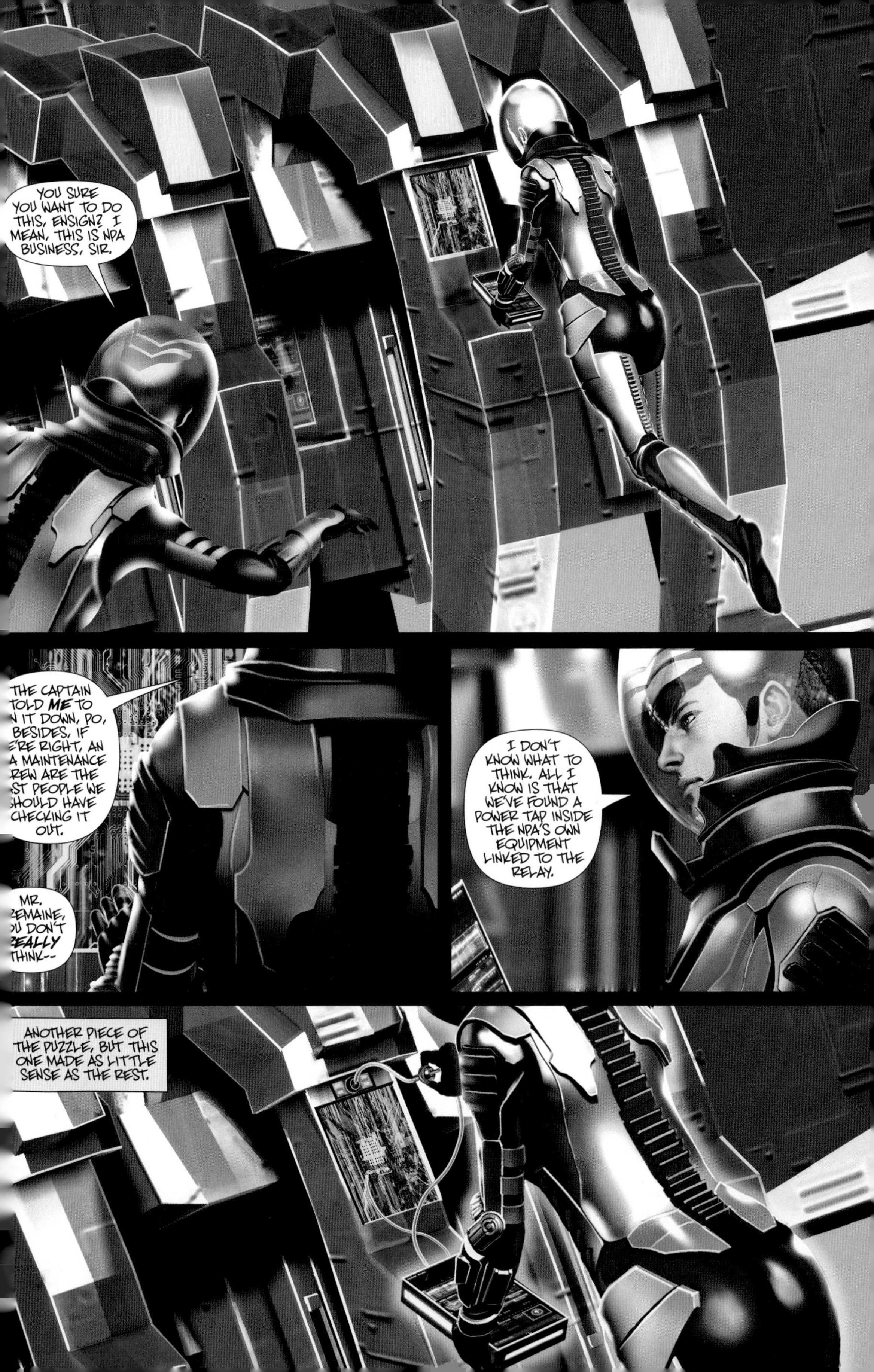
YOU SURE YOU WANT TO DO THIS, ENSIGN? I MEAN, THIS IS NPA BUSINESS, SIR.
THE CAPTAIN TOLD ME TO N IT DOWN, PO, BESIDES, IF E'RE RIGHT, AN A MAINTENANCE REW ARE THE ST PEOPLE WE SHOULD HAVE CHECKING IT OUT.
MR. EMAINE, OU DON'T EALLY THINK--
I DON'T KNOW WHAT TO THINK. ALL I KNOW IS THAT WE'VE FOUND A POWER TAP INSIDE THE NPA'S OWN EQUIPMENT LINKED TO THE RELAY.
ANOTHER PIECE OF THE PUZZLE, BUT THIS ONE MADE AS LITTLE SENSE AS THE REST.

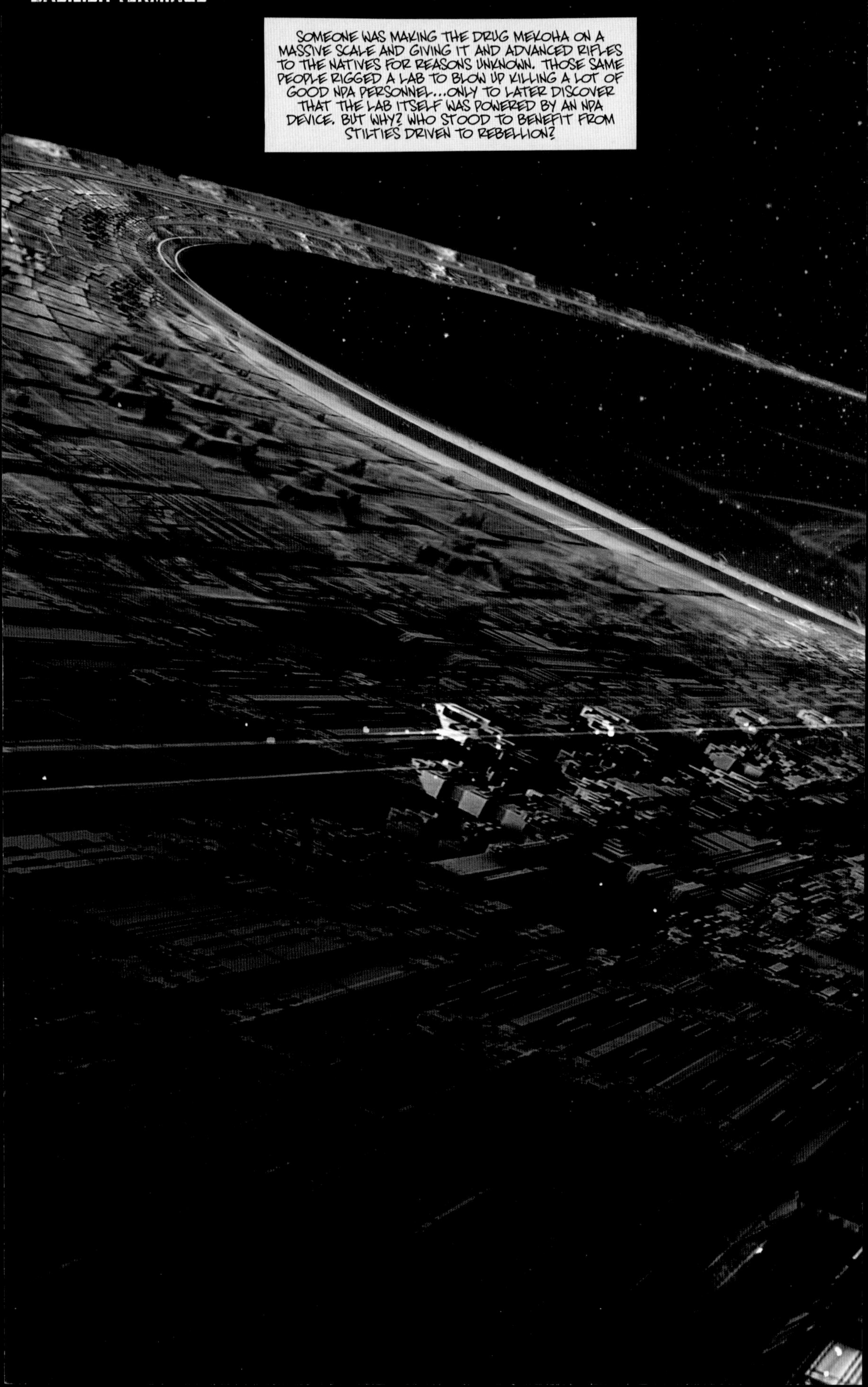
SOMEONE WAS MAKING THE DRUG MEKOHA ON A MASSIVE SCALE AND GIVING IT AND ADVANCED RIFLES TO THE NATIVES FOR REASONS UNKNOWN. THOSE SAME PEOPLE RIGGED A LAB TO BLOW UP KILLING A LOT OF GOOD NPA PERSONNEL...ONLY TO LATER DISCOVER THAT THE LAB ITSELF WAS POWERED BY AN NPA DEVICE. BUT WHY? WHO STOOD TO BENEFIT FROM STILTIES DRIVEN TO REBELLION?

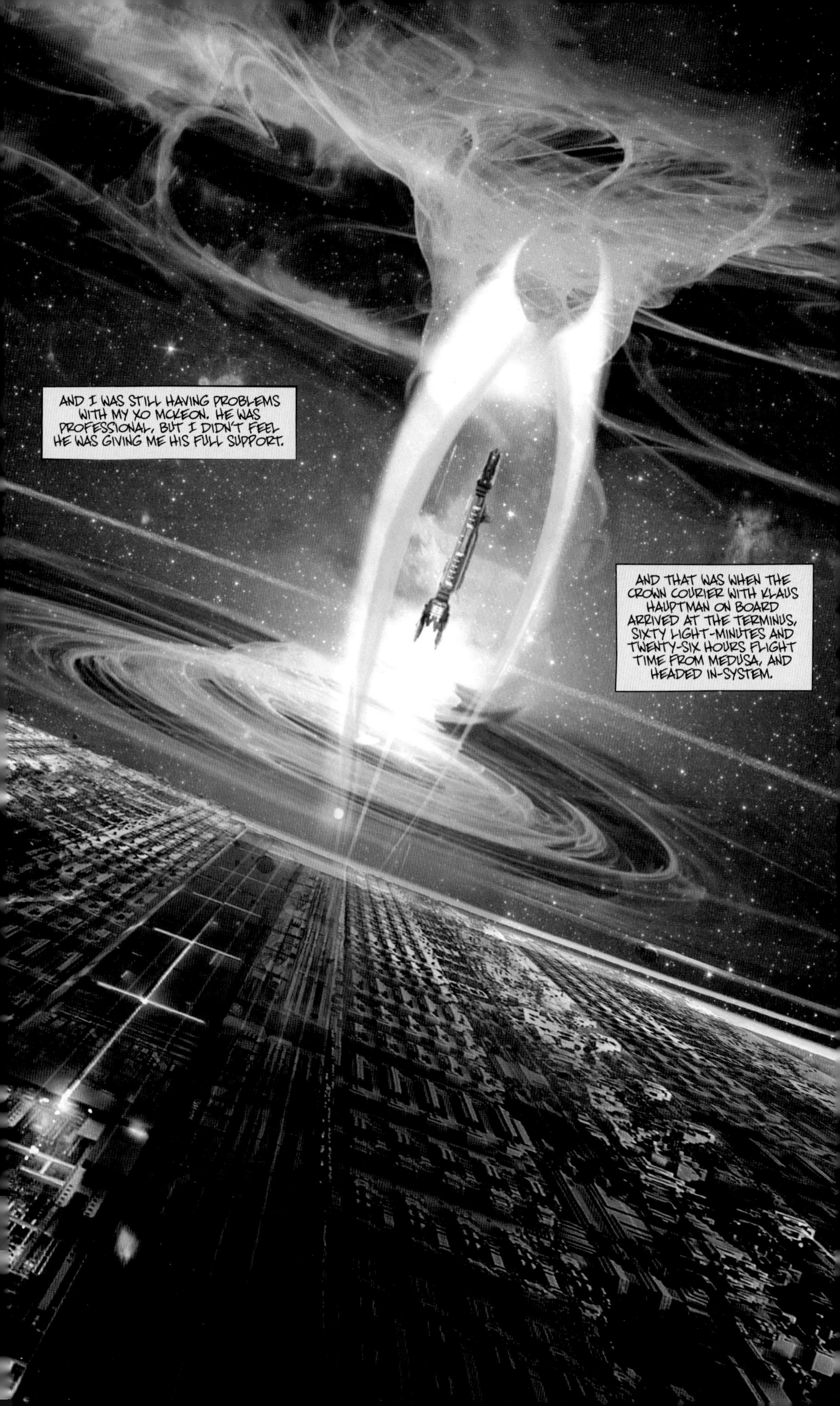
AND I WAS STILL HAVING PROBLEMS WITH MY XO MCKEON. HE WAS PROFESSIONAL, BUT I DIDN'T FEEL HE WAS GIVING ME HIS FULL SUPPORT.
AND THAT WAS WHEN THE CROWN COURIER WITH KLAUS HAUPTMAN ON BOARD ARRIVED AT THE TERMINUS, SIXTY LIGHT-MINUTES AND TWENTY-SIX HOURS FLIGHT TIME FROM MEDUSA, AND HEADED IN-SYSTEM.

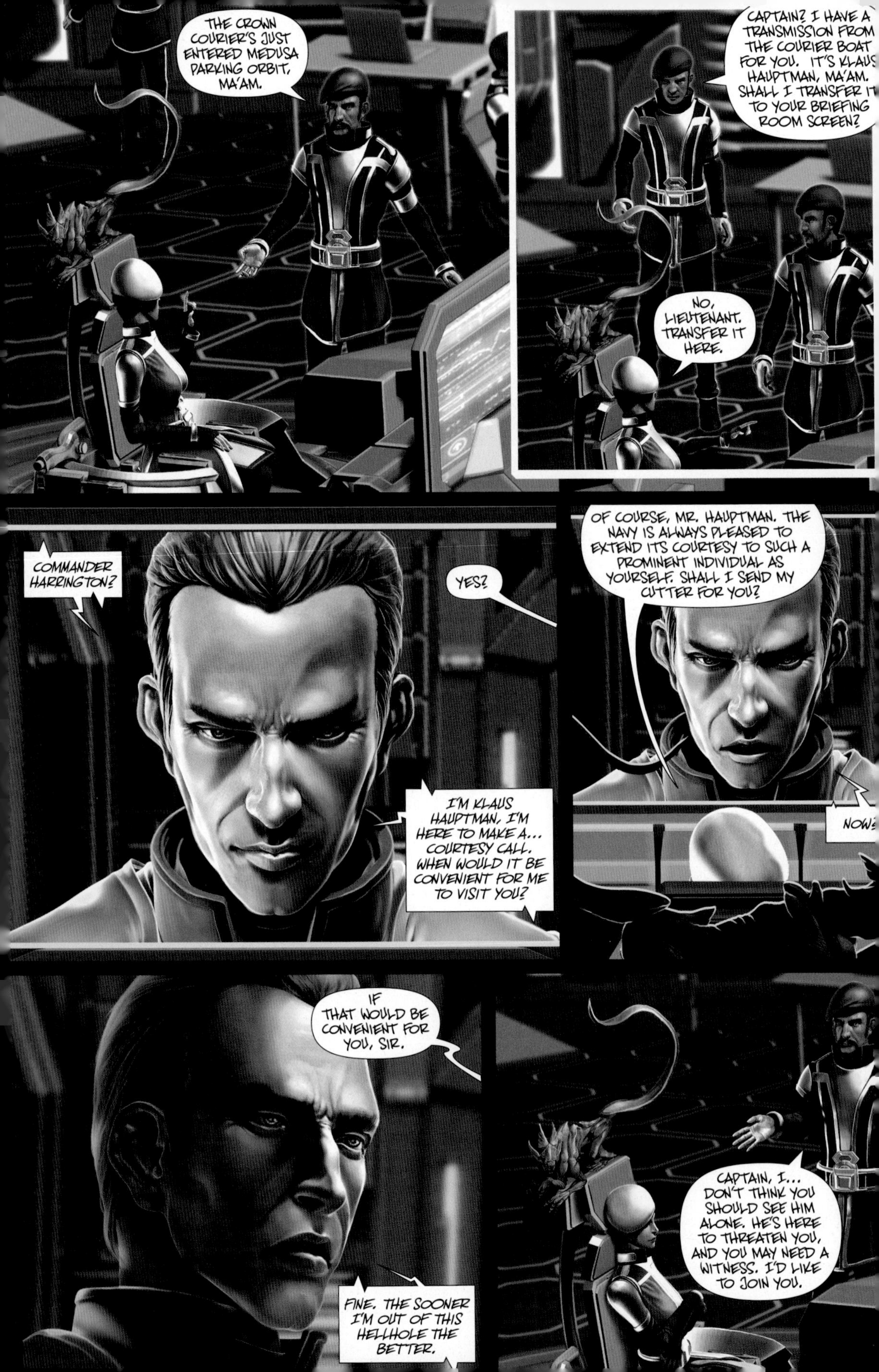

THE CROWN COURIER'S JUST ENTERED MEDUSA PARKING ORBIT, MA'AM.
CAPTAIN? I HAVE A TRANSMISSION FROM THE COURIER BOAT FOR YOU. IT'S KLAUS HAUPTMAN, MA'AM. SHALL I TRANSFER IT TO YOUR BRIEFING ROOM SCREEN?
NO, LIEUTENANT. TRANSFER IT HERE.
COMMANDER HARRINGTON?
YES?
I'M KLAUS HAUPTMAN, I'M HERE TO MAKE A... COURTESY CALL. WHEN WOULD IT BE CONVENIENT FOR ME TO VISIT YOU?
OF COURSE, MR. HAUPTMAN. THE NAVY IS ALWAYS PLEASED TO EXTEND ITS COURTESY TO SUCH A PROMINENT INDIVIDUAL AS YOURSELF. SHALL I SEND MY CUTTER FOR YOU?
NOW?
IF THAT WOULD BE CONVENIENT FOR YOU, SIR.
FINE. THE SOONER I'M OUT OF THIS HELLHOLE THE BETTER.
CAPTAIN, I... DON'T THINK YOU SHOULD SEE HIM ALONE. HE'S HERE TO THREATEN YOU, AND YOU MAY NEED A WITNESS. I'D LIKE TO JOIN YOU.

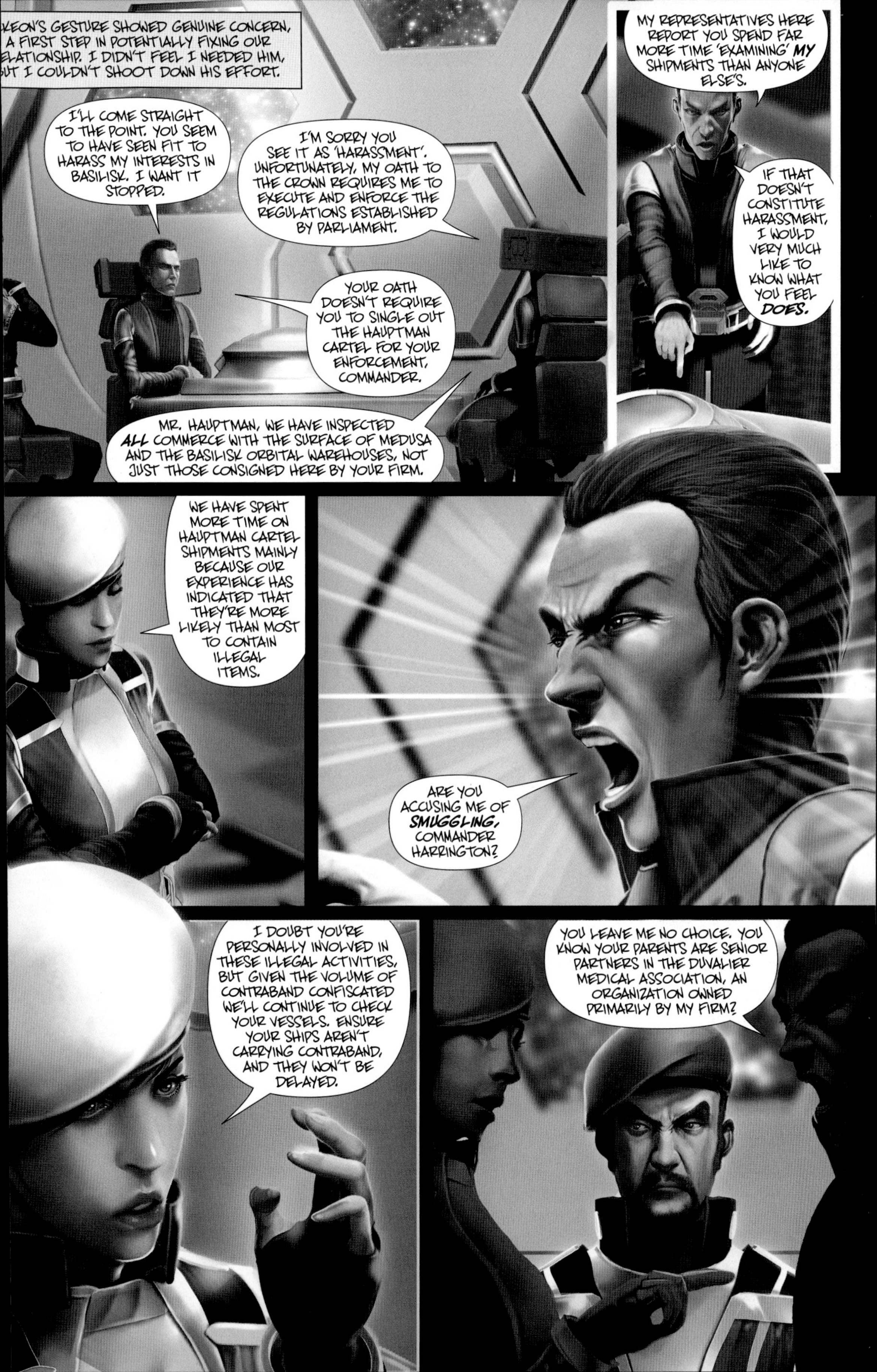
KEON'S GESTURE SHOWED GENUINE CONCERN, A FIRST STEP IN POTENTIALLY FIXING OUR ELATIONSHIP. I DIDN'T FEEL I NEEDED HIM, UT I COULDN'T SHOOT DOWN HIS EFFORT.
I'LL COME STRAIGHT TO THE POINT. YOU SEEM TO HAVE SEEN FIT TO HARASS MY INTERESTS IN BASILISK. I WANT IT STOPPED.
I'M SORRY YOU SEE IT AS 'HARASSMENT'. UNFORTUNATELY, MY OATH TO THE CROWN REQUIRES ME TO EXECUTE AND ENFORCE THE REGULATIONS ESTABLISHED BY PARLIAMENT.
YOUR OATH DOESN'T REQUIRE YOU TO SINGLE OUT THE HAUPTMAN CARTEL FOR YOUR ENFORCEMENT, COMMANDER.
MR. HAUPTMAN, WE HAVE INSPECTED ALL COMMERCE WITH THE SURFACE OF MEDUSA AND THE BASILISK ORBITAL WAREHOUSES, NOT JUST THOSE CONSIGNED HERE BY YOUR FIRM.
MY REPRESENTATIVES HERE REPORT YOU SPEND FAR MORE TIME 'EXAMINING' MY SHIPMENTS THAN ANYONE ELSE'S.
IF THAT DOESN'T CONSTITUTE HARASSMENT, I WOULD VERY MUCH LIKE TO KNOW WHAT YOU FEEL DOES.
WE HAVE SPENT MORE TIME ON HAUPTMAN CARTEL SHIPMENTS MAINLY BECAUSE OUR EXPERIENCE HAS INDICATED THAT THEY'RE MORE LIKELY THAN MOST TO CONTAIN ILLEGAL ITEMS.
ARE YOU ACCUSING ME OF SMUGGLING, COMMANDER HARRINGTON?
I DOUBT YOU'RE PERSONALLY INVOLVED IN THESE ILLEGAL ACTIVITIES, BUT GIVEN THE VOLUME OF CONTRABAND CONFISCATED WE'LL CONTINUE TO CHECK YOUR VESSELS. ENSURE YOUR SHIPS AREN'T CARRYING CONTRABAND, AND THEY WON'T BE DELAYED.
YOU LEAVE ME NO CHOICE. YOU KNOW YOUR PARENTS ARE SENIOR PARTNERS IN THE DUVALIER MEDICAL ASSOCIATION, AN ORGANIZATION OWNED PRIMARILY BY MY FIRM?

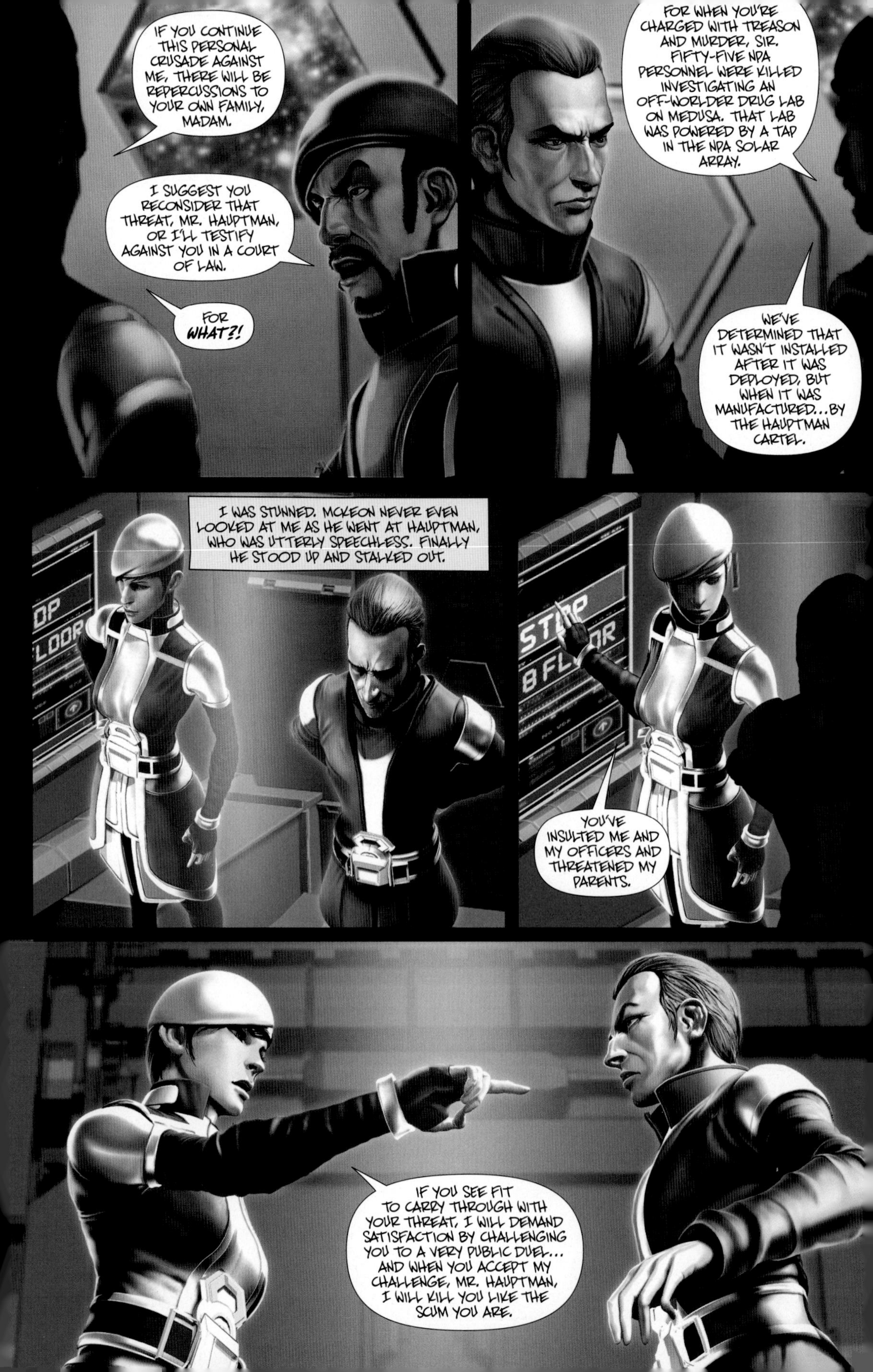
IF YOU CONTINUE THIS PERSONAL CRUSADE AGAINST ME, THERE WILL BE REPERCUSSIONS TO YOUR OWN FAMILY, MADAM.
I SUGGEST YOU RECONSIDER THAT THREAT, MR. HAUPTMAN, OR I'LL TESTIFY AGAINST YOU IN A COURT OF LAW.
FOR *WHAT?!*
FOR WHEN YOU'RE CHARGED WITH TREASON AND MURDER, SIR. FIFTY-FIVE NDA PERSONNEL WERE KILLED INVESTIGATING AN OFF-WORLDER DRUG LAB ON MEDUSA. THAT LAB WAS POWERED BY A TAP IN THE NDA SOLAR ARRAY.
WE'VE DETERMINED THAT IT WASN'T INSTALLED AFTER IT WAS DEPLOYED, BUT WHEN IT WAS MANUFACTURED...BY THE HAUPTMAN CARTEL.
I WAS STUNNED. MCKEON NEVER EVEN LOOKED AT ME AS HE WENT AT HAUPTMAN, WHO WAS UTTERLY SPEECHLESS. FINALLY HE STOOD UP AND STALKED OUT.
YOU'VE INSULTED ME AND MY OFFICERS AND THREATENED MY PARENTS.
IF YOU SEE FIT TO CARRY THROUGH WITH YOUR THREAT, I WILL DEMAND SATISFACTION BY CHALLENGING YOU TO A VERY PUBLIC DUEL... AND WHEN YOU ACCEPT MY CHALLENGE, MR. HAUPTMAN, I WILL KILL YOU LIKE THE SCUM YOU ARE.

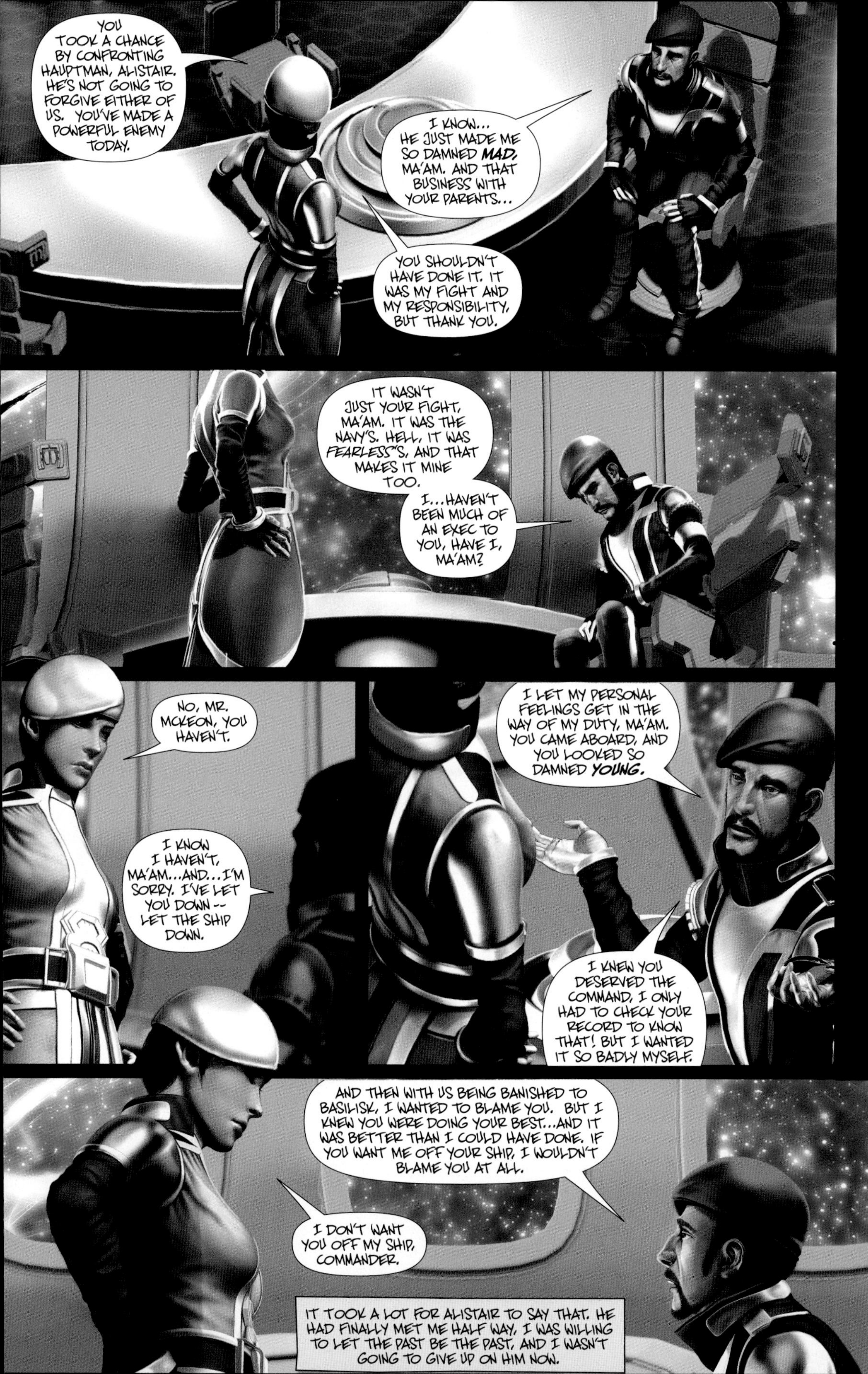
YOU TOOK A CHANCE BY CONFRONTING HAUPTMAN, ALISTAIR. HE'S NOT GOING TO FORGIVE EITHER OF US. YOU'VE MADE A POWERFUL ENEMY TODAY.
I KNOW... HE JUST MADE ME SO DAMNED **MAD,** MA'AM. AND THAT BUSINESS WITH YOUR PARENTS...
YOU SHOULDN'T HAVE DONE IT. IT WAS MY FIGHT AND MY RESPONSIBILITY, BUT THANK YOU.
IT WASN'T JUST YOUR FIGHT, MA'AM. IT WAS THE NAVY'S. HELL, IT WAS *FEARLESS*'S, AND THAT MAKES IT MINE TOO.
I...HAVEN'T BEEN MUCH OF AN EXEC TO YOU, HAVE I, MA'AM?
NO, MR. MCKEON, YOU HAVEN'T.
I KNOW I HAVEN'T, MA'AM...AND...I'M SORRY. I'VE LET YOU DOWN -- LET THE SHIP DOWN.
I LET MY PERSONAL FEELINGS GET IN THE WAY OF MY DUTY, MA'AM. YOU CAME ABOARD, AND YOU LOOKED SO DAMNED **YOUNG.**
I KNEW YOU DESERVED THE COMMAND, I ONLY HAD TO CHECK YOUR RECORD TO KNOW THAT! BUT I WANTED IT SO BADLY MYSELF.
AND THEN WITH US BEING BANISHED TO BASILISK, I WANTED TO BLAME YOU. BUT I KNEW YOU WERE DOING YOUR BEST...AND IT WAS BETTER THAN I COULD HAVE DONE. IF YOU WANT ME OFF YOUR SHIP, I WOULDN'T BLAME YOU AT ALL.
I DON'T WANT YOU OFF MY SHIP, COMMANDER.
IT TOOK A LOT FOR ALISTAIR TO SAY THAT. HE HAD FINALLY MET ME HALF WAY, I WAS WILLING TO LET THE PAST BE THE PAST, AND I WASN'T GOING TO GIVE UP ON HIM NOW.

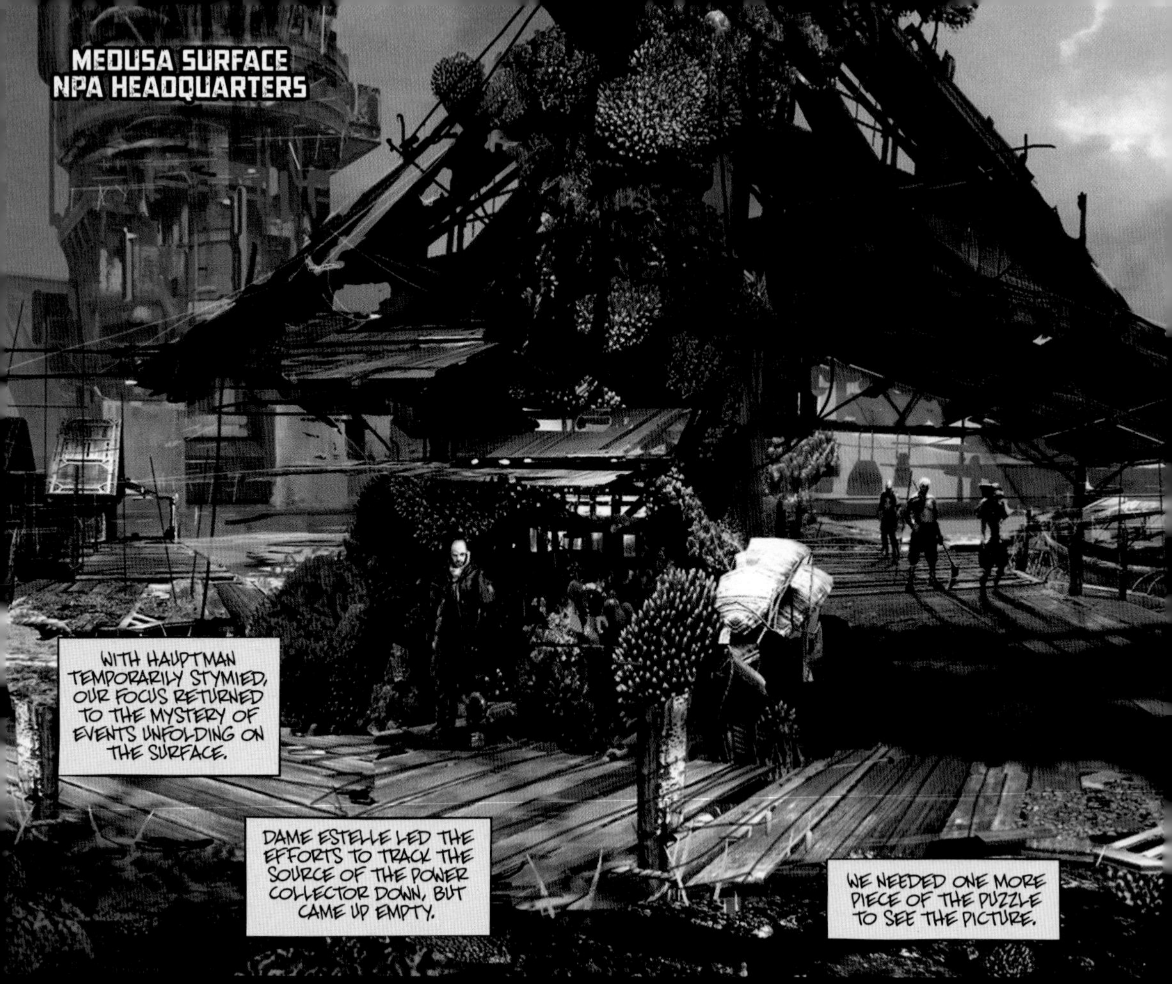
MEDUSA SURFACE
NPA HEADQUARTERS
WITH HAUPTMAN TEMPORARILY STYMIED, OUR FOCUS RETURNED TO THE MYSTERY OF EVENTS UNFOLDING ON THE SURFACE.
DAME ESTELLE LED THE EFFORTS TO TRACK THE SOURCE OF THE POWER COLLECTOR DOWN, BUT CAME UP EMPTY.
WE NEEDED ONE MORE PIECE OF THE PUZZLE TO SEE THE PICTURE.

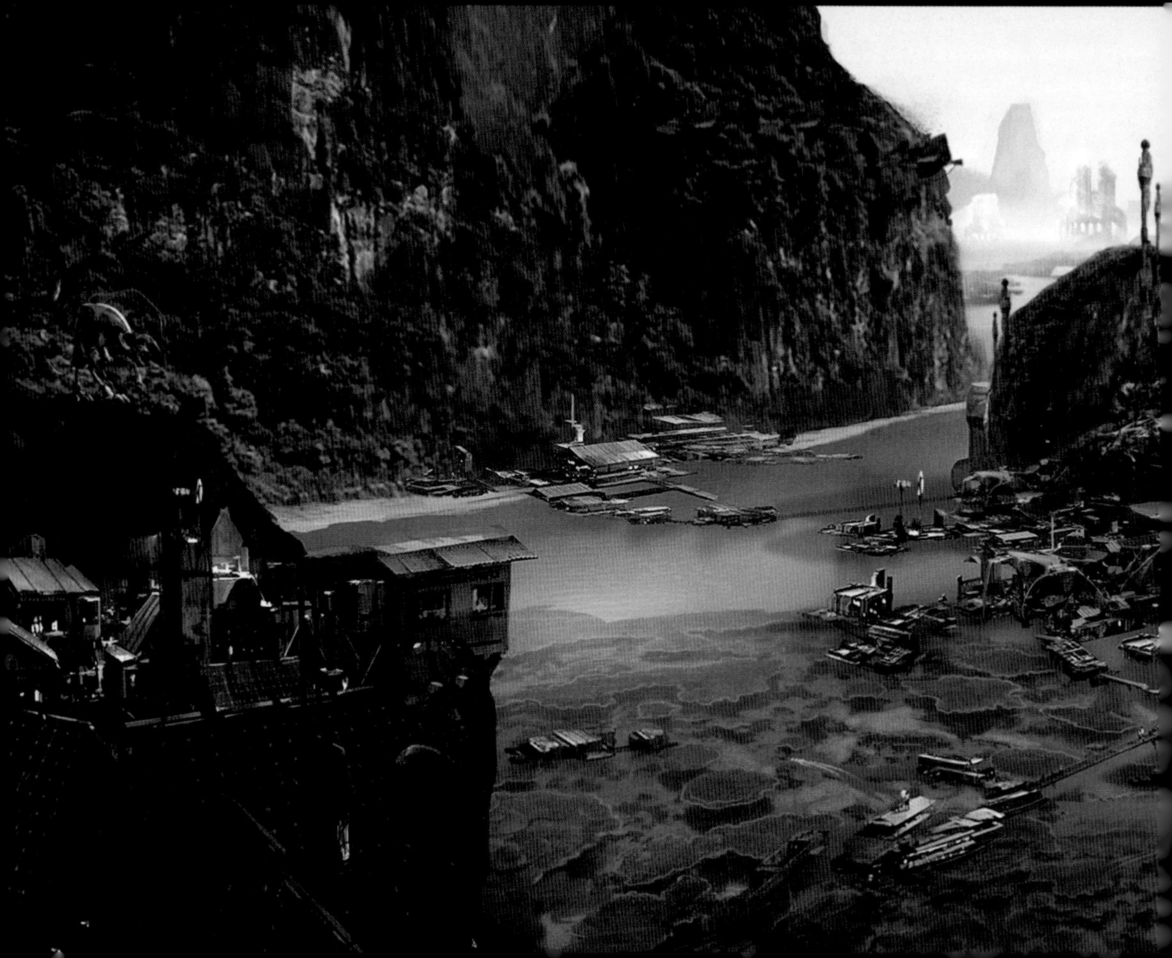

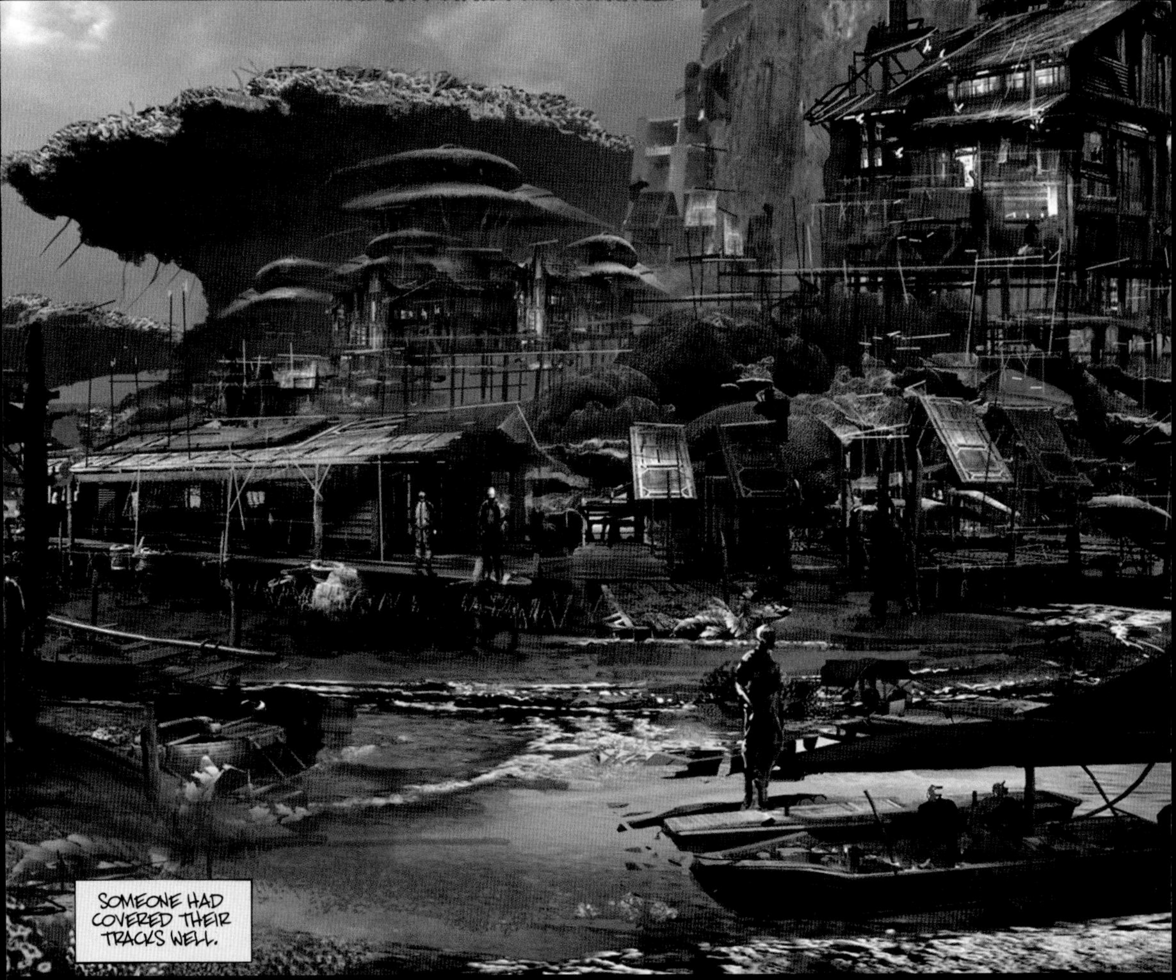
SOMEONE HAD COVERED THEIR TRACKS WELL.

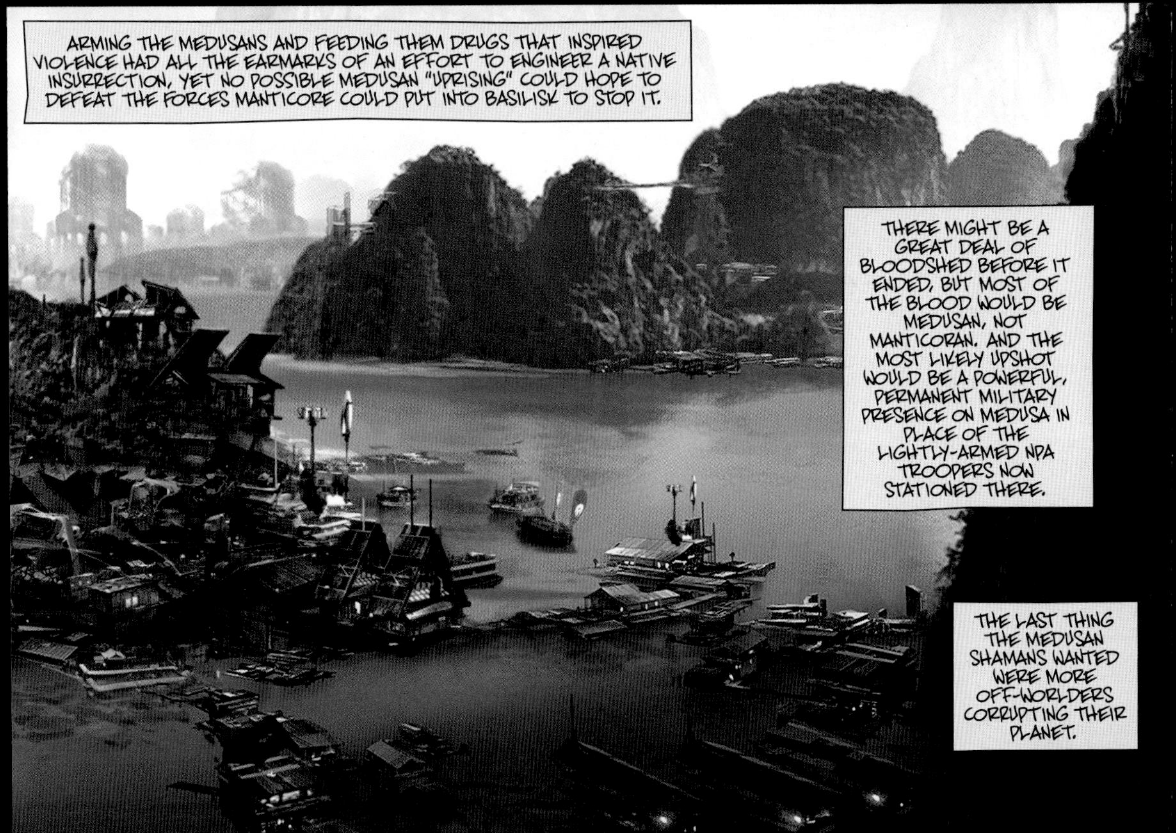
ARMING THE MEDUSANS AND FEEDING THEM DRUGS THAT INSPIRED VIOLENCE HAD ALL THE EARMARKS OF AN EFFORT TO ENGINEER A NATIVE INSURRECTION, YET NO POSSIBLE MEDUSAN "UPRISING" COULD HOPE TO DEFEAT THE FORCES MANTICORE COULD PUT INTO BASILISK TO STOP IT.
THERE MIGHT BE A GREAT DEAL OF BLOODSHED BEFORE IT ENDED, BUT MOST OF THE BLOOD WOULD BE MEDUSAN, NOT MANTICORAN. AND THE MOST LIKELY UPSHOT WOULD BE A POWERFUL, PERMANENT MILITARY PRESENCE ON MEDUSA IN PLACE OF THE LIGHTLY-ARMED NPA TROOPERS NOW STATIONED THERE.
THE LAST THING THE MEDUSAN SHAMANS WANTED WERE MORE OFF-WORLDERS CORRUPTING THEIR PLANET.

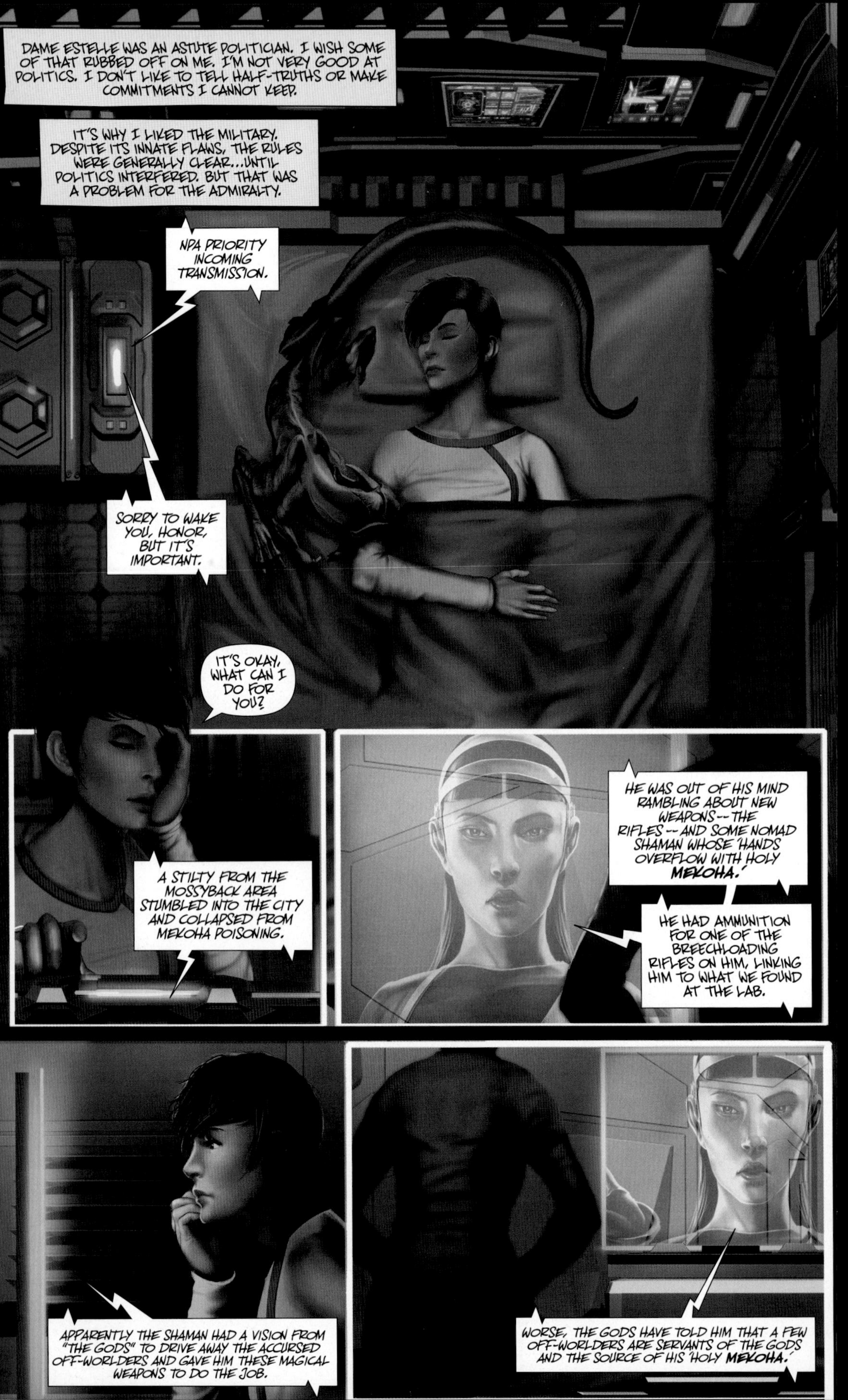
DAME ESTELLE WAS AN ASTUTE POLITICIAN. I WISH SOME OF THAT RUBBED OFF ON ME. I'M NOT VERY GOOD AT POLITICS. I DON'T LIKE TO TELL HALF-TRUTHS OR MAKE COMMITMENTS I CANNOT KEEP.
IT'S WHY I LIKED THE MILITARY. DESPITE ITS INNATE FLAWS, THE RULES WERE GENERALLY CLEAR...UNTIL POLITICS INTERFERED. BUT THAT WAS A PROBLEM FOR THE ADMIRALTY.
NPA PRIORITY INCOMING TRANSMISSION.
SORRY TO WAKE YOU, HONOR, BUT IT'S IMPORTANT.
IT'S OKAY, WHAT CAN I DO FOR YOU?
A STILTY FROM THE MOSSYBACK AREA STUMBLED INTO THE CITY AND COLLAPSED FROM MEKOHA POISONING.
HE WAS OUT OF HIS MIND RAMBLING ABOUT NEW WEAPONS-- THE RIFLES -- AND SOME NOMAD SHAMAN WHOSE 'HANDS OVERFLOW WITH HOLY **MEKOHA**.'
HE HAD AMMUNITION FOR ONE OF THE BREECHLOADING RIFLES ON HIM, LINKING HIM TO WHAT WE FOUND AT THE LAB.
APPARENTLY THE SHAMAN HAD A VISION FROM "THE GODS" TO DRIVE AWAY THE ACCURSED OFF-WORLDERS AND GAVE HIM THESE MAGICAL WEAPONS TO DO THE JOB.
WORSE, THE GODS HAVE TOLD HIM THAT A FEW OFF-WORLDERS ARE SERVANTS OF THE GODS AND THE SOURCE OF HIS 'HOLY **MEKOHA**.'

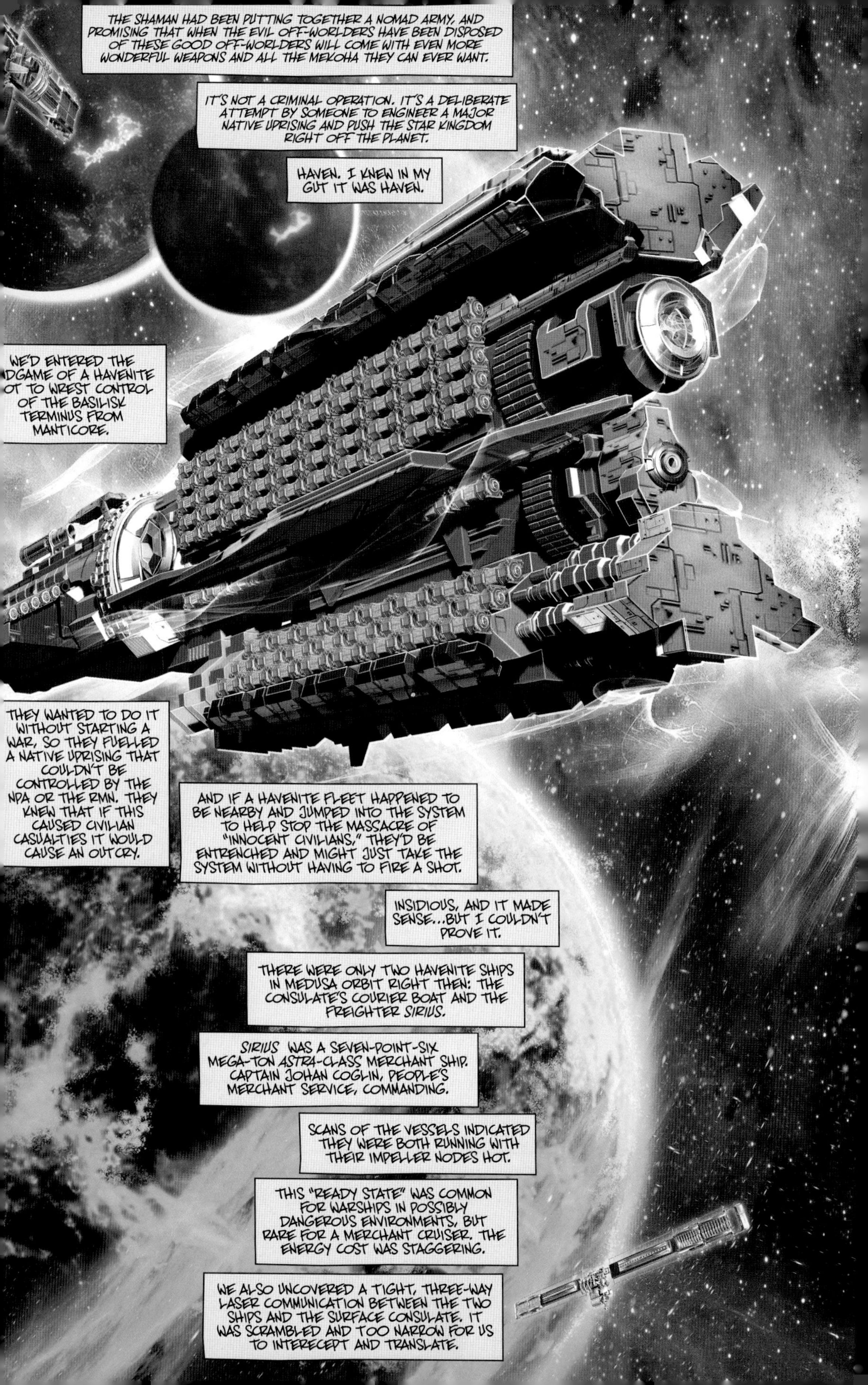
THE SHAMAN HAD BEEN PUTTING TOGETHER A NOMAD ARMY, AND PROMISING THAT WHEN THE EVIL OFF-WORLDERS HAVE BEEN DISPOSED OF THESE GOOD OFF-WORLDERS WILL COME WITH EVEN MORE WONDERFUL WEAPONS AND ALL THE MEKOHA THEY CAN EVER WANT.
IT'S NOT A CRIMINAL OPERATION. IT'S A DELIBERATE ATTEMPT BY SOMEONE TO ENGINEER A MAJOR NATIVE UPRISING AND PUSH THE STAR KINGDOM RIGHT OFF THE PLANET.
HAVEN. I KNEW IN MY GUT IT WAS HAVEN.
WE'D ENTERED THE DGAME OF A HAVENITE OT TO WREST CONTROL OF THE BASILISK TERMINUS FROM MANTICORE.
THEY WANTED TO DO IT WITHOUT STARTING A WAR, SO THEY FUELLED A NATIVE UPRISING THAT COULDN'T BE CONTROLLED BY THE NPA OR THE RMN. THEY KNEW THAT IF THIS CAUSED CIVILIAN CASUALTIES IT WOULD CAUSE AN OUTCRY.
AND IF A HAVENITE FLEET HAPPENED TO BE NEARBY AND JUMPED INTO THE SYSTEM TO HELP STOP THE MASSACRE OF "INNOCENT CIVILIANS," THEY'D BE ENTRENCHED AND MIGHT JUST TAKE THE SYSTEM WITHOUT HAVING TO FIRE A SHOT.
INSIDIOUS, AND IT MADE SENSE...BUT I COULDN'T PROVE IT.
THERE WERE ONLY TWO HAVENITE SHIPS IN MEDUSA ORBIT RIGHT THEN: THE CONSULATE'S COURIER BOAT AND THE FREIGHTER *SIRIUS*.
SIRIUS WAS A SEVEN-POINT-SIX MEGA-TON *ASTRA*-CLASS MERCHANT SHIP. CAPTAIN JOHAN COGLIN, PEOPLE'S MERCHANT SERVICE, COMMANDING.
SCANS OF THE VESSELS INDICATED THEY WERE BOTH RUNNING WITH THEIR IMPELLER NODES HOT.
THIS "READY STATE" WAS COMMON FOR WARSHIPS IN POSSIBLY DANGEROUS ENVIRONMENTS, BUT RARE FOR A MERCHANT CRUISER. THE ENERGY COST WAS STAGGERING.
WE ALSO UNCOVERED A TIGHT, THREE-WAY LASER COMMUNICATION BETWEEN THE TWO SHIPS AND THE SURFACE CONSULATE. IT WAS SCRAMBLED AND TOO NARROW FOR US TO INTERECEPT AND TRANSLATE.

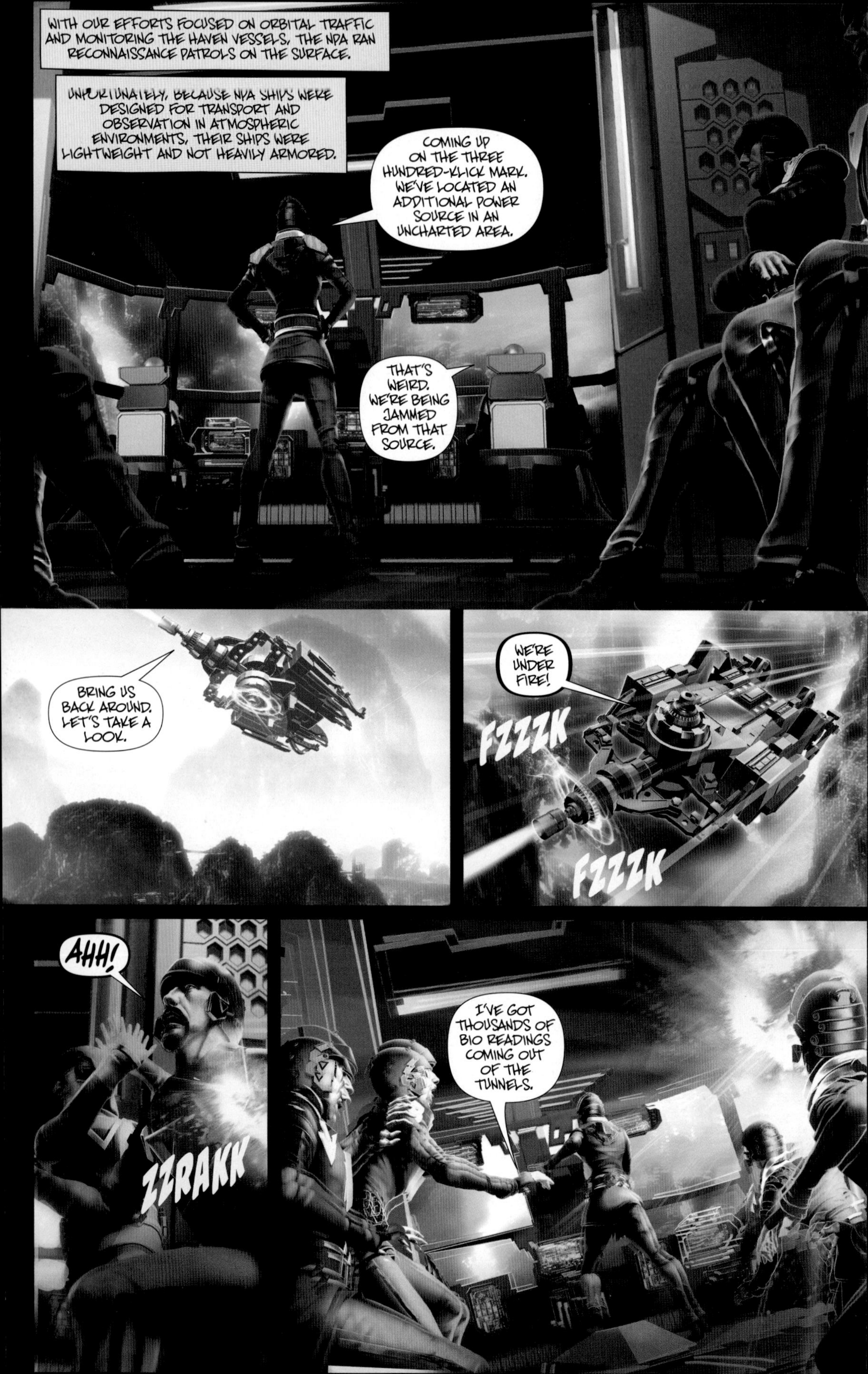
WITH OUR EFFORTS FOCUSED ON ORBITAL TRAFFIC AND MONITORING THE HAVEN VESSELS, THE NPA RAN RECONNAISSANCE PATROLS ON THE SURFACE.
UNFORTUNATELY, BECAUSE NPA SHIPS WERE DESIGNED FOR TRANSPORT AND OBSERVATION IN ATMOSPHERIC ENVIRONMENTS, THEIR SHIPS WERE LIGHTWEIGHT AND NOT HEAVILY ARMORED.
COMING UP ON THE THREE HUNDRED-KLICK MARK. WE'VE LOCATED AN ADDITIONAL POWER SOURCE IN AN UNCHARTED AREA.
THAT'S WEIRD. WE'RE BEING JAMMED FROM THAT SOURCE.
BRING US BACK AROUND. LET'S TAKE A LOOK.
WE'RE UNDER FIRE!
FZZZK
FZZZK
AHH!
ZZRAKK
I'VE GOT THOUSANDS OF BIO READINGS COMING OUT OF THE TUNNELS.

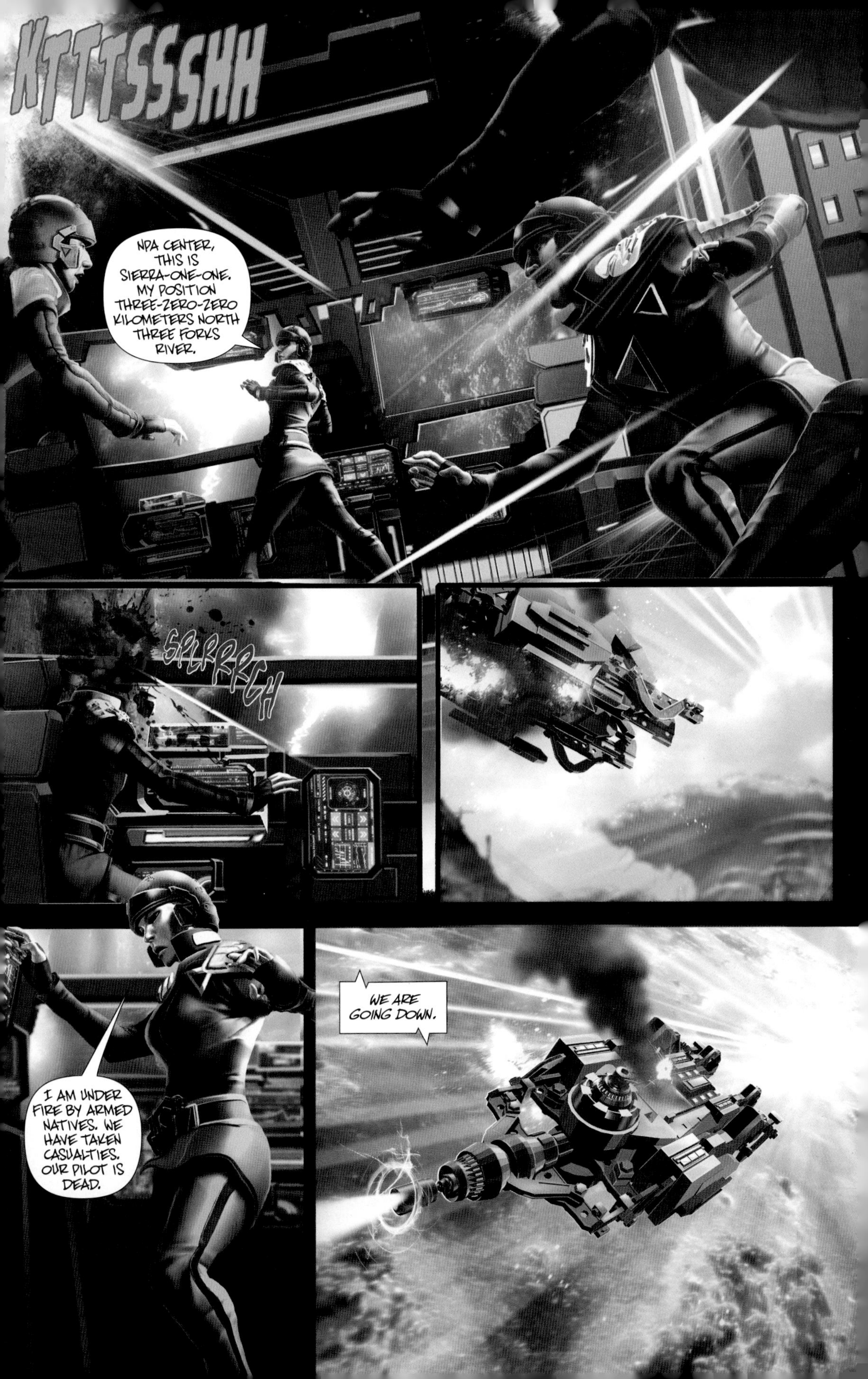
KTTTSSSHH
NPA CENTER, THIS IS SIERRA-ONE-ONE. MY POSITION THREE-ZERO-ZERO KILOMETERS NORTH THREE FORKS RIVER.
SPLRRRCH
I AM UNDER FIRE BY ARMED NATIVES. WE HAVE TAKEN CASUALTIES. OUR PILOT IS DEAD.
WE ARE GOING DOWN.

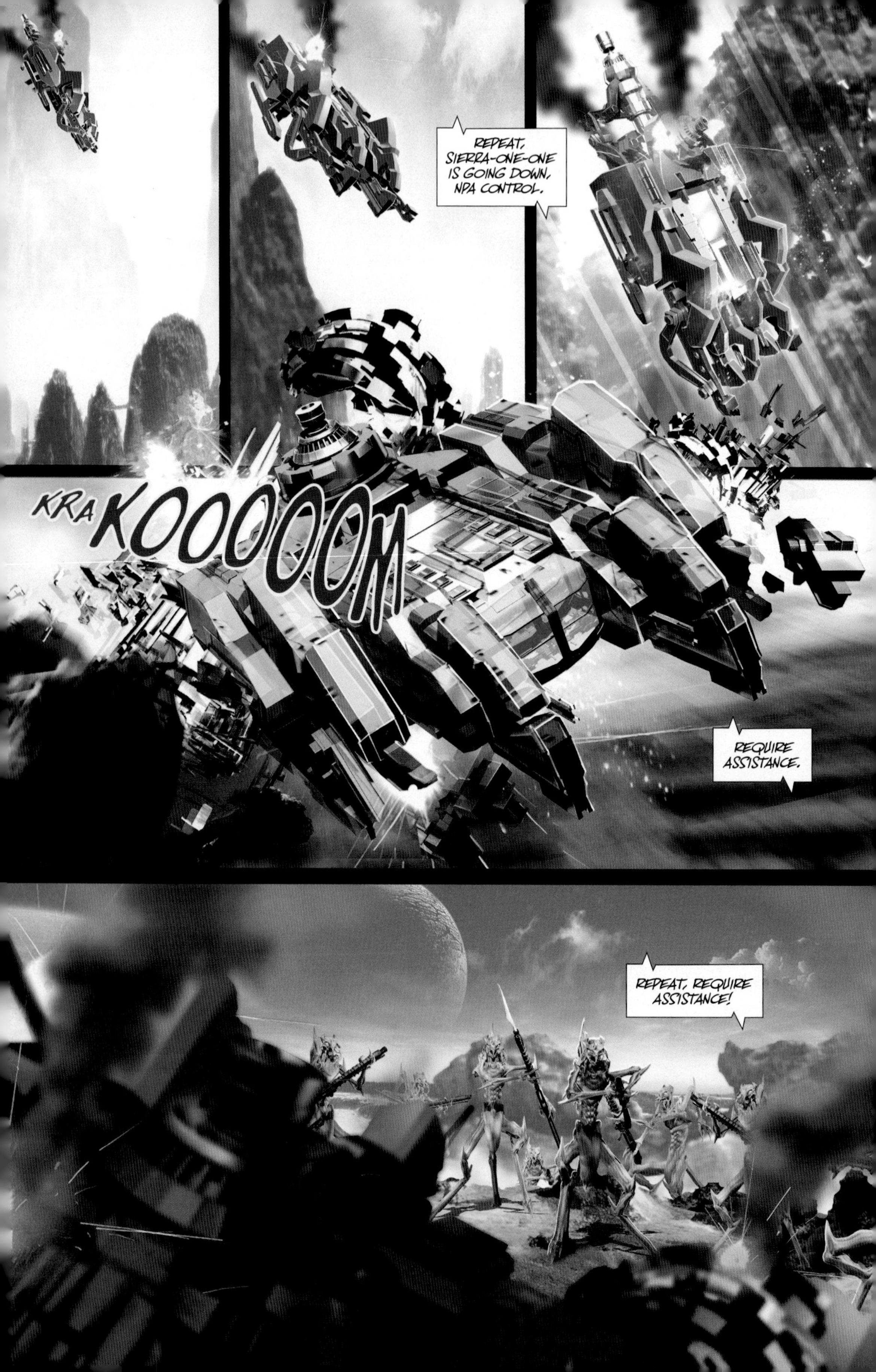
REPEAT, SIERRA-ONE-ONE IS GOING DOWN, NPA CONTROL.
KRA KOOOOOM
REQUIRE ASSISTANCE.
REPEAT, REQUIRE ASSISTANCE!

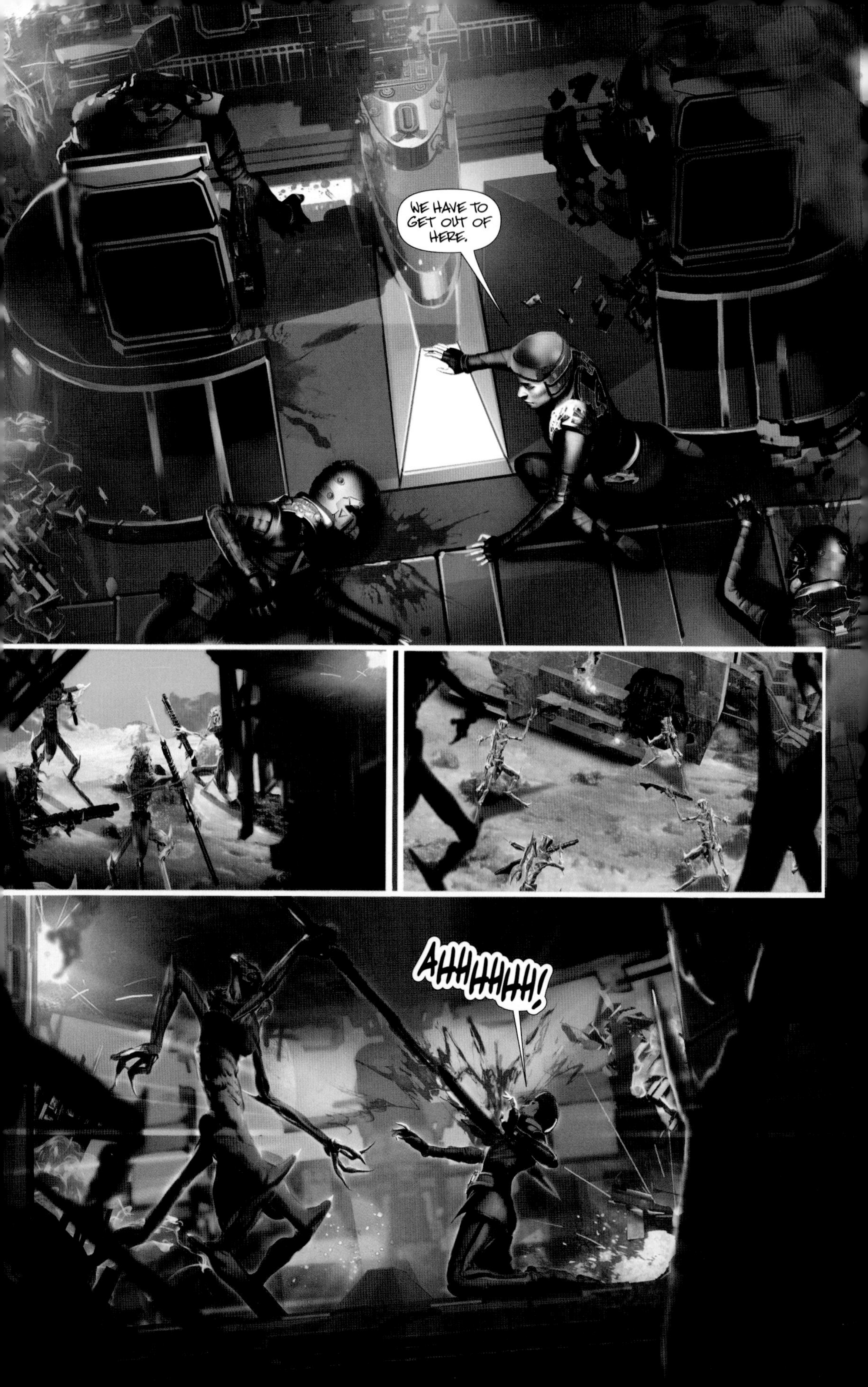
WE HAVE TO GET OUT OF HERE.
AHHHHHH!

TALES OF HONOR

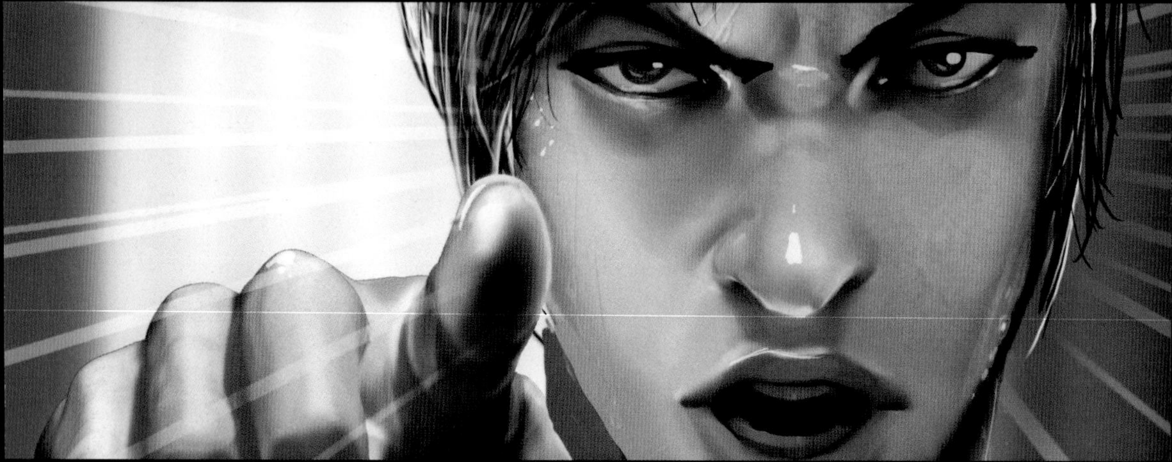

CHAPTER FOUR

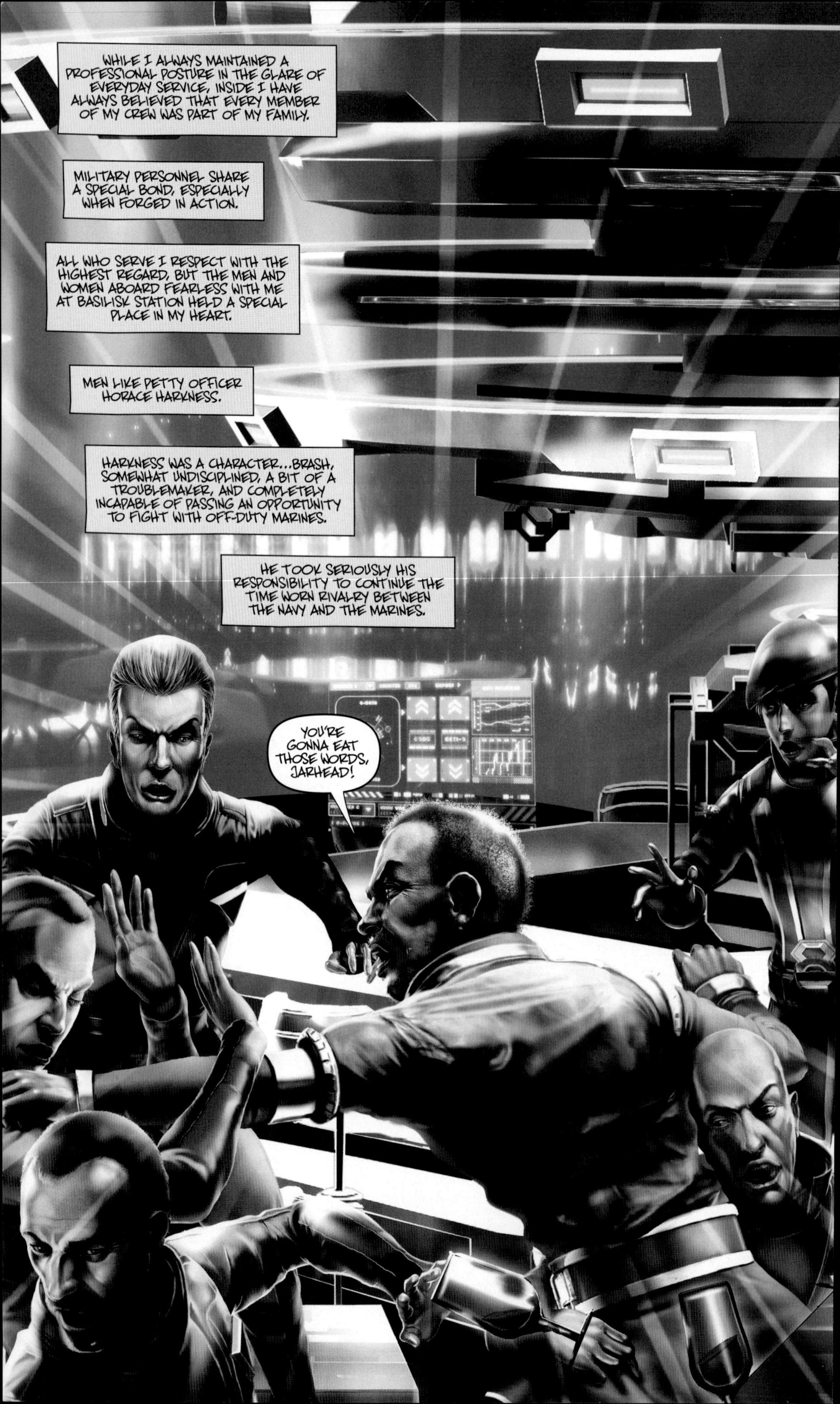
WHILE I ALWAYS MAINTAINED A PROFESSIONAL POSTURE IN THE GLARE OF EVERYDAY SERVICE, INSIDE I HAVE ALWAYS BELIEVED THAT EVERY MEMBER OF MY CREW WAS PART OF MY FAMILY.
MILITARY PERSONNEL SHARE A SPECIAL BOND, ESPECIALLY WHEN FORGED IN ACTION.
ALL WHO SERVE I RESPECT WITH THE HIGHEST REGARD, BUT THE MEN AND WOMEN ABOARD FEARLESS WITH ME AT BASILISK STATION HELD A SPECIAL PLACE IN MY HEART.
MEN LIKE PETTY OFFICER HORACE HARKNESS.
HARKNESS WAS A CHARACTER...BRASH, SOMEWHAT UNDISCIPLINED, A BIT OF A TROUBLEMAKER, AND COMPLETELY INCAPABLE OF PASSING AN OPPORTUNITY TO FIGHT WITH OFF-DUTY MARINES.
HE TOOK SERIOUSLY HIS RESPONSIBILITY TO CONTINUE THE TIME WORN RIVALRY BETWEEN THE NAVY AND THE MARINES.
YOU'RE GONNA EAT THOSE WORDS, JARHEAD!

WHOK

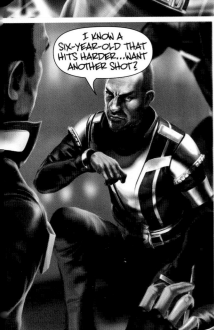

I KNOW A SIX-YEAR-OLD THAT HITS HARDER...WANT ANOTHER SHOT?

KRAK

GGRRRAAAAAAH!

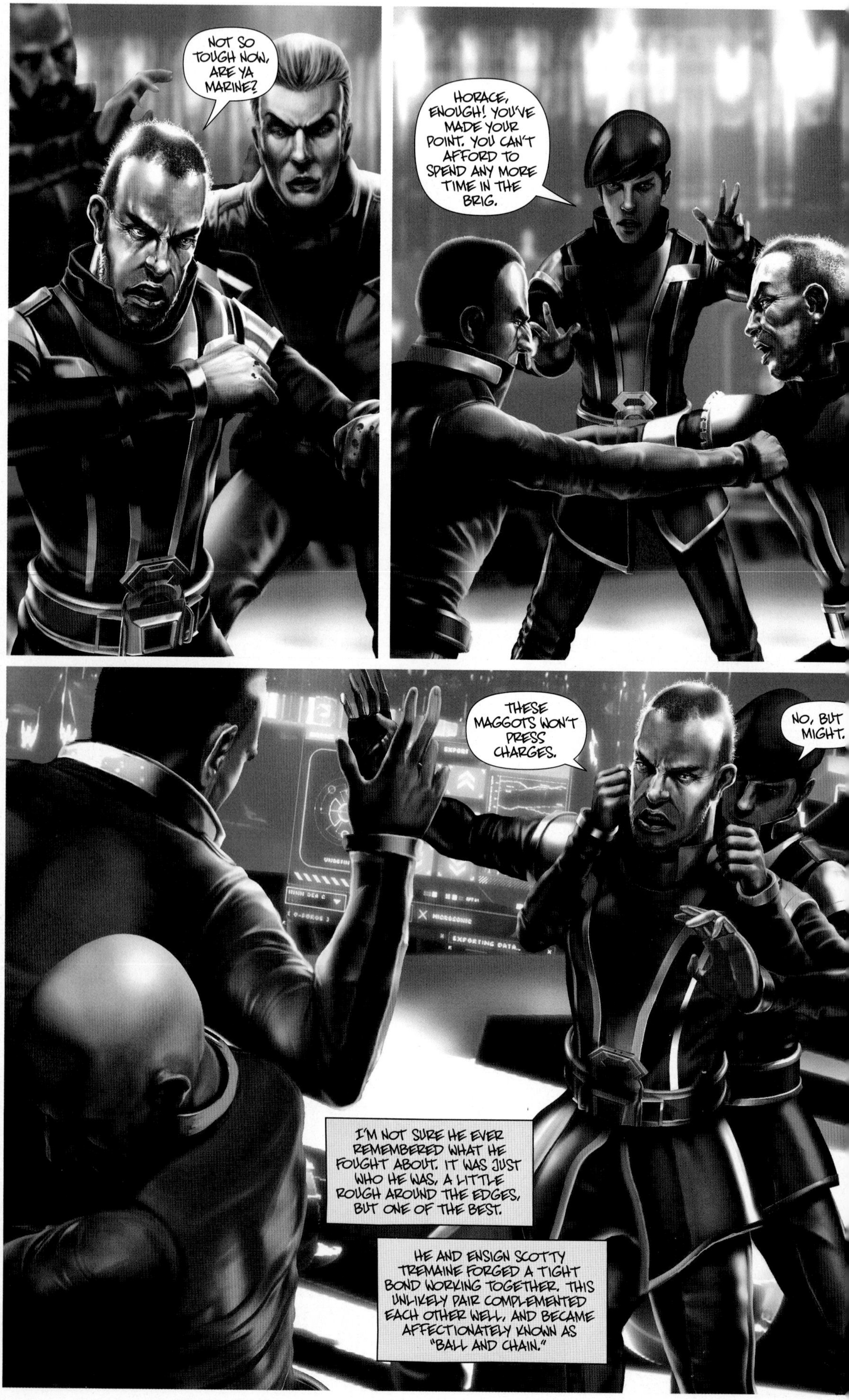
NOT SO TOUGH NOW, ARE YA MARINE?
HORACE, ENOUGH! YOU'VE MADE YOUR POINT. YOU CAN'T AFFORD TO SPEND ANY MORE TIME IN THE BRIG.
THESE MAGGOTS WON'T PRESS CHARGES.
NO, BUT MIGHT.
I'M NOT SURE HE EVER REMEMBERED WHAT HE FOUGHT ABOUT. IT WAS JUST WHO HE WAS, A LITTLE ROUGH AROUND THE EDGES, BUT ONE OF THE BEST.
HE AND ENSIGN SCOTTY TREMAINE FORGED A TIGHT BOND WORKING TOGETHER. THIS UNLIKELY PAIR COMPLEMENTED EACH OTHER WELL, AND BECAME AFFECTIONATELY KNOWN AS "BALL AND CHAIN."

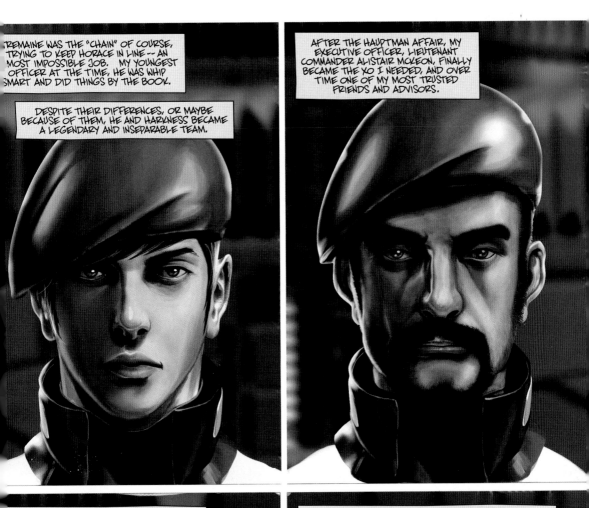

TREMAINE WAS THE "CHAIN" OF COURSE, TRYING TO KEEP HORACE IN LINE -- AN ALMOST IMPOSSIBLE JOB. MY YOUNGEST OFFICER AT THE TIME, HE WAS WHIP SMART AND DID THINGS BY THE BOOK.

DESPITE THEIR DIFFERENCES, OR MAYBE BECAUSE OF THEM, HE AND HARKNESS BECAME A LEGENDARY AND INSEPARABLE TEAM.

AFTER THE HAUPTMAN AFFAIR, MY EXECUTIVE OFFICER, LIEUTENANT COMMANDER ALISTAIR MCKEON, FINALLY BECAME THE XO I NEEDED, AND OVER TIME ONE OF MY MOST TRUSTED FRIENDS AND ADVISORS.

CHIEF ENGINEER DOMINICA SANTOS HAD BECOME ANOTHER PILLAR OF STRENGTH. FROM HER ANALYSIS OF SIRIUS'S IMPELLER NODES TO DAMAGE CONTROL MIRACLES NO ONE WOULD HAVE BELIEVED WERE POSSIBLE, SHE WAS MY STRONG RIGHT ARM THAT KEPT FEARLESS'S HEART BEATING.

AND LAST BUT NOT LEAST, LIEUTENANT RAFE CARDONES. HE'D GROWN UP ON BASILISK STATION, AND EARNED THE TRADITIONAL INFORMAL HONORIFIC "GUNS" BESTOWED ON THE RMN'S TACTICAL OFFICERS. AND I CAN'T EVEN COUNT THE TIMES SINCE BASILISK WHEN HE'S TAKEN OUT ONE WAVE OF INCOMING ORDNANCE AFTER ANOTHER.

SIGH...UNLOCKING THE MYSTERY OF BASILISK CHANGED EVERYTHING...

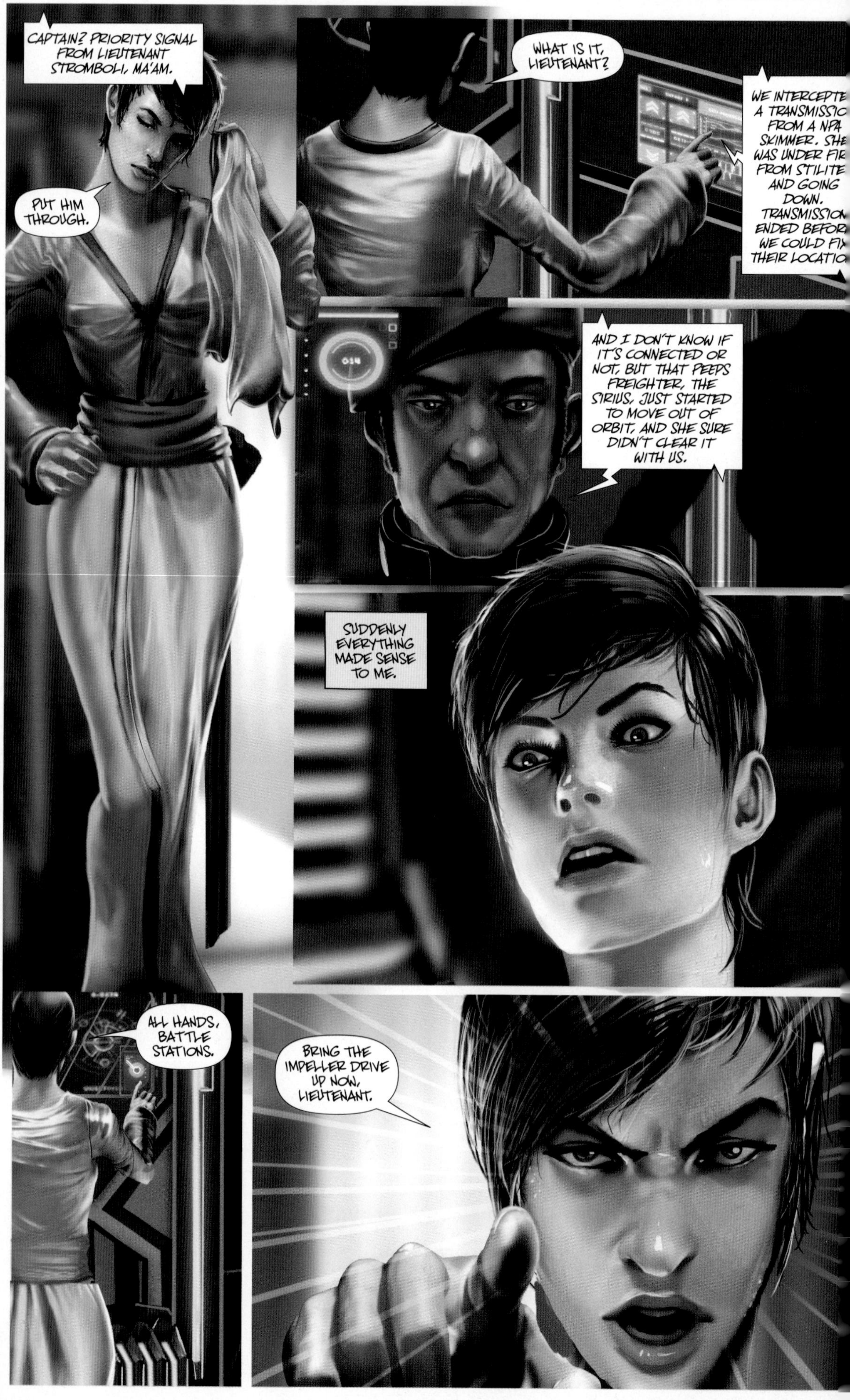
CAPTAIN? PRIORITY SIGNAL FROM LIEUTENANT STROMBOLI, MA'AM.
PUT HIM THROUGH.
WHAT IS IT, LIEUTENANT?
WE INTERCEPTE A TRANSMISSIO FROM A NPA SKIMMER. SHE WAS UNDER FIR FROM STILITE AND GOING DOWN. TRANSMISSION ENDED BEFOR WE COULD FI THEIR LOCATIO
AND I DON'T KNOW IF IT'S CONNECTED OR NOT, BUT THAT PEEPS FREIGHTER, THE SIRIUS, JUST STARTED TO MOVE OUT OF ORBIT, AND SHE SURE DIDN'T CLEAR IT WITH US.
SUDDENLY EVERYTHING MADE SENSE TO ME.
ALL HANDS, BATTLE STATIONS.
BRING THE IMPELLER DRIVE UP NOW, LIEUTENANT.

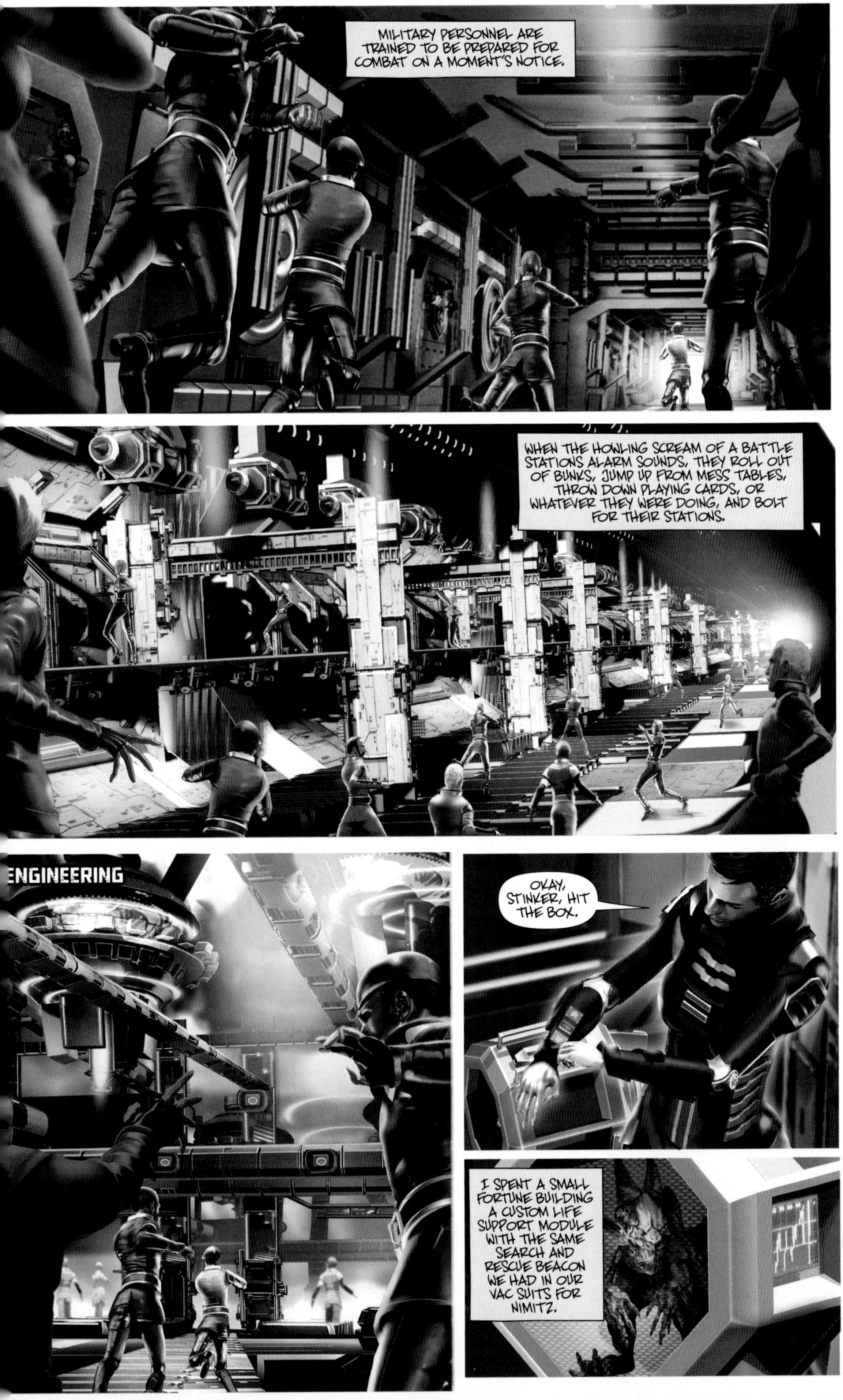
MILITARY PERSONNEL ARE TRAINED TO BE PREPARED FOR COMBAT ON A MOMENT'S NOTICE.
WHEN THE HOWLING SCREAM OF A BATTLE STATIONS ALARM SOUNDS, THEY ROLL OUT OF BUNKS, JUMP UP FROM MESS TABLES, THROW DOWN PLAYING CARDS, OR WHATEVER THEY WERE DOING, AND BOLT FOR THEIR STATIONS.
ENGINEERING
OKAY, STINKER, HIT THE BOX.
I SPENT A SMALL FORTUNE BUILDING A CUSTOM LIFE SUPPORT MODULE WITH THE SAME SEARCH AND RESCUE BEACON WE HAD IN OUR VAC SUITS FOR NIMITZ.

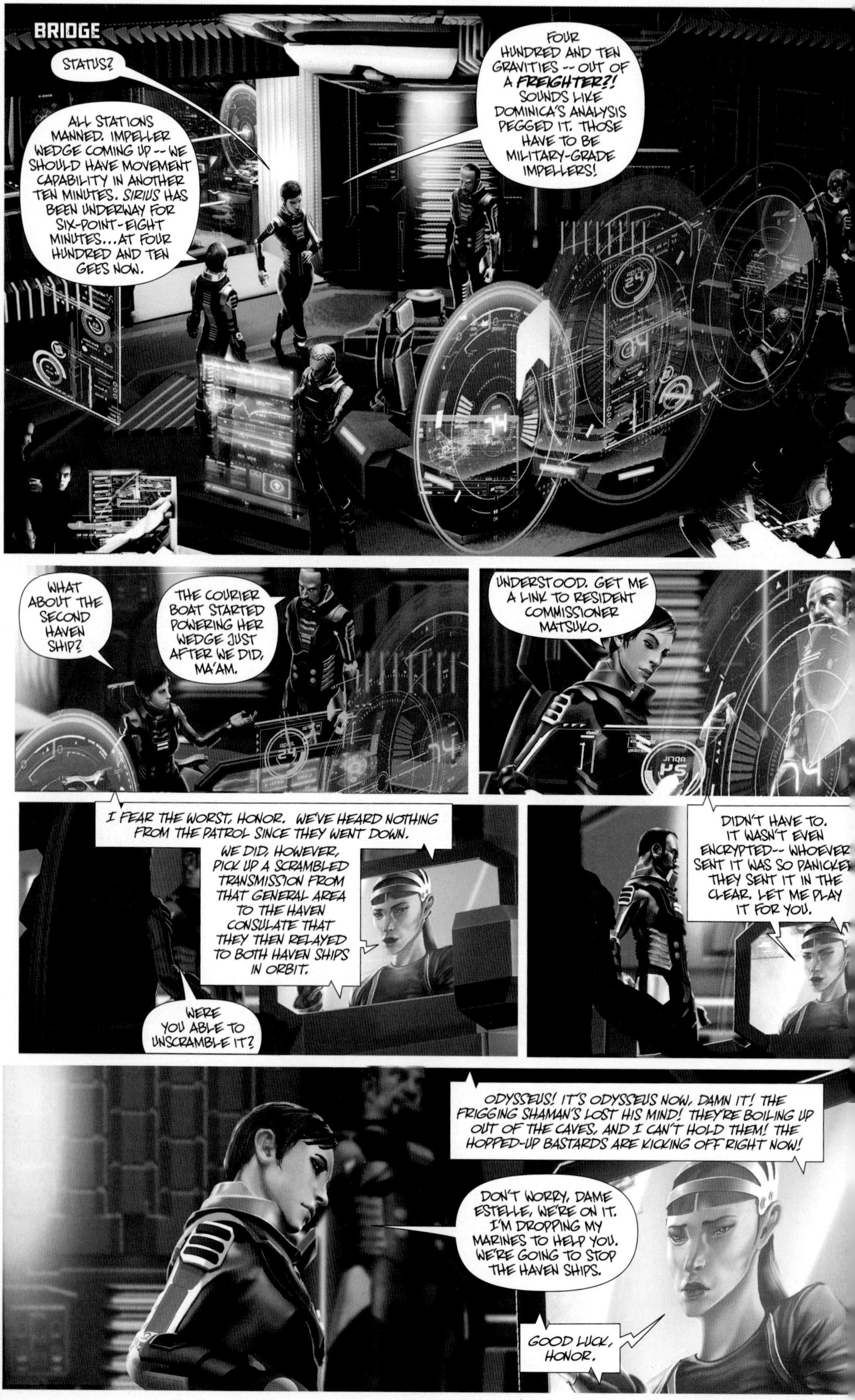

BRIDGE
STATUS?
ALL STATIONS MANNED. IMPELLER WEDGE COMING UP -- WE SHOULD HAVE MOVEMENT CAPABILITY IN ANOTHER TEN MINUTES. SIRIUS HAS BEEN UNDERWAY FOR SIX-POINT-EIGHT MINUTES... AT FOUR HUNDRED AND TEN GEES NOW.
FOUR HUNDRED AND TEN GRAVITIES -- OUT OF A FREIGHTER?! SOUNDS LIKE DOMINICA'S ANALYSIS PEGGED IT. THOSE HAVE TO BE MILITARY-GRADE IMPELLERS!
WHAT ABOUT THE SECOND HAVEN SHIP?
THE COURIER BOAT STARTED POWERING HER WEDGE JUST AFTER WE DID, MA'AM.
UNDERSTOOD. GET ME A LINK TO RESIDENT COMMISSIONER MATSUKO.
I FEAR THE WORST, HONOR. WE'VE HEARD NOTHING FROM THE PATROL SINCE THEY WENT DOWN.
WE DID, HOWEVER, PICK UP A SCRAMBLED TRANSMISSION FROM THAT GENERAL AREA TO THE HAVEN CONSULATE THAT THEY THEN RELAYED TO BOTH HAVEN SHIPS IN ORBIT.
WERE YOU ABLE TO UNSCRAMBLE IT?
DIDN'T HAVE TO. IT WASN'T EVEN ENCRYPTED-- WHOEVER SENT IT WAS SO PANICKED THEY SENT IT IN THE CLEAR. LET ME PLAY IT FOR YOU.
ODYSSEUS! IT'S ODYSSEUS NOW, DAMN IT! THE FRIGGING SHAMAN'S LOST HIS MIND! THEY'RE BOILING UP OUT OF THE CAVES, AND I CAN'T HOLD THEM! THE HOPPED-UP BASTARDS ARE KICKING OFF RIGHT NOW!
DON'T WORRY, DAME ESTELLE, WE'RE ON IT. I'M DROPPING MY MARINES TO HELP YOU. WE'RE GOING TO STOP THE HAVEN SHIPS.
GOOD LUCK, HONOR.

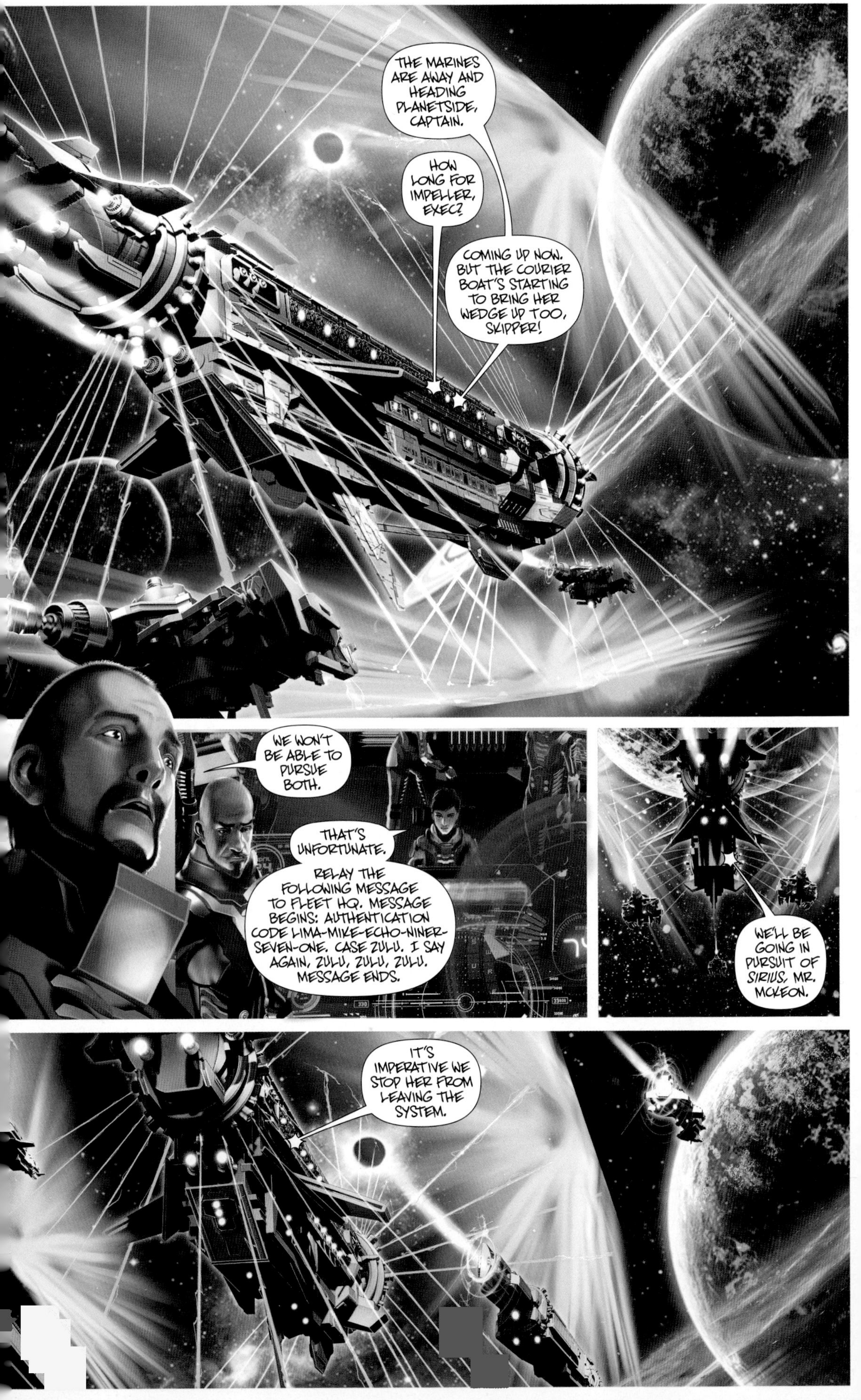
THE MARINES ARE AWAY AND HEADING PLANETSIDE, CAPTAIN.
HOW LONG FOR IMPELLER, EXEC?
COMING UP NOW. BUT THE COURIER BOAT'S STARTING TO BRING HER WEDGE UP TOO, SKIPPER!
WE WON'T BE ABLE TO PURSUE BOTH.
THAT'S UNFORTUNATE.
RELAY THE FOLLOWING MESSAGE TO FLEET HQ. MESSAGE BEGINS: AUTHENTICATION CODE LIMA-MIKE-ECHO-NINER-SEVEN-ONE. CASE ZULU. I SAY AGAIN, ZULU, ZULU, ZULU. MESSAGE ENDS.
WE'LL BE GOING IN PURSUIT OF *SIRIUS*, MR. MCKEON.
IT'S IMPERATIVE WE STOP HER FROM LEAVING THE SYSTEM.

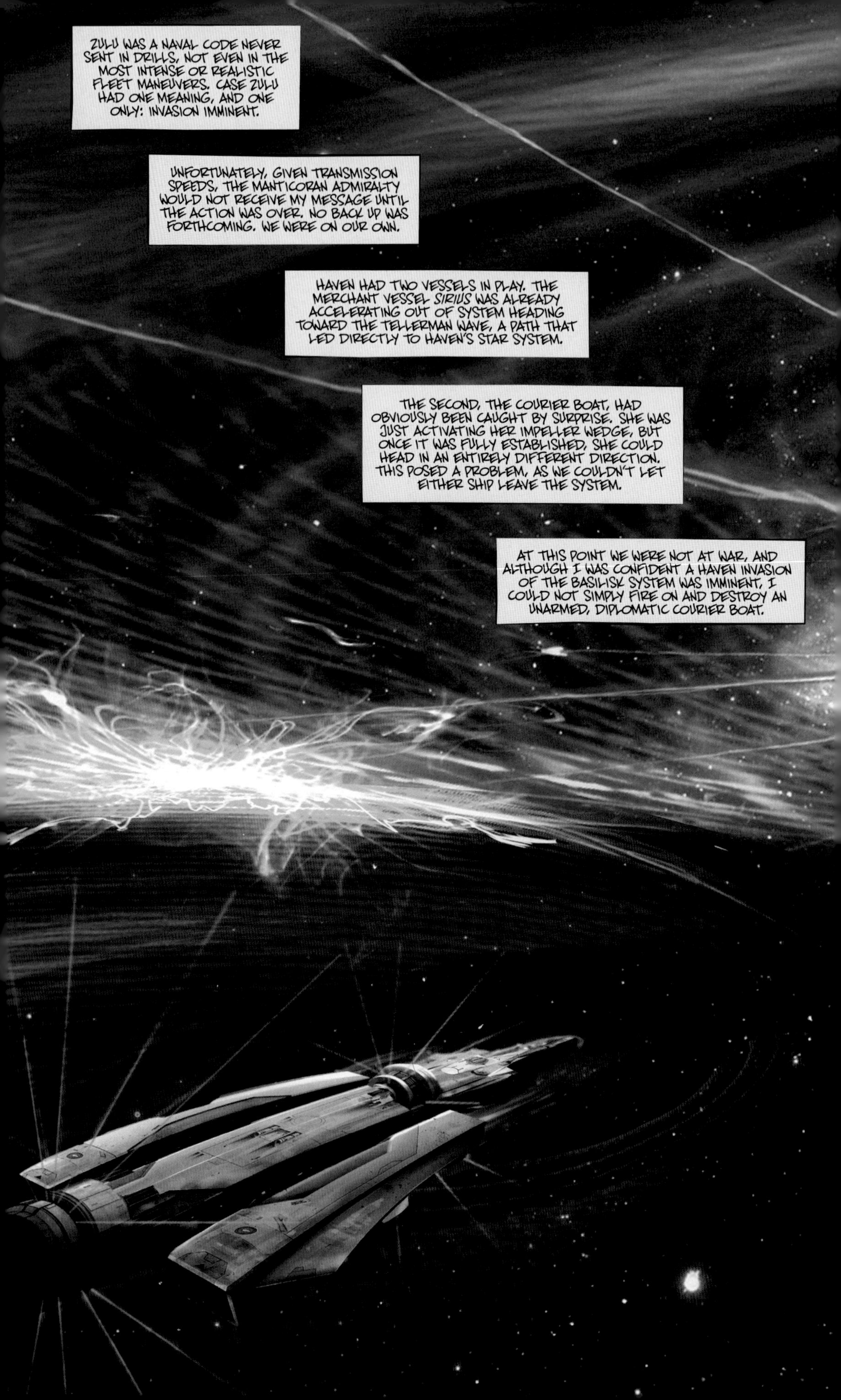
ZULU WAS A NAVAL CODE NEVER SENT IN DRILLS, NOT EVEN IN THE MOST INTENSE OR REALISTIC FLEET MANEUVERS. CASE ZULU HAD ONE MEANING, AND ONE ONLY: INVASION IMMINENT.
UNFORTUNATELY, GIVEN TRANSMISSION SPEEDS, THE MANTICORAN ADMIRALTY WOULD NOT RECEIVE MY MESSAGE UNTIL THE ACTION WAS OVER. NO BACK UP WAS FORTHCOMING. WE WERE ON OUR OWN.
HAVEN HAD TWO VESSELS IN PLAY. THE MERCHANT VESSEL *SIRIUS* WAS ALREADY ACCELERATING OUT OF SYSTEM HEADING TOWARD THE TELLERMAN WAVE, A PATH THAT LED DIRECTLY TO HAVEN'S STAR SYSTEM.
THE SECOND, THE COURIER BOAT, HAD OBVIOUSLY BEEN CAUGHT BY SURPRISE. SHE WAS JUST ACTIVATING HER IMPELLER WEDGE, BUT ONCE IT WAS FULLY ESTABLISHED, SHE COULD HEAD IN AN ENTIRELY DIFFERENT DIRECTION. THIS POSED A PROBLEM, AS WE COULDN'T LET EITHER SHIP LEAVE THE SYSTEM.
AT THIS POINT WE WERE NOT AT WAR, AND ALTHOUGH I WAS CONFIDENT A HAVEN INVASION OF THE BASILISK SYSTEM WAS IMMINENT, I COULD NOT SIMPLY FIRE ON AND DESTROY AN UNARMED, DIPLOMATIC COURIER BOAT.

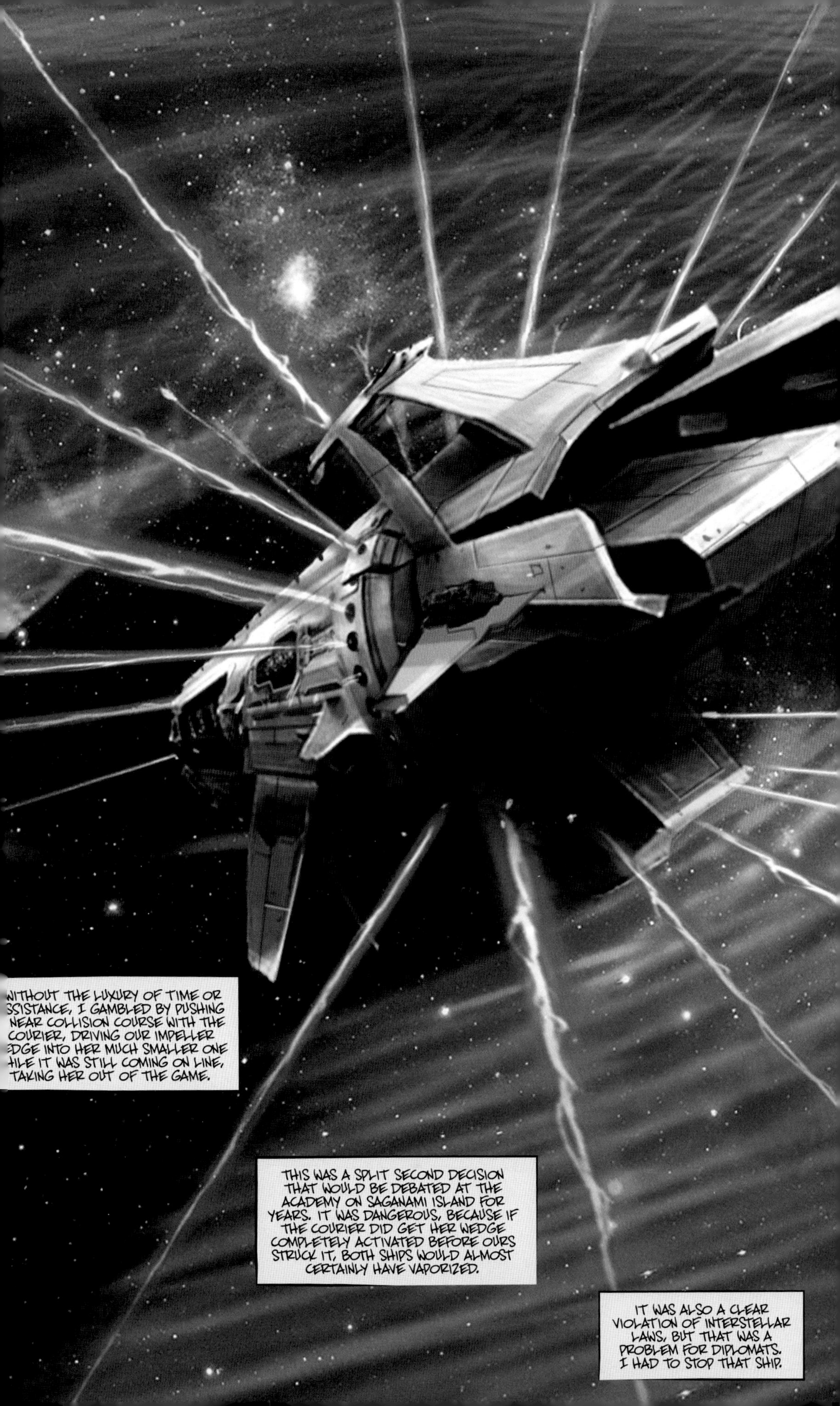
WITHOUT THE LUXURY OF TIME OR SSISTANCE, I GAMBLED BY PUSHING NEAR COLLISION COURSE WITH THE COURIER, DRIVING OUR IMPELLER EDGE INTO HER MUCH SMALLER ONE HILE IT WAS STILL COMING ON LINE, TAKING HER OUT OF THE GAME.
THIS WAS A SPLIT SECOND DECISION THAT WOULD BE DEBATED AT THE ACADEMY ON SAGANAMI ISLAND FOR YEARS. IT WAS DANGEROUS, BECAUSE IF THE COURIER DID GET HER WEDGE COMPLETELY ACTIVATED BEFORE OURS STRUCK IT, BOTH SHIPS WOULD ALMOST CERTAINLY HAVE VAPORIZED.
IT WAS ALSO A CLEAR VIOLATION OF INTERSTELLAR LAWS, BUT THAT WAS A PROBLEM FOR DIPLOMATS. I HAD TO STOP THAT SHIP.

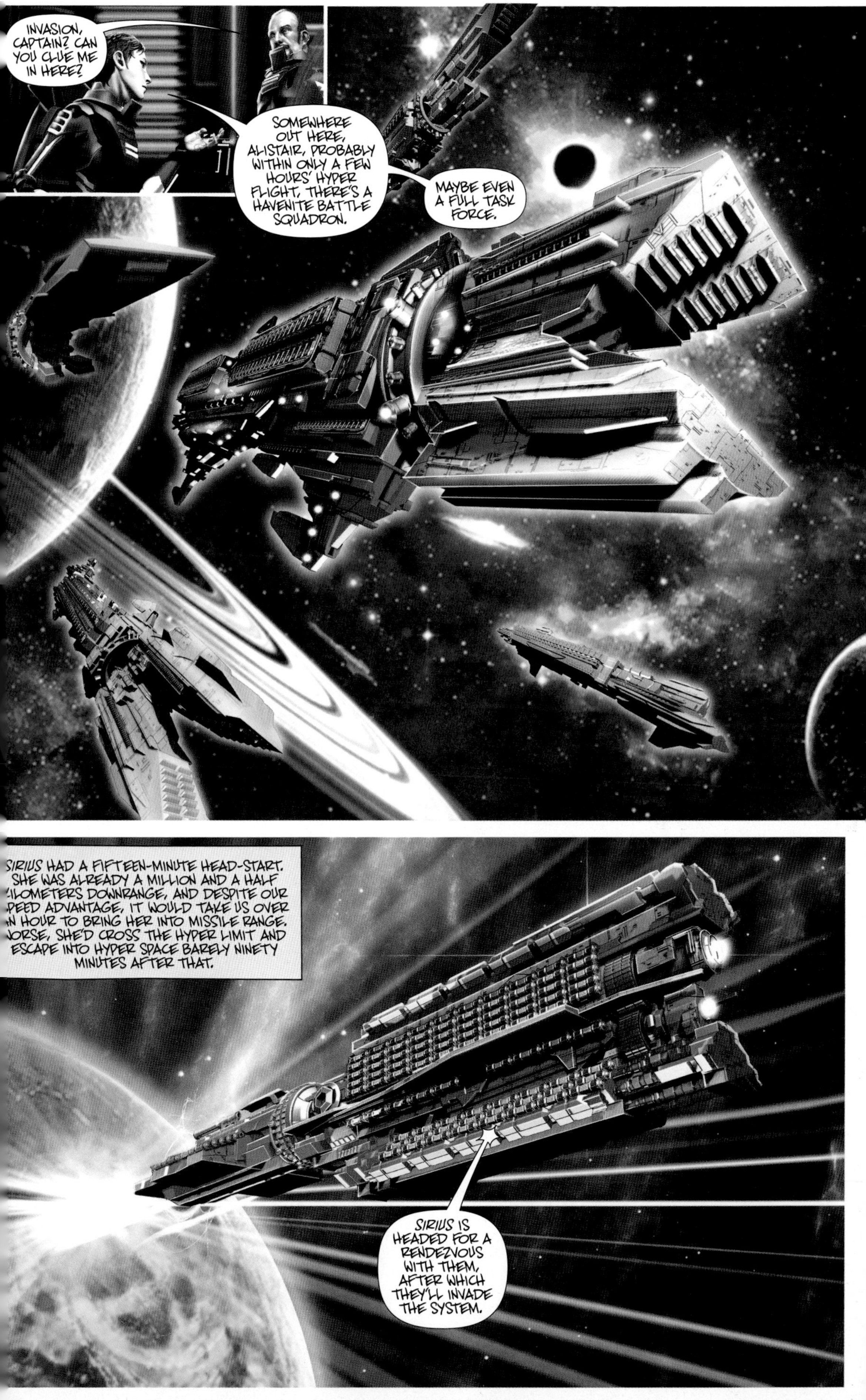
INVASION, CAPTAIN? CAN YOU CLUE ME IN HERE?
SOMEWHERE OUT HERE, ALISTAIR, PROBABLY WITHIN ONLY A FEW HOURS' HYPER FLIGHT, THERE'S A HAVENITE BATTLE SQUADRON.
MAYBE EVEN A FULL TASK FORCE.
SIRIUS HAD A FIFTEEN-MINUTE HEAD-START. SHE WAS ALREADY A MILLION AND A HALF ILOMETERS DOWNRANGE, AND DESPITE OUR PEED ADVANTAGE, IT WOULD TAKE US OVER N HOUR TO BRING HER INTO MISSILE RANGE. ORSE, SHE'D CROSS THE HYPER LIMIT AND ESCAPE INTO HYPER SPACE BARELY NINETY MINUTES AFTER THAT.
SIRIUS IS HEADED FOR A RENDEZVOUS WITH THEM, AFTER WHICH THEY'LL INVADE THE SYSTEM.

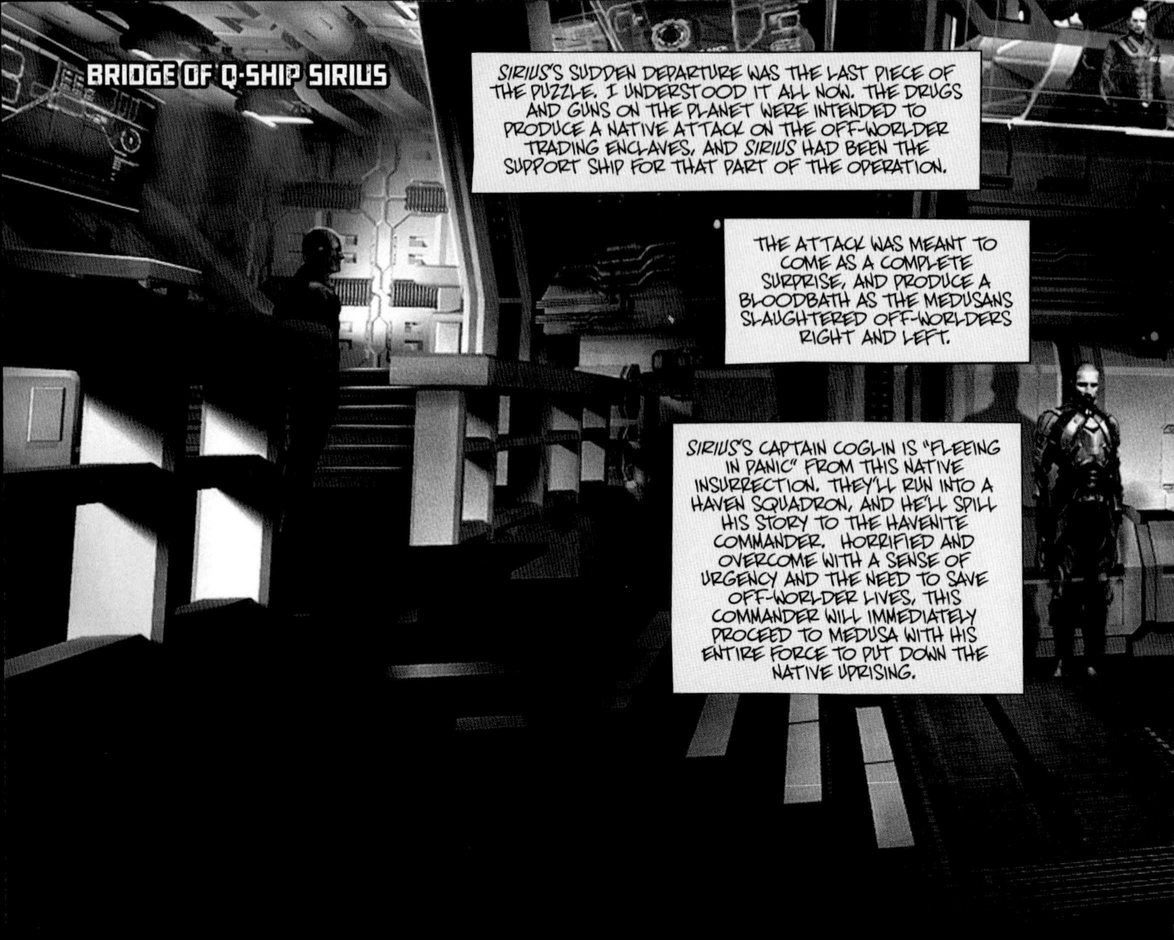
BRIDGE OF Q-SHIP SIRIUS
SIRIUS'S SUDDEN DEPARTURE WAS THE LAST PIECE OF THE PUZZLE. I UNDERSTOOD IT ALL NOW. THE DRUGS AND GUNS ON THE PLANET WERE INTENDED TO PRODUCE A NATIVE ATTACK ON THE OFF-WORLDER TRADING ENCLAVES, AND SIRIUS HAD BEEN THE SUPPORT SHIP FOR THAT PART OF THE OPERATION.
THE ATTACK WAS MEANT TO COME AS A COMPLETE SURPRISE, AND PRODUCE A BLOODBATH AS THE MEDUSANS SLAUGHTERED OFF-WORLDERS RIGHT AND LEFT.
SIRIUS'S CAPTAIN COGLIN IS "FLEEING IN PANIC" FROM THIS NATIVE INSURRECTION. THEY'LL RUN INTO A HAVEN SQUADRON, AND HE'LL SPILL HIS STORY TO THE HAVENITE COMMANDER. HORRIFIED AND OVERCOME WITH A SENSE OF URGENCY AND THE NEED TO SAVE OFF-WORLDER LIVES, THIS COMMANDER WILL IMMEDIATELY PROCEED TO MEDUSA WITH HIS ENTIRE FORCE TO PUT DOWN THE NATIVE UPRISING.
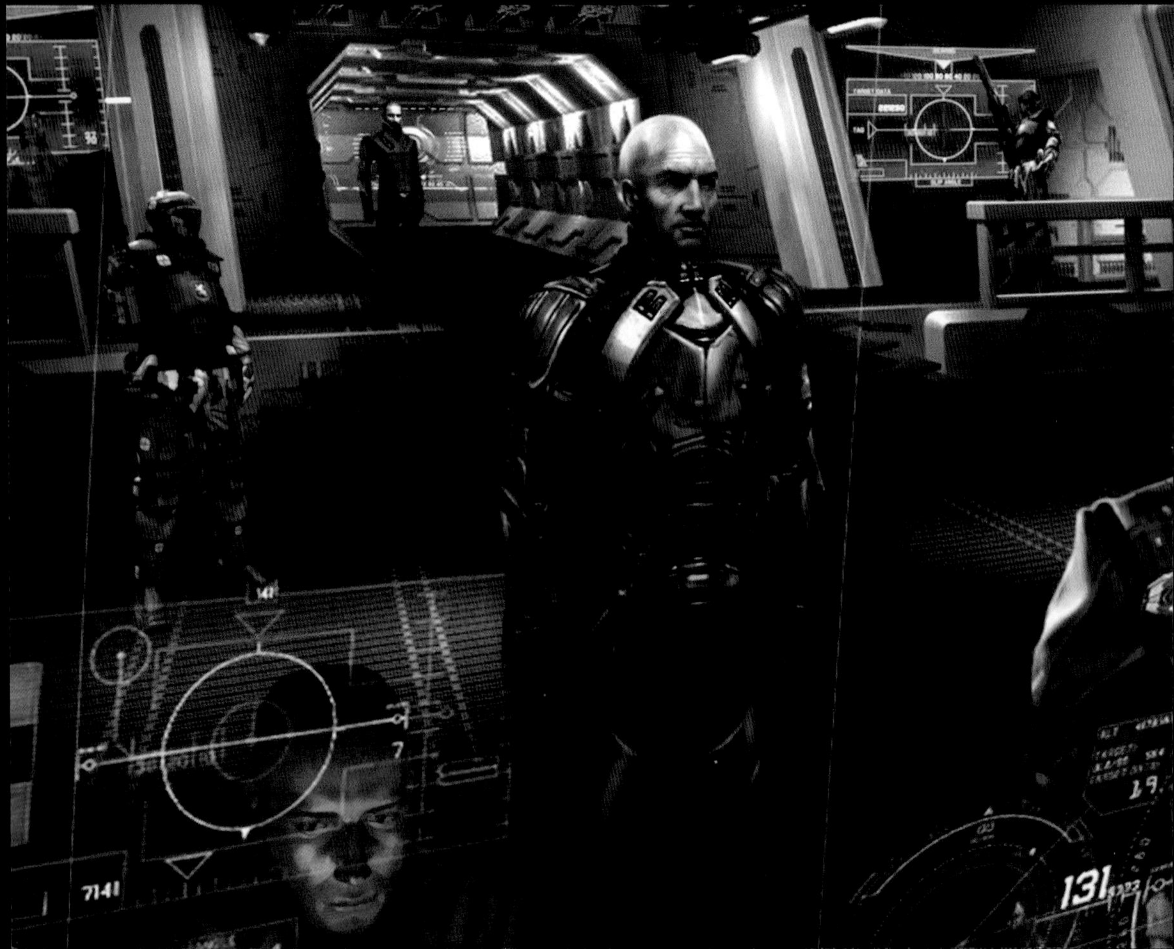

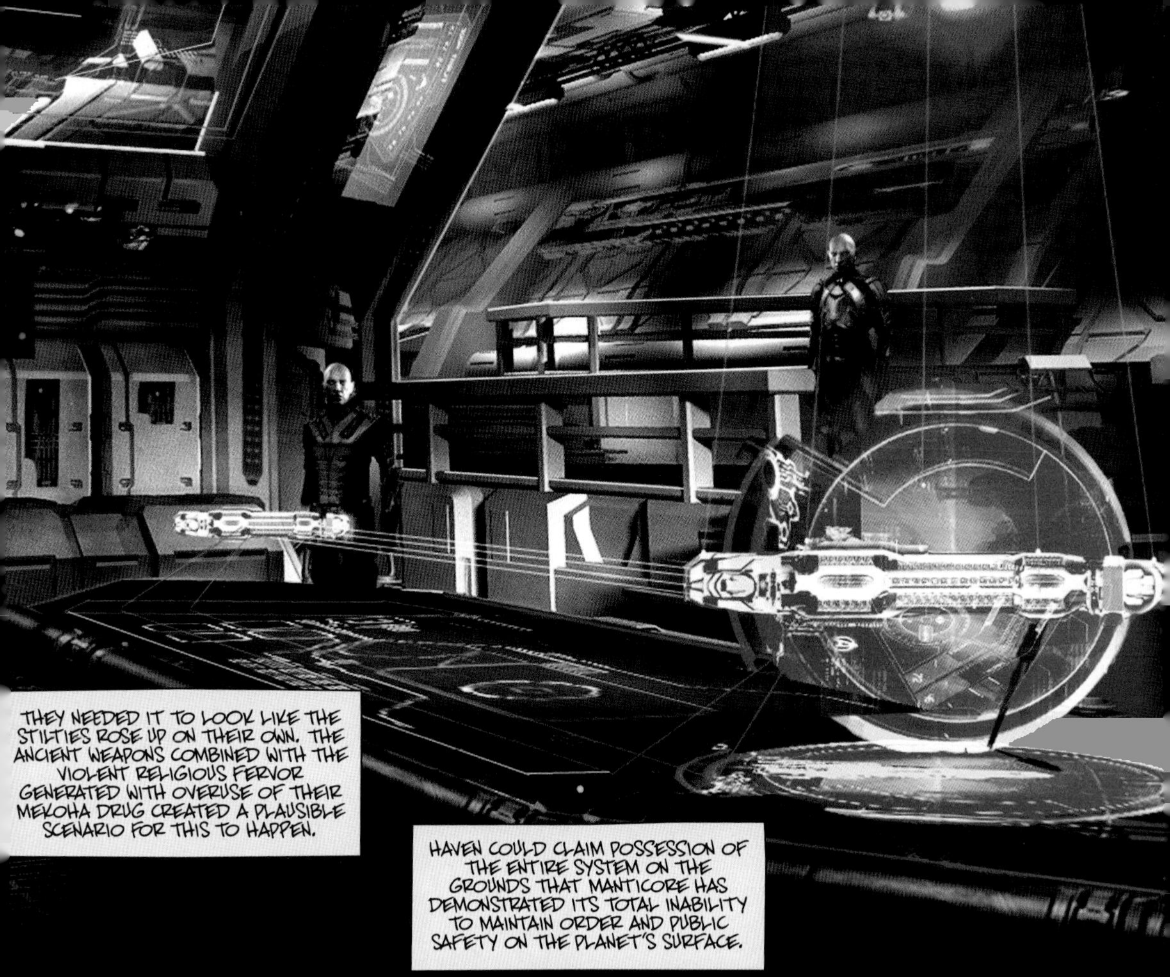
THEY NEEDED IT TO LOOK LIKE THE STILTIES ROSE UP ON THEIR OWN. THE ANCIENT WEAPONS COMBINED WITH THE VIOLENT RELIGIOUS FERVOR GENERATED WITH OVERUSE OF THEIR MEKOHA DRUG CREATED A PLAUSIBLE SCENARIO FOR THIS TO HAPPEN.
HAVEN COULD CLAIM POSSESSION OF THE ENTIRE SYSTEM ON THE GROUNDS THAT MANTICORE HAS DEMONSTRATED ITS TOTAL INABILITY TO MAINTAIN ORDER AND PUBLIC SAFETY ON THE PLANET'S SURFACE.

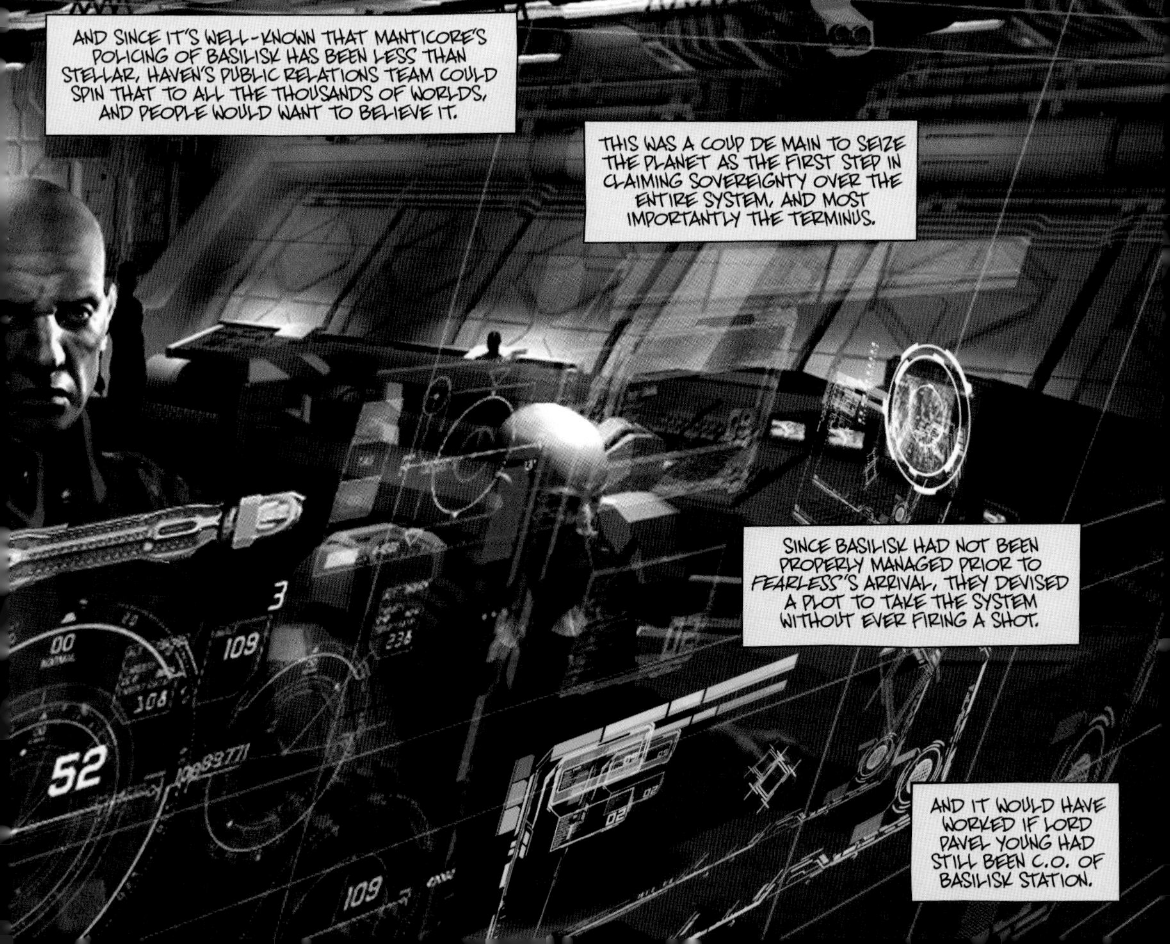
AND SINCE IT'S WELL-KNOWN THAT MANTICORE'S POLICING OF BASILISK HAS BEEN LESS THAN STELLAR, HAVEN'S PUBLIC RELATIONS TEAM COULD SPIN THAT TO ALL THE THOUSANDS OF WORLDS, AND PEOPLE WOULD WANT TO BELIEVE IT.
THIS WAS A COUP DE MAIN TO SEIZE THE PLANET AS THE FIRST STEP IN CLAIMING SOVEREIGNTY OVER THE ENTIRE SYSTEM, AND MOST IMPORTANTLY THE TERMINUS.
SINCE BASILISK HAD NOT BEEN PROPERLY MANAGED PRIOR TO FEARLESS'S ARRIVAL, THEY DEVISED A PLOT TO TAKE THE SYSTEM WITHOUT EVER FIRING A SHOT.
AND IT WOULD HAVE WORKED IF LORD PAVEL YOUNG HAD STILL BEEN C.O. OF BASILISK STATION.

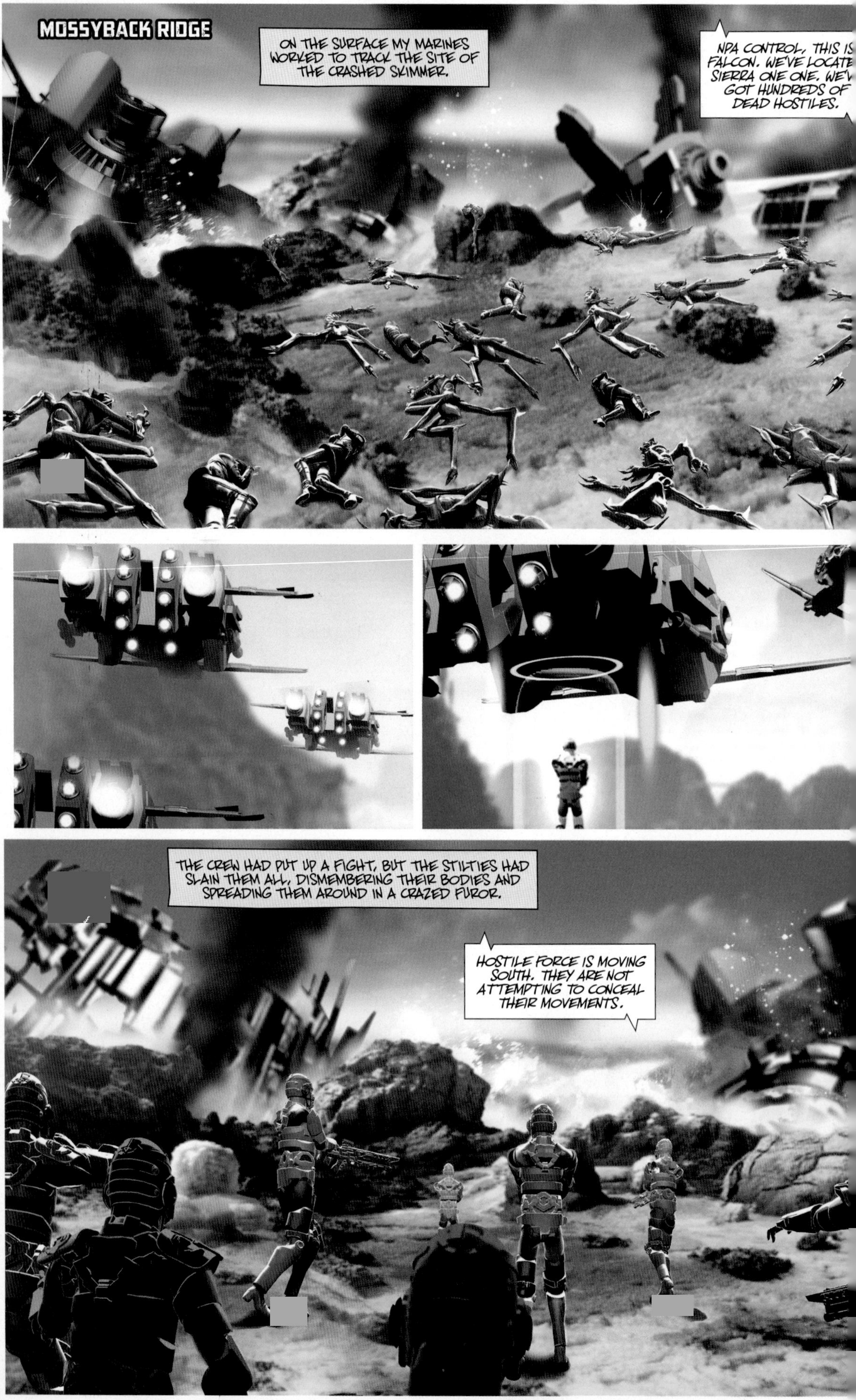
MOSSYBACK RIDGE
ON THE SURFACE MY MARINES WORKED TO TRACK THE SITE OF THE CRASHED SKIMMER.
NPA CONTROL, THIS IS FALCON. WE'VE LOCATE SIERRA ONE ONE. WE'V GOT HUNDREDS OF DEAD HOSTILES.
THE CREW HAD PUT UP A FIGHT, BUT THE STILTIES HAD SLAIN THEM ALL, DISMEMBERING THEIR BODIES AND SPREADING THEM AROUND IN A CRAZED FUROR.
HOSTILE FORCE IS MOVING SOUTH. THEY ARE NOT ATTEMPTING TO CONCEAL THEIR MOVEMENTS.

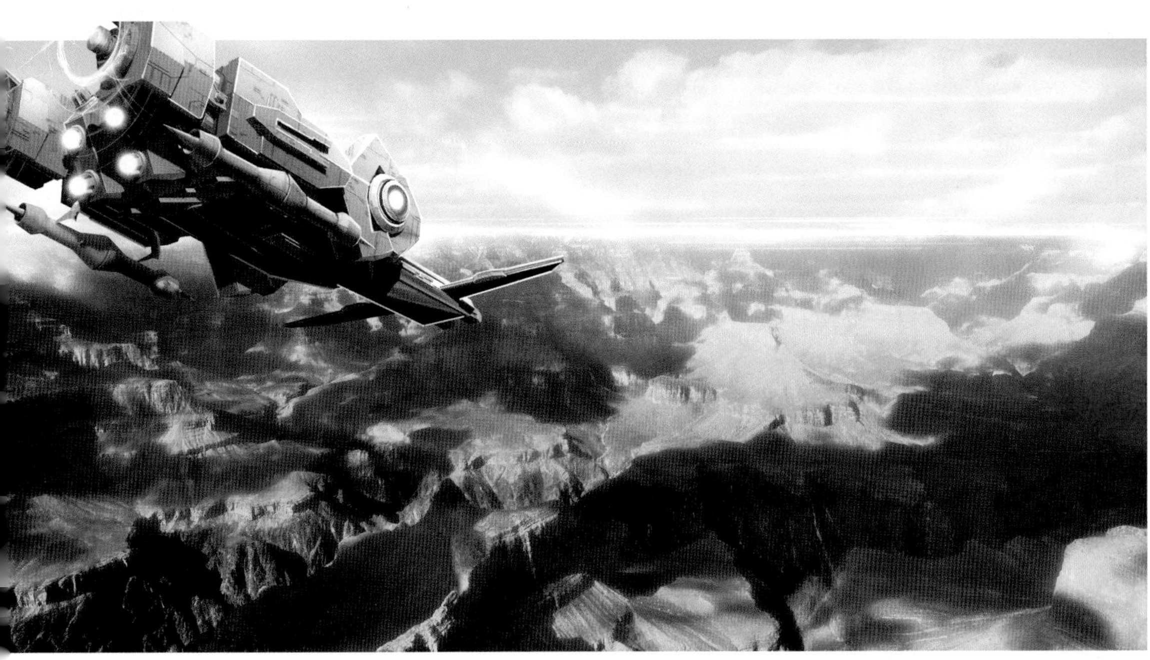

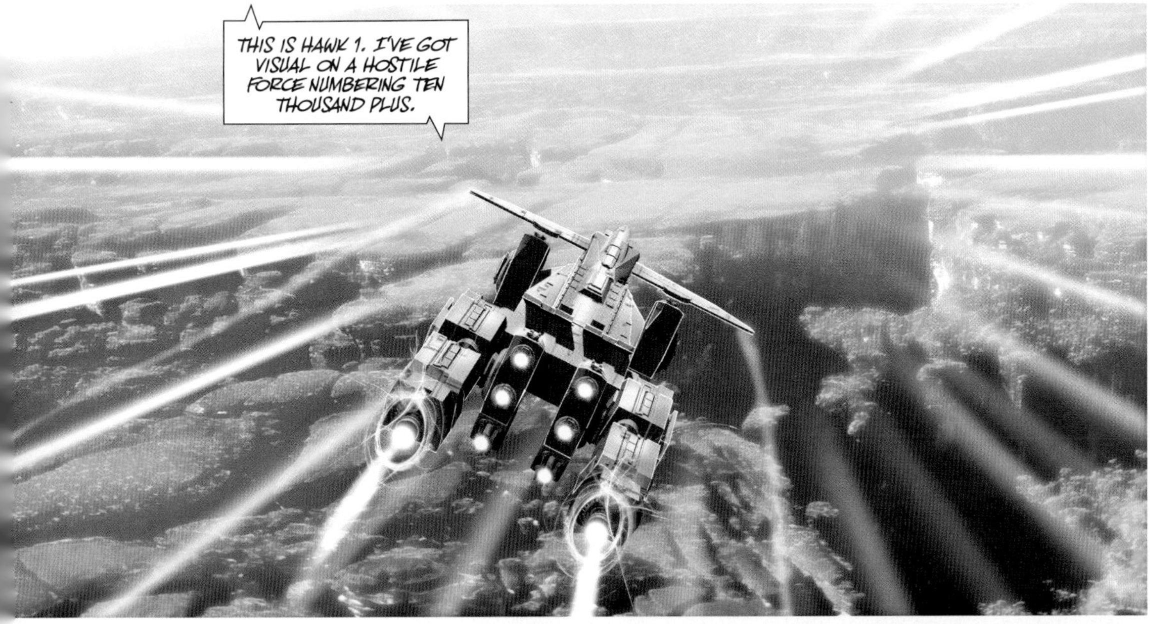
THIS IS HAWK 1. I'VE GOT VISUAL ON A HOSTILE FORCE NUMBERING TEN THOUSAND PLUS.

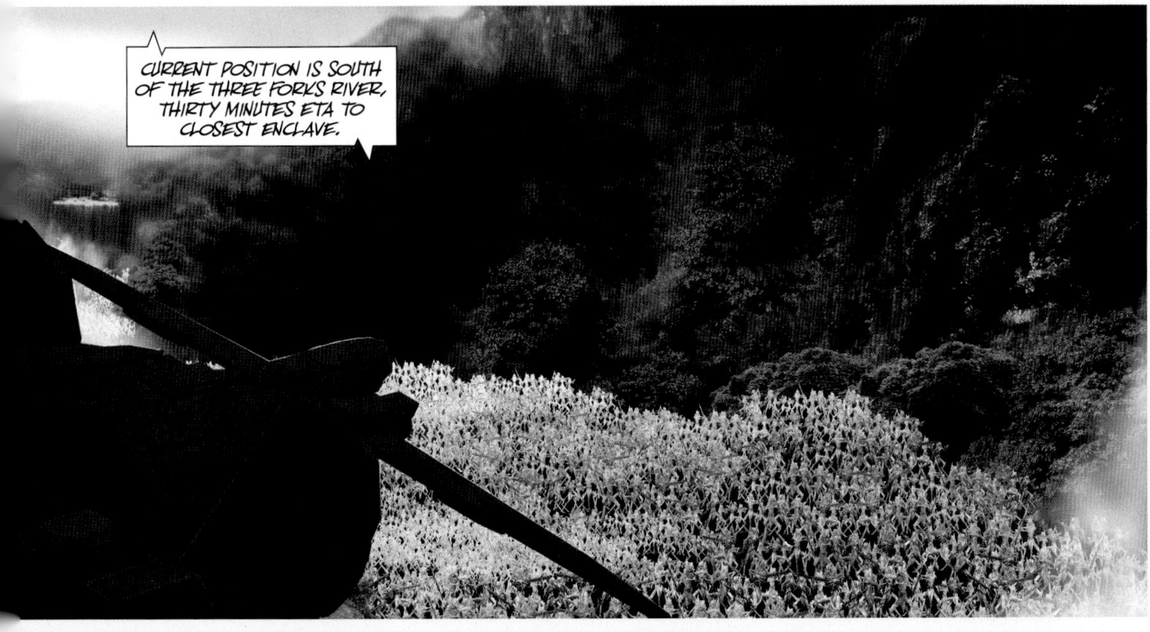
CURRENT POSITION IS SOUTH OF THE THREE FORKS RIVER, THIRTY MINUTES ETA TO CLOSEST ENCLAVE.

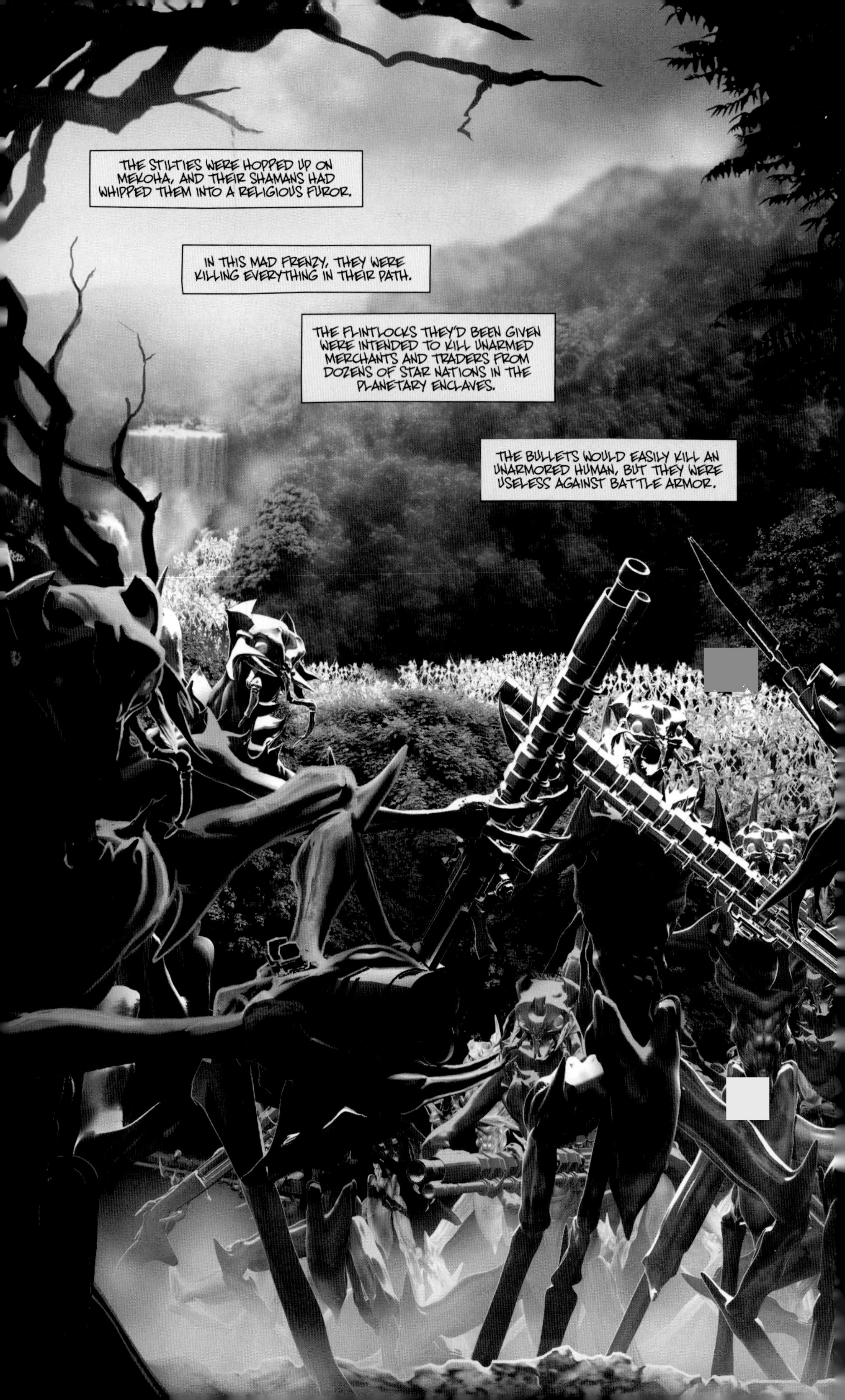
THE STILTIES WERE HOPPED UP ON MEKOHA, AND THEIR SHAMANS HAD WHIPPED THEM INTO A RELIGIOUS FUROR.
IN THIS MAD FRENZY, THEY WERE KILLING EVERYTHING IN THEIR PATH.
THE FLINTLOCKS THEY'D BEEN GIVEN WERE INTENDED TO KILL UNARMED MERCHANTS AND TRADERS FROM DOZENS OF STAR NATIONS IN THE PLANETARY ENCLAVES.
THE BULLETS WOULD EASILY KILL AN UNARMORED HUMAN, BUT THEY WERE USELESS AGAINST BATTLE ARMOR.

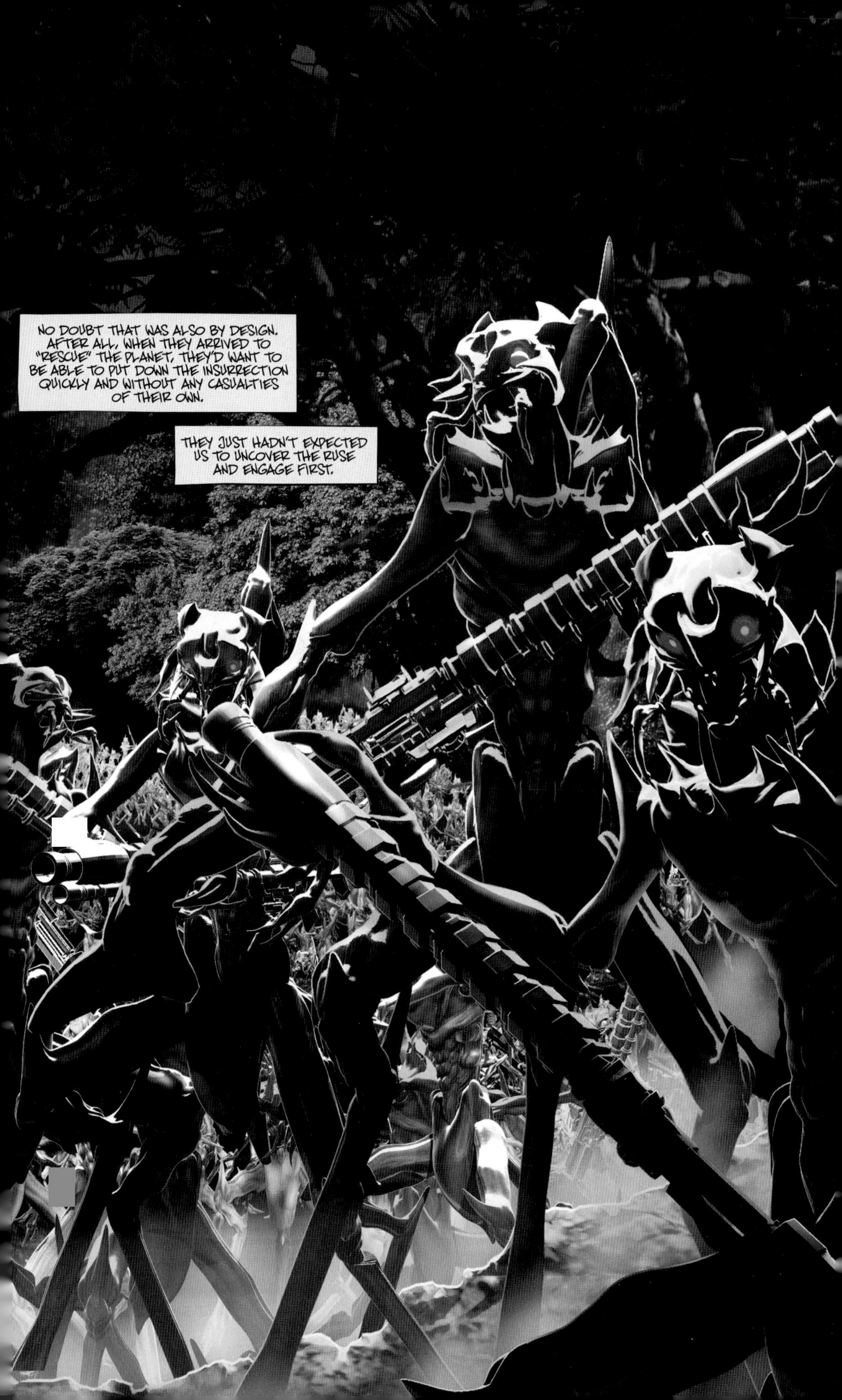
NO DOUBT THAT WAS ALSO BY DESIGN. AFTER ALL, WHEN THEY ARRIVED TO "RESCUE" THE PLANET, THEY'D WANT TO BE ABLE TO PUT DOWN THE INSURRECTION QUICKLY AND WITHOUT ANY CASUALTIES OF THEIR OWN.
THEY JUST HADN'T EXPECTED US TO UNCOVER THE RUSE AND ENGAGE FIRST.

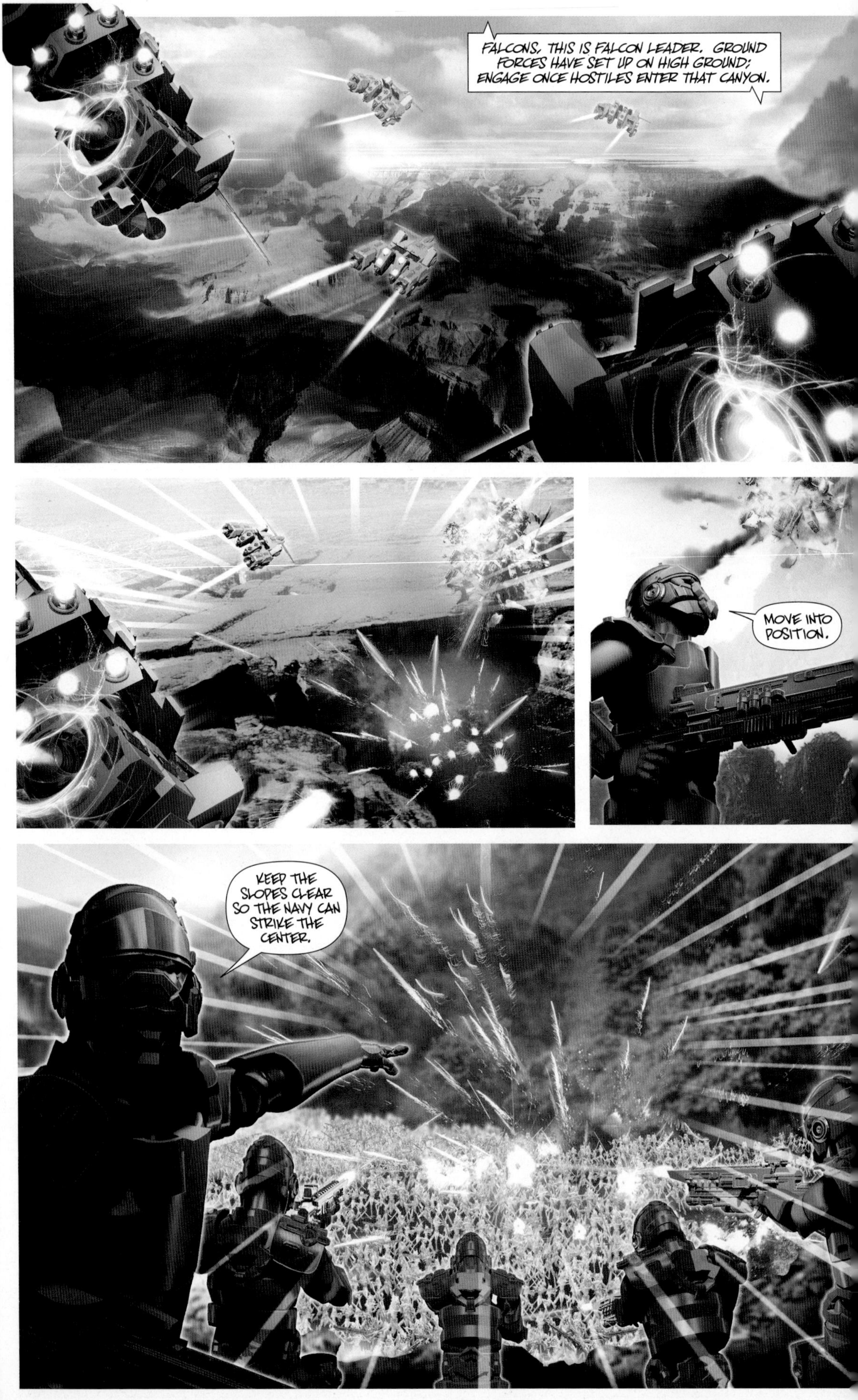
FALCONS, THIS IS FALCON LEADER. GROUND FORCES HAVE SET UP ON HIGH GROUND; ENGAGE ONCE HOSTILES ENTER THAT CANYON.
MOVE INTO POSITION.
KEEP THE SLOPES CLEAR SO THE NAVY CAN STRIKE THE CENTER.

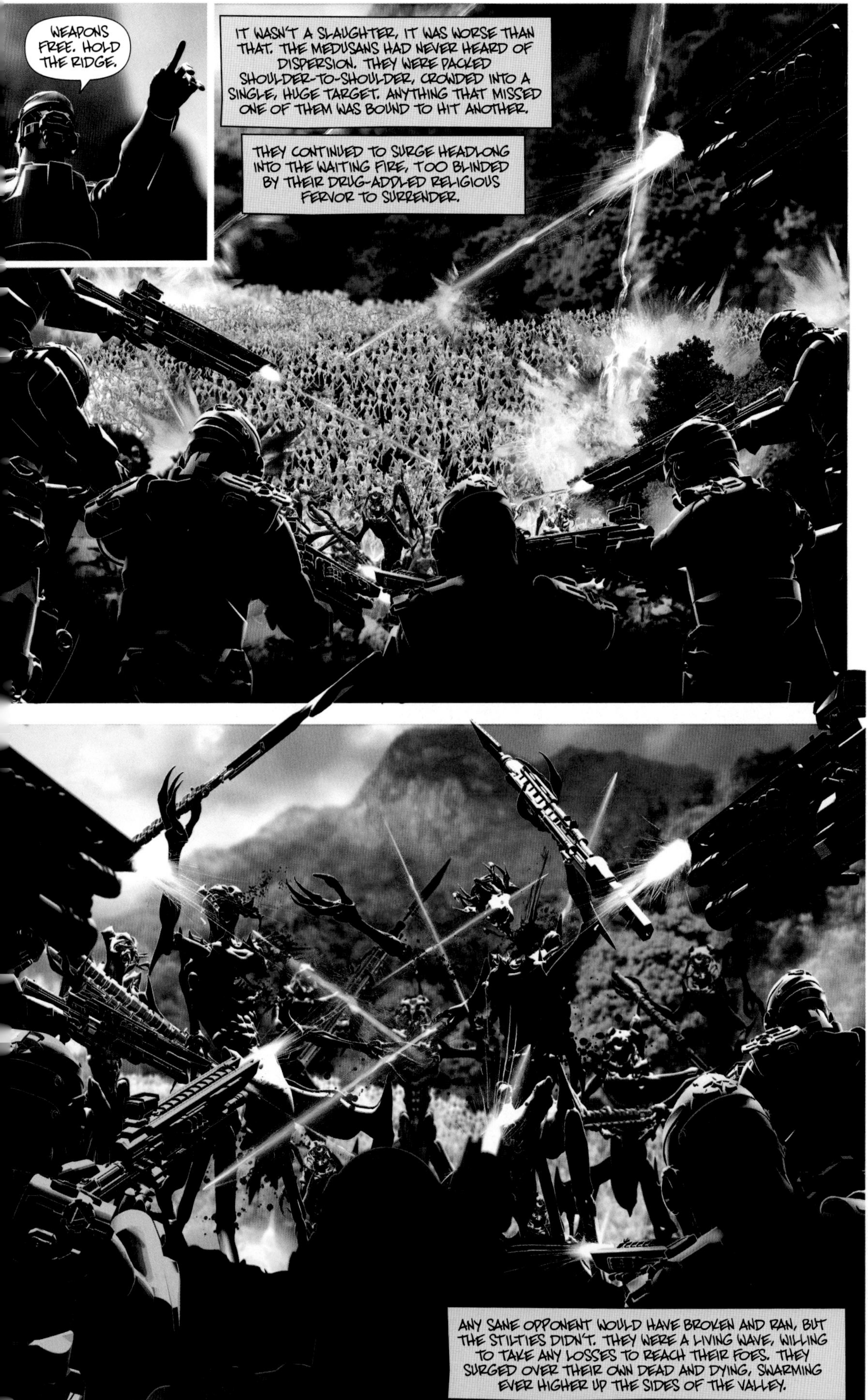
WEAPONS FREE. HOLD THE RIDGE.
IT WASN'T A SLAUGHTER, IT WAS WORSE THAN THAT. THE MEDUSANS HAD NEVER HEARD OF DISPERSION. THEY WERE PACKED SHOULDER-TO-SHOULDER, CROWDED INTO A SINGLE, HUGE TARGET. ANYTHING THAT MISSED ONE OF THEM WAS BOUND TO HIT ANOTHER.
THEY CONTINUED TO SURGE HEADLONG INTO THE WAITING FIRE, TOO BLINDED BY THEIR DRUG-ADDLED RELIGIOUS FERVOR TO SURRENDER.
ANY SANE OPPONENT WOULD HAVE BROKEN AND RAN, BUT THE STILTIES DIDN'T. THEY WERE A LIVING WAVE, WILLING TO TAKE ANY LOSSES TO REACH THEIR FOES. THEY SURGED OVER THEIR OWN DEAD AND DYING, SWARMING EVER HIGHER UP THE SIDES OF THE VALLEY.

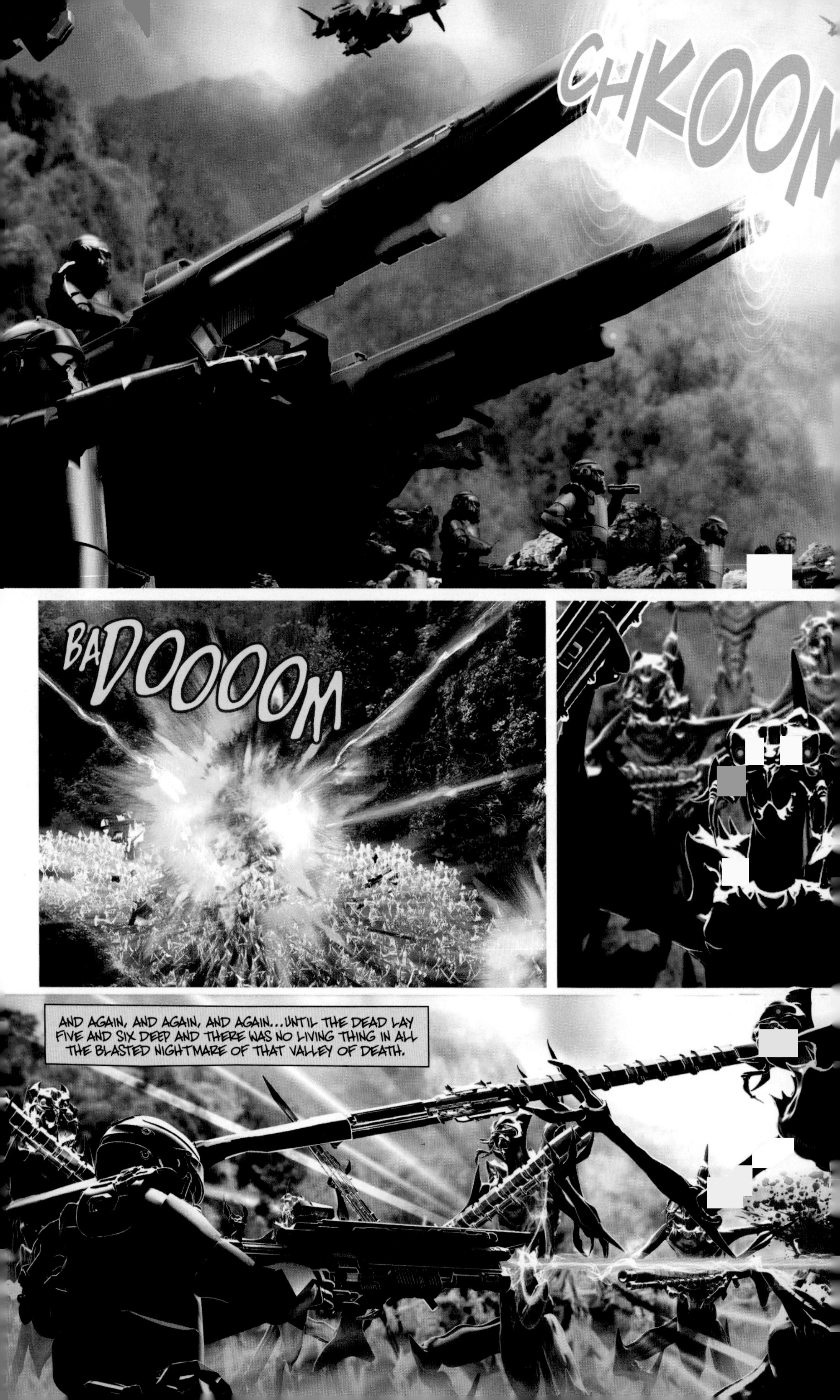
CHKOOM
BADOOOOM
AND AGAIN, AND AGAIN, AND AGAIN...UNTIL THE DEAD LAY FIVE AND SIX DEEP AND THERE WAS NO LIVING THING IN ALL THE BLASTED NIGHTMARE OF THAT VALLEY OF DEATH.

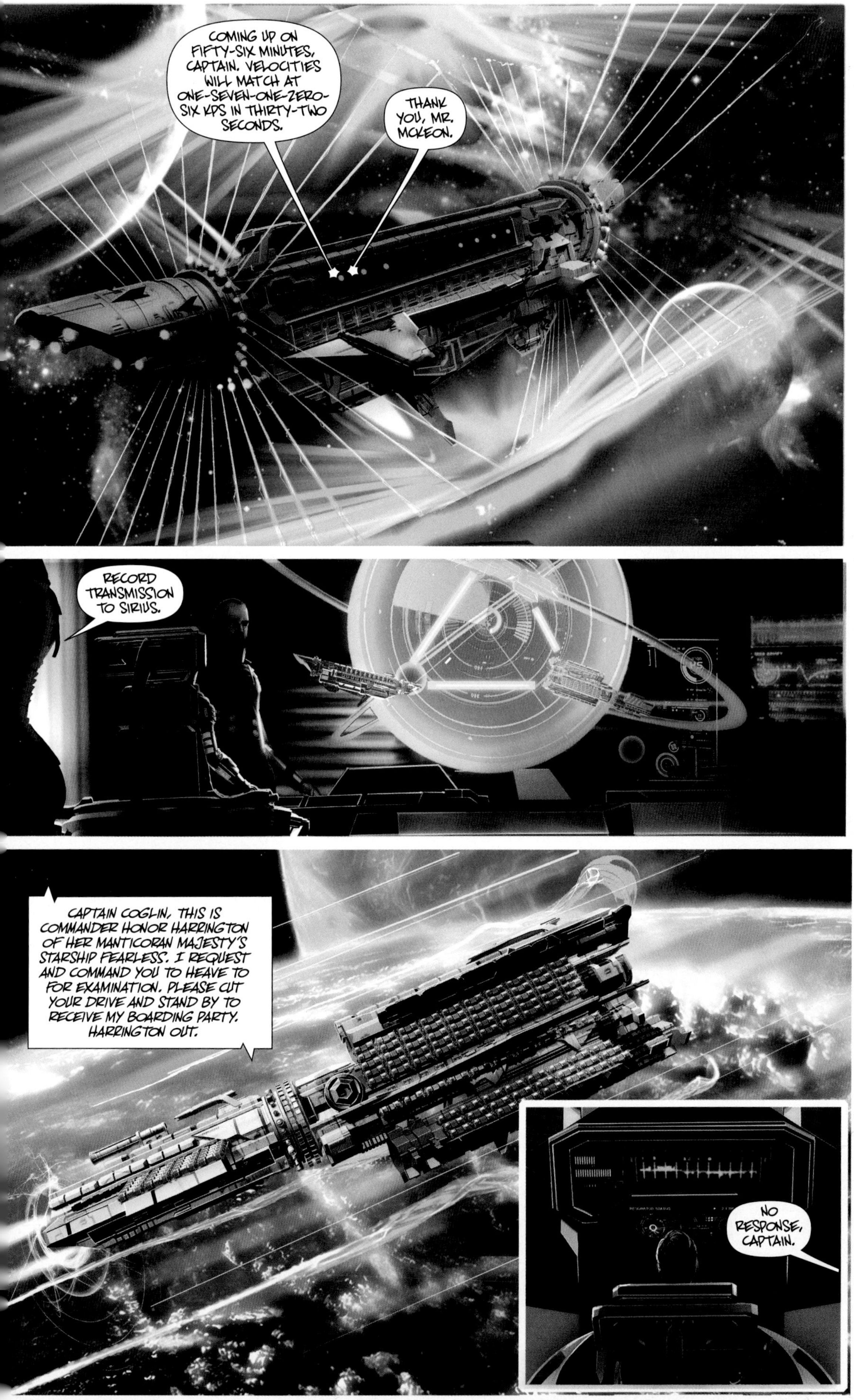
COMING UP ON FIFTY-SIX MINUTES, CAPTAIN. VELOCITIES WILL MATCH AT ONE-SEVEN-ONE-ZERO-SIX KPS IN THIRTY-TWO SECONDS.
THANK YOU, MR. MCKEON.
RECORD TRANSMISSION TO SIRIUS.
CAPTAIN COGLIN, THIS IS COMMANDER HONOR HARRINGTON OF HER MANTICORAN MAJESTY'S STARSHIP FEARLESS. I REQUEST AND COMMAND YOU TO HEAVE TO FOR EXAMINATION. PLEASE CUT YOUR DRIVE AND STAND BY TO RECEIVE MY BOARDING PARTY. HARRINGTON OUT.
NO RESPONSE, CAPTAIN.

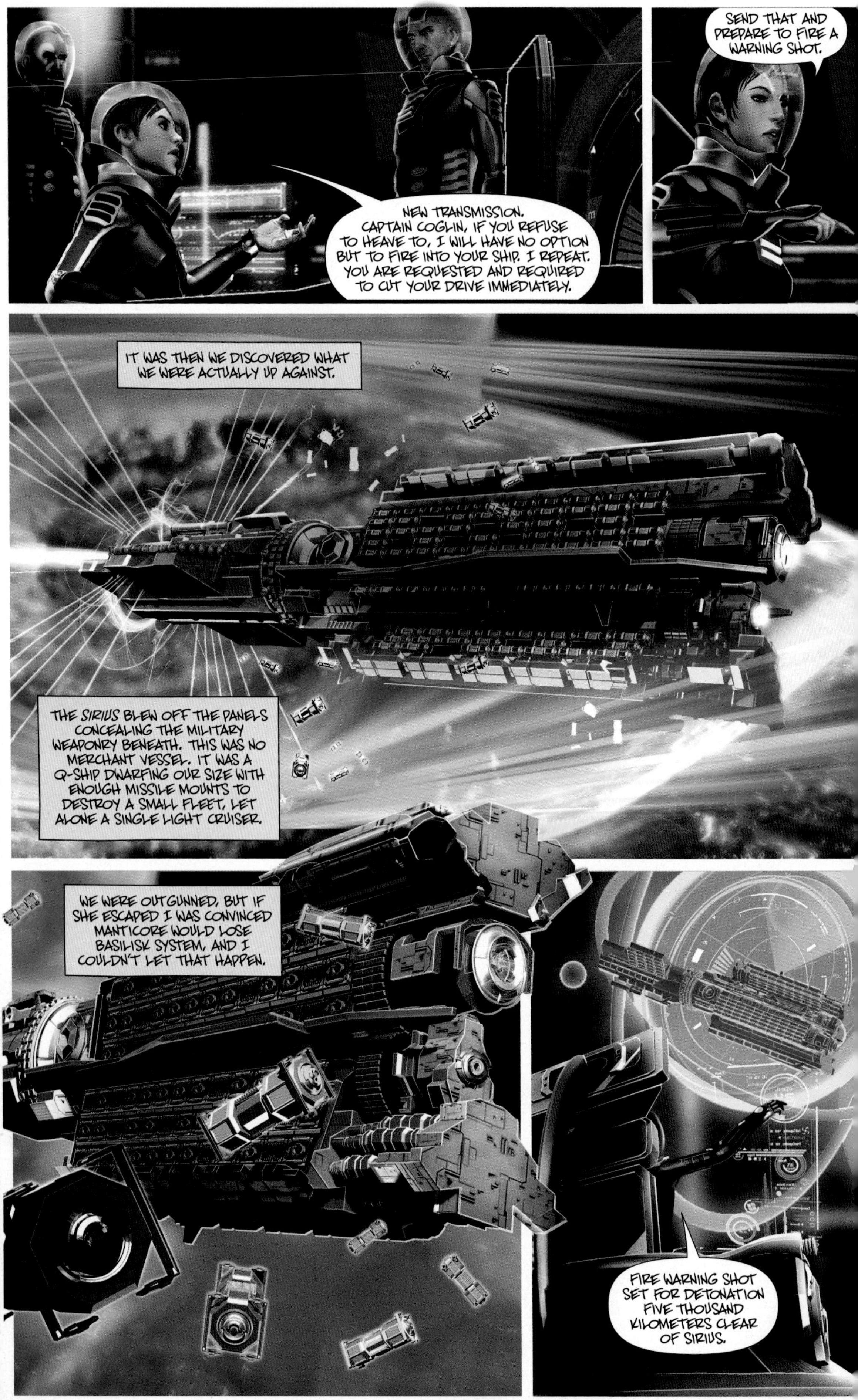
NEW TRANSMISSION. CAPTAIN COGLIN, IF YOU REFUSE TO HEAVE TO, I WILL HAVE NO OPTION BUT TO FIRE INTO YOUR SHIP. I REPEAT. YOU ARE REQUESTED AND REQUIRED TO CUT YOUR DRIVE IMMEDIATELY.
SEND THAT AND PREPARE TO FIRE A WARNING SHOT.
IT WAS THEN WE DISCOVERED WHAT WE WERE ACTUALLY UP AGAINST.
THE SIRIUS BLEW OFF THE PANELS CONCEALING THE MILITARY WEAPONRY BENEATH. THIS WAS NO MERCHANT VESSEL. IT WAS A Q-SHIP DWARFING OUR SIZE WITH ENOUGH MISSILE MOUNTS TO DESTROY A SMALL FLEET, LET ALONE A SINGLE LIGHT CRUISER.
WE WERE OUTGUNNED, BUT IF SHE ESCAPED I WAS CONVINCED MANTICORE WOULD LOSE BASILISK SYSTEM, AND I COULDN'T LET THAT HAPPEN.
FIRE WARNING SHOT SET FOR DETONATION FIVE THOUSAND KILOMETERS CLEAR OF SIRIUS.

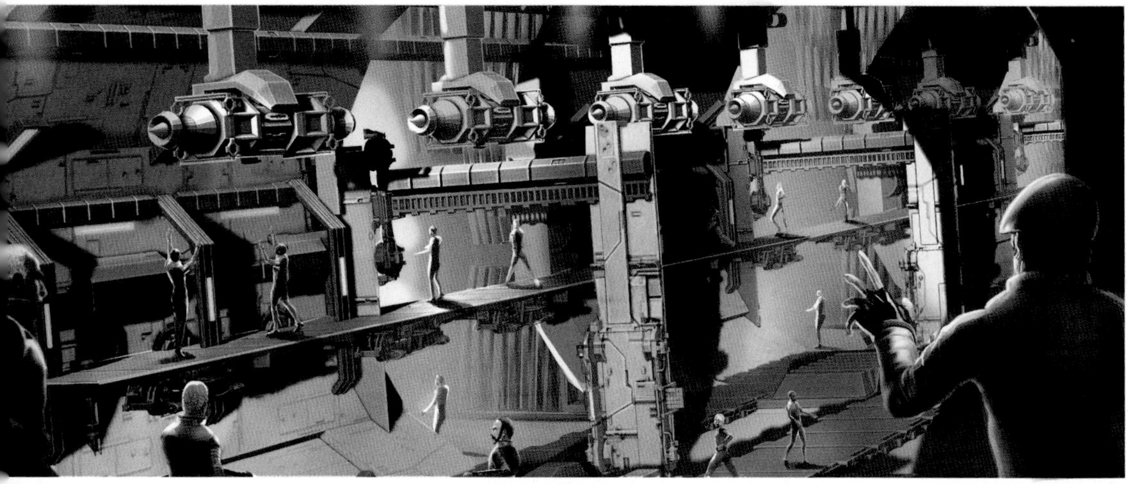
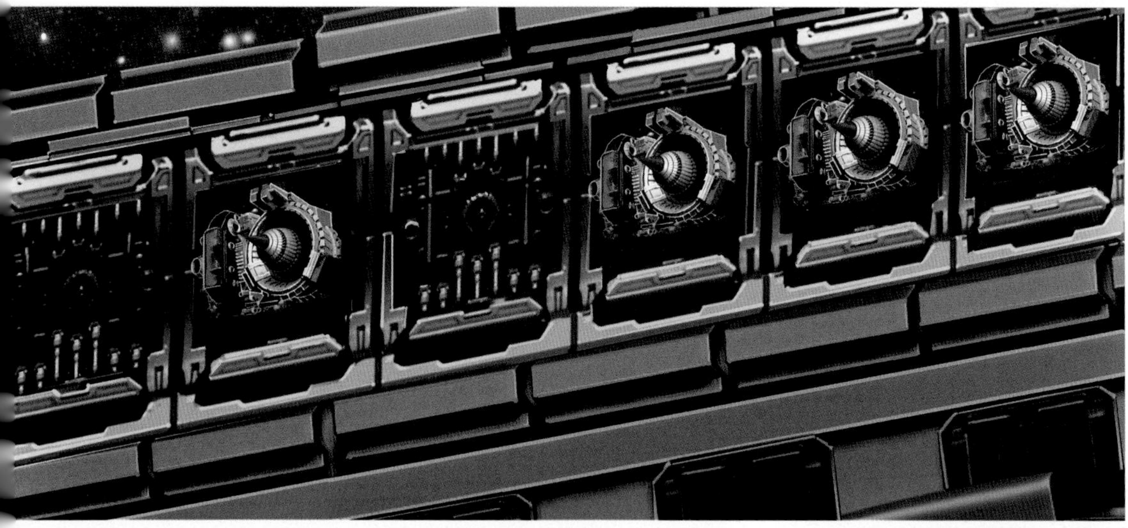
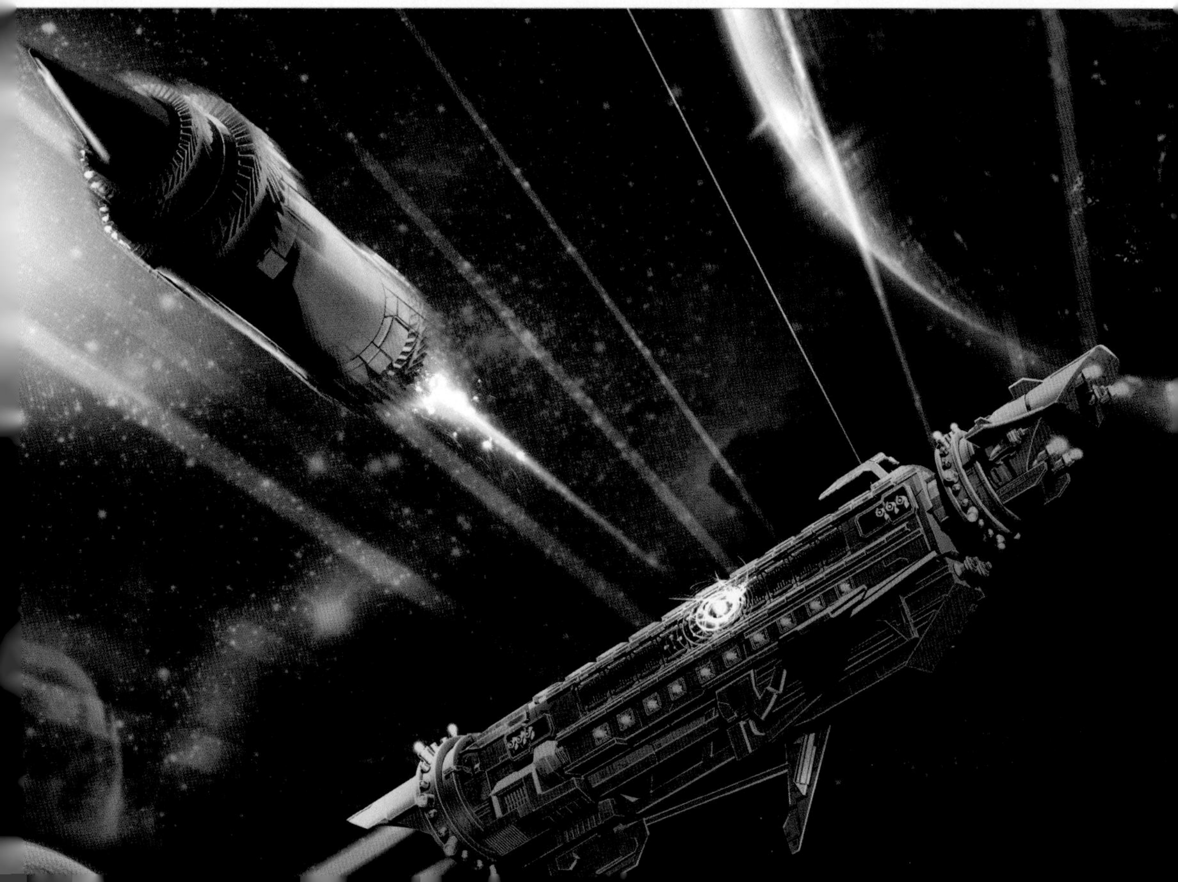

TALES OF HONOR

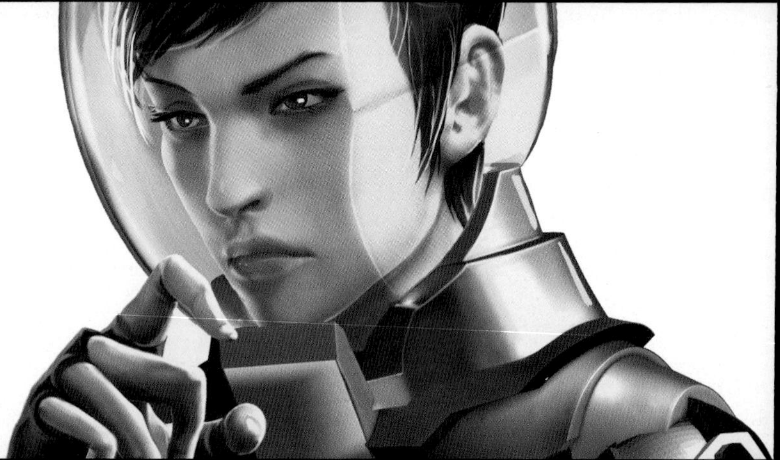

CHAPTER FIVE

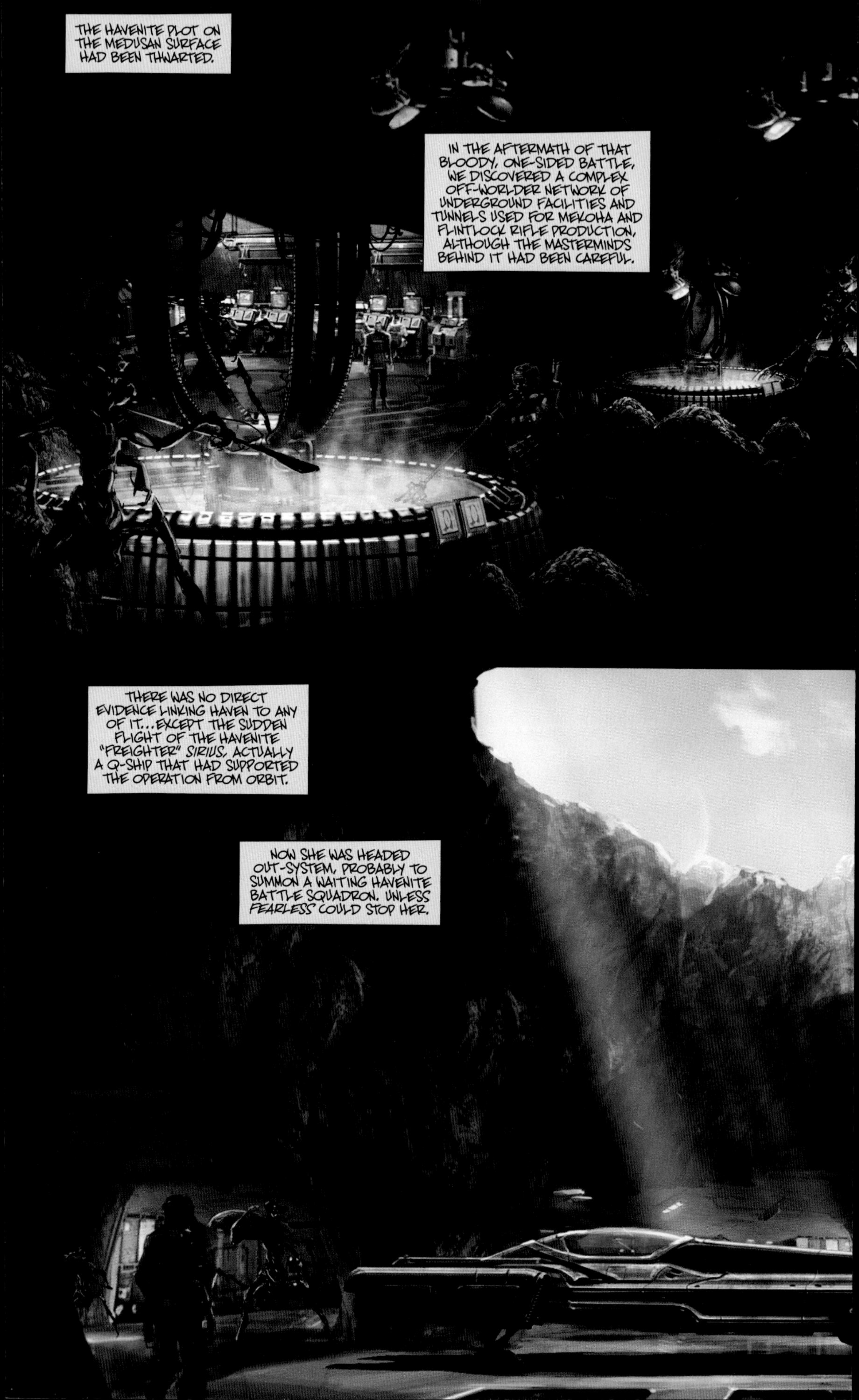
THE HAVENITE PLOT ON THE MEDUSAN SURFACE HAD BEEN THWARTED.
IN THE AFTERMATH OF THAT BLOODY, ONE-SIDED BATTLE, WE DISCOVERED A COMPLEX OFF-WORLDER NETWORK OF UNDERGROUND FACILITIES AND TUNNELS USED FOR MEKOHA AND FLINTLOCK RIFLE PRODUCTION, ALTHOUGH THE MASTERMINDS BEHIND IT HAD BEEN CAREFUL.
THERE WAS NO DIRECT EVIDENCE LINKING HAVEN TO ANY OF IT...EXCEPT THE SUDDEN FLIGHT OF THE HAVENITE "FREIGHTER" *SIRIUS*, ACTUALLY A Q-SHIP THAT HAD SUPPORTED THE OPERATION FROM ORBIT.
NOW SHE WAS HEADED OUT-SYSTEM, PROBABLY TO SUMMON A WAITING HAVENITE BATTLE SQUADRON. UNLESS *FEARLESS* COULD STOP HER.

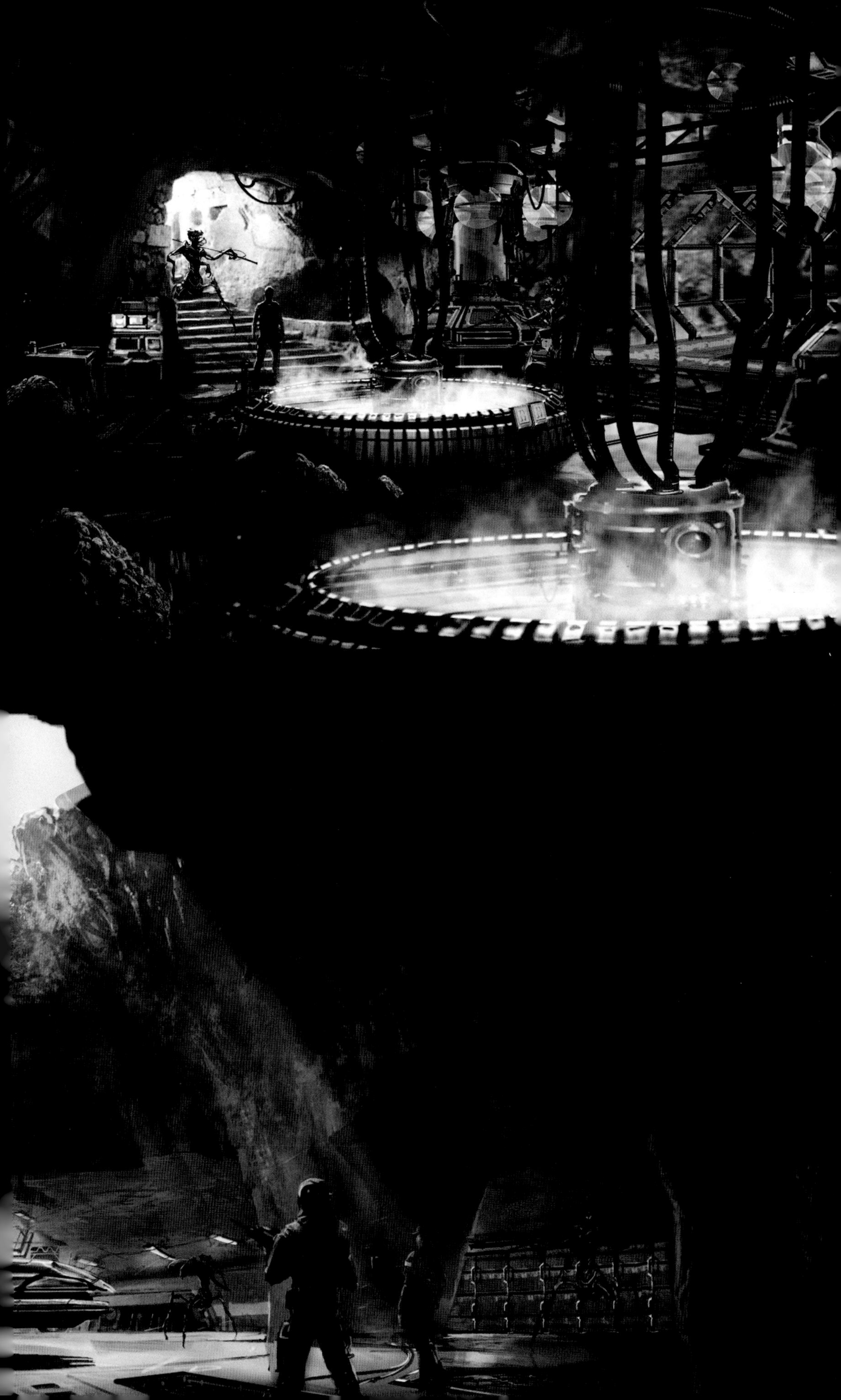

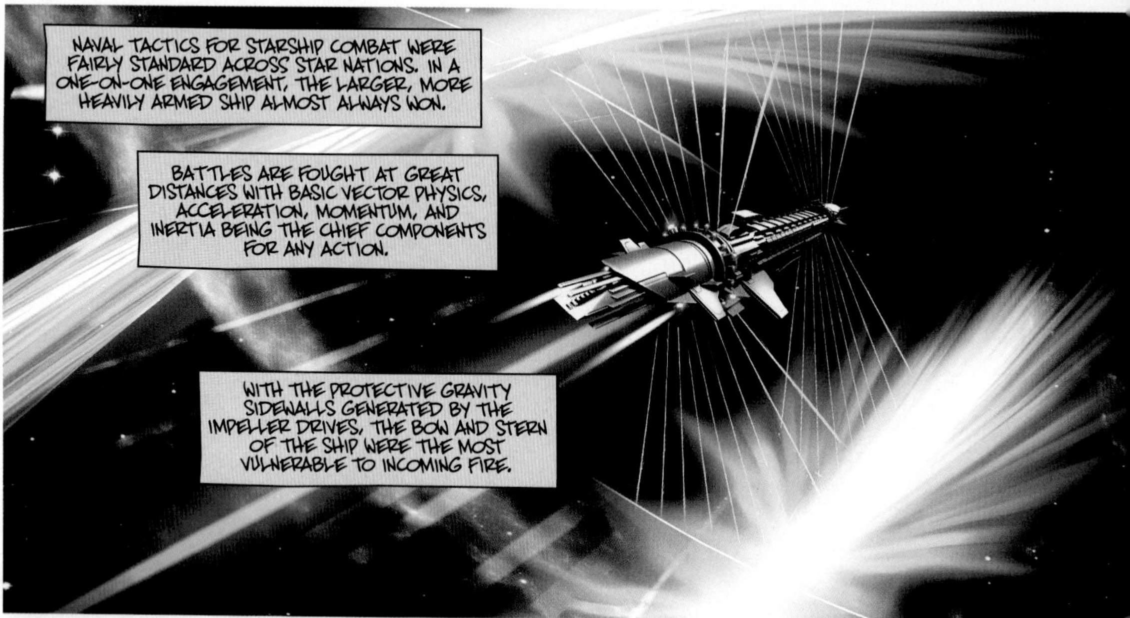
NAVAL TACTICS FOR STARSHIP COMBAT WERE FAIRLY STANDARD ACROSS STAR NATIONS. IN A ONE-ON-ONE ENGAGEMENT, THE LARGER, MORE HEAVILY ARMED SHIP ALMOST ALWAYS WON.
BATTLES ARE FOUGHT AT GREAT DISTANCES WITH BASIC VECTOR PHYSICS, ACCELERATION, MOMENTUM, AND INERTIA BEING THE CHIEF COMPONENTS FOR ANY ACTION.
WITH THE PROTECTIVE GRAVITY SIDEWALLS GENERATED BY THE IMPELLER DRIVES, THE BOW AND STERN OF THE SHIP WERE THE MOST VULNERABLE TO INCOMING FIRE.

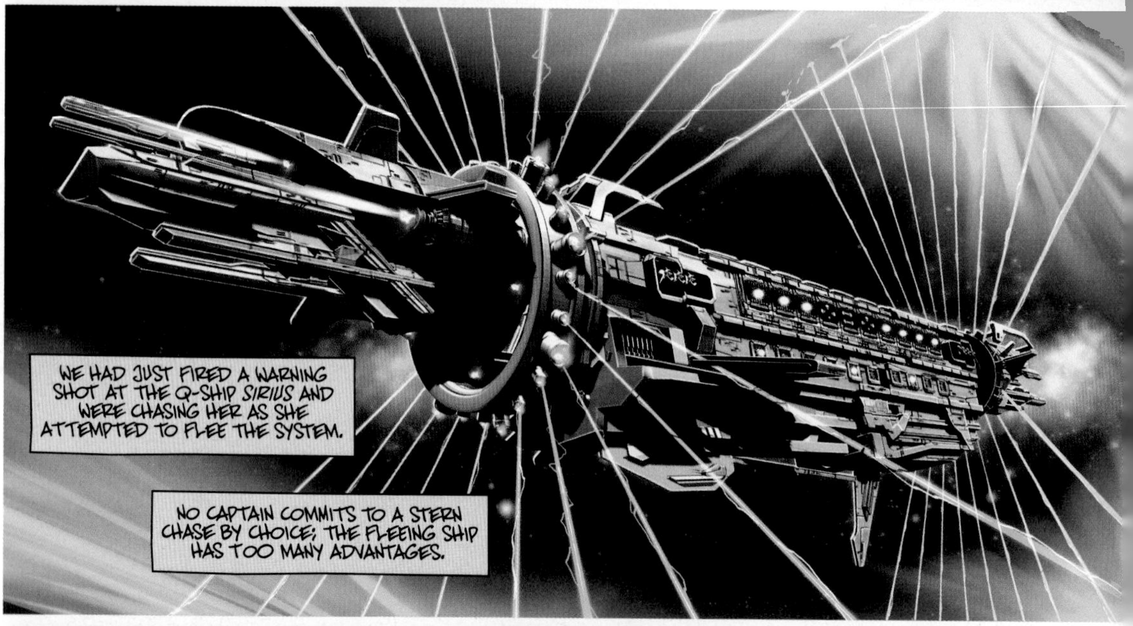
WE HAD JUST FIRED A WARNING SHOT AT THE Q-SHIP *SIRIUS* AND WERE CHASING HER AS SHE ATTEMPTED TO FLEE THE SYSTEM.
NO CAPTAIN COMMITS TO A STERN CHASE BY CHOICE; THE FLEEING SHIP HAS TOO MANY ADVANTAGES.

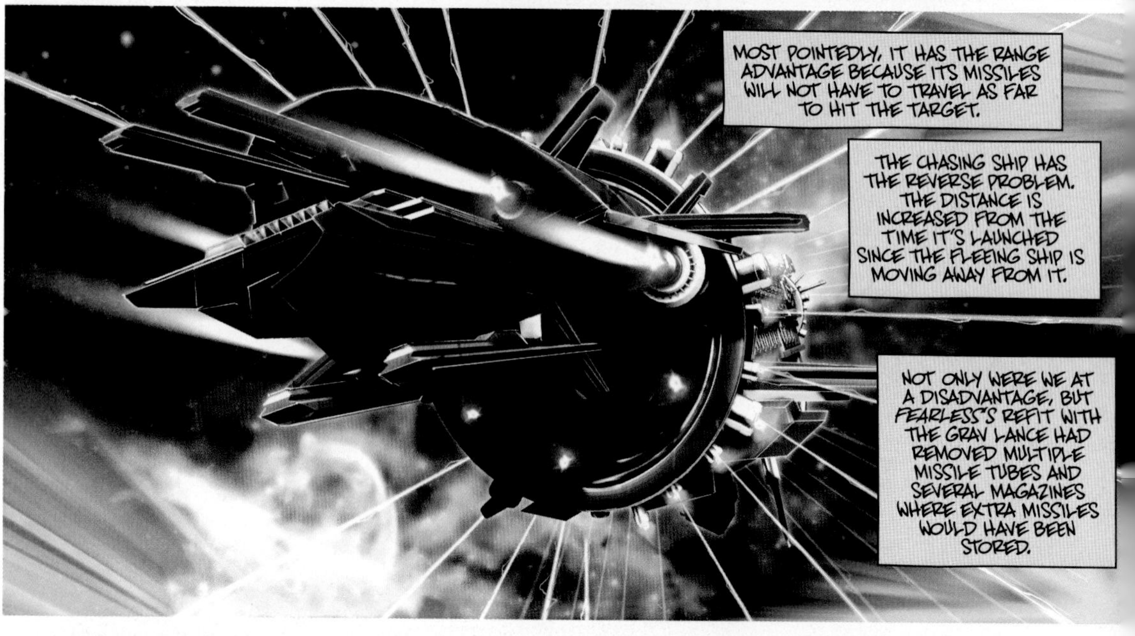
MOST POINTEDLY, IT HAS THE RANGE ADVANTAGE BECAUSE ITS MISSILES WILL NOT HAVE TO TRAVEL AS FAR TO HIT THE TARGET.
THE CHASING SHIP HAS THE REVERSE PROBLEM. THE DISTANCE IS INCREASED FROM THE TIME IT'S LAUNCHED SINCE THE FLEEING SHIP IS MOVING AWAY FROM IT.
NOT ONLY WERE WE AT A DISADVANTAGE, BUT *FEARLESS'S* REFIT WITH THE GRAV LANCE HAD REMOVED MULTIPLE MISSILE TUBES AND SEVERAL MAGAZINES WHERE EXTRA MISSILES WOULD HAVE BEEN STORED.

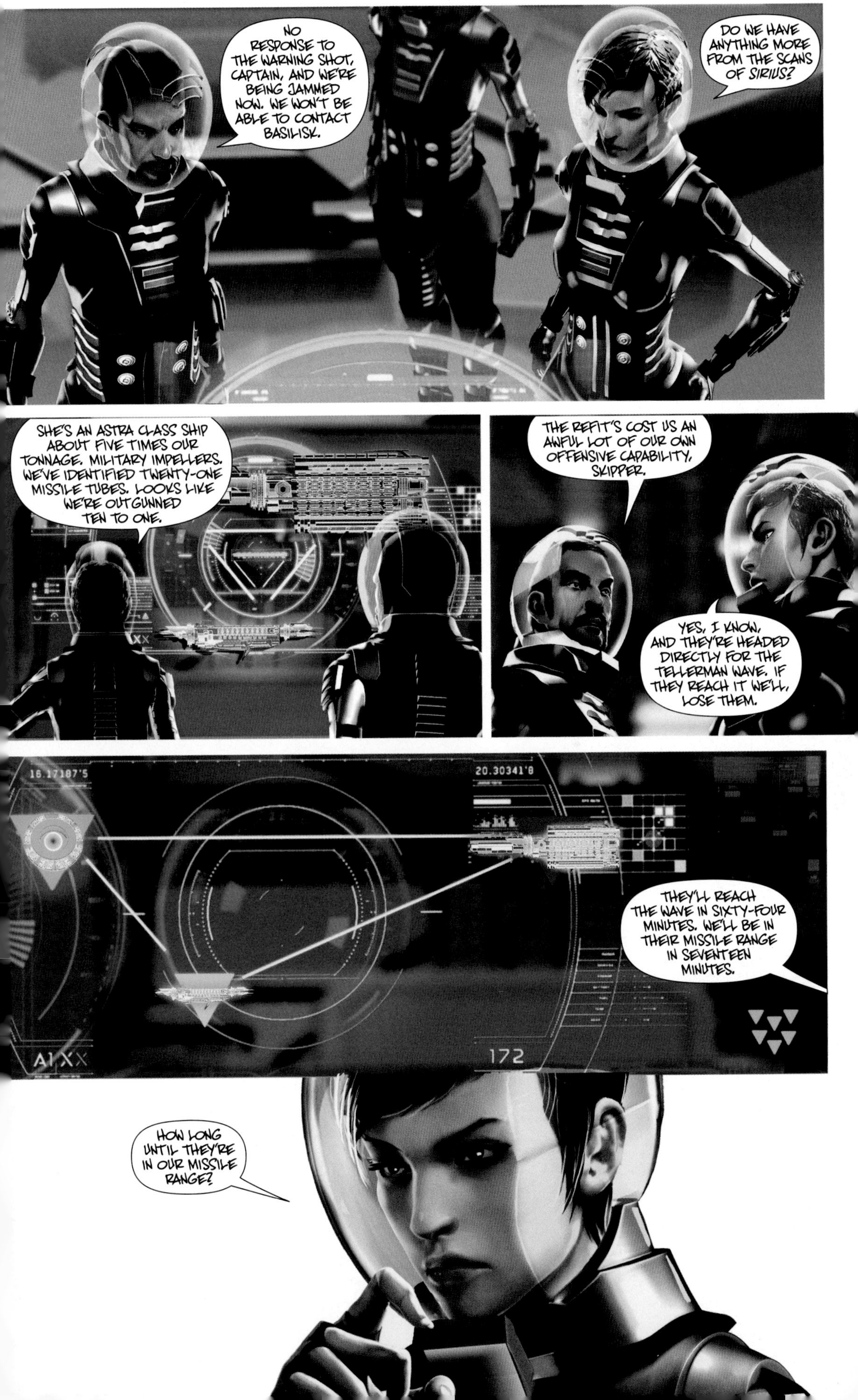
NO RESPONSE TO THE WARNING SHOT, CAPTAIN, AND WE'RE BEING JAMMED NOW. WE WON'T BE ABLE TO CONTACT BASILISK.
DO WE HAVE ANYTHING MORE FROM THE SCANS OF SIRIUS?
SHE'S AN ASTRA CLASS SHIP ABOUT FIVE TIMES OUR TONNAGE. MILITARY IMPELLERS. WE'VE IDENTIFIED TWENTY-ONE MISSILE TUBES. LOOKS LIKE WE'RE OUTGUNNED TEN TO ONE.
THE REFIT'S COST US AN AWFUL LOT OF OUR OWN OFFENSIVE CAPABILITY, SKIPPER.
YES, I KNOW, AND THEY'RE HEADED DIRECTLY FOR THE TELLERMAN WAVE. IF THEY REACH IT WE'LL LOSE THEM.
16.17187'S
20.30341'8
THEY'LL REACH THE WAVE IN SIXTY-FOUR MINUTES. WE'LL BE IN THEIR MISSILE RANGE IN SEVENTEEN MINUTES.
AIXX
172
HOW LONG UNTIL THEY'RE IN OUR MISSILE RANGE?

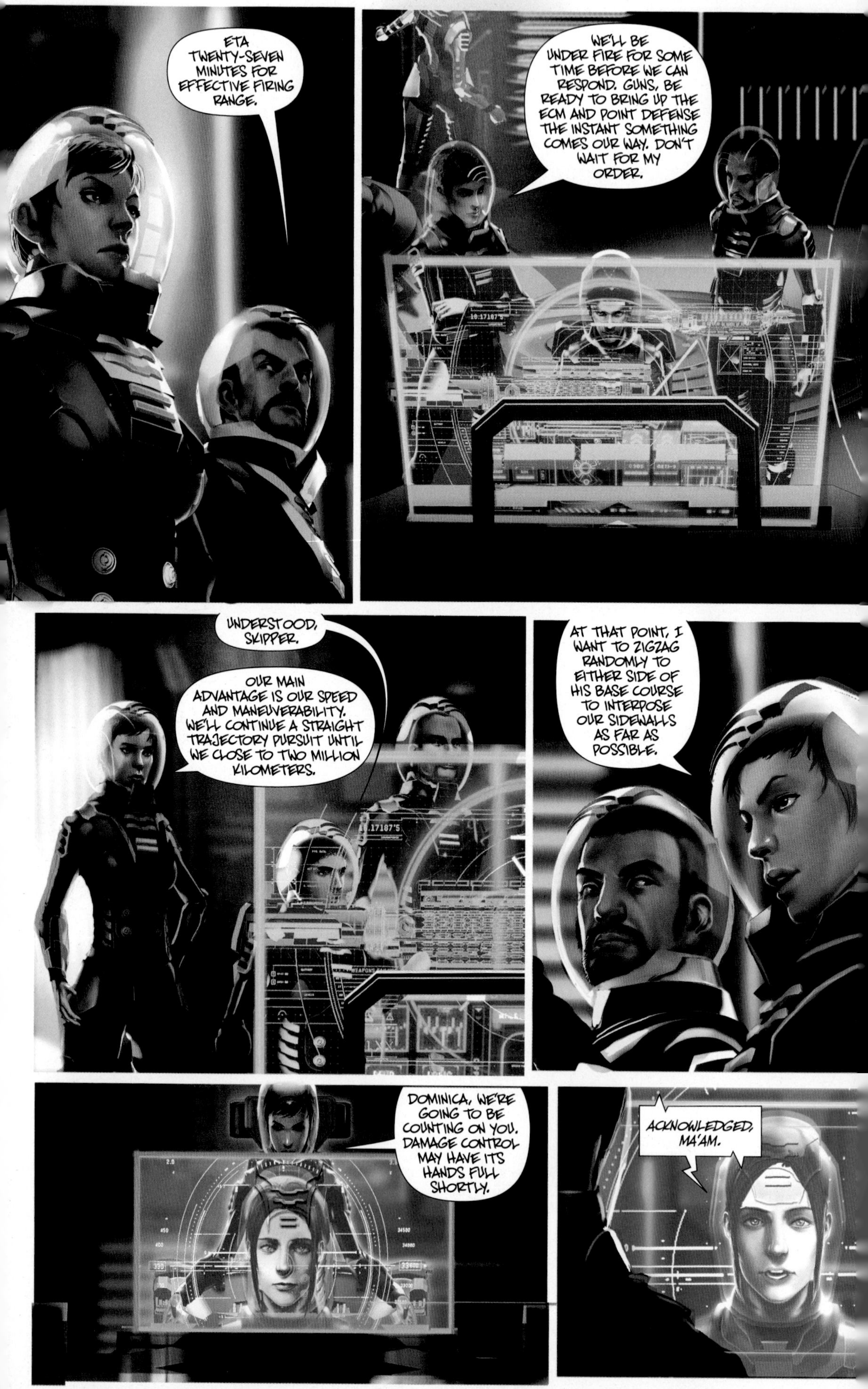
ETA TWENTY-SEVEN MINUTES FOR EFFECTIVE FIRING RANGE.
WE'LL BE UNDER FIRE FOR SOME TIME BEFORE WE CAN RESPOND. GUNS, BE READY TO BRING UP THE ECM AND POINT DEFENSE THE INSTANT SOMETHING COMES OUR WAY. DON'T WAIT FOR MY ORDER.
UNDERSTOOD, SKIPPER.
OUR MAIN ADVANTAGE IS OUR SPEED AND MANEUVERABILITY. WE'LL CONTINUE A STRAIGHT TRAJECTORY PURSUIT UNTIL WE CLOSE TO TWO MILLION KILOMETERS.
AT THAT POINT, I WANT TO ZIGZAG RANDOMLY TO EITHER SIDE OF HIS BASE COURSE TO INTERPOSE OUR SIDEWALLS AS FAR AS POSSIBLE.
DOMINICA, WE'RE GOING TO BE COUNTING ON YOU. DAMAGE CONTROL MAY HAVE ITS HANDS FULL SHORTLY.
ACKNOWLEDGED, MA'AM.

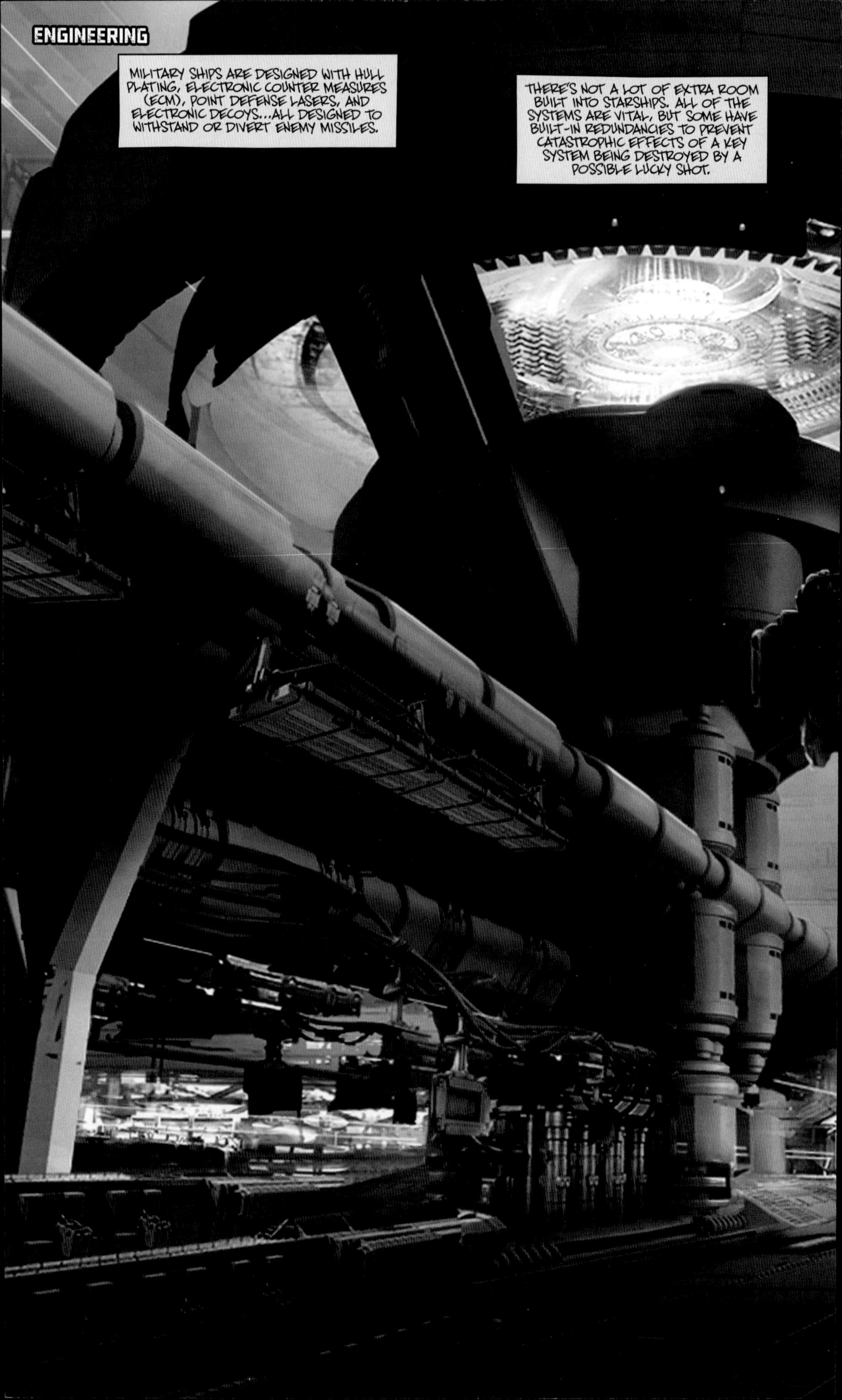
MILITARY SHIPS ARE DESIGNED WITH HULL PLATING, ELECTRONIC COUNTER MEASURES (ECM), POINT DEFENSE LASERS, AND ELECTRONIC DECOYS...ALL DESIGNED TO WITHSTAND OR DIVERT ENEMY MISSILES.
THERE'S NOT A LOT OF EXTRA ROOM BUILT INTO STARSHIPS. ALL OF THE SYSTEMS ARE VITAL, BUT SOME HAVE BUILT-IN REDUNDANCIES TO PREVENT CATASTROPHIC EFFECTS OF A KEY SYSTEM BEING DESTROYED BY A POSSIBLE LUCKY SHOT.

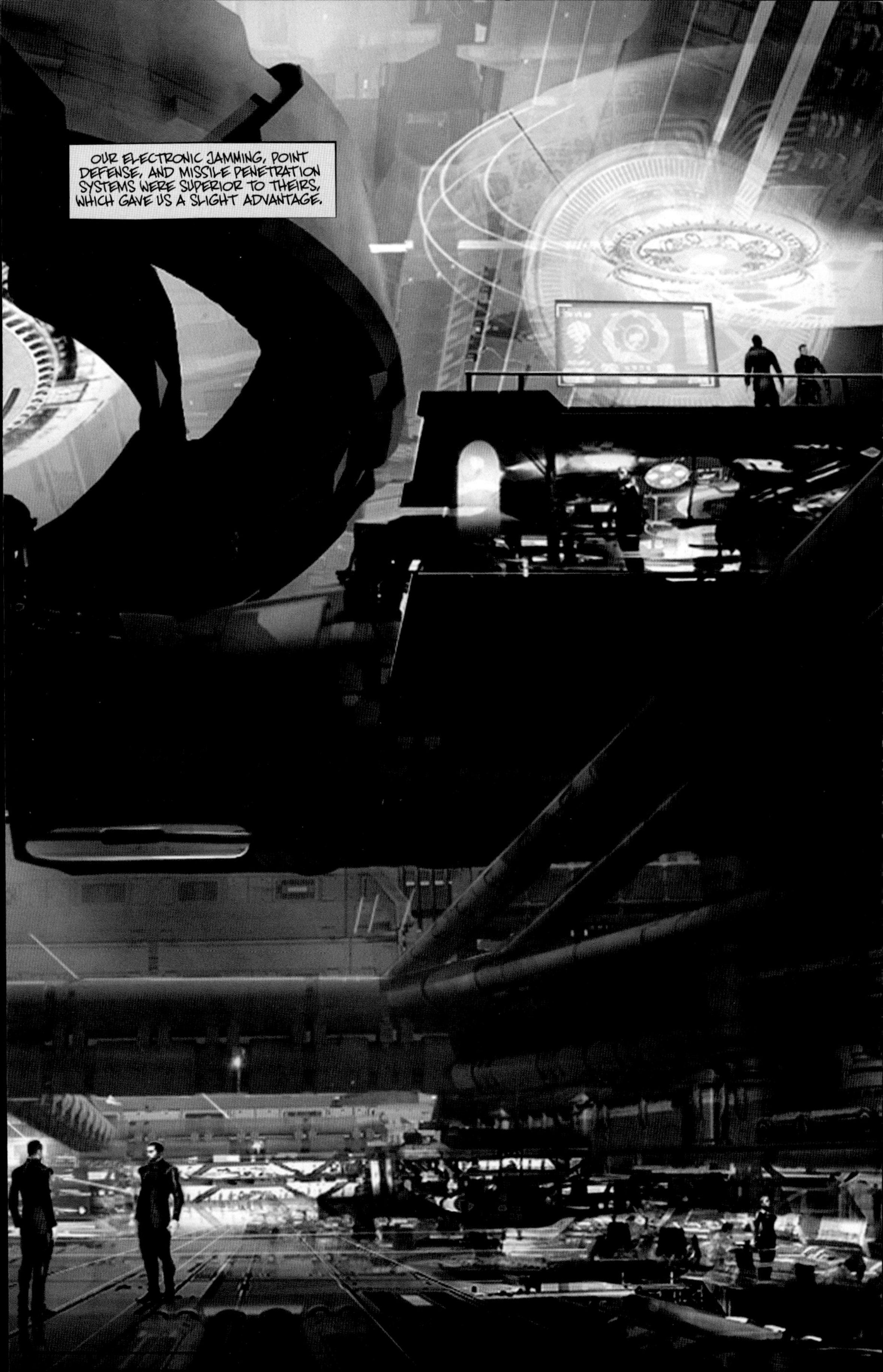
OUR ELECTRONIC JAMMING, POINT DEFENSE, AND MISSILE PENETRATION SYSTEMS WERE SUPERIOR TO THEIRS, WHICH GAVE US A SLIGHT ADVANTAGE.

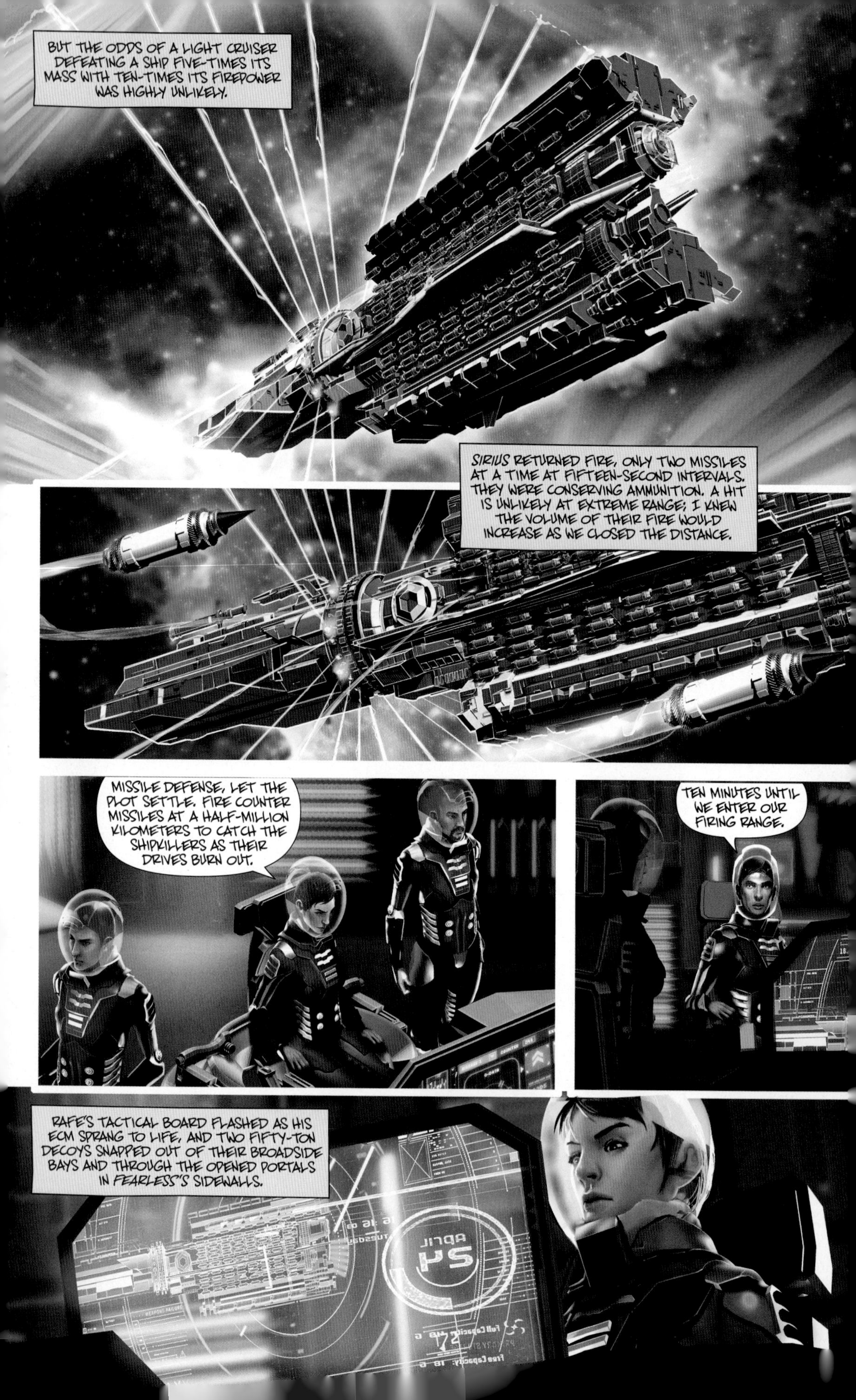
BUT THE ODDS OF A LIGHT CRUISER DEFEATING A SHIP FIVE-TIMES ITS MASS WITH TEN-TIMES ITS FIREPOWER WAS HIGHLY UNLIKELY.
SIRIUS RETURNED FIRE, ONLY TWO MISSILES AT A TIME AT FIFTEEN-SECOND INTERVALS. THEY WERE CONSERVING AMMUNITION. A HIT IS UNLIKELY AT EXTREME RANGE; I KNEW THE VOLUME OF THEIR FIRE WOULD INCREASE AS WE CLOSED THE DISTANCE.
MISSILE DEFENSE, LET THE PLOT SETTLE. FIRE COUNTER MISSILES AT A HALF-MILLION KILOMETERS TO CATCH THE SHIPKILLERS AS THEIR DRIVES BURN OUT.
TEN MINUTES UNTIL WE ENTER OUR FIRING RANGE.
RAFE'S TACTICAL BOARD FLASHED AS HIS ECM SPRANG TO LIFE, AND TWO FIFTY-TON DECOYS SNAPPED OUT OF THEIR BROADSIDE BAYS AND THROUGH THE OPENED PORTALS IN *FEARLESS'S* SIDEWALLS.

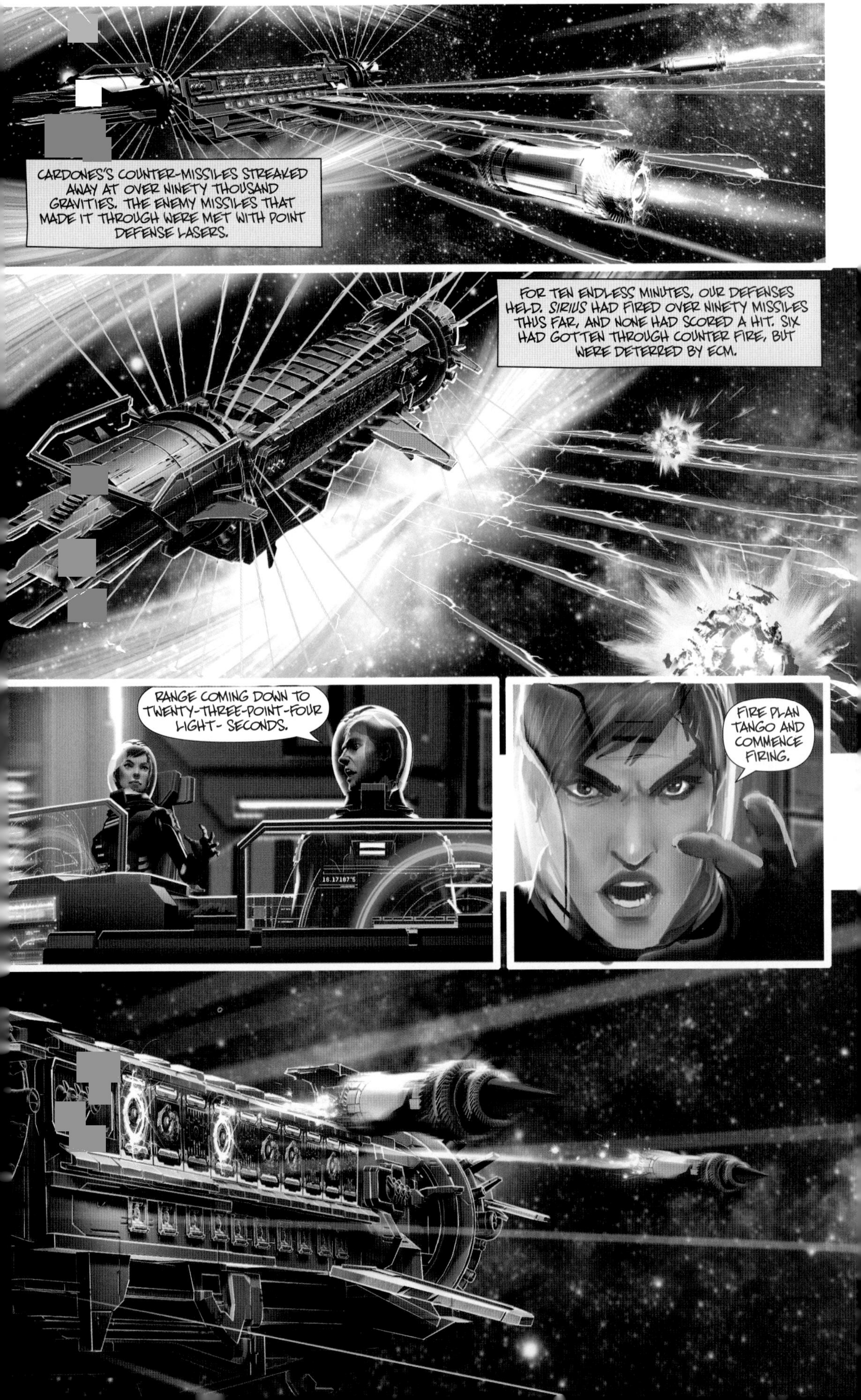
CARDONES'S COUNTER-MISSILES STREAKED AWAY AT OVER NINETY THOUSAND GRAVITIES. THE ENEMY MISSILES THAT MADE IT THROUGH WERE MET WITH POINT DEFENSE LASERS.
FOR TEN ENDLESS MINUTES, OUR DEFENSES HELD. *SIRIUS* HAD FIRED OVER NINETY MISSILES THUS FAR, AND NONE HAD SCORED A HIT. SIX HAD GOTTEN THROUGH COUNTER FIRE, BUT WERE DETERRED BY ECM.
RANGE COMING DOWN TO TWENTY-THREE-POINT-FOUR LIGHT- SECONDS.
FIRE PLAN TANGO AND COMMENCE FIRING.

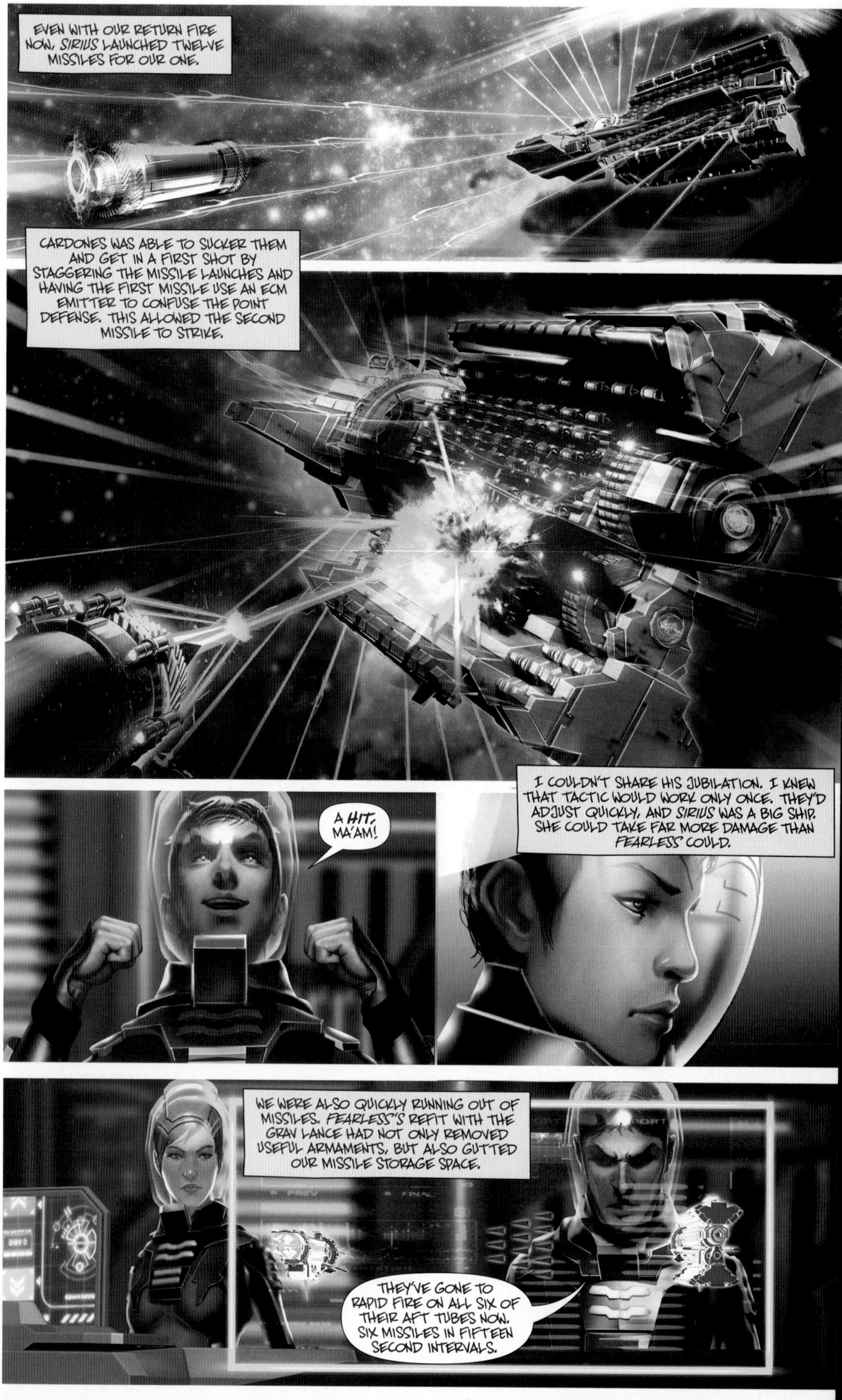
EVEN WITH OUR RETURN FIRE NOW, SIRIUS LAUNCHED TWELVE MISSILES FOR OUR ONE.
CARDONES WAS ABLE TO SUCKER THEM AND GET IN A FIRST SHOT BY STAGGERING THE MISSILE LAUNCHES AND HAVING THE FIRST MISSILE USE AN ECM EMITTER TO CONFUSE THE POINT DEFENSE. THIS ALLOWED THE SECOND MISSILE TO STRIKE.
A HIT, MA'AM!
I COULDN'T SHARE HIS JUBILATION. I KNEW THAT TACTIC WOULD WORK ONLY ONCE. THEY'D ADJUST QUICKLY, AND SIRIUS WAS A BIG SHIP. SHE COULD TAKE FAR MORE DAMAGE THAN FEARLESS COULD.
WE WERE ALSO QUICKLY RUNNING OUT OF MISSILES. FEARLESS'S REFIT WITH THE GRAV LANCE HAD NOT ONLY REMOVED USEFUL ARMAMENTS, BUT ALSO GUTTED OUR MISSILE STORAGE SPACE.
THEY'VE GONE TO RAPID FIRE ON ALL SIX OF THEIR AFT TUBES NOW. SIX MISSILES IN FIFTEEN SECOND INTERVALS.

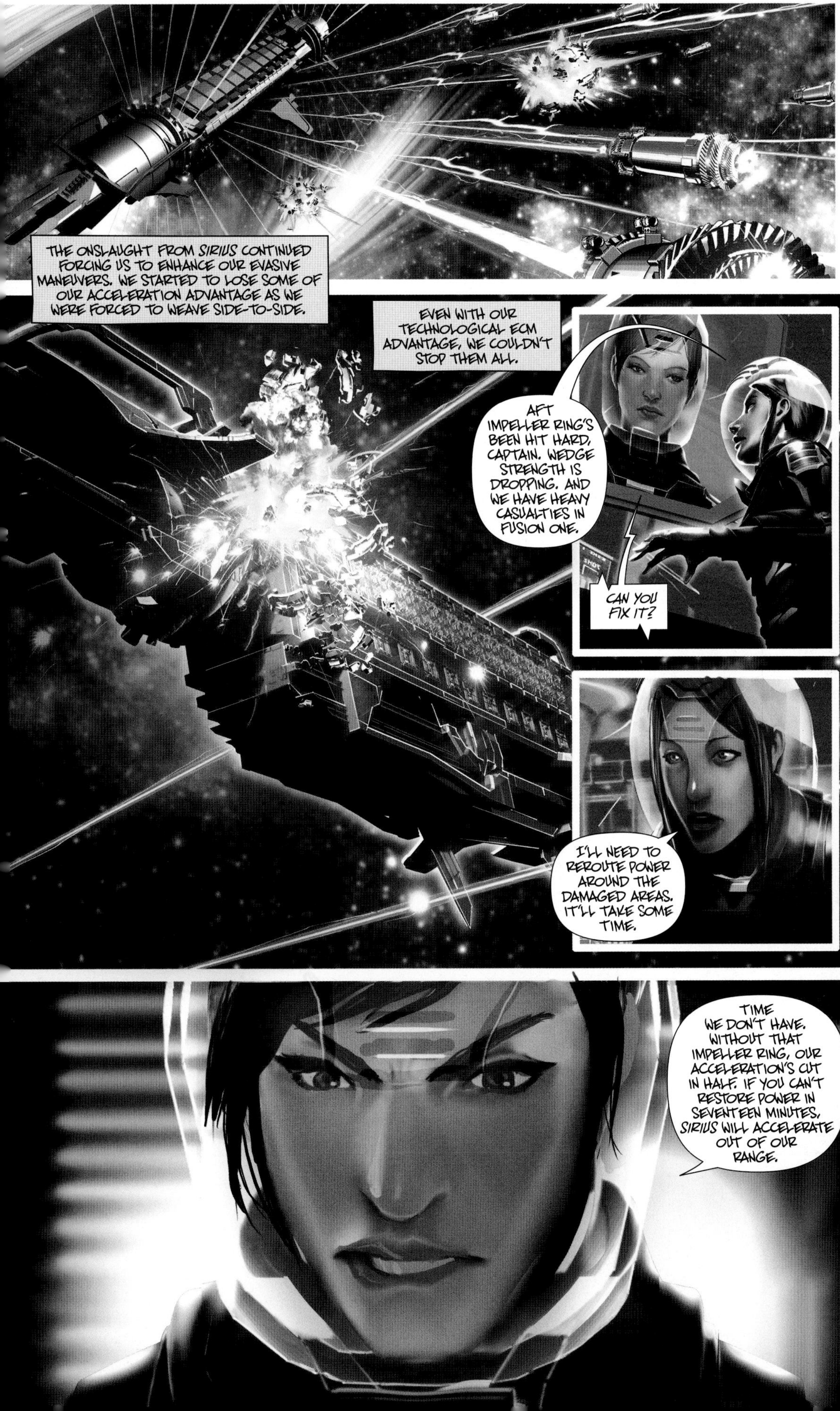
THE ONSLAUGHT FROM SIRIUS CONTINUED FORCING US TO ENHANCE OUR EVASIVE MANEUVERS. WE STARTED TO LOSE SOME OF OUR ACCELERATION ADVANTAGE AS WE WERE FORCED TO WEAVE SIDE-TO-SIDE.
EVEN WITH OUR TECHNOLOGICAL ECM ADVANTAGE, WE COULDN'T STOP THEM ALL.
AFT IMPELLER RING'S BEEN HIT HARD, CAPTAIN. WEDGE STRENGTH IS DROPPING. AND WE HAVE HEAVY CASUALTIES IN FUSION ONE.
CAN YOU FIX IT?
I'LL NEED TO REROUTE POWER AROUND THE DAMAGED AREAS. IT'LL TAKE SOME TIME.
TIME WE DON'T HAVE. WITHOUT THAT IMPELLER RING, OUR ACCELERATION'S CUT IN HALF. IF YOU CAN'T RESTORE POWER IN SEVENTEEN MINUTES, SIRIUS WILL ACCELERATE OUT OF OUR RANGE.

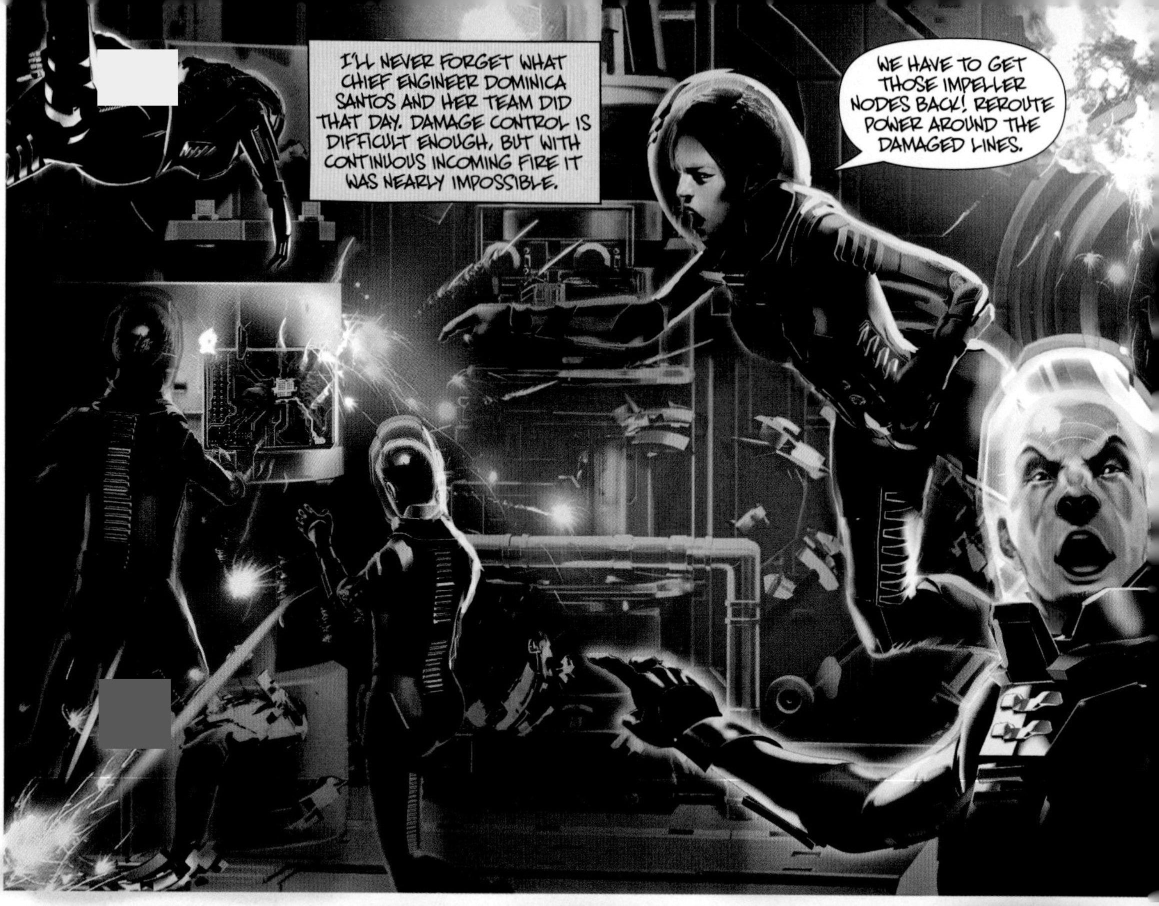
I'LL NEVER FORGET WHAT CHIEF ENGINEER DOMINICA SANTOS AND HER TEAM DID THAT DAY. DAMAGE CONTROL IS DIFFICULT ENOUGH, BUT WITH CONTINUOUS INCOMING FIRE IT WAS NEARLY IMPOSSIBLE.
WE HAVE TO GET THOSE IMPELLER NODES BACK! REROUTE POWER AROUND THE DAMAGED LINES.

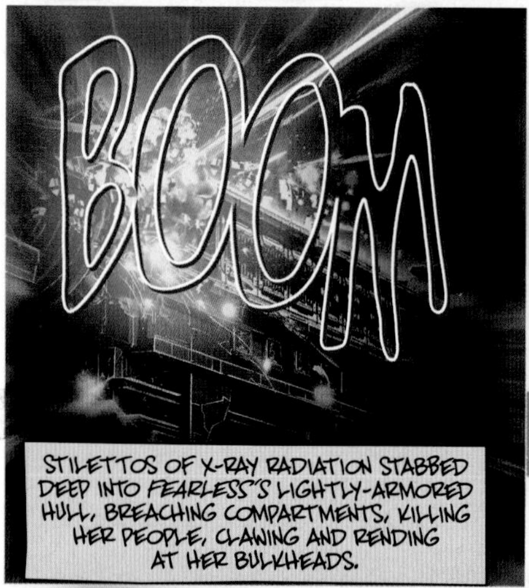
BOOM
STILETTOS OF X-RAY RADIATION STABBED DEEP INTO *FEARLESS*'S LIGHTLY-ARMORED HULL, BREACHING COMPARTMENTS, KILLING HER PEOPLE, CLAWING AND RENDING AT HER BULKHEADS.

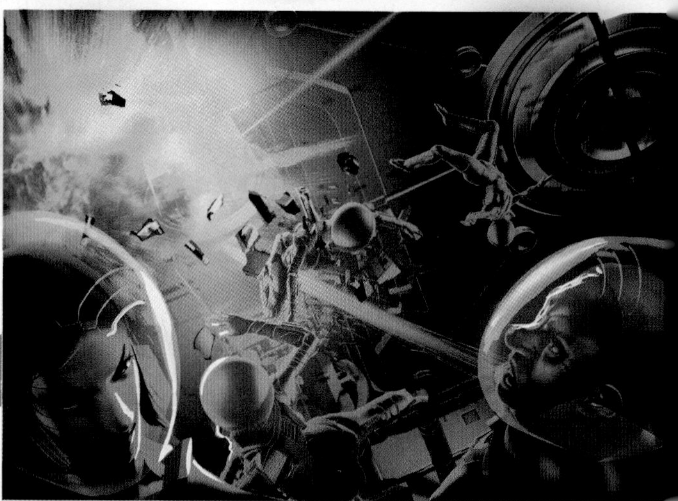

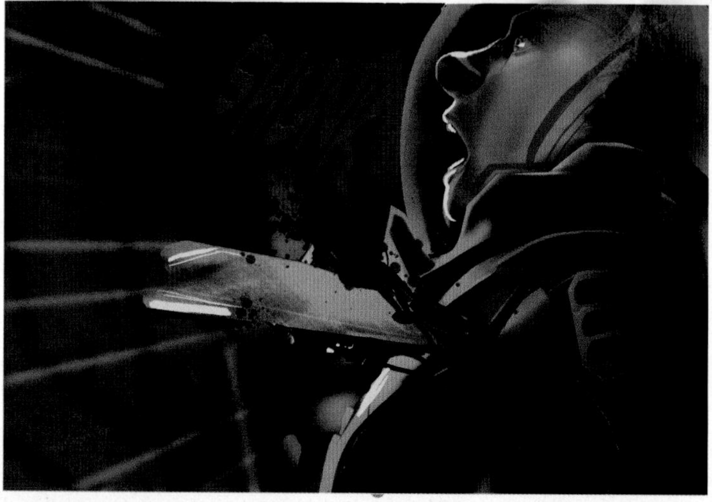

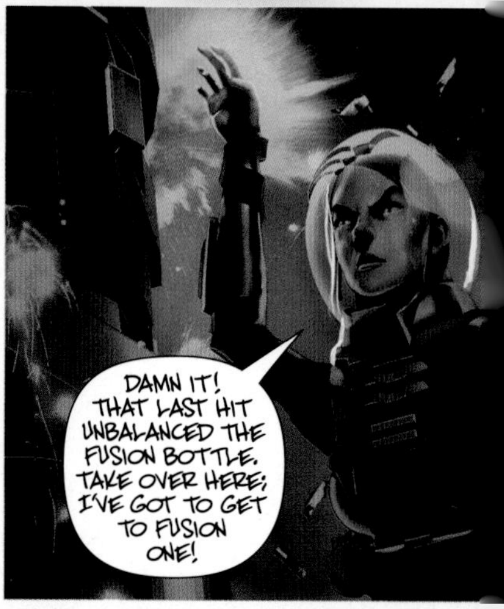
DAMN IT! THAT LAST HIT UNBALANCED THE FUSION BOTTLE. TAKE OVER HERE; I'VE GOT TO GET TO FUSION ONE!

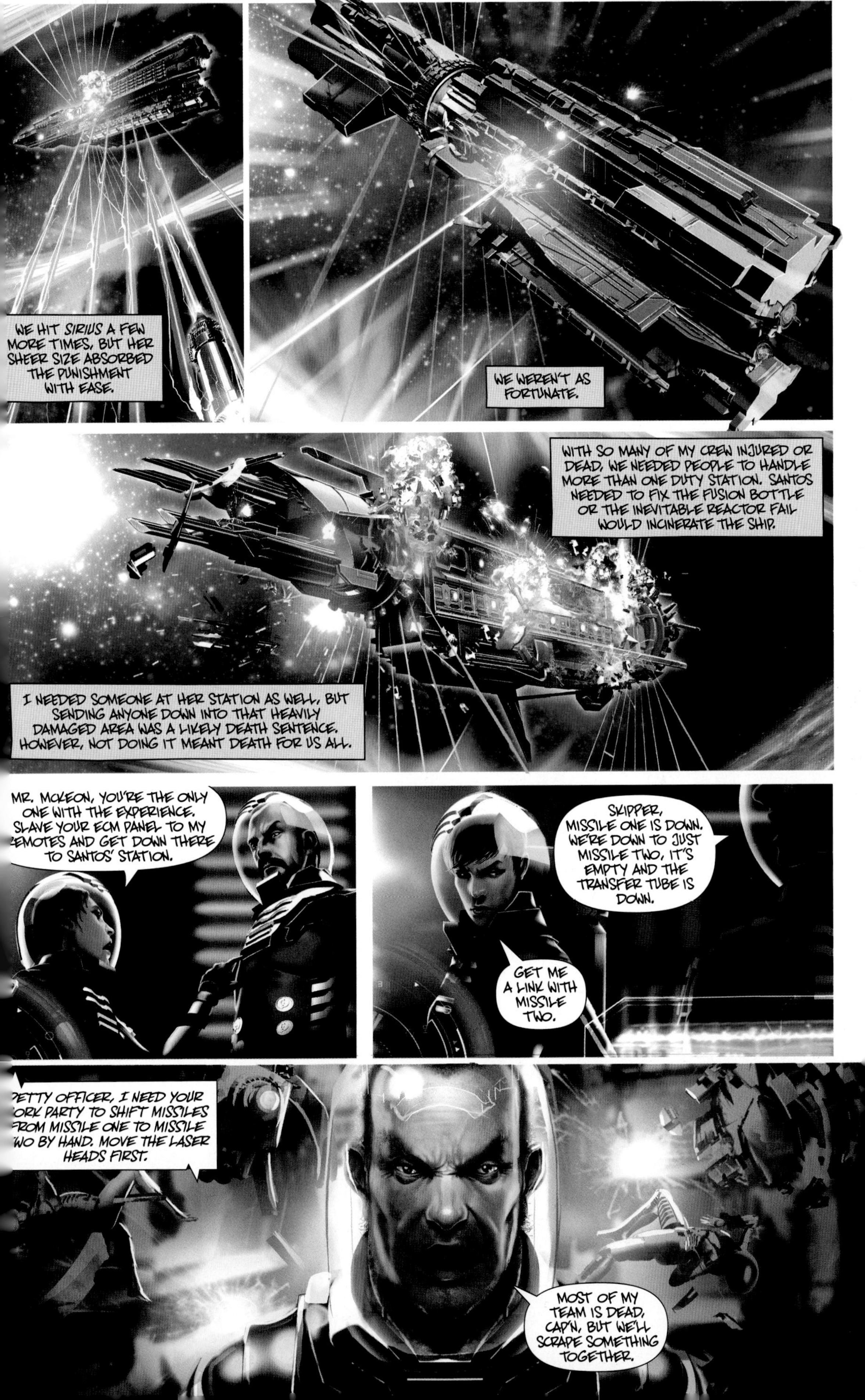
WE HIT SIRIUS A FEW MORE TIMES, BUT HER SHEER SIZE ABSORBED THE PUNISHMENT WITH EASE.
WE WEREN'T AS FORTUNATE.
WITH SO MANY OF MY CREW INJURED OR DEAD, WE NEEDED PEOPLE TO HANDLE MORE THAN ONE DUTY STATION. SANTOS NEEDED TO FIX THE FUSION BOTTLE OR THE INEVITABLE REACTOR FAIL WOULD INCINERATE THE SHIP.
I NEEDED SOMEONE AT HER STATION AS WELL, BUT SENDING ANYONE DOWN INTO THAT HEAVILY DAMAGED AREA WAS A LIKELY DEATH SENTENCE. HOWEVER, NOT DOING IT MEANT DEATH FOR US ALL.
MR. MCKEON, YOU'RE THE ONLY ONE WITH THE EXPERIENCE. SLAVE YOUR ECM PANEL TO MY REMOTES AND GET DOWN THERE TO SANTOS' STATION.
SKIPPER, MISSILE ONE IS DOWN. WE'RE DOWN TO JUST MISSILE TWO, IT'S EMPTY AND THE TRANSFER TUBE IS DOWN.
GET ME A LINK WITH MISSILE TWO.
PETTY OFFICER, I NEED YOUR WORK PARTY TO SHIFT MISSILES FROM MISSILE ONE TO MISSILE TWO BY HAND. MOVE THE LASER HEADS FIRST.
MOST OF MY TEAM IS DEAD, CAP'N, BUT WE'LL SCRAPE SOMETHING TOGETHER.

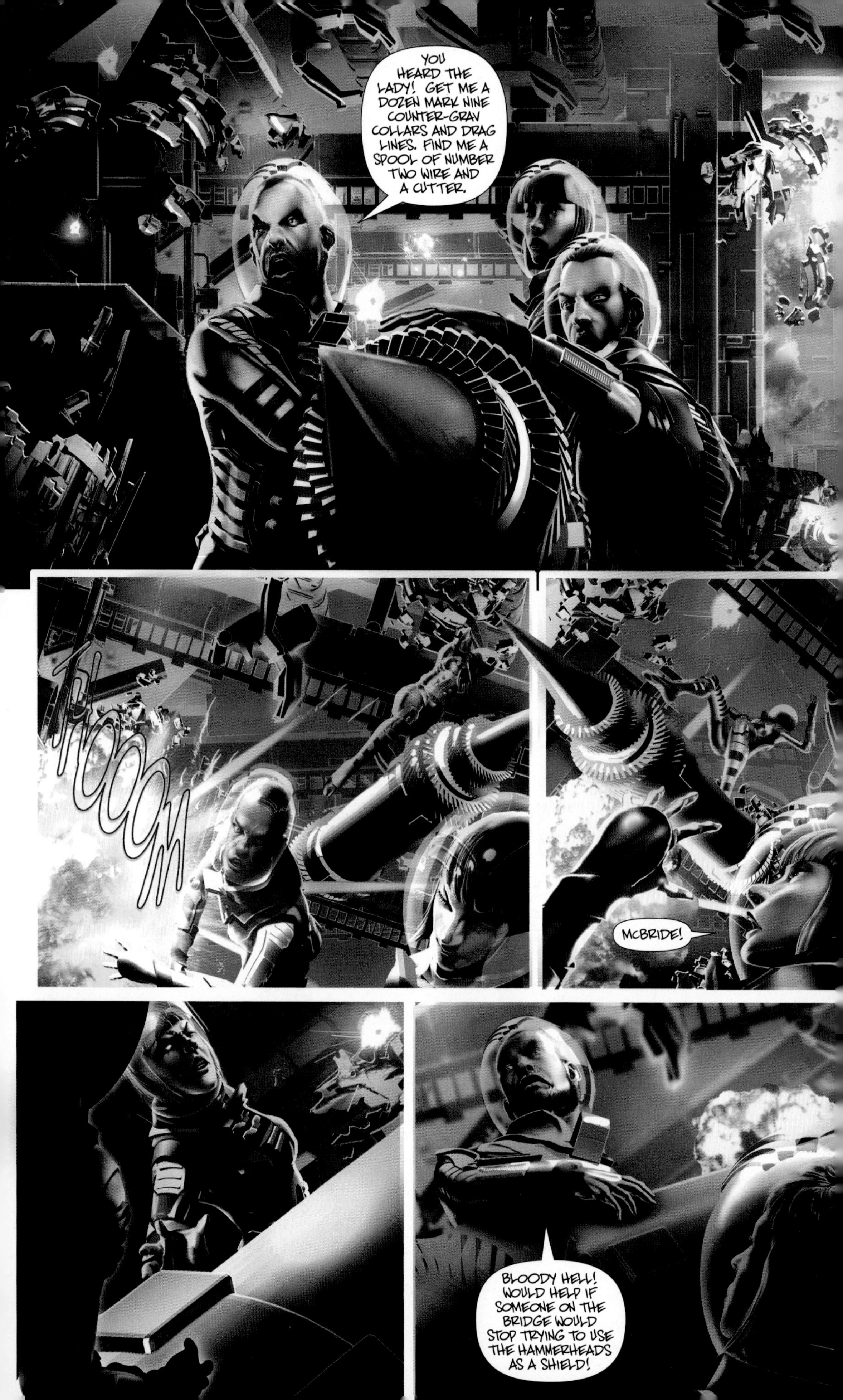
YOU HEARD THE LADY! GET ME A DOZEN MARK NINE COUNTER-GRAV COLLARS AND DRAG LINES. FIND ME A SPOOL OF NUMBER TWO WIRE AND A CUTTER.
THOOOM
MCBRIDE!
BLOODY HELL! WOULD HELP IF SOMEONE ON THE BRIDGE WOULD STOP TRYING TO USE THE HAMMERHEADS AS A SHIELD!

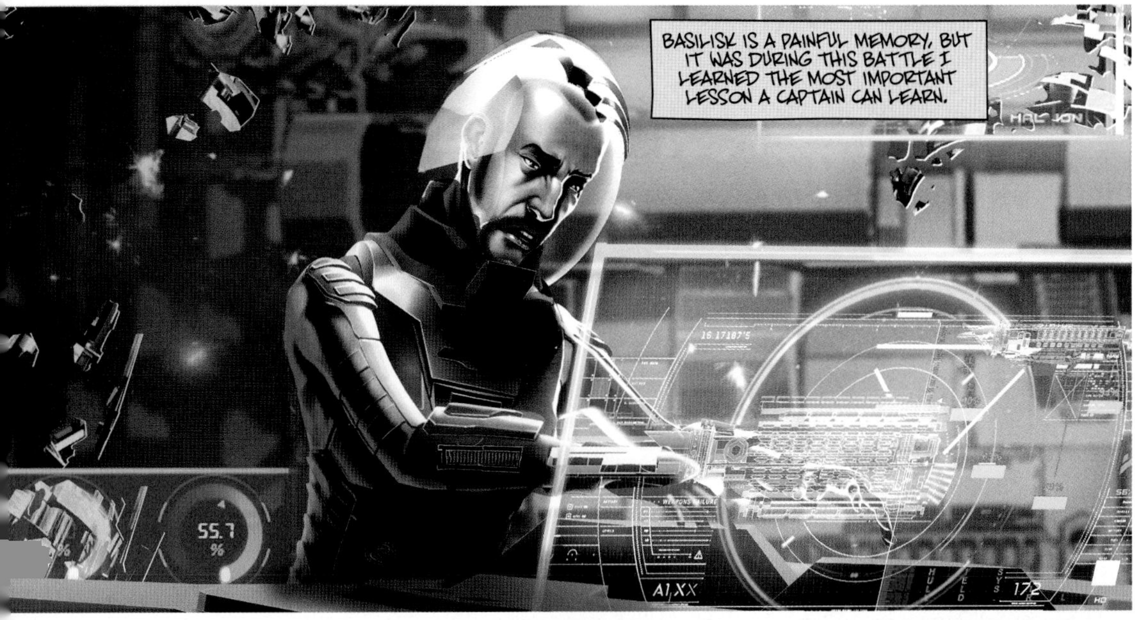
BASILISK IS A PAINFUL MEMORY, BUT IT WAS DURING THIS BATTLE I LEARNED THE MOST IMPORTANT LESSON A CAPTAIN CAN LEARN.
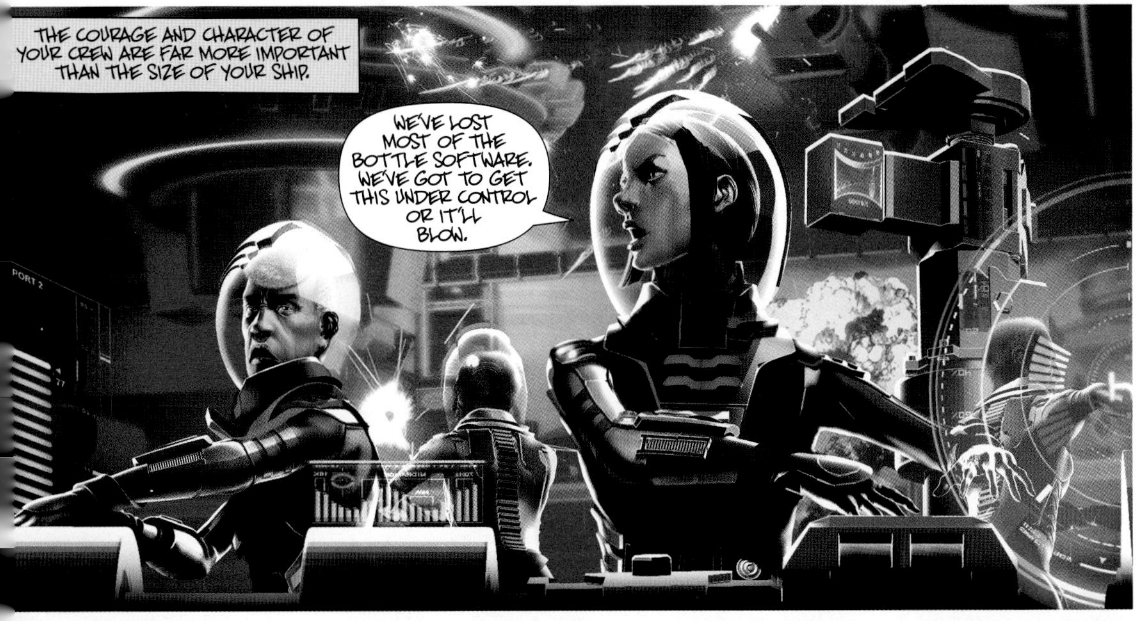
THE COURAGE AND CHARACTER OF YOUR CREW ARE FAR MORE IMPORTANT THAN THE SIZE OF YOUR SHIP.
WE'VE LOST MOST OF THE BOTTLE SOFTWARE. WE'VE GOT TO GET THIS UNDER CONTROL OR IT'LL BLOW.
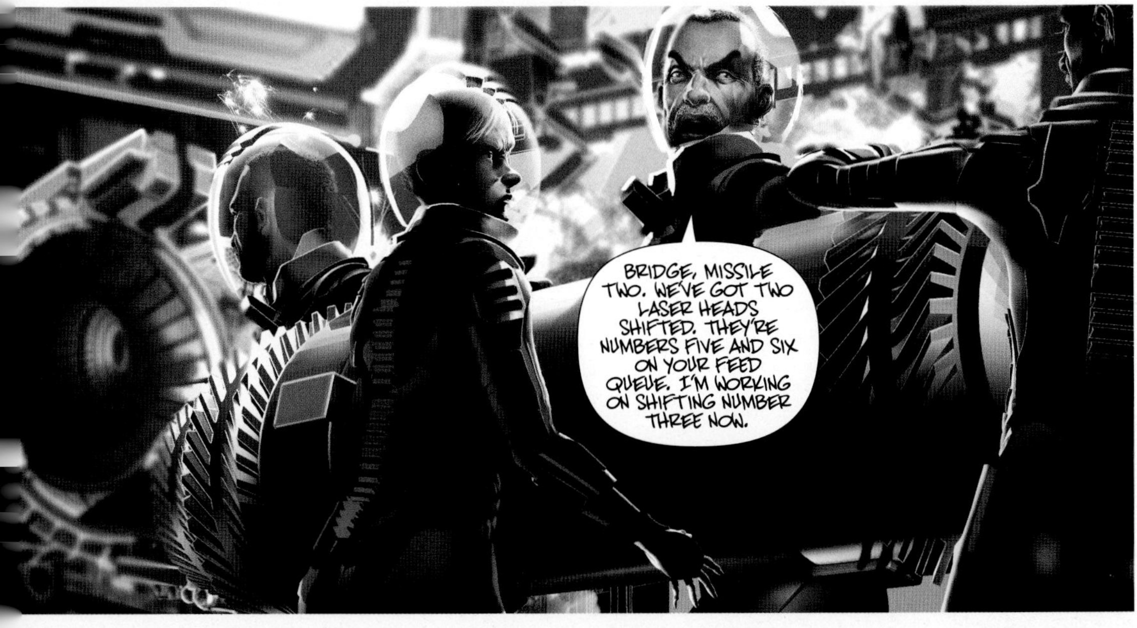
BRIDGE, MISSILE TWO. WE'VE GOT TWO LASER HEADS SHIFTED. THEY'RE NUMBERS FIVE AND SIX ON YOUR FEED QUEUE. I'M WORKING ON SHIFTING NUMBER THREE NOW.

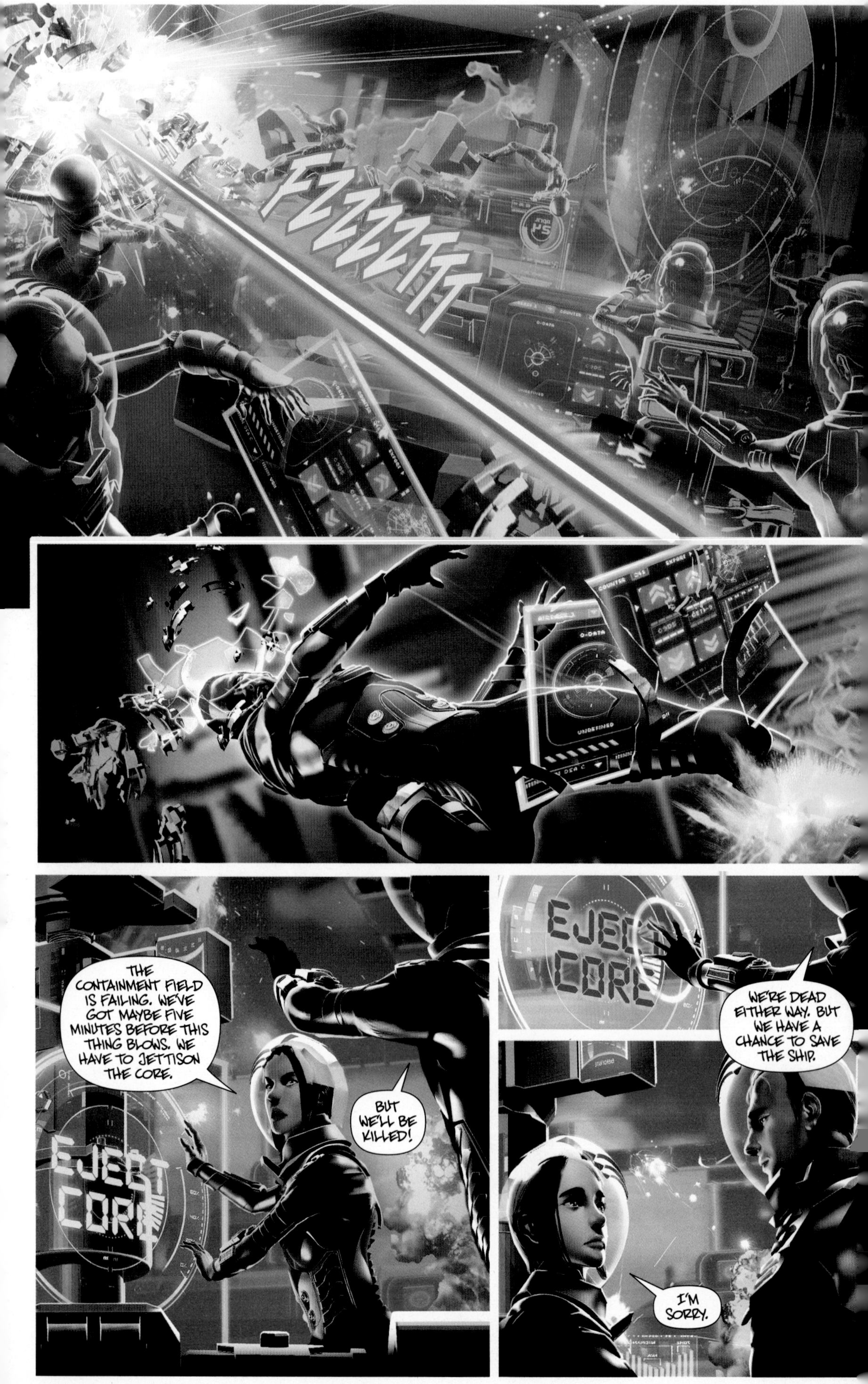
FZZZZTTT
THE CONTAINMENT FIELD IS FAILING. WE'VE GOT MAYBE FIVE MINUTES BEFORE THIS THING BLOWS. WE HAVE TO JETTISON THE CORE.
BUT WE'LL BE KILLED!
WE'RE DEAD EITHER WAY. BUT WE HAVE A CHANCE TO SAVE THE SHIP.
I'M SORRY.

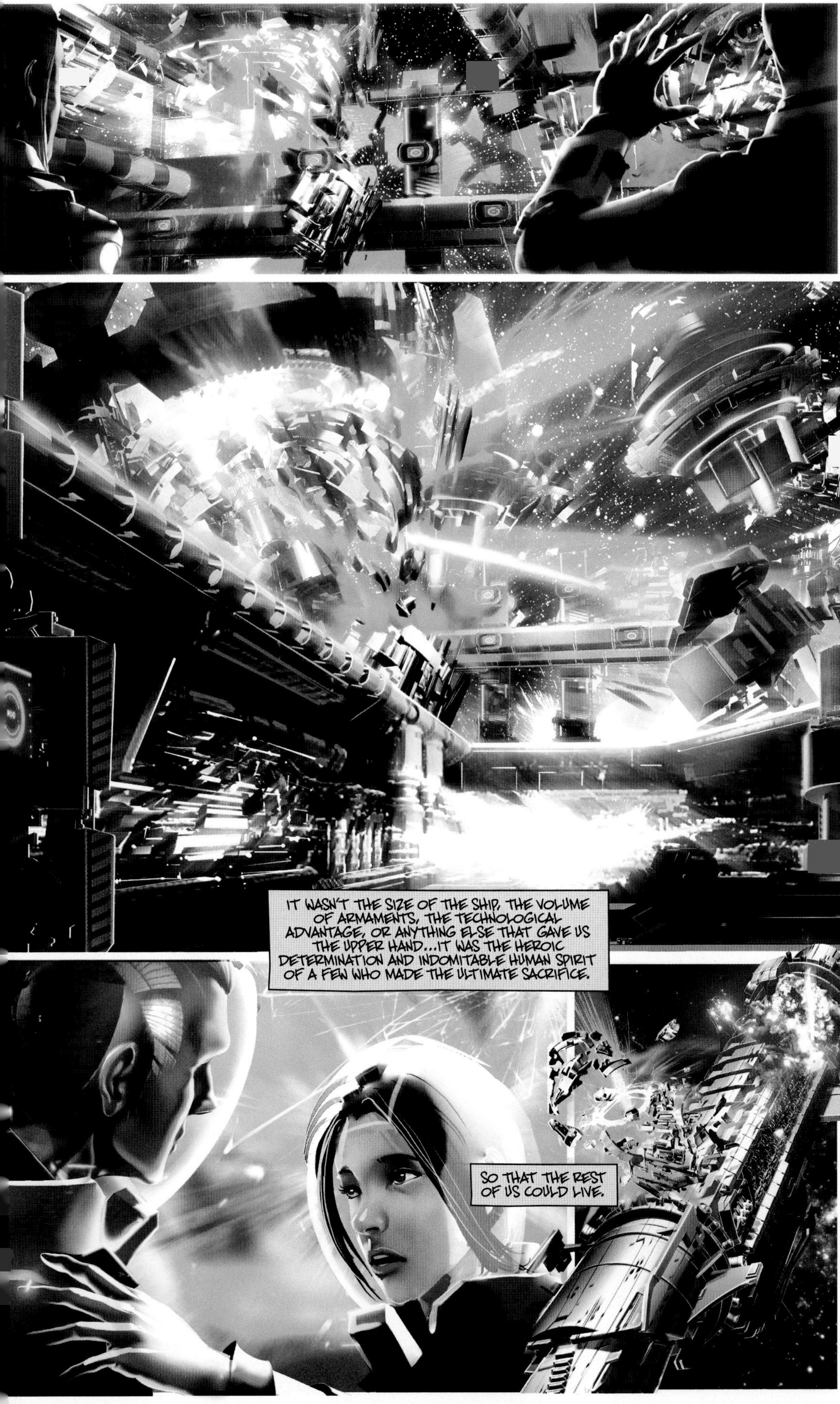
IT WASN'T THE SIZE OF THE SHIP, THE VOLUME OF ARMAMENTS, THE TECHNOLOGICAL ADVANTAGE, OR ANYTHING ELSE THAT GAVE US THE UPPER HAND...IT WAS THE HEROIC DETERMINATION AND INDOMITABLE HUMAN SPIRIT OF A FEW WHO MADE THE ULTIMATE SACRIFICE.
SO THAT THE REST OF US COULD LIVE.

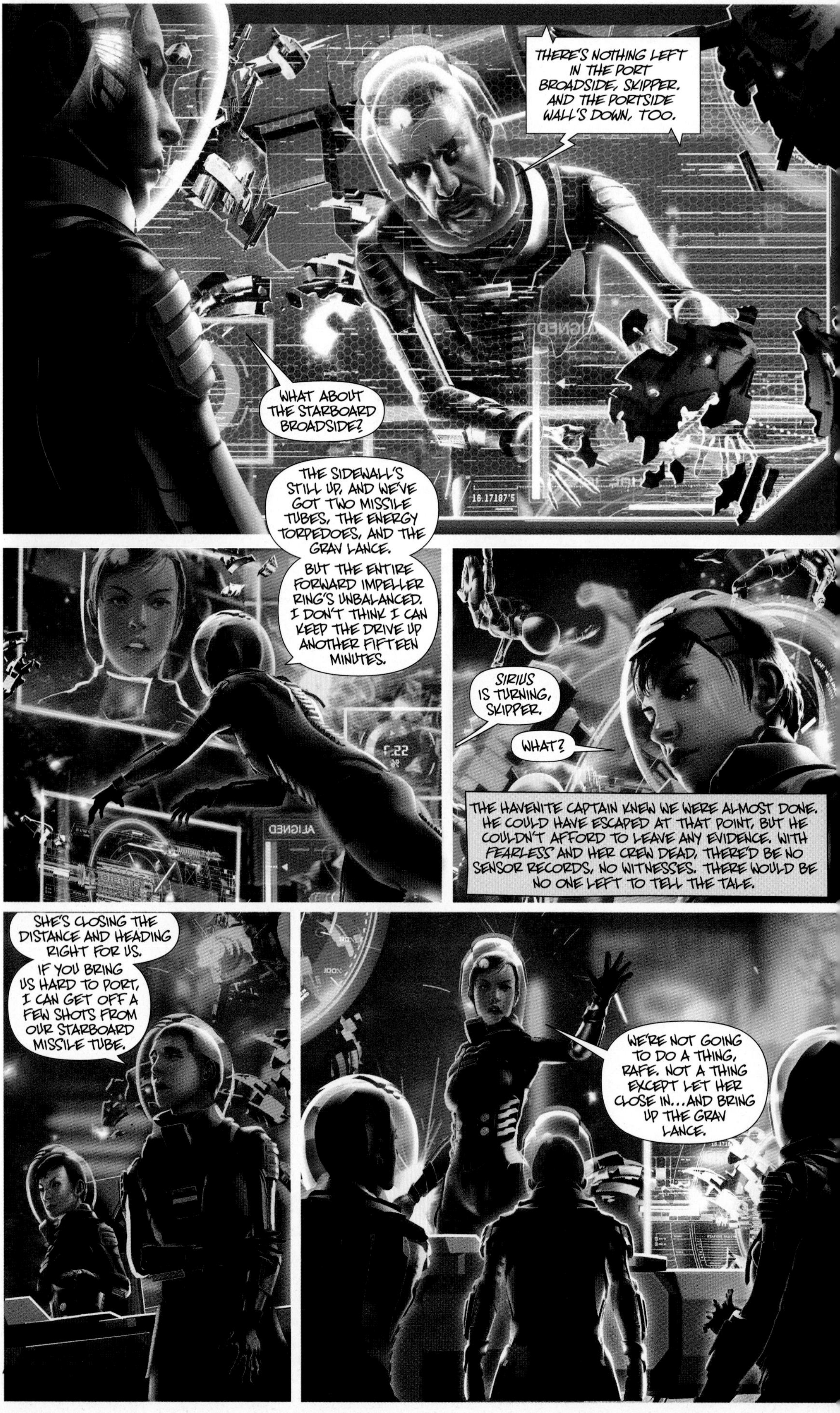
THERE'S NOTHING LEFT IN THE PORT BROADSIDE, SKIPPER. AND THE PORTSIDE WALL'S DOWN, TOO.
WHAT ABOUT THE STARBOARD BROADSIDE?
THE SIDEWALL'S STILL UP, AND WE'VE GOT TWO MISSILE TUBES, THE ENERGY TORPEDOES, AND THE GRAV LANCE.
BUT THE ENTIRE FORWARD IMPELLER RING'S UNBALANCED. I DON'T THINK I CAN KEEP THE DRIVE UP ANOTHER FIFTEEN MINUTES.
SIRIUS IS TURNING, SKIPPER.
WHAT?
THE HAVENITE CAPTAIN KNEW WE WERE ALMOST DONE. HE COULD HAVE ESCAPED AT THAT POINT, BUT HE COULDN'T AFFORD TO LEAVE ANY EVIDENCE. WITH FEARLESS AND HER CREW DEAD, THERE'D BE NO SENSOR RECORDS, NO WITNESSES. THERE WOULD BE NO ONE LEFT TO TELL THE TALE.
SHE'S CLOSING THE DISTANCE AND HEADING RIGHT FOR US.
IF YOU BRING US HARD TO PORT, I CAN GET OFF A FEW SHOTS FROM OUR STARBOARD MISSILE TUBE.
WE'RE NOT GOING TO DO A THING, RAFE. NOT A THING EXCEPT LET HER CLOSE IN...AND BRING UP THE GRAV LANCE.

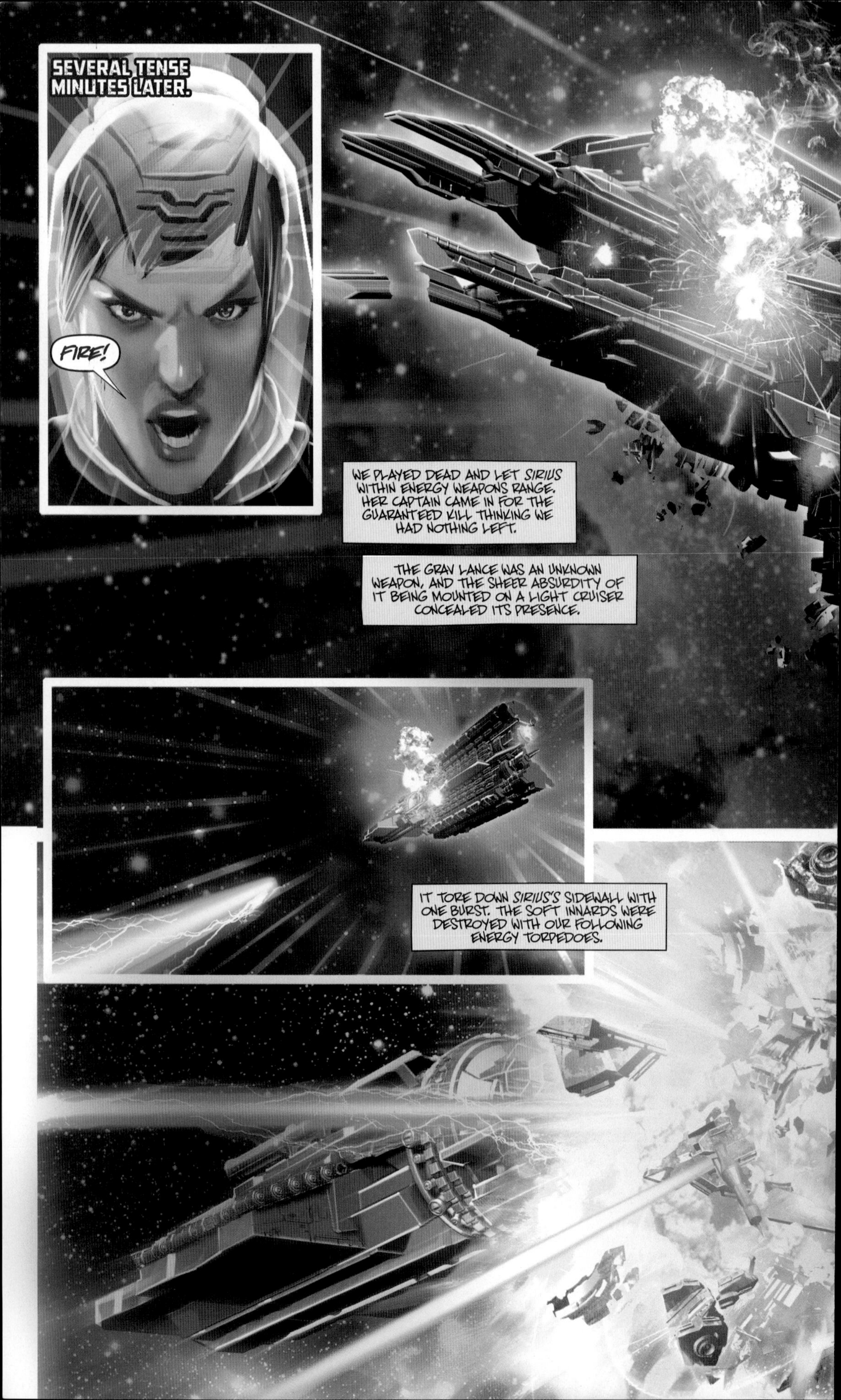
SEVERAL TENSE MINUTES LATER.
FIRE!
WE PLAYED DEAD AND LET SIRIUS WITHIN ENERGY WEAPONS RANGE. HER CAPTAIN CAME IN FOR THE GUARANTEED KILL THINKING WE HAD NOTHING LEFT.
THE GRAV LANCE WAS AN UNKNOWN WEAPON, AND THE SHEER ABSURDITY OF IT BEING MOUNTED ON A LIGHT CRUISER CONCEALED ITS PRESENCE.
IT TORE DOWN SIRIUS'S SIDEWALL WITH ONE BURST. THE SOFT INNARDS WERE DESTROYED WITH OUR FOLLOWING ENERGY TORPEDOES.

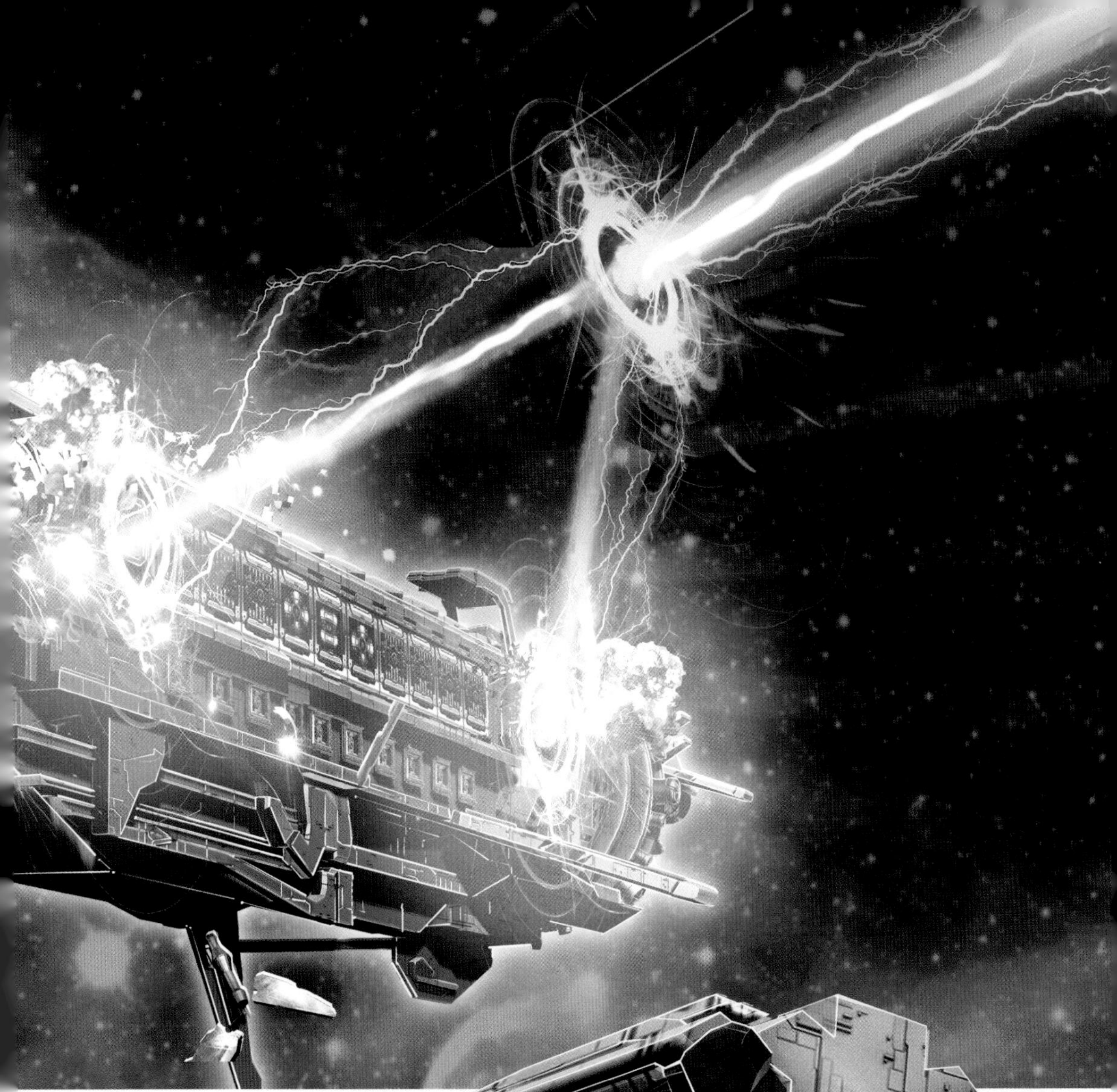

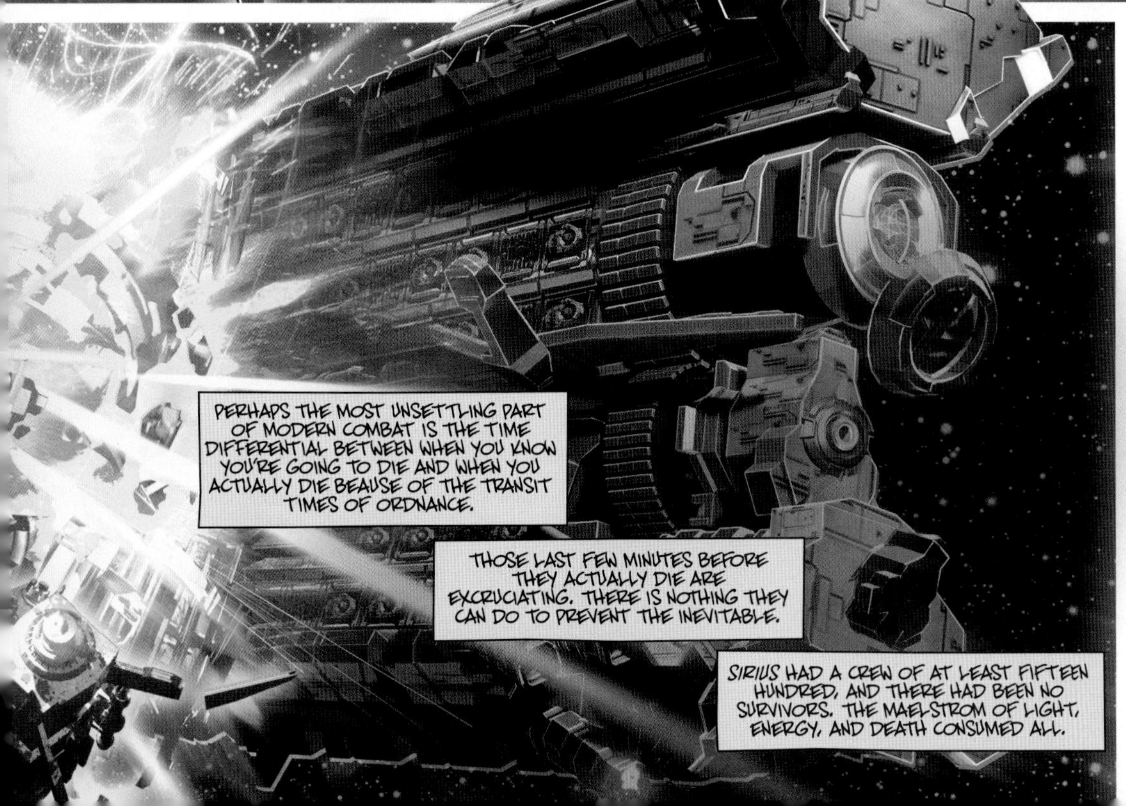
PERHAPS THE MOST UNSETTLING PART OF MODERN COMBAT IS THE TIME DIFFERENTIAL BETWEEN WHEN YOU KNOW YOU'RE GOING TO DIE AND WHEN YOU ACTUALLY DIE BEAUSE OF THE TRANSIT TIMES OF ORDNANCE.
THOSE LAST FEW MINUTES BEFORE THEY ACTUALLY DIE ARE EXCRUCIATING. THERE IS NOTHING THEY CAN DO TO PREVENT THE INEVITABLE.
SIRIUS HAD A CREW OF AT LEAST FIFTEEN HUNDRED, AND THERE HAD BEEN NO SURVIVORS. THE MAELSTROM OF LIGHT, ENERGY, AND DEATH CONSUMED ALL.

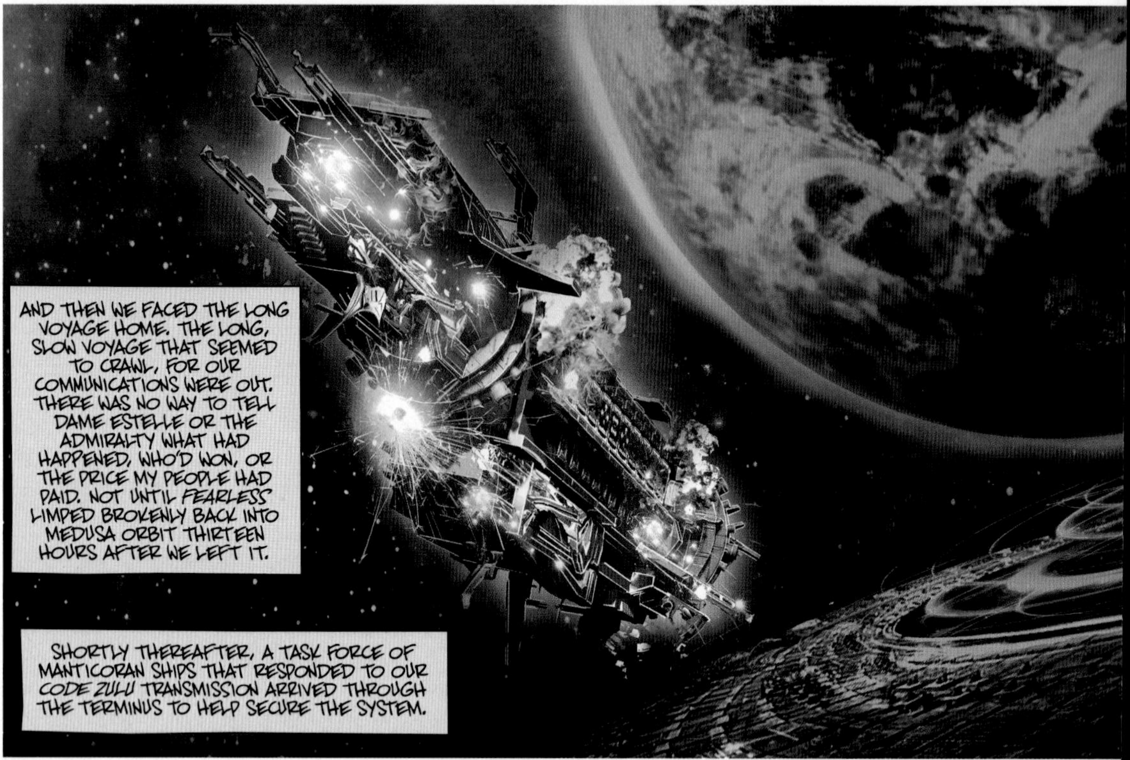
AND THEN WE FACED THE LONG VOYAGE HOME. THE LONG, SLOW VOYAGE THAT SEEMED TO CRAWL, FOR OUR COMMUNICATIONS WERE OUT. THERE WAS NO WAY TO TELL DAME ESTELLE OR THE ADMIRALTY WHAT HAD HAPPENED, WHO'D WON, OR THE PRICE MY PEOPLE HAD PAID. NOT UNTIL *FEARLESS* LIMPED BROKENLY BACK INTO MEDUSA ORBIT THIRTEEN HOURS AFTER WE LEFT IT.
SHORTLY THEREAFTER, A TASK FORCE OF MANTICORAN SHIPS THAT RESPONDED TO OUR *CODE ZULU* TRANSMISSION ARRIVED THROUGH THE TERMINUS TO HELP SECURE THE SYSTEM.
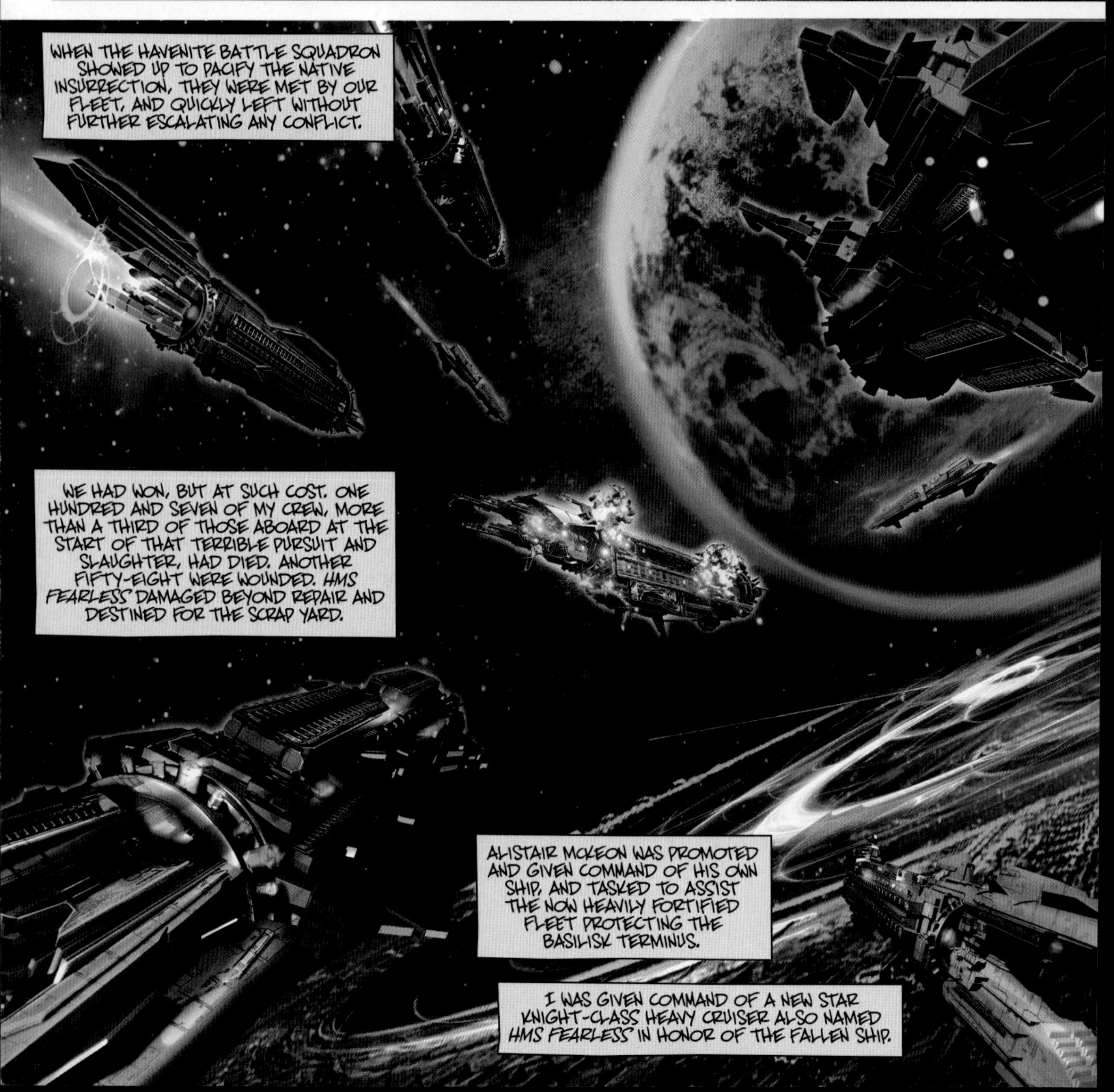
WHEN THE HAVENITE BATTLE SQUADRON SHOWED UP TO PACIFY THE NATIVE INSURRECTION, THEY WERE MET BY OUR FLEET, AND QUICKLY LEFT WITHOUT FURTHER ESCALATING ANY CONFLICT.
WE HAD WON, BUT AT SUCH COST. ONE HUNDRED AND SEVEN OF MY CREW, MORE THAN A THIRD OF THOSE ABOARD AT THE START OF THAT TERRIBLE PURSUIT AND SLAUGHTER, HAD DIED. ANOTHER FIFTY-EIGHT WERE WOUNDED. HMS *FEARLESS* DAMAGED BEYOND REPAIR AND DESTINED FOR THE SCRAP YARD.
ALISTAIR MCKEON WAS PROMOTED AND GIVEN COMMAND OF HIS OWN SHIP, AND TASKED TO ASSIST THE NOW HEAVILY FORTIFIED FLEET PROTECTING THE BASILISK TERMINUS.
I WAS GIVEN COMMAND OF A NEW STAR KNIGHT-CLASS HEAVY CRUISER ALSO NAMED HMS *FEARLESS* IN HONOR OF THE FALLEN SHIP.

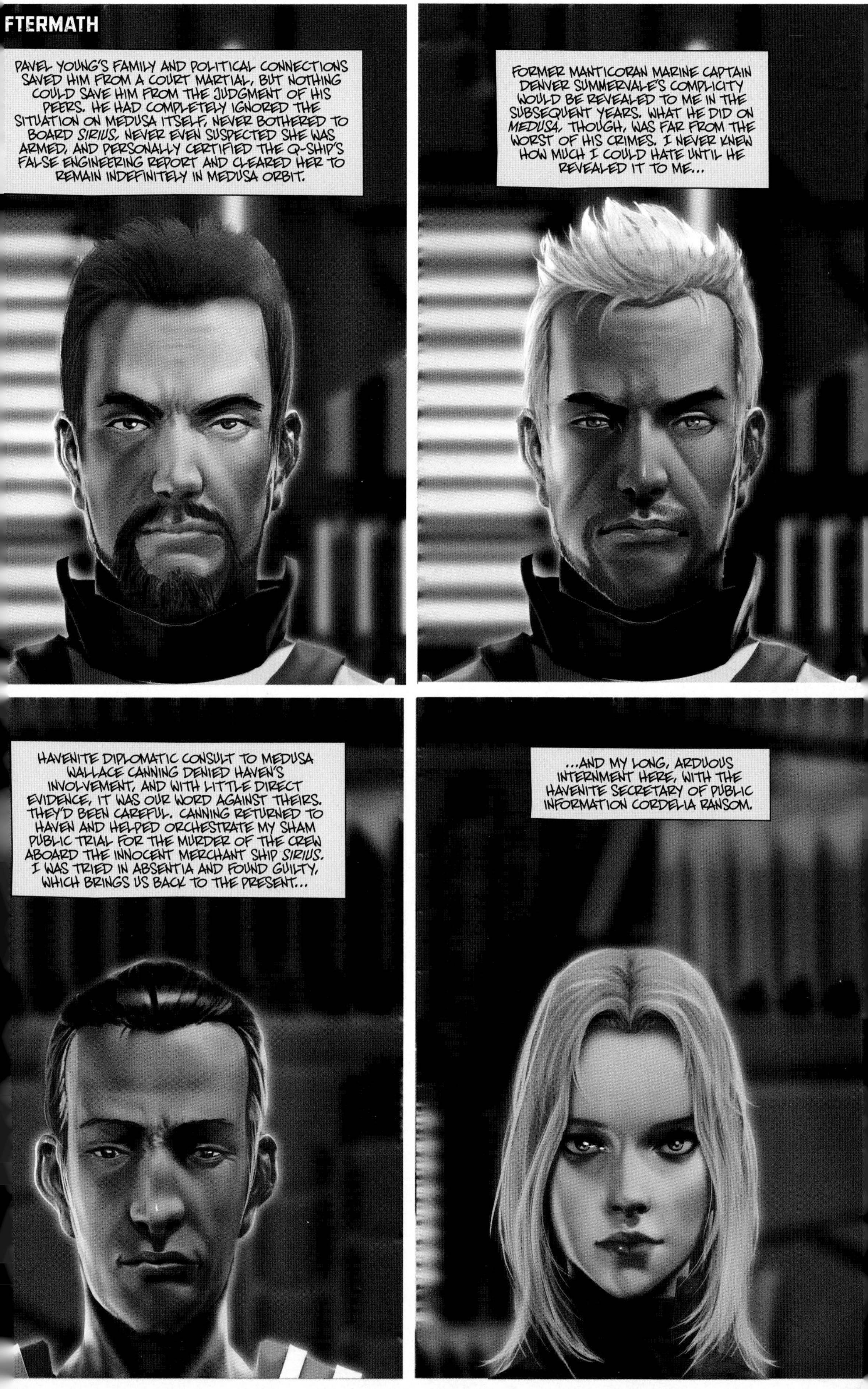
FTERMATH
PAVEL YOUNG'S FAMILY AND POLITICAL CONNECTIONS SAVED HIM FROM A COURT MARTIAL, BUT NOTHING COULD SAVE HIM FROM THE JUDGMENT OF HIS PEERS. HE HAD COMPLETELY IGNORED THE SITUATION ON MEDUSA ITSELF, NEVER BOTHERED TO BOARD SIRIUS, NEVER EVEN SUSPECTED SHE WAS ARMED, AND PERSONALLY CERTIFIED THE Q-SHIP'S FALSE ENGINEERING REPORT AND CLEARED HER TO REMAIN INDEFINITELY IN MEDUSA ORBIT.
FORMER MANTICORAN MARINE CAPTAIN DENVER SUMMERVALE'S COMPLICITY WOULD BE REVEALED TO ME IN THE SUBSEQUENT YEARS. WHAT HE DID ON MEDUSA, THOUGH, WAS FAR FROM THE WORST OF HIS CRIMES. I NEVER KNEW HOW MUCH I COULD HATE UNTIL HE REVEALED IT TO ME...
HAVENITE DIPLOMATIC CONSULT TO MEDUSA WALLACE CANNING DENIED HAVEN'S INVOLVEMENT, AND WITH LITTLE DIRECT EVIDENCE, IT WAS OUR WORD AGAINST THEIRS. THEY'D BEEN CAREFUL. CANNING RETURNED TO HAVEN AND HELPED ORCHESTRATE MY SHAM PUBLIC TRIAL FOR THE MURDER OF THE CREW ABOARD THE INNOCENT MERCHANT SHIP SIRIUS. I WAS TRIED IN ABSENTIA AND FOUND GUILTY, WHICH BRINGS US BACK TO THE PRESENT...
...AND MY LONG, ARDUOUS INTERNMENT HERE, WITH THE HAVENITE SECRETARY OF PUBLIC INFORMATION CORDELIA RANSOM.

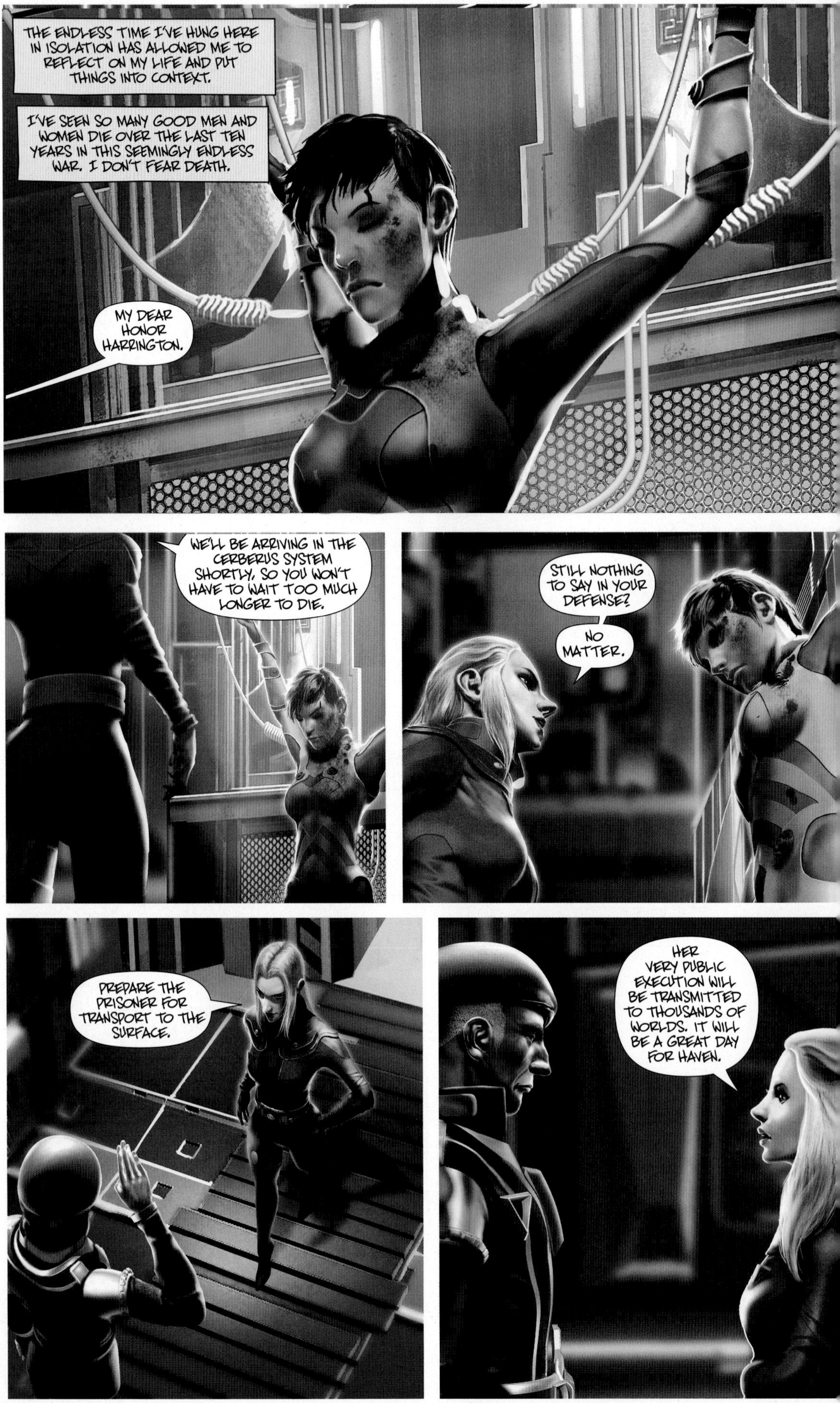
THE ENDLESS TIME I'VE HUNG HERE IN ISOLATION HAS ALLOWED ME TO REFLECT ON MY LIFE AND PUT THINGS INTO CONTEXT.
I'VE SEEN SO MANY GOOD MEN AND WOMEN DIE OVER THE LAST TEN YEARS IN THIS SEEMINGLY ENDLESS WAR. I DON'T FEAR DEATH.
MY DEAR HONOR HARRINGTON.
WE'LL BE ARRIVING IN THE CERBERUS SYSTEM SHORTLY, SO YOU WON'T HAVE TO WAIT TOO MUCH LONGER TO DIE.
STILL NOTHING TO SAY IN YOUR DEFENSE?
NO MATTER.
PREPARE THE PRISONER FOR TRANSPORT TO THE SURFACE.
HER VERY PUBLIC EXECUTION WILL BE TRANSMITTED TO THOUSANDS OF WORLDS. IT WILL BE A GREAT DAY FOR HAVEN.

TALES OF HONOR

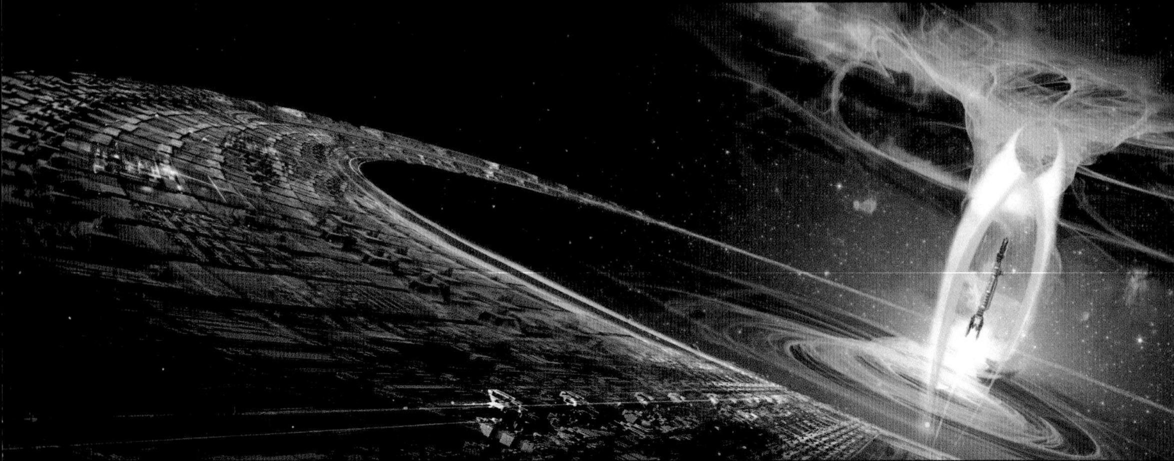

SCIENCE CLASS – TALES OF HONOR EDITION

Wel[redacted]to *Tales of Honor Volume* 1! I'm very proud of this book you hold in you[redacted]s (or view on your tablet). You've probably figured out by this point that this comic book is based on the long-vrunning series of *Honor Harrington* novels written by David Weber, collectively called the Honorverse. The first one, *On Basilisk Station*, is available for free download on Kindle and on Ibooks, and is a fantastic read. I recommend you all go download it.

Kindle: http://goo.gl/klmjWS

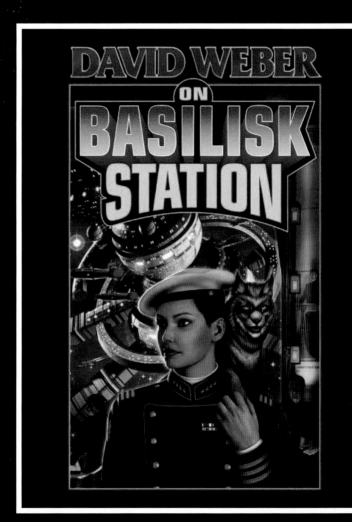

For those of you already famil[redacted]th the *Honor Harrington* novels, you'll recognize that this comic story[redacted]actually starts in the 7th novel, *In Enemy Hands*. It then jumps back [redacted]*n Basilisk Station*, but doesn't follow that in a linear fashion. This is by[redacted]gn, and something th[redacted]e folk at Evergreen Studios[redacted]David Weber, and I all agreed upon before this all got started. So you understa[redacted]d, the intent is to tell he[redacted]recollections of events while under duress, which allows me a bit of latitud[redacted]o adapt the story into a comic book format.

DAVID WEBER
ON
BASILISK
STATION

I should talk about Evergreen Studios for a[redacted]inute. They're the [redacted]pany behind the recent *Walking with Dinosaurs* film, and they are developing the Honorverse into a series of films. They'[redacted]een great to work with[redacted]ithout them this comi[redacted]d not exist.

http://www.tales-of-honor.com

Write in your questions, thoughts, and commentary to fanmail@topcow.com and I'll answer some of that here. We also have an active community on our web[redacted]site with message boards that will include a new section specifically for *Tales of Honor*.

Our site is: http://www.topcow.com/

The following few pages show some behind-the-scenes development materials a[redacted]designs, in addition to some extra info on the series and other media for *Tales of Honor*. Thanks for giving this book a shot. I hope you enjoy it.

HONOR HARRINGTON DESIGN PROCESS

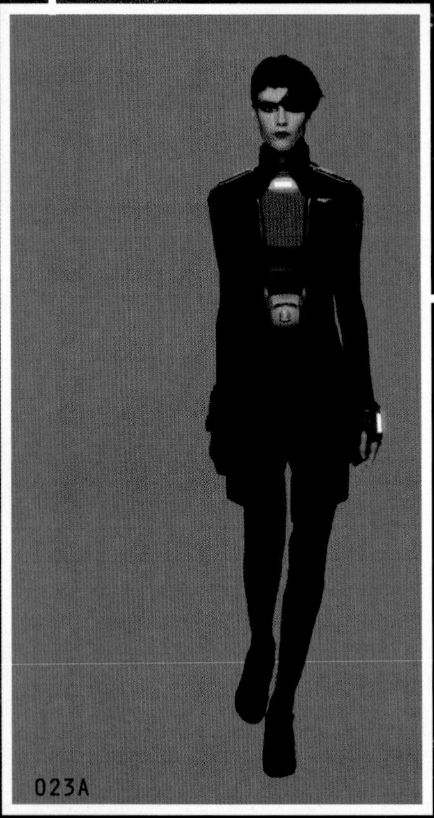
023A

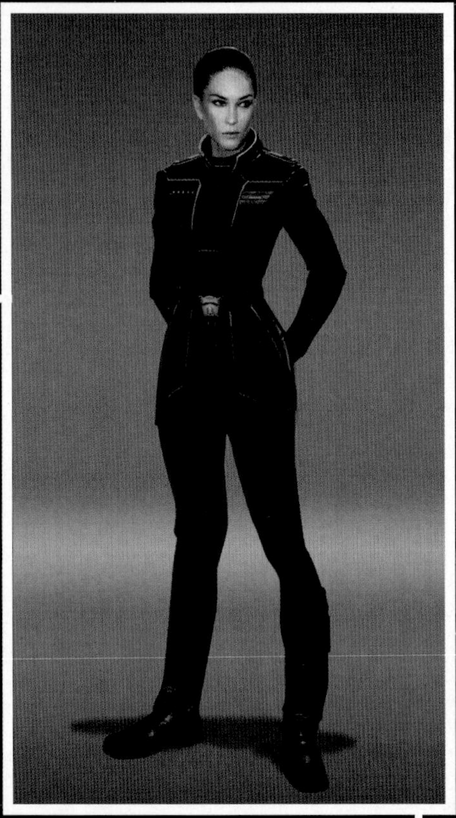

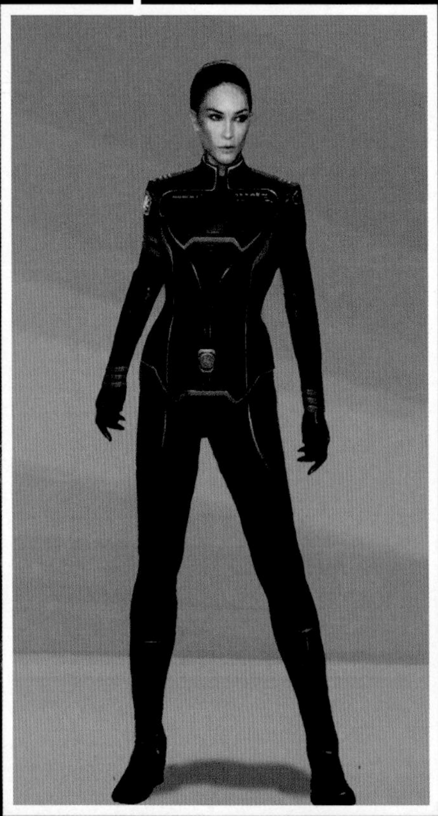

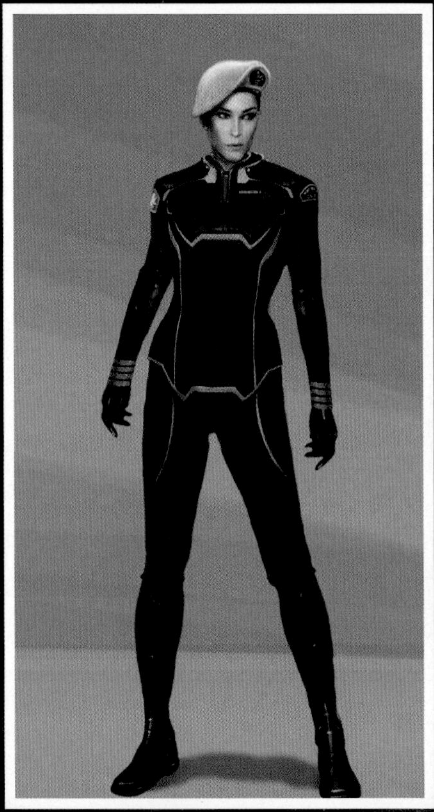

EARLY NIMITZ DESIGN BY BLUR STUDIO

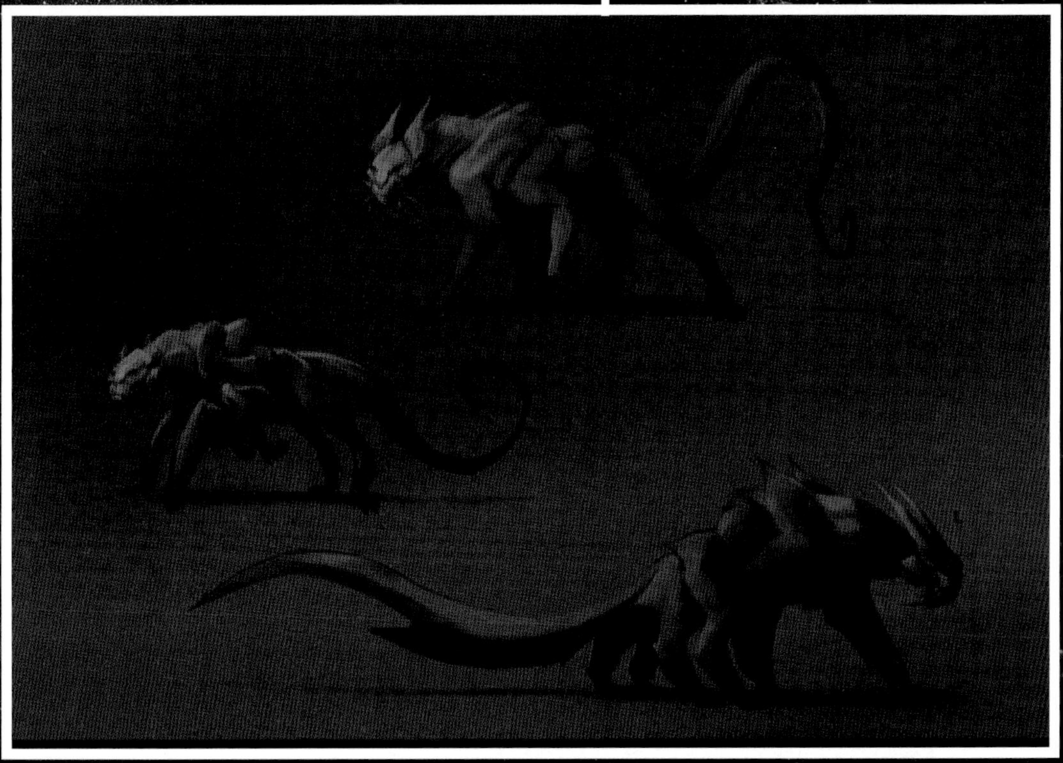

STILTIE DESIGN BY STJEPAN SEJIC

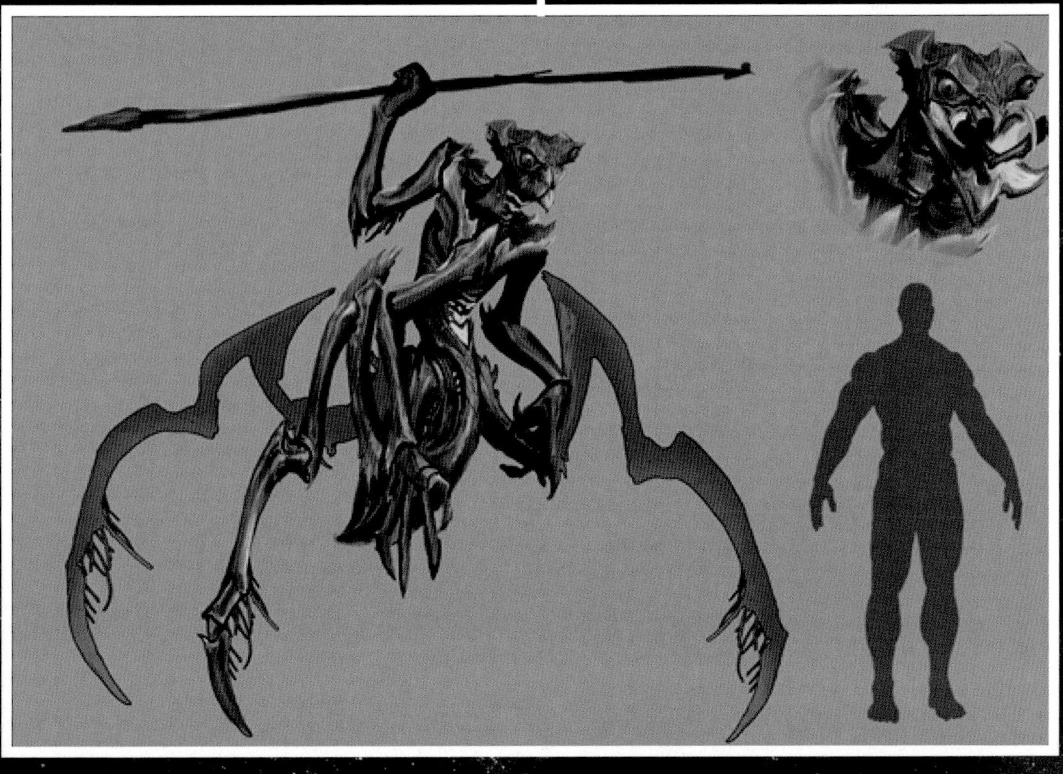

HMS FEARLESS DESIGN

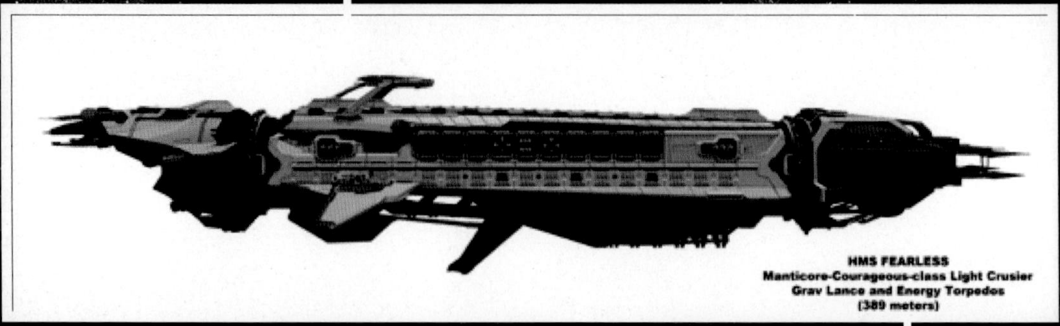
HMS FEARLESS
Manticore-Courageous-class Light Crusier
Grav Lance and Energy Torpedos
(389 meters)

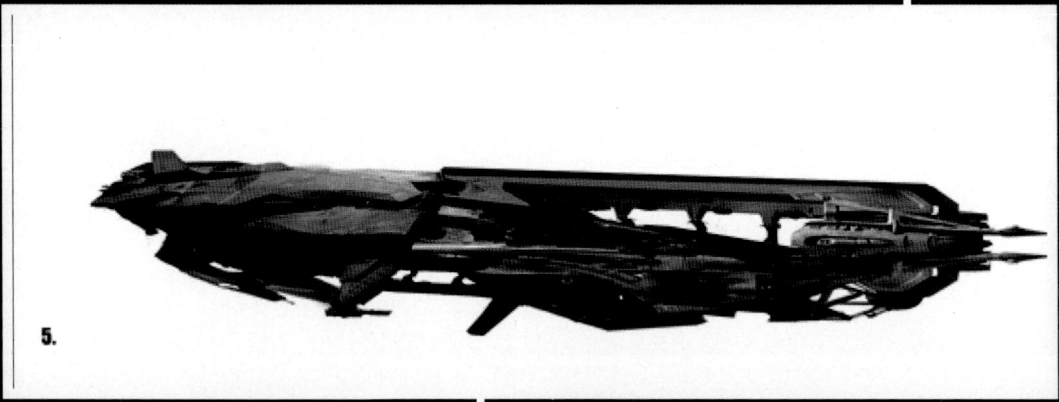
5.

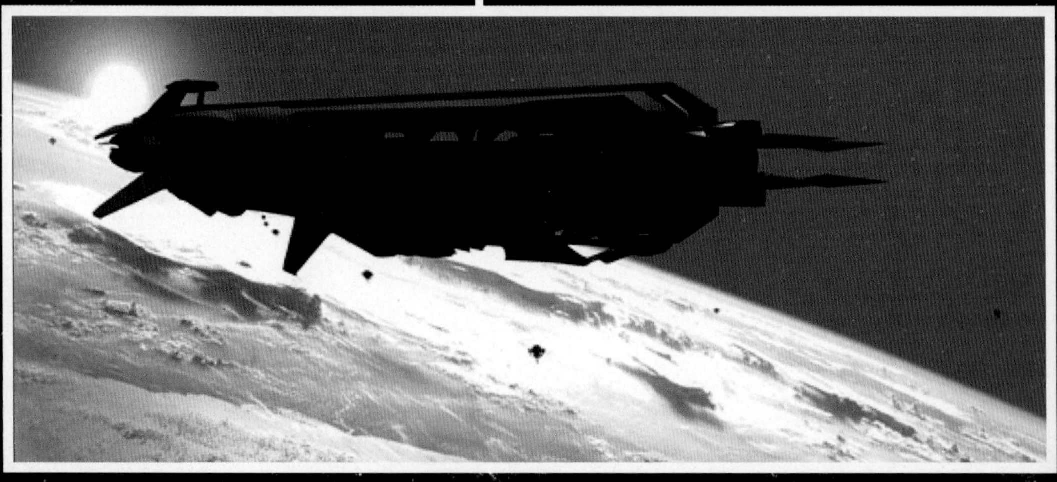

HEPHAESTUS SPACE STATION DESIGN

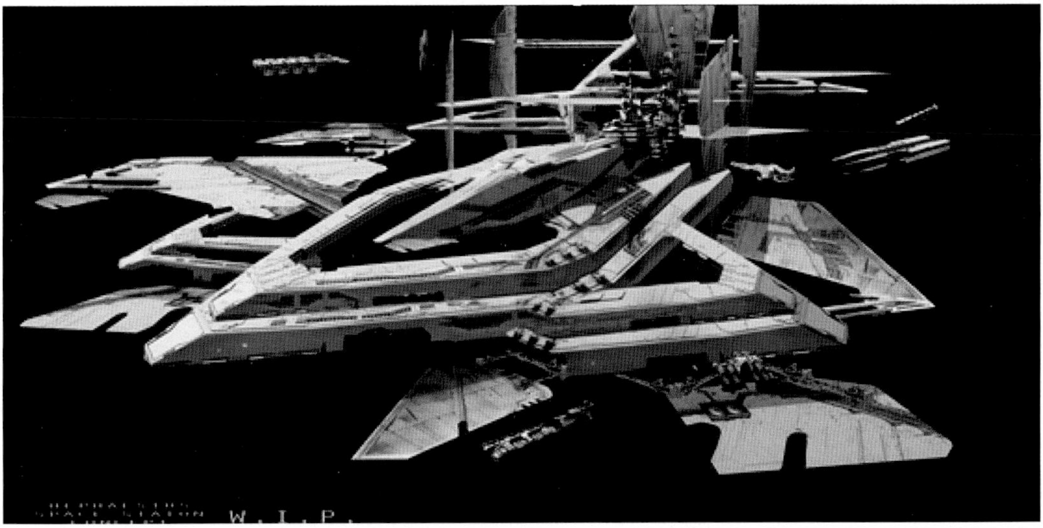
W.I.P.

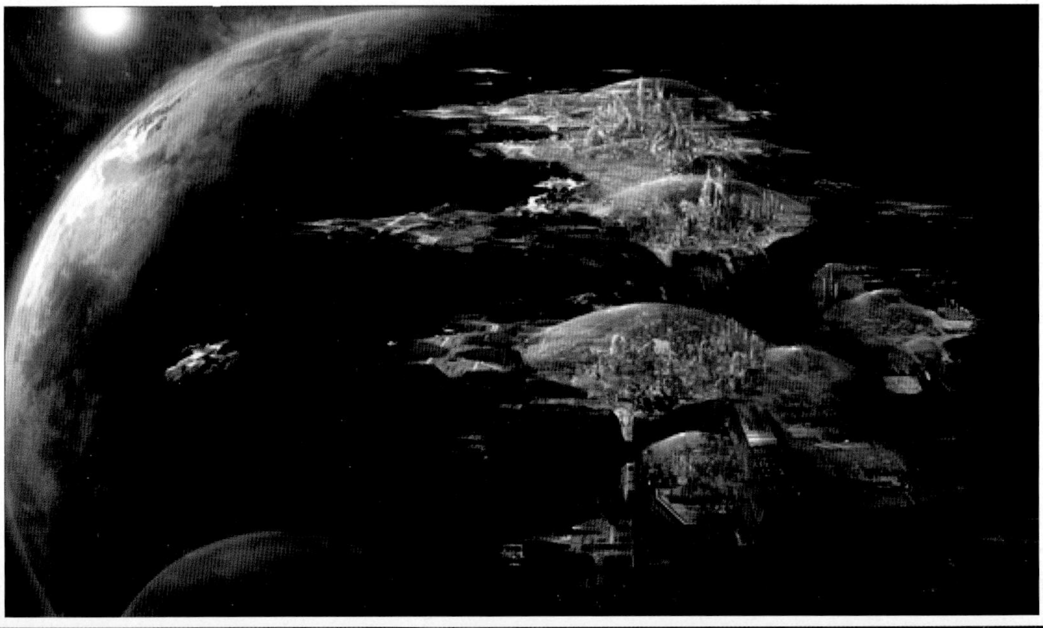

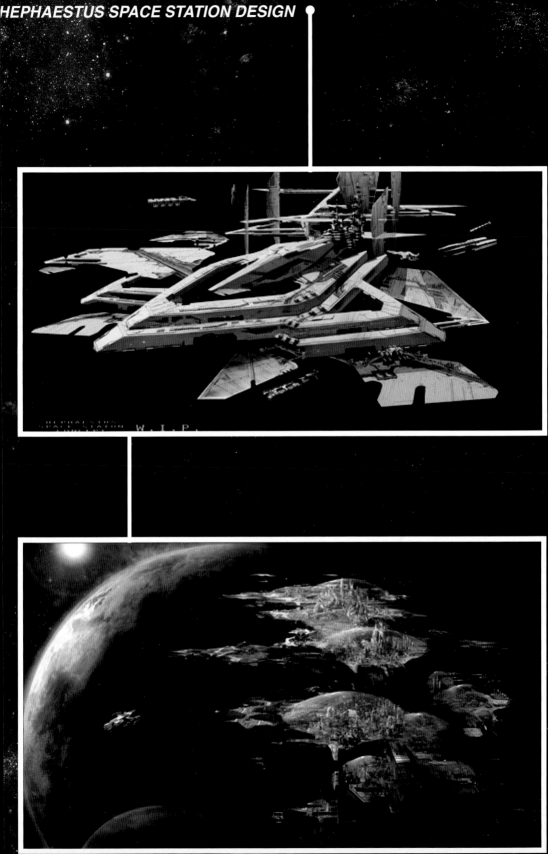

"Gravity sidewalls were the first and primary line of defense for every warship. The impeller drive created a pair of stressed gravity bands above and below a ship—a wedge, open at both ends, though the forward edge was far deeper than the after one—capable in theory of instant acceleration to light speed. Of course, that kind of acceleration would turn any crew to gory goo...

...Even with modern inertial compensators, the best acceleration any warship could pull under impeller was well under six hundred gravities, but it had been a tremendous step forward. And not simply in terms of propulsion; even today no known weapon could penetrate the main drive bands of a military-grade impeller wedge, which meant simply powering its impellers protected a ship against any fire from above or below.

But that had left the sides of the impeller wedge, for they, too, were open—until someone invented the gravity sidewall and extended protection to its flanks. The bow and stern aspects still couldn't be closed, even by a sidewall, and the most powerful sidewall ever generated was far weaker than a drive band.

Sidewalls could be penetrated, particularly by missiles fitted with penetration aids, but it took a powerful energy weapon at very short range (relatively speaking) to pierce them with any effect, and that limited beams to a range of no more than four hundred thousand kilometers.

It also meant that deep-space battles had a nasty tendency to end in tactical draws, however important they might be strategically. When one fleet realized it was in trouble, it simply turned its ships up on their sides, presenting only the impenetrable aspects of its individual units' impeller wedges, while it endeavored to break off the action.

The only counter was a resolute pursuit, but that, in turn, exposed the unguarded frontal arcs of the pursuers' wedges, inviting raking fire straight down their throats as they attempted to close. Cruiser actions were more often fought to the finish, but engagements between capital ships all too often had the formalism of some intricate dance in which both sides knew all the steps."

Excerpt from *On Basilisk Station* by David Weber

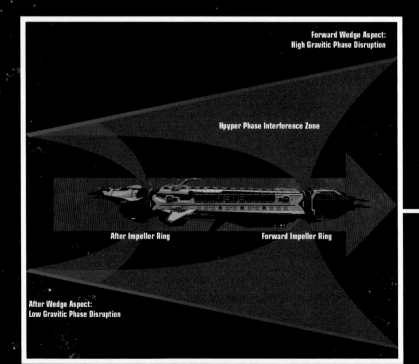

Forward Wedge Aspect:
High Gravitic Phase Disruption

Hpyper Phase Interference Zone

After Impeller Ring

Forward Impeller Ring

After Wedge Aspect:
Low Gravitic Phase Disruption

NIMITZ

The biggest source of concern from he pre-existing fans has been Nimitz's ppearance. This has been a work-in-progress from day one and has been ltered many times. Balancing the idea f a cute and cuddly cat-like creature with six legs, w[redacted]e correspondingly being a ad ass is not the easiest thing to convey isually. I'm not an artist, but I feel for the nu[redacted]e people who've taken a stab at his[redacted]This image with additional fur will be sed in the second arc of the comic series *Tales of Honor: Honor of the Queen.*

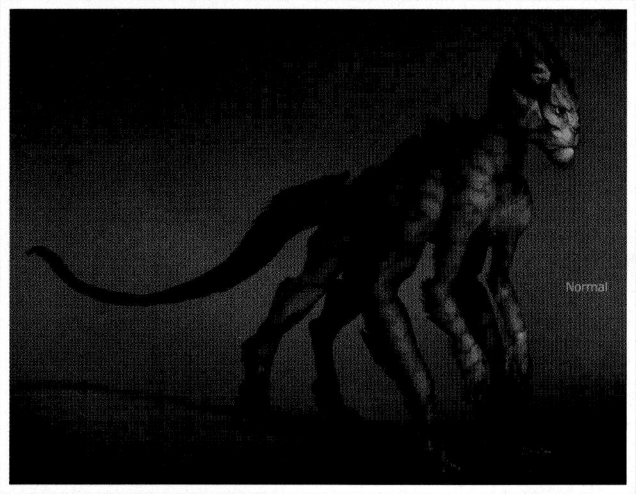
Normal

CHARACTER BIOS

There are a lot of characters in this series[redacted]We'll be highlighting some ere and in future volumes.

HONOR HARRINGTON:

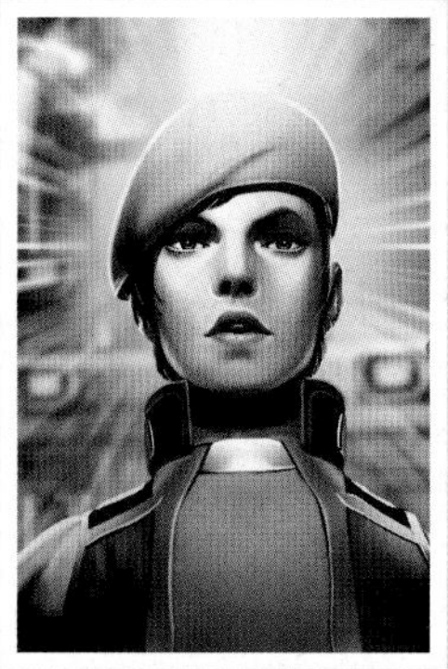

onor Harrington was born on October 1st, 1859 (Post-Diaspora) n the planet Sphinx to physician parents. From the time she was young girl Honor knew she wanted to be in the Royal Manticoran Navy. Although both of her parents were physicians, Honor enlisted n the R[redacted]Manticoran Naval Academy and emerged an officer. The mil[redacted]life suited her – Honor rose through the ranks quickly, aining command of the *HMS Fearless*, a light cruiser, in the year 900[redacted]An intelligent, determined soldier, Honor dislikes favoritism nd commands the respect of her crew firmly yet fairly.

NIMITZ:

Treecats are a native species of the planet Sphinx, where Honor Harrington was born. As a pecies, they are "tele-empathic"- meaning they can sense the feelings of those around them - and ossess the unique ability to mentally bond with human beings, becoming companions for life and orming a permanent psychic link. Nimitz and Honor formed such a bond when she was 12 years ld. Th[redacted]ugh he is known as "Laughs Brightly' to his clan, Honor named him after Admiral Chester Nimi[redacted]Commander-in-Chief of the United States Navy during World War II. A highly intelligent reature, Nimitz is precocious and brave, but above all loyal to Honor.

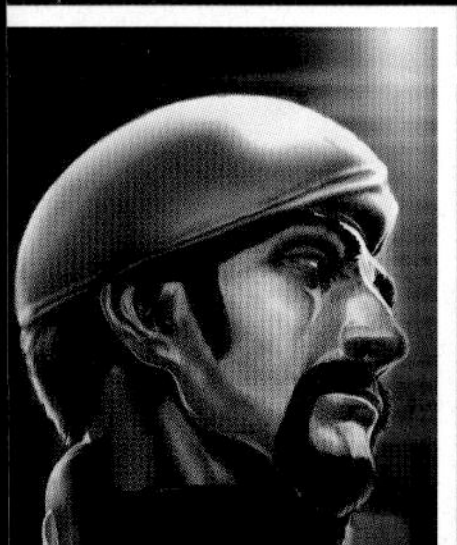

ALISTAIR MCKEON:

McKeon was the First Lieutenant aboard the *HMS Fearless*, first under Captain Rath and, after running the ship mid-transition, under Commander Honor Harrington. While McKeon assists Honor to the best of his ability and never questions her authority in public, he frequently questions her placement in charge of the *Fearless,* professing personal jealousy on being passed up for the position himself, as well as suspicion toward Honor's intentions. In spite of this, he is good man and a dedicated soldier, determined to ensure success for all aboard the *Fearless.*

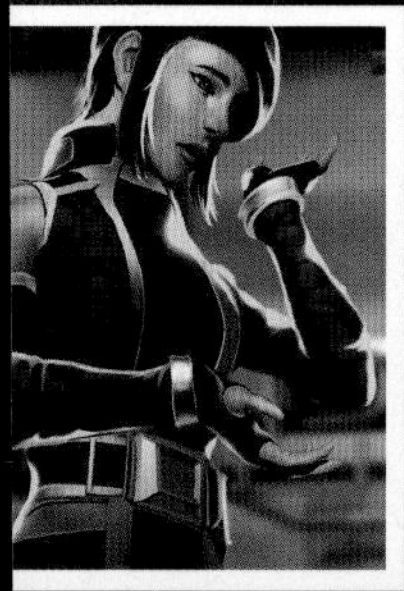

DOMINICA SANTOS:

Chief Engineer aboard the *HMS Fearless*, holding the rank of Lieutenant Commander, Dominica Santos was in charge of programming and preparing recon droids for use on the planet Medusa. Close friends with Alistair McKeon and mistrustful of Honor Harrington, Santos is more open about her misgivings for the Fearless' new commander, but, like McKeon, is an incredibly talented and capable crewmember, invaluable to the *Fearless*' operations.

CORDELIA RANSOM:

A propagandist with the government of the Republic of Haven, Cordelia is beautiful, deadly, and a master at manipulating information. She has nothing but loathing for the military establishment, viewing it only as a mean to her ends – which is why, from her perspective, the public assassination of Commander Honor Harrington of the Manticoran Alliance represents the ultimate publicity stunt, and an opportunity to change the tides of war in favor of Haven.

PAVEL YOUNG:

The spoiled son of the powerful Earl of North Hollow, Young lived a life of entitlement. While attending the Royal Manticoran Naval Academy, he attempted to rape fellow cadet Honor Harrington – who, although putting a stop to the assault, never reported it. Later, as captain of the *HMS Warlock*, Young accompanied his vessel on an extended refit, forcing Honor and the *HMS Fearless* to take his place on Basilisk Station, intending for her to fail in her mission there and be disgraced.

DENVER SUMMERVALE:

A captain in the Royal Manticoran Marine Corps, Summervale accumulated a vast debt, and agreed to duel fellow royals for pay – eventually becoming addicted to the thrill of professional dueling. Classically dishonorable and travelling in royal circles with such questionable characters as Pavel Young, Summervale is a scoundrel of the worst variety, with a suspicious interest in the planet Medusa.

MEDUSANS:

Sentient race of the Basilisk System and situated on the planet Medusa, the people colloquially referred to as Stilties were technologically unadvanced until the arrival of human beings. With advanced weaponry bestowed upon them by the People's Republic of Haven, the previously nomadic and peaceful Stilties began to organize and attack Manticoran forces on the planet. Human interaction with the Medusans also led the Stilties to develop addiction to mekoha, a drug developed from local vegetation.

SUPPORTING WEB SITES

http://tales-of-honor.com

This is the web site built by Evergreen Studios, and a hub for all things going on with film, comic, book and video game. It's definitely worth checking out.

http://honorverse.wikia.com/wiki/Main_Page

This is a custom Wiki that is filled with awesome information, and the folks who keep it updated do a fantastic job.

http://www.davidweber.net/

This is the home site for David Weber, creator and novel author of *Honor Harrington* and many other great books! There is a very active community here that loves to talk about all things Honor.

TALES OF HONOR VIDEO GAME

A "free to play" mobile game app is available now on both the iOS and Android platforms. This starship combat game allows the player to battle their way through the Honorverse, unveiling new ships, new worlds, and ever evolving new experiences.

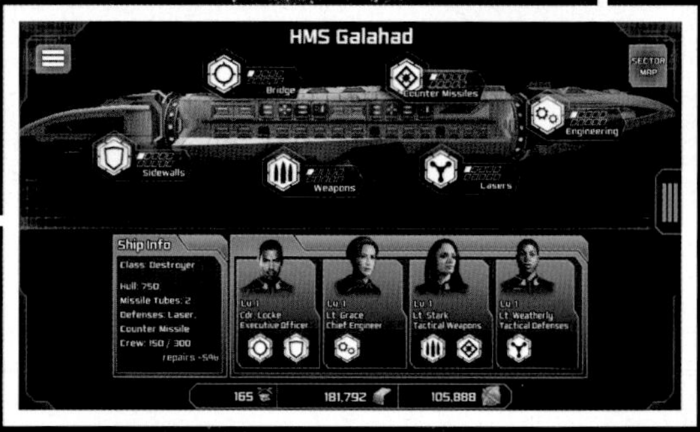
HMS Galahad
SECTOR MAP
Bridge
Counter Missiles
Engineering
Sidewalls
Weapons
Lasers
Ship Info
Class: Destroyer
Hull: 750
Missile Tubes: 2
Defenses: Laser, Counter Missile
Crew: 150 / 300
Cdr. Locke
Executive Officer
Lt. Grace
Chief Engineer
Lt. Stark
Tactical Weapons
Lt. Weatherly
Tactical Defenses
165
181,792
105,888

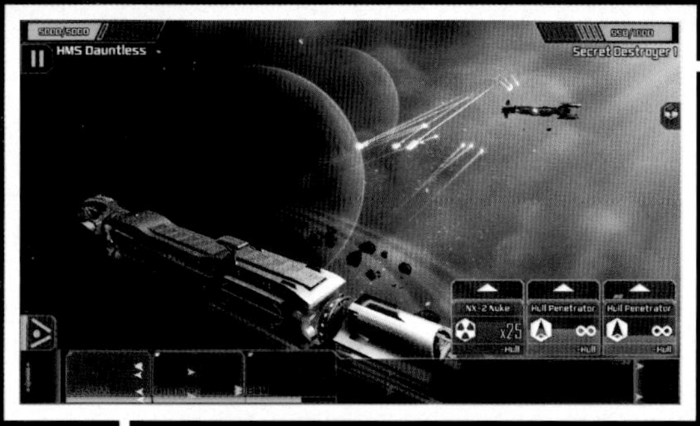
HMS Dauntless
NX-2 Nuke
Hull Penetrator
Hull Penetrator
x25

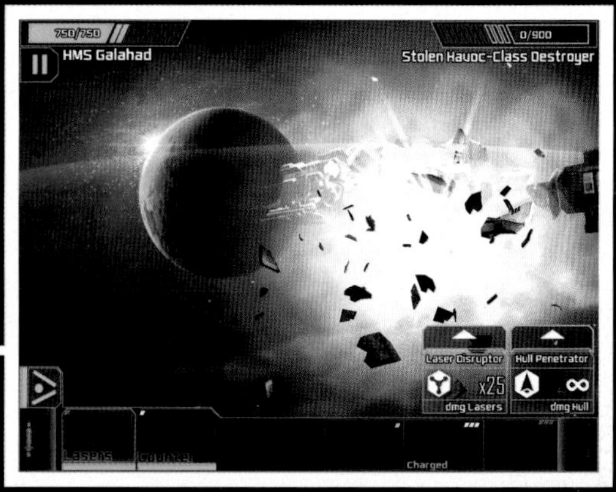
750/750
HMS Galahad
0/900
Stolen Havoc-Class Destroyer
Laser Disruptor
Hull Penetrator
x25
dmg Lasers
dmg Hull
Charged

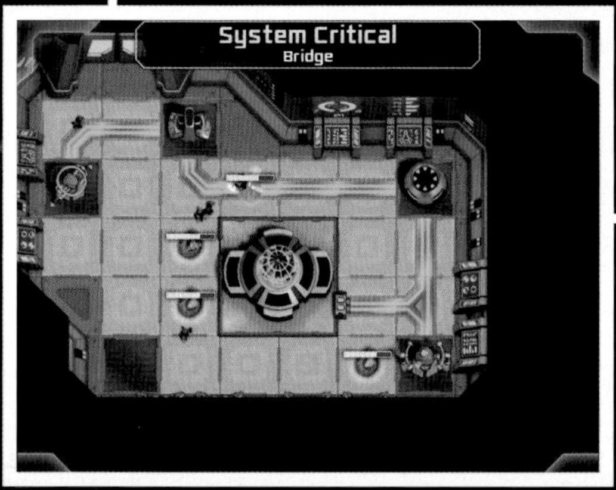
System Critical
Bridge

CONCEPT ART

Evergreen Studios works with phenomenal concept artist Matt Codd. He's done a lot of these designs and is simply awesome. He's done a lot of the environment shots that we've used in the series. He also painted these pages from this issue and the last:

His home site is: http://www.mattcodd.com/Matt_Codd/Concept_Art/Concept_Art.html

You may have realized that the Honorverse factors in economics and geopolitics into its storyline. I love this stuff and a big part of it are the merchant cartels of the various star systems. Each issue I want to delve into some behind the scenes stuff, so we're hitting the merchants in this one.

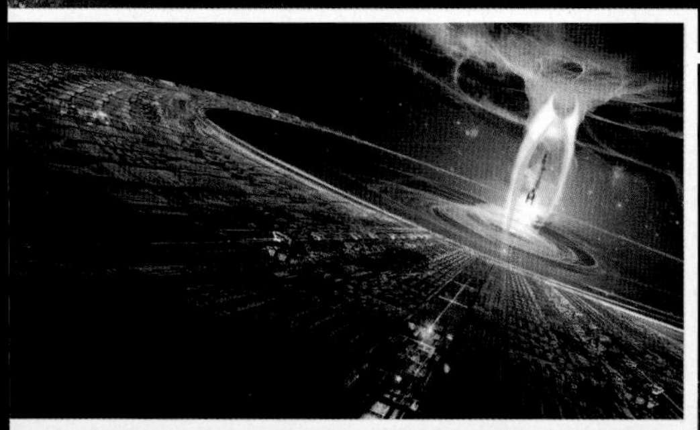

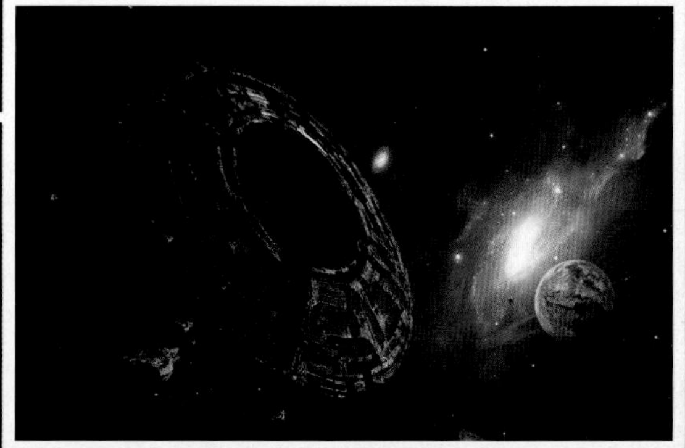

KLAUS HAUPTMAN

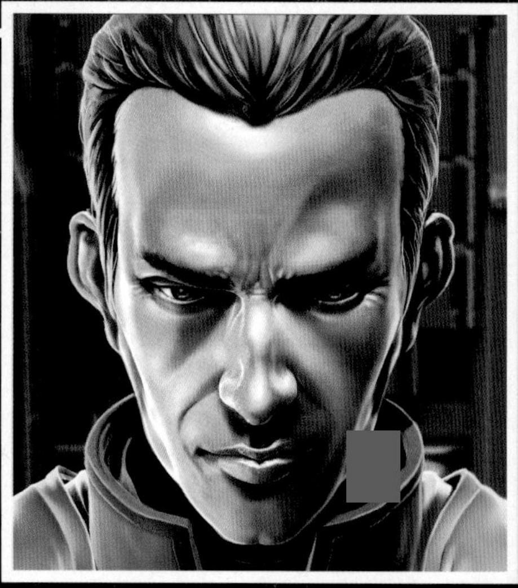

"He was shorter than she'd expected, but solid, with the dramatic white sideburns she'd always suspected were artificial. His square face and powerful jaw had certainly benefited from cosmetic surgery—no one's features could be that regular—but the fundamental architecture had been maintained. There was strength in that face, an uncompromising, self-confident assurance that went beyond mere arrogance and pugnacity, and his eyes were hard."
-*On Basilisk Station*

While Klaus's primary role in Honor Harrington's life is as antagonist (time and time again, the word associated with Hauptman is "petty"), it should be noted that from a morally objective standpoint, he rarely plays the villain. Despite being essentially the wealthiest man in the Star Kingdom, and acting head of the Hauptman merchant cartel, Hauptman detests the notion of dynasties and generational wealth. An opponent of slavery and injustice, Hauptman and Honor should have gotten along swimmingly, if it weren't for his pride – and the fact that their first interaction involved her detainment and inspection of his merchant fleets off of Medusa.

HAUPTMAN CARTEL

"I am saying, Mr. Hauptman, that the record demonstrates that the incidence of contraband in shipments registered to your firm is thirty-five percent above that of any other firm trading with Medusa. Whether you are personally involved in those illegal activities or not, I cannot, of course say."
-Honor Harrington, *On Basilisk Station*

The Hauptman Cartel is a conglomerate formed by Heinrich Hauptman following the Great Manticoran Plague, and the largest merchant cartel in the contemporary Star Kingdom of Manticore. Under its current chairman, Klaus Hauptman, the cartel's vessels and trade routes – particularly those coming to and from the planet Medusa - have come under the scru[redacted] of Basilisk Station Commander Honor Harrington, particularly for several vessels' attempts to s[redacted]ggle in hundreds of pelts of Peak Bear fur. The cost of the pelts was estimated at over $43 million (in Manticoran dollars).

DEMPSEY CARTEL

"There were no remote order terminals in Dempsey's Bar. Patrons were served by real, live waiters and waitresses—a factor, given civilian labor costs on the Navy's busiest orbital shipyard, which explained much about Dempsey's price levels."
-*Field of Dishonor*

The Dempsey Cartel, run by Erika Dempsey, is the second largest business conglomerate in the Kingdom of Manticore. While the Dempsey conglomerate is a widely respected and cutthroat organization, earning even the admiration of competitor Klaus Hauptman, the cartel owes its humble beginning to the Dempsey's Bar restaurant chain – still popular on many planets within Manticoran space. The professional duelist and all-around scoundrel, Denver Summervale, is known to frequent several Dempsey's Bar locations.

JANKOWSKI CARTEL

"In fact, Gearman thought, Jankowski's who handled the major share of R&D on adapting the Grayson compensator design for the fleet, aren't they?"
-*Echoes of Honor*

Focusing mainly on research and development, the Jankowski cartel is especially loyalist – as long as the Manticoran Navy renews its contracts. When the Grayson Navy adjusted its inertial compensator designs, giving their ships a serious edge in battle, it was the Jankowski cartel that adapted this model for the Manticoran Navy, thereby evening the odds.

DILLINGHAM CARTEL

"We've got something much better...bait. We know that every pirate in the sector knows about the Dillingham Cartel's installations here in Melchor."
-*Changer of Worlds*, "Ms. Midshipwoman Harrington"

While a Manticoran owned and operated conglomerate, the Dillingham Cartel maintains substantial interests in the Melchor system, located in Silesian space. Dillingham mining operations led to conflicts with local pirates and Silesian authorities; in response, the conglomerate sinks a disproportionate amount of funds into local defense projects.

JORDAN CARTEL

"The baron's involvement in the Jordan Cartel had been hidden behind more than a dozen layers of dummy shareholders, but the last Earl of North Hollow had discovered it."
-*Field of Dishonor*

Having utterly failed to deliver a new batch of Apollo cruisers for the Manticoran Navy, the Jordan Cartel's military production contracts were terminated, and given over to the vastly more lucrative Hauptman Cartel. As time wore on, the cartel was whittled down from within due to insider trading and shareholder scandal, leading to its eventual collapse.

INERTIA

This is the reason I fell in love with the Honorverse. Every other Sci-Fi epic uses pseudo-science to overlook this. *Star Trek* has "inertial dampeners".

Inertia is (from Wikipedia) "the resistance of any physical object to any change in its state of motion, including changes to its speed and direction. It is the tendency of objects to keep moving in a straight line at constant velocity."

In plain speak, you can't just turn on a dime. So if you're flying in a ship at insane speeds, it would take time for you to turn and you would continue along the original direction until you countered it going the other way. If you were flying in a straight line north (for easy example I'm aware there's no north in space) then turned west using your engine to fly that westward direction, you'd actually fly in a north-northwest direction in a curve until you eventually would be flying northwest/west. These videos demonstrate that curve.

https://www.youtube.com/watch?v=8zsE3mpZ6Hw

https://www.youtube.com/watch?v=T1ux9D7-O38

http://en.wikipedia.org/wiki/Inertia

We're going to mix it up a bit with the next volume and do something more original and less a pure adaptation of the novels. The novels exist and they're perfect the way they are, so doing a pure comic book adaptation seems to fall a bit short of the depth and emotional resonance of the novels themselves. This volume we just wrapped up tells the story of the first novel, *On Basilisk Station*, but framed with story from the seventh novel, *In Enemy Hands*.

Here are the main novels in order and release years:

On Basilisk Station (1993)

The Honor of the Queen (1993)

The Short Victorious War (1994)

Field of Dishonor (1994)

Flag in Exile (1995)

Honor Among Enemies (1996)

In Enemy Hands (1997)

Echoes of Honor (1998)

Ashes of Victory (2000)

War of Honor (2002)

At All Costs (2005)

Mission of Honor (2010)

A Rising Thunder (2012)

Shadow of Freedom (2013)

BAEN
SCIENCE FICTION
DAVID WEBER IN ENEMY HANDS
DAVID WEBER HONOR AMONG ENEMIES
DAVID WEBER FLAG IN EXILE
DAVID WEBER FIELD OF DISHONOR
DAVID WEBER THE SHORT VICTORIOUS WAR
DAVID WEBER THE HONOR OF THE QUEEN
DAVID WEBER
ON BASILISK STATION

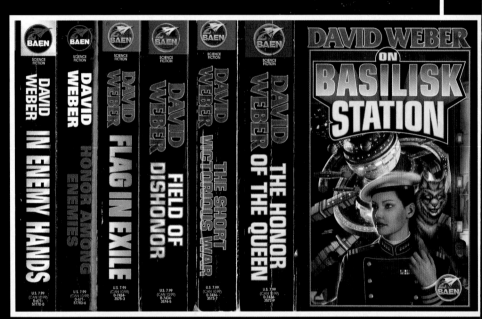

You can buy and read these now! Both *On Basilisk Station* and *The Honor of the Queen* are free on Kindle and iBooks. We're still finalizing what we're doing for the next volume, and we're targeting to launch the next single issue in March 2015. It will be written by me and painted by Linda Sejic, who just collaborated with me on Wildfire.

Carpe Diem!

Matt Hawkins

@topcowmatt
https://www.facebook.com/Selfloathingnarcissist

TALES OF HONOR

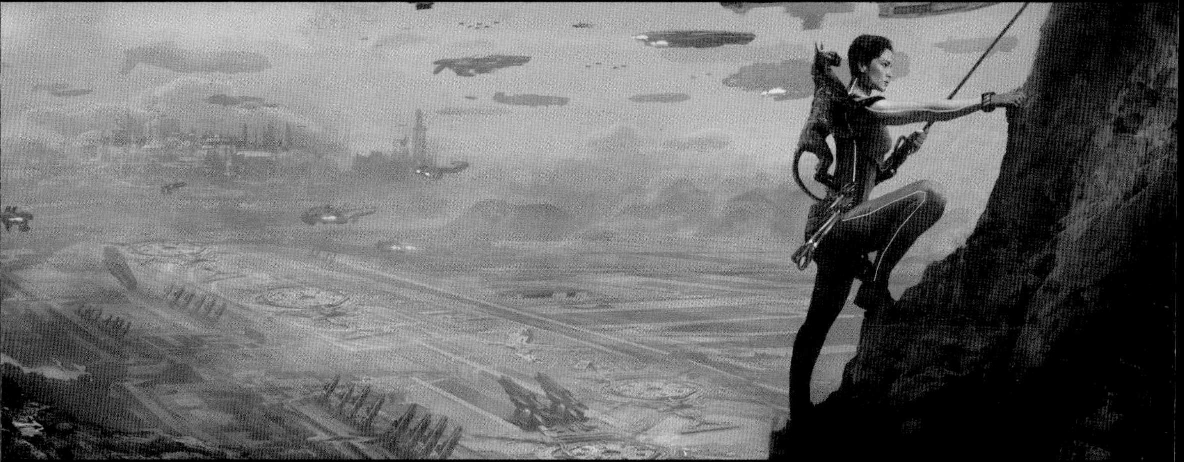

COVER GALLERY

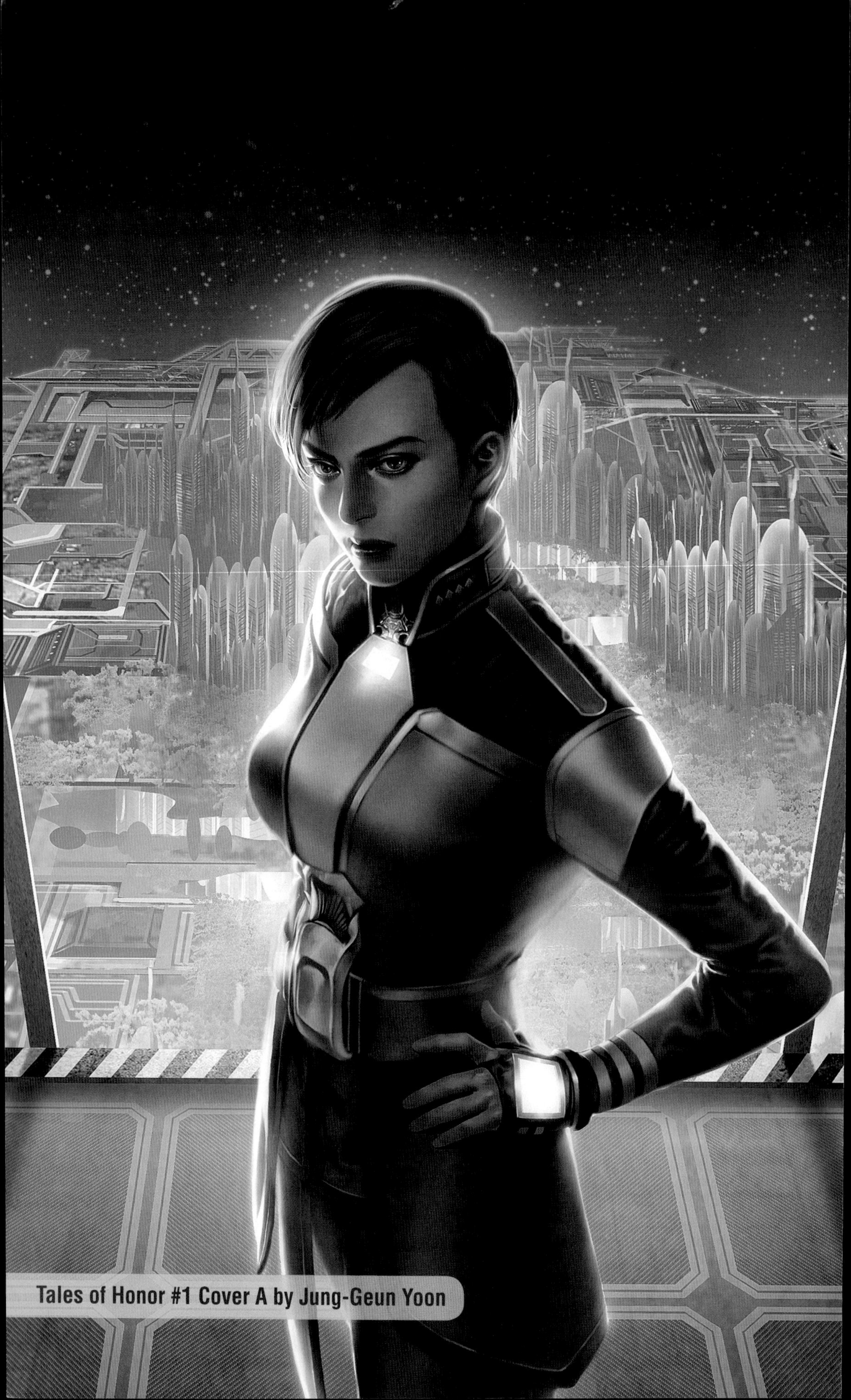

Tales of Honor #1 Cover A by Jung-Geun Yoon

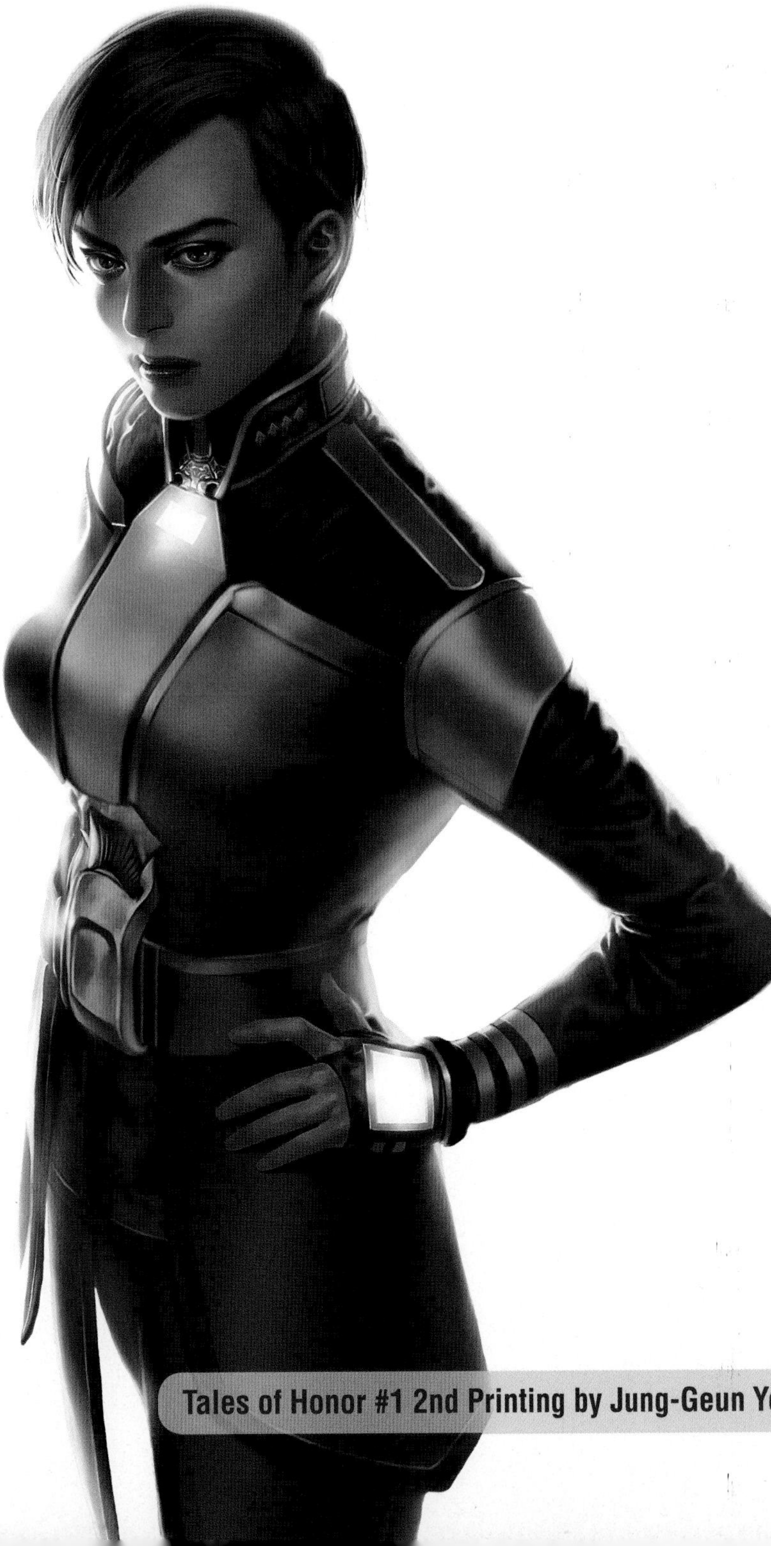

Tales of Honor #1 2nd Printing by Jung-Geun Yoon

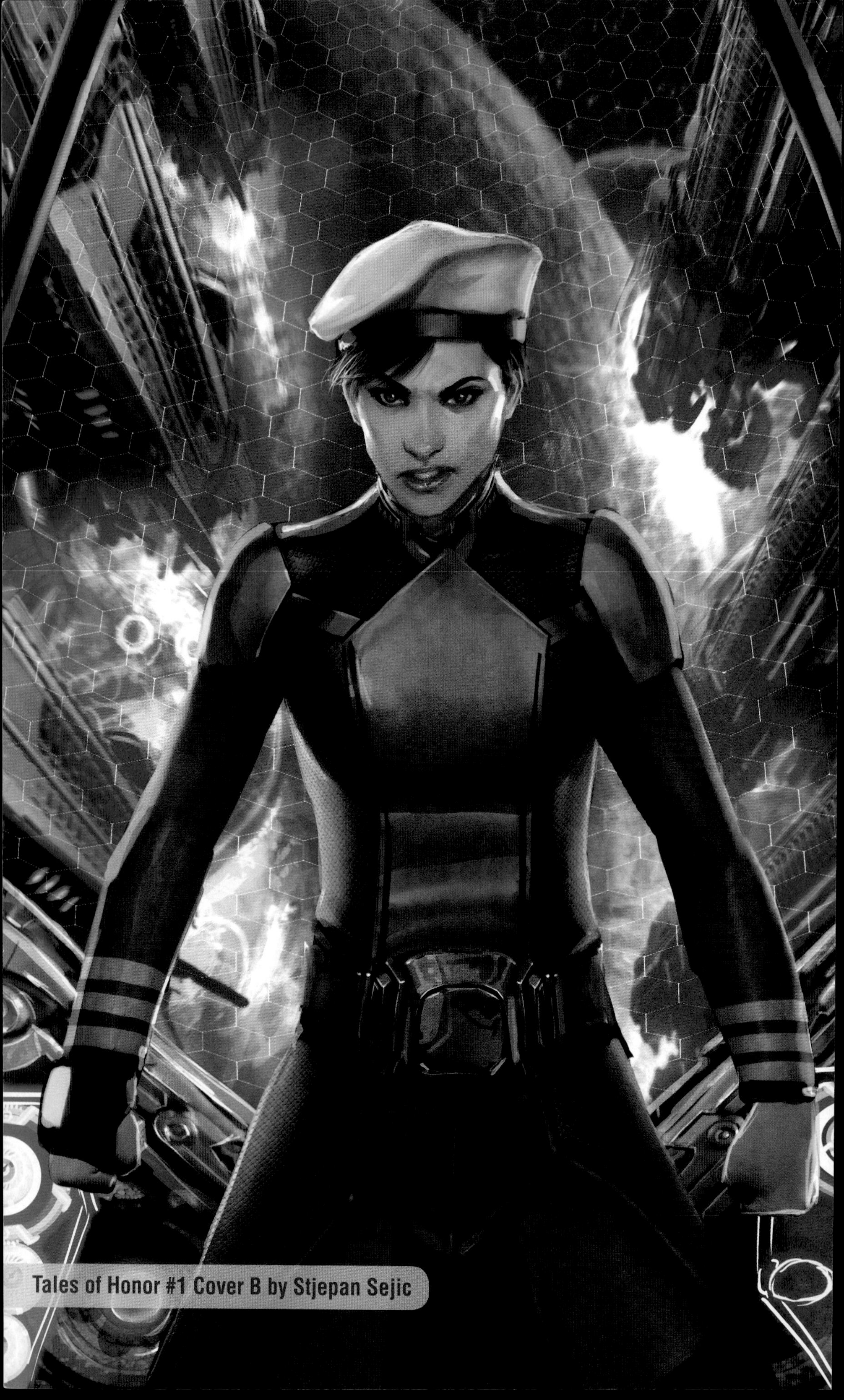

Tales of Honor #1 Cover B by Stjepan Sejic

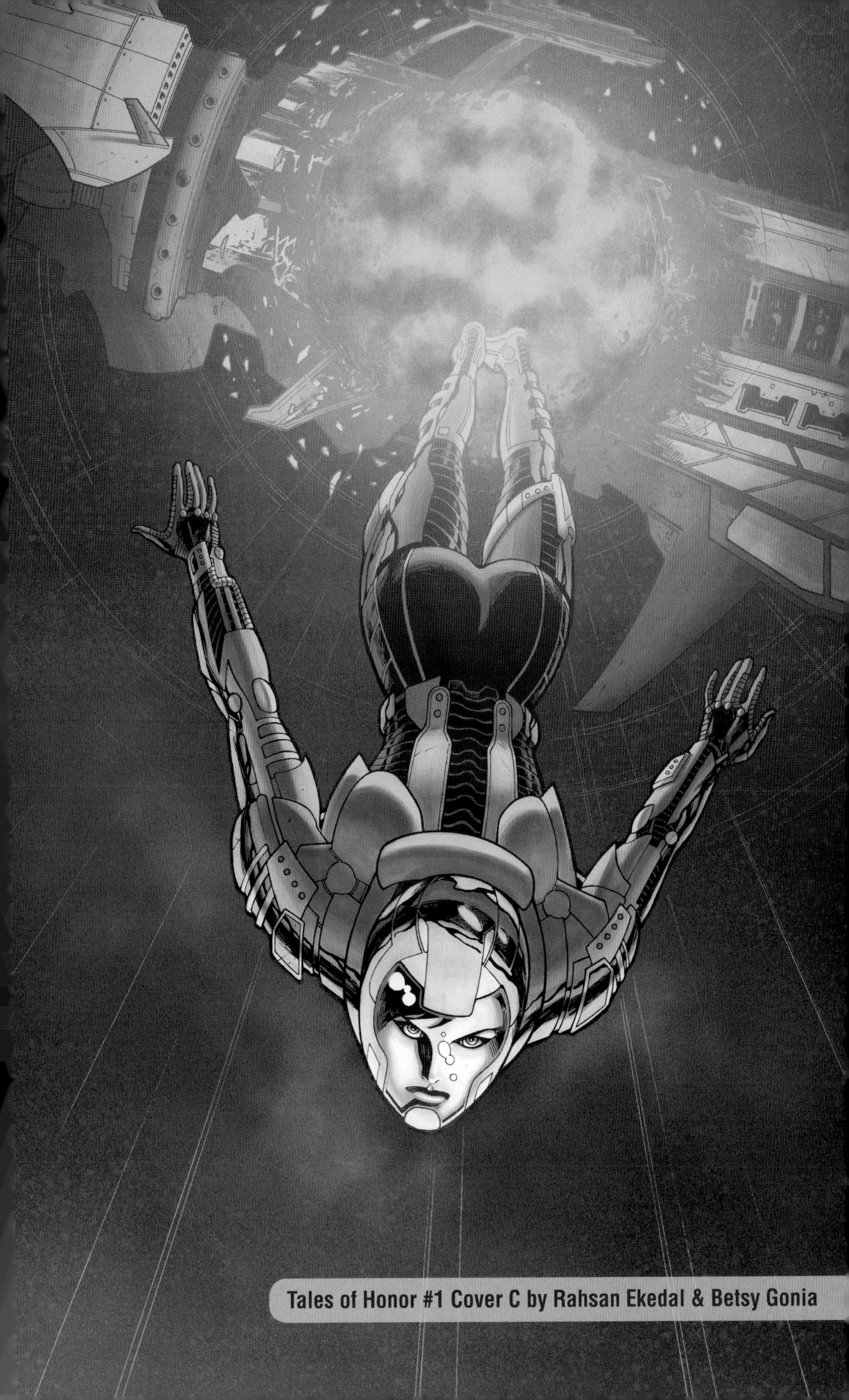

Tales of Honor #1 Cover C by Rahsan Ekedal & Betsy Gonia

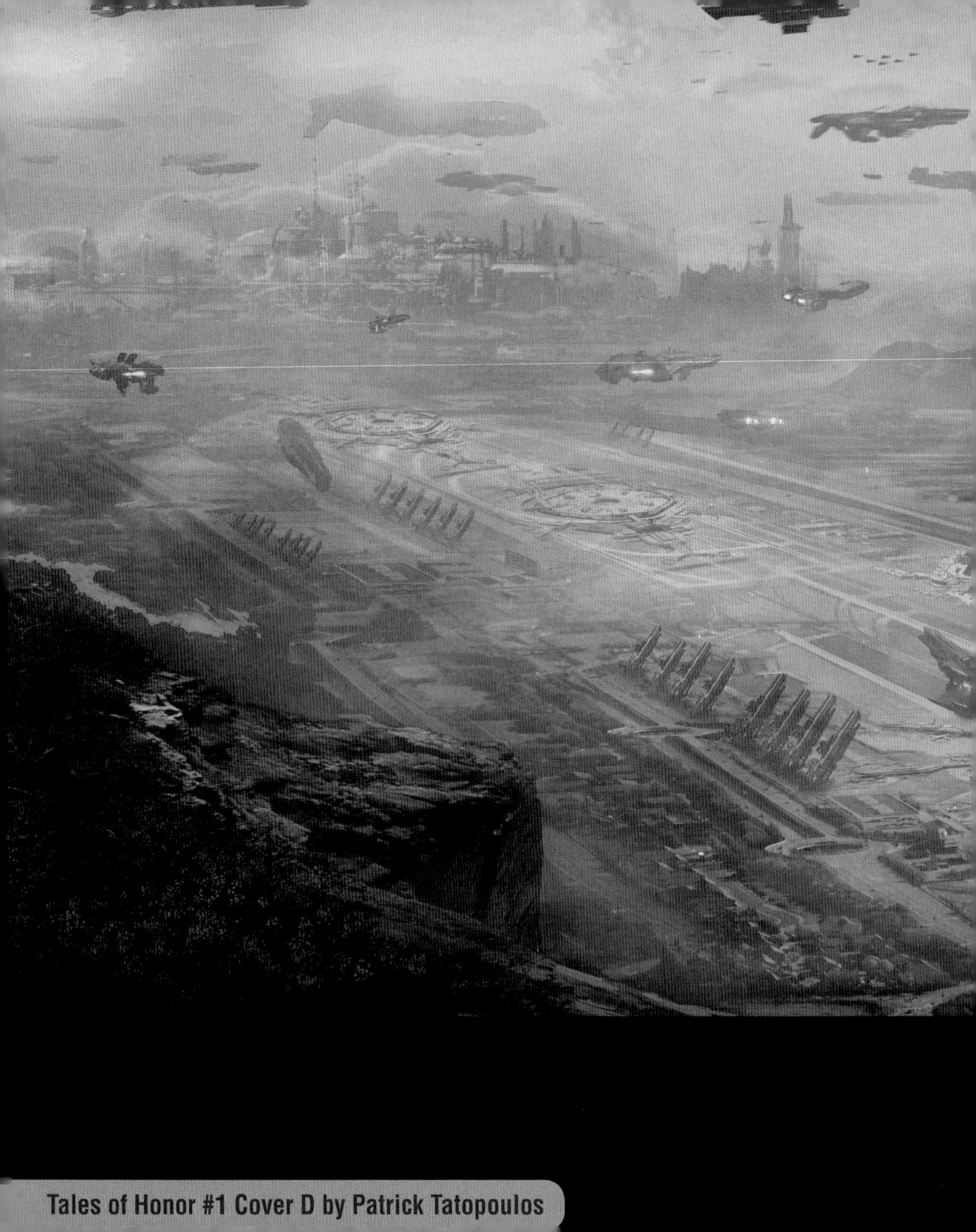

Tales of Honor #1 Cover D by Patrick Tatopoulos

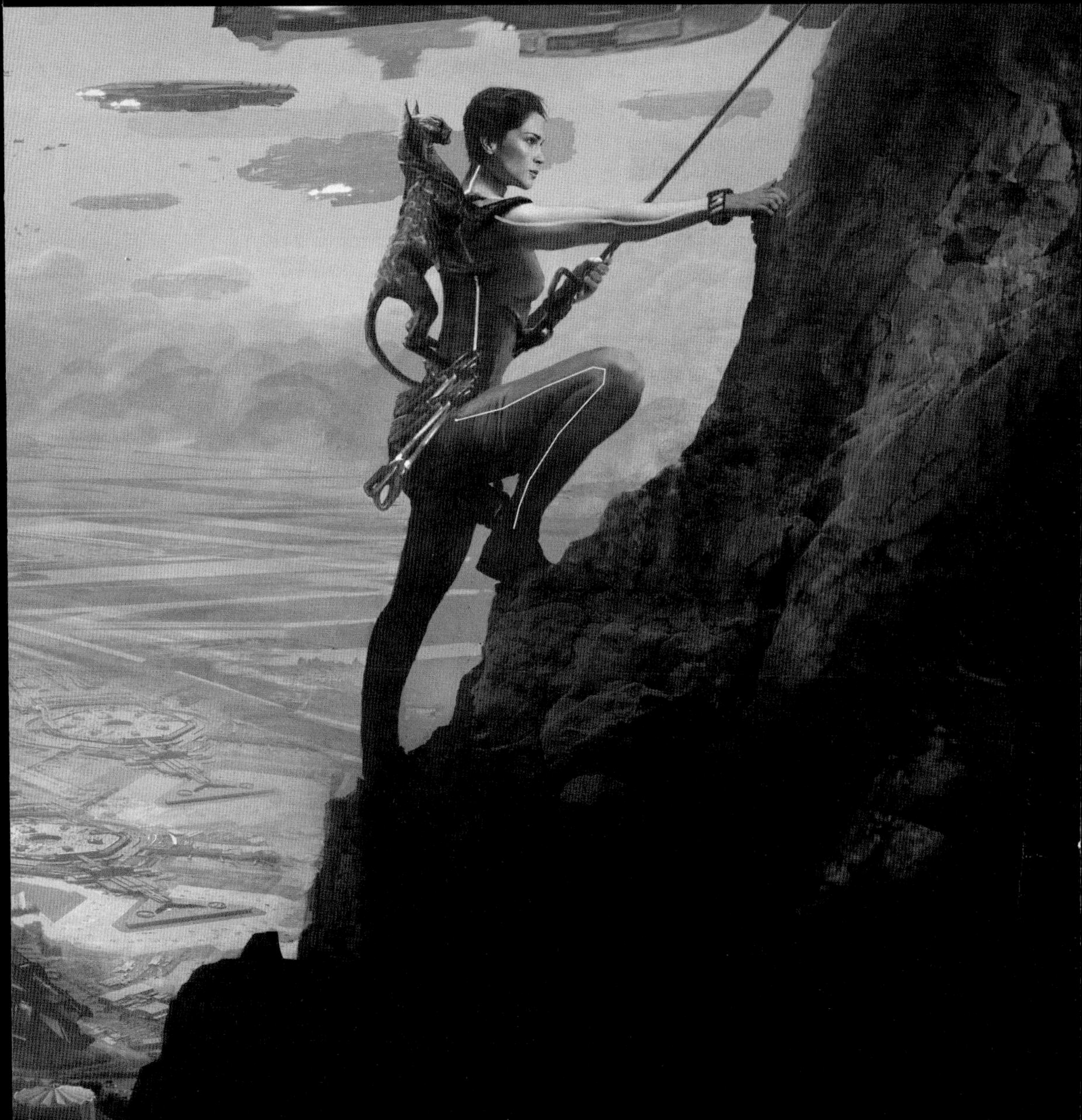

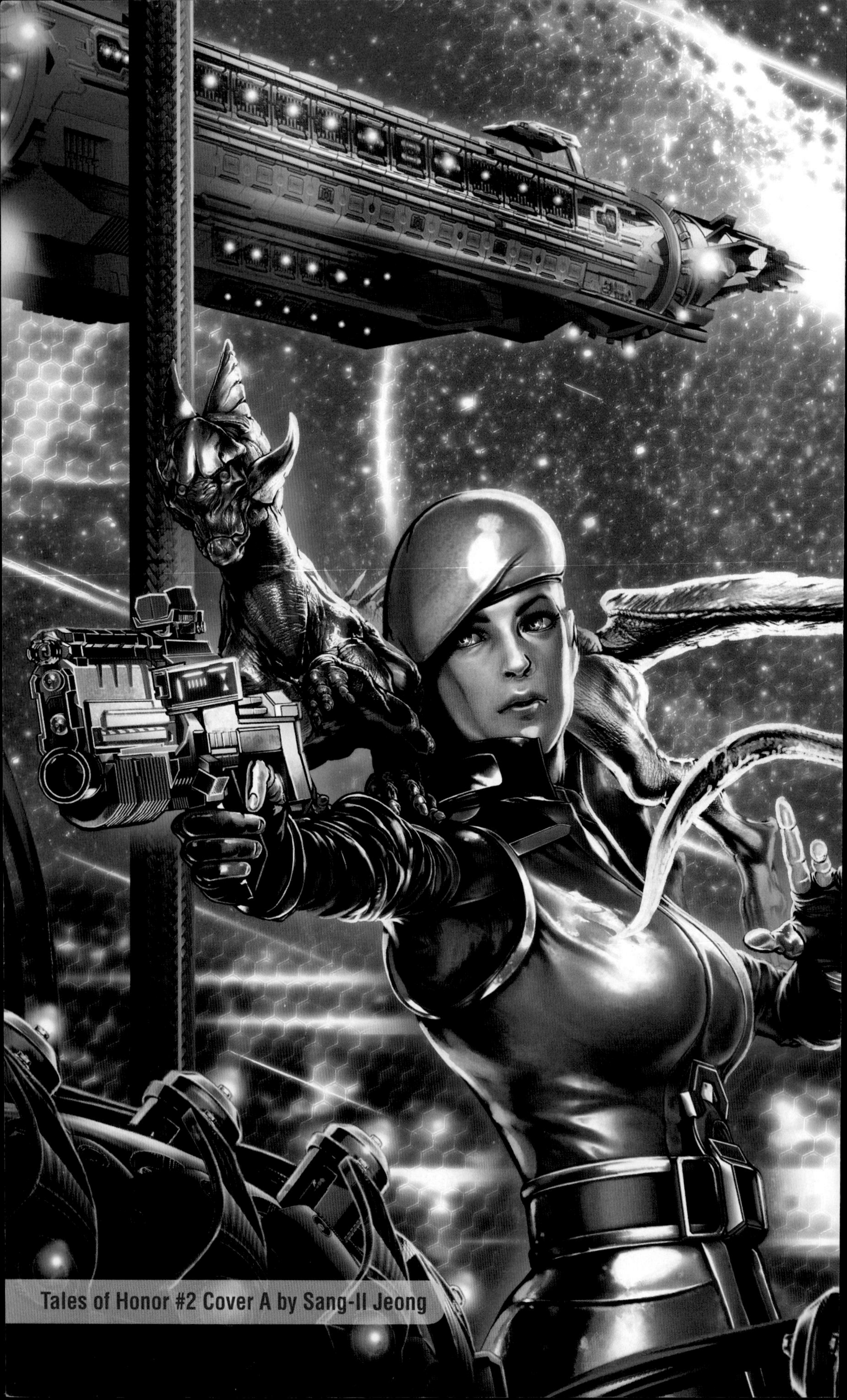

Tales of Honor #2 Cover A by Sang-Il Jeong

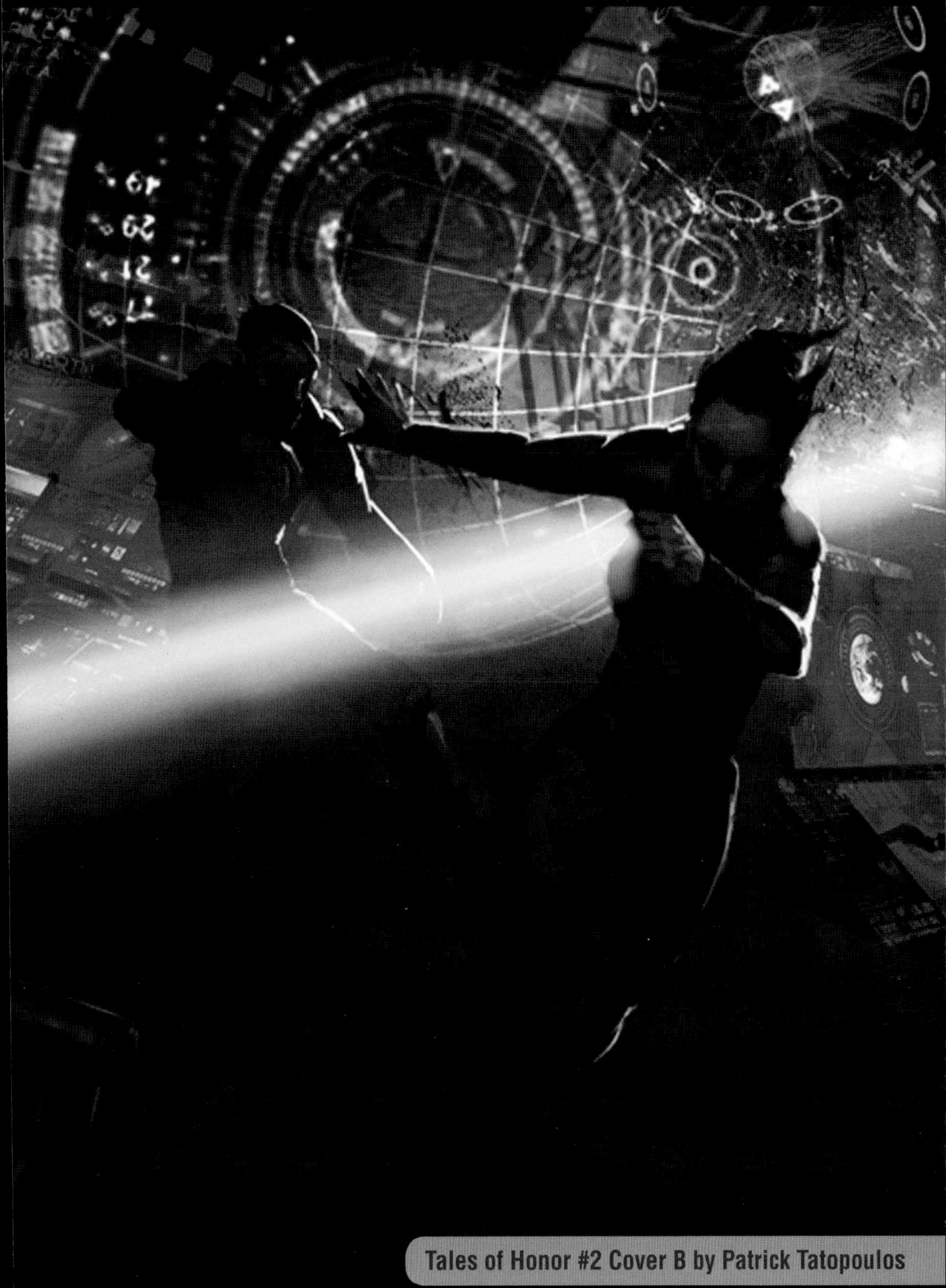

Tales of Honor #2 Cover B by Patrick Tatopoulos

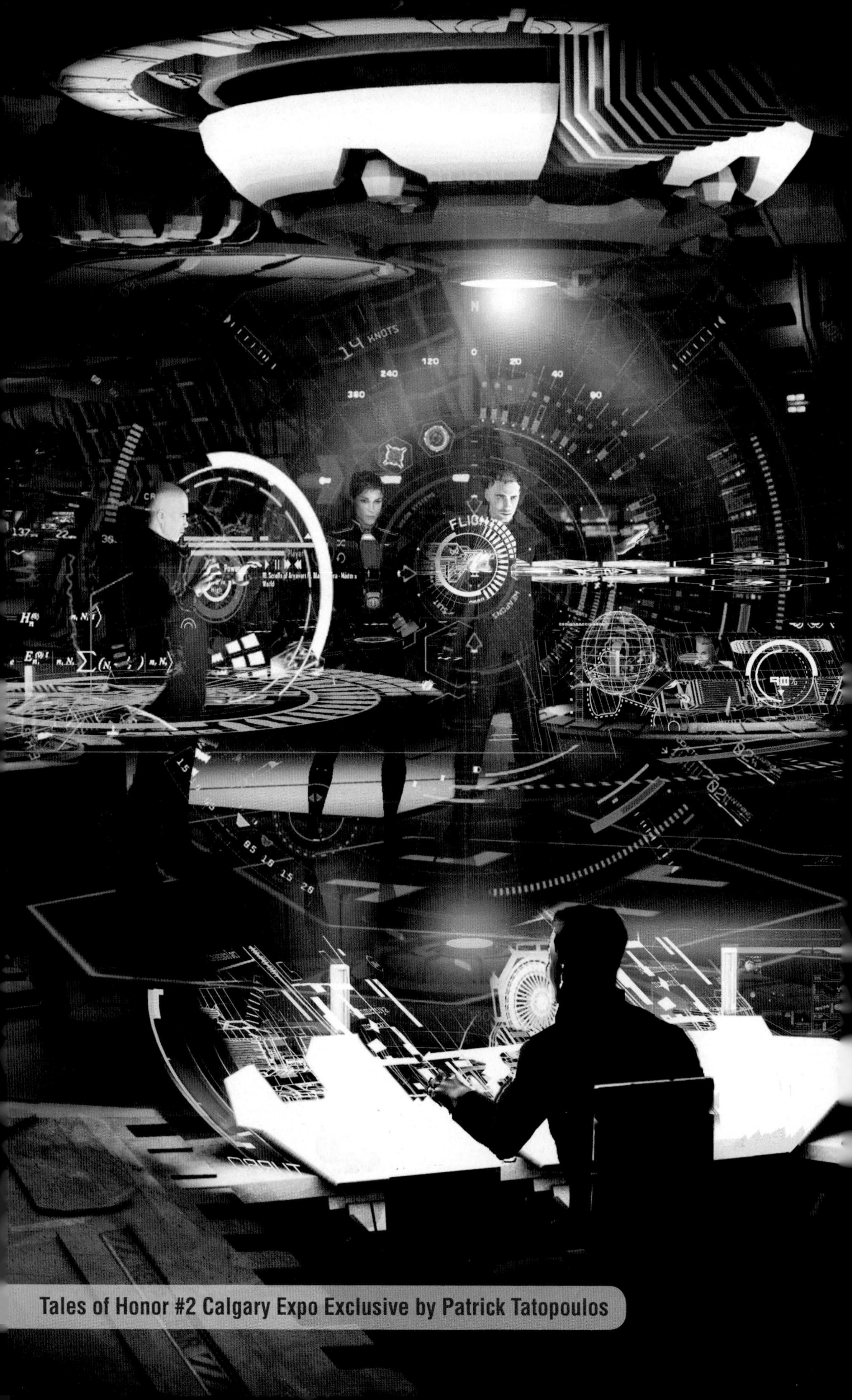
14 KNOTS

Tales of Honor #2 Calgary Expo Exclusive by Patrick Tatopoulos

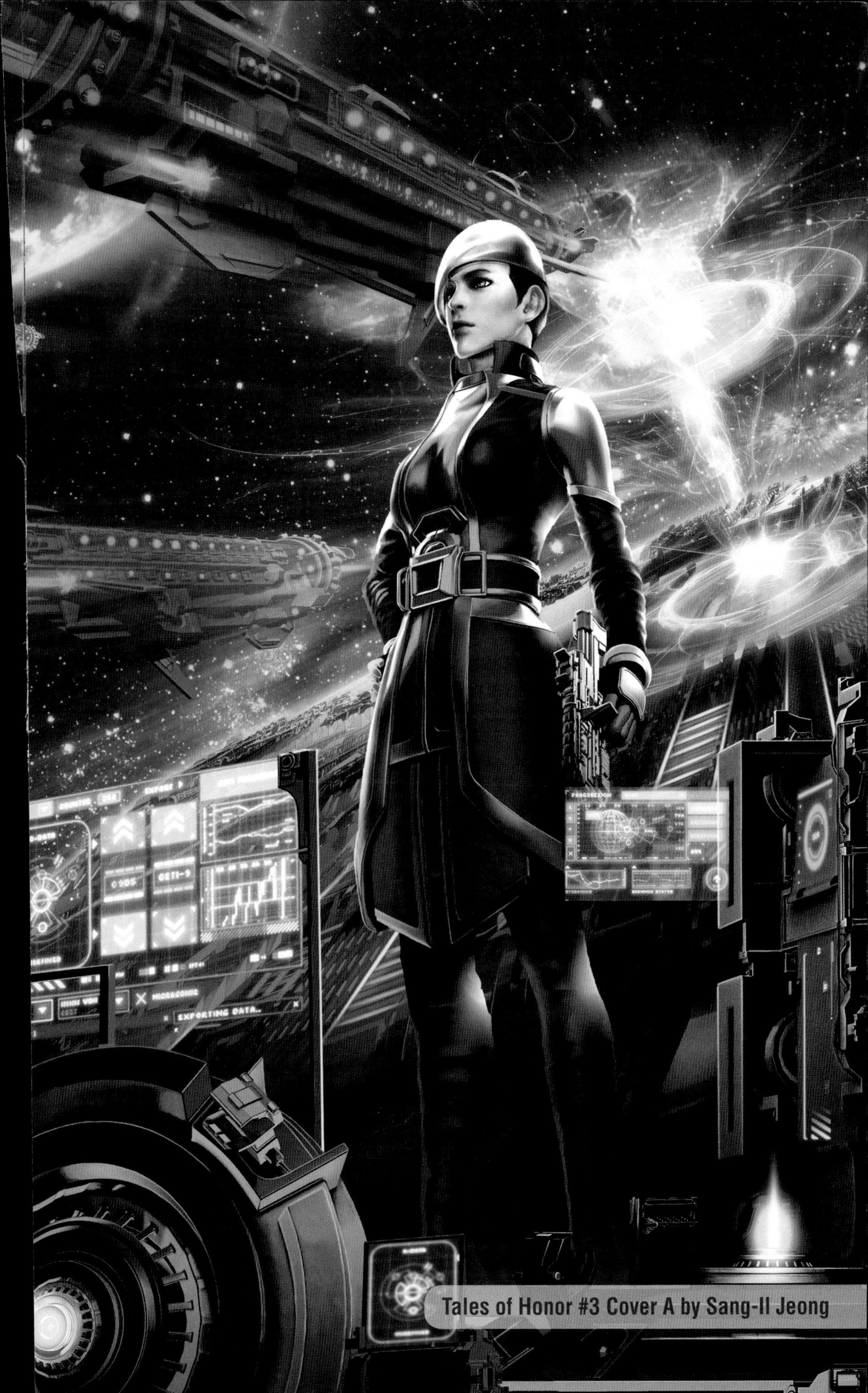
EXPORTING DATA..

Tales of Honor #3 Cover A by Sang-Il Jeong

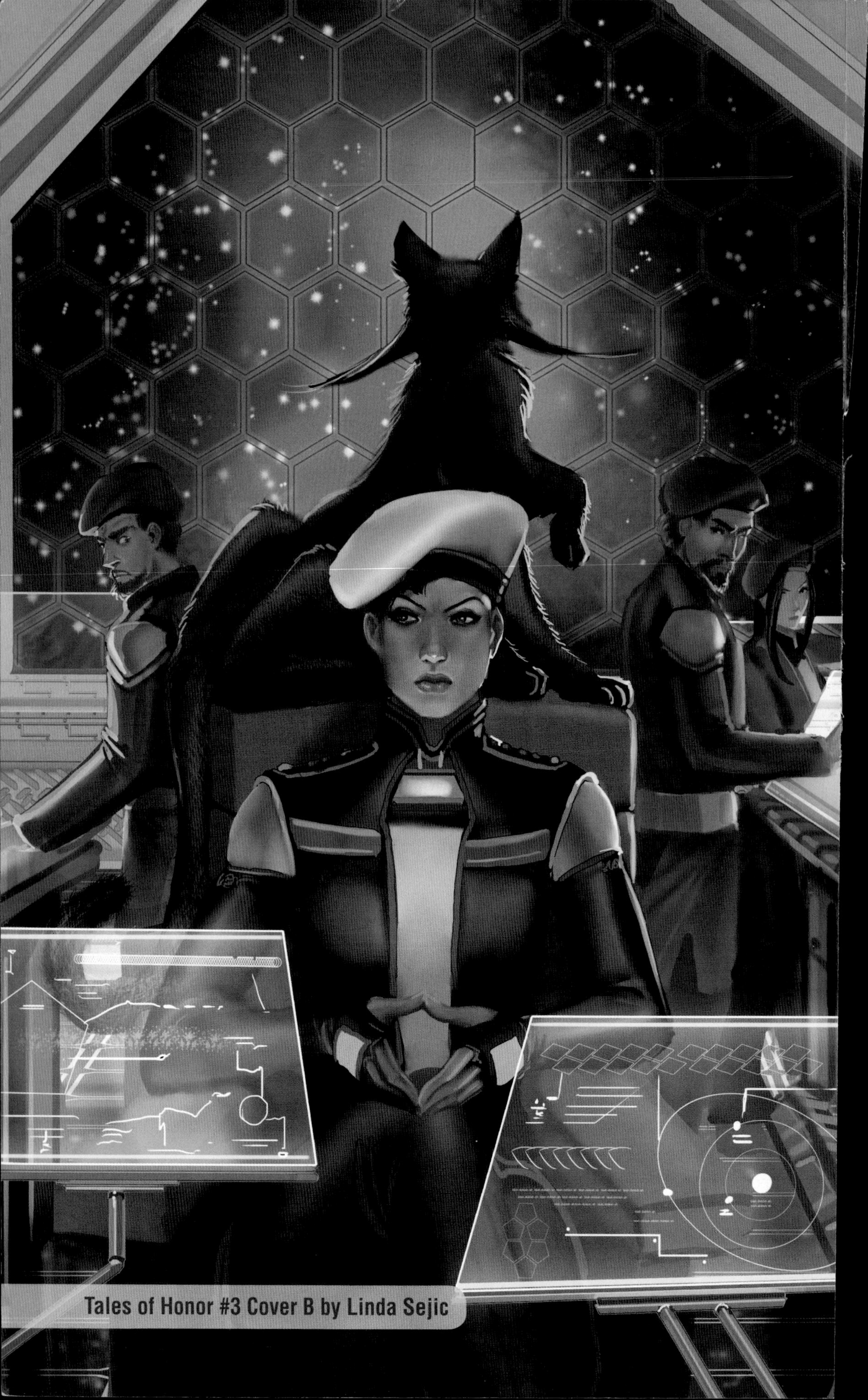

Tales of Honor #3 Cover B by Linda Sejic

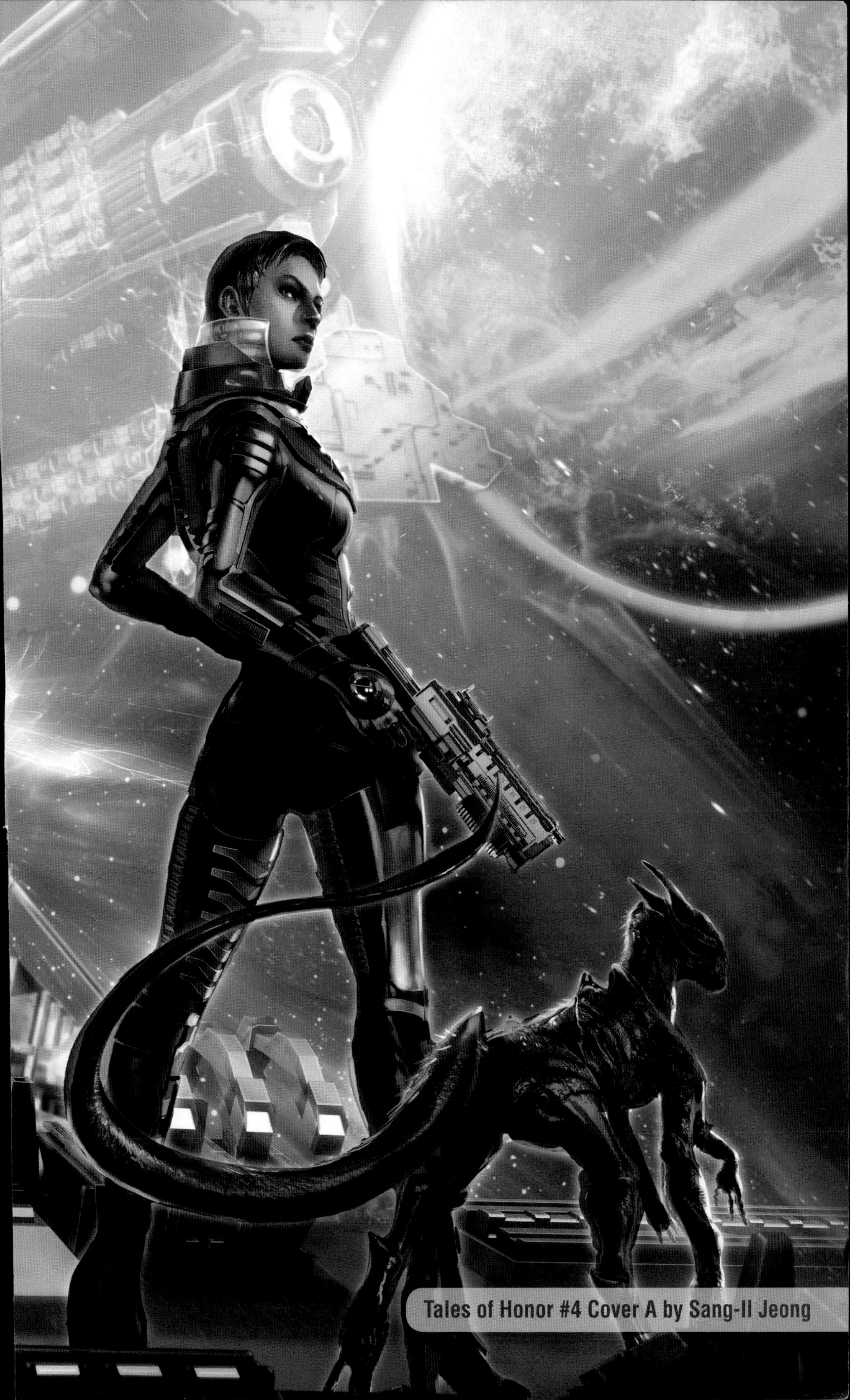

Tales of Honor #4 Cover A by Sang-Il Jeong

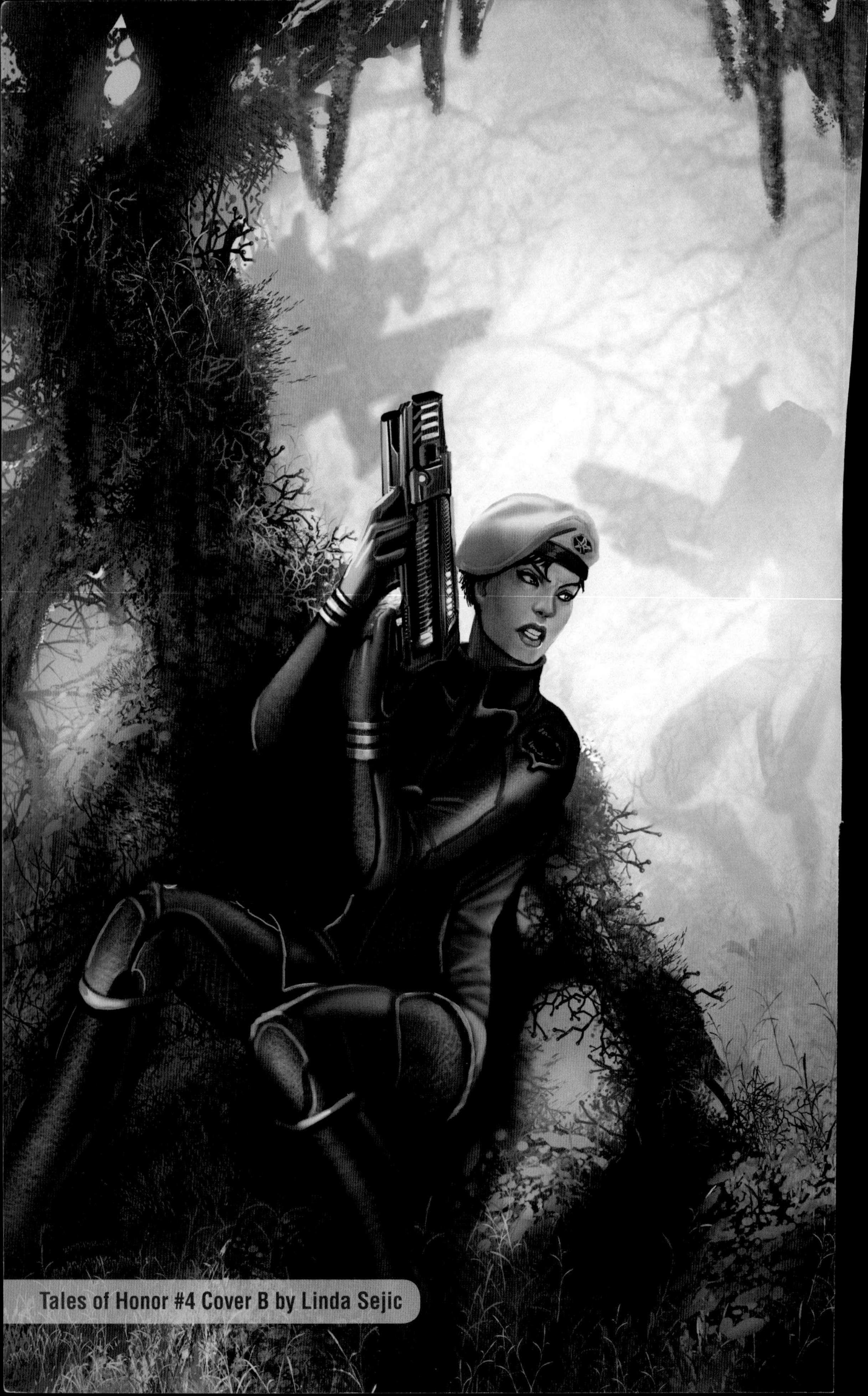

Tales of Honor #4 Cover B by Linda Sejic

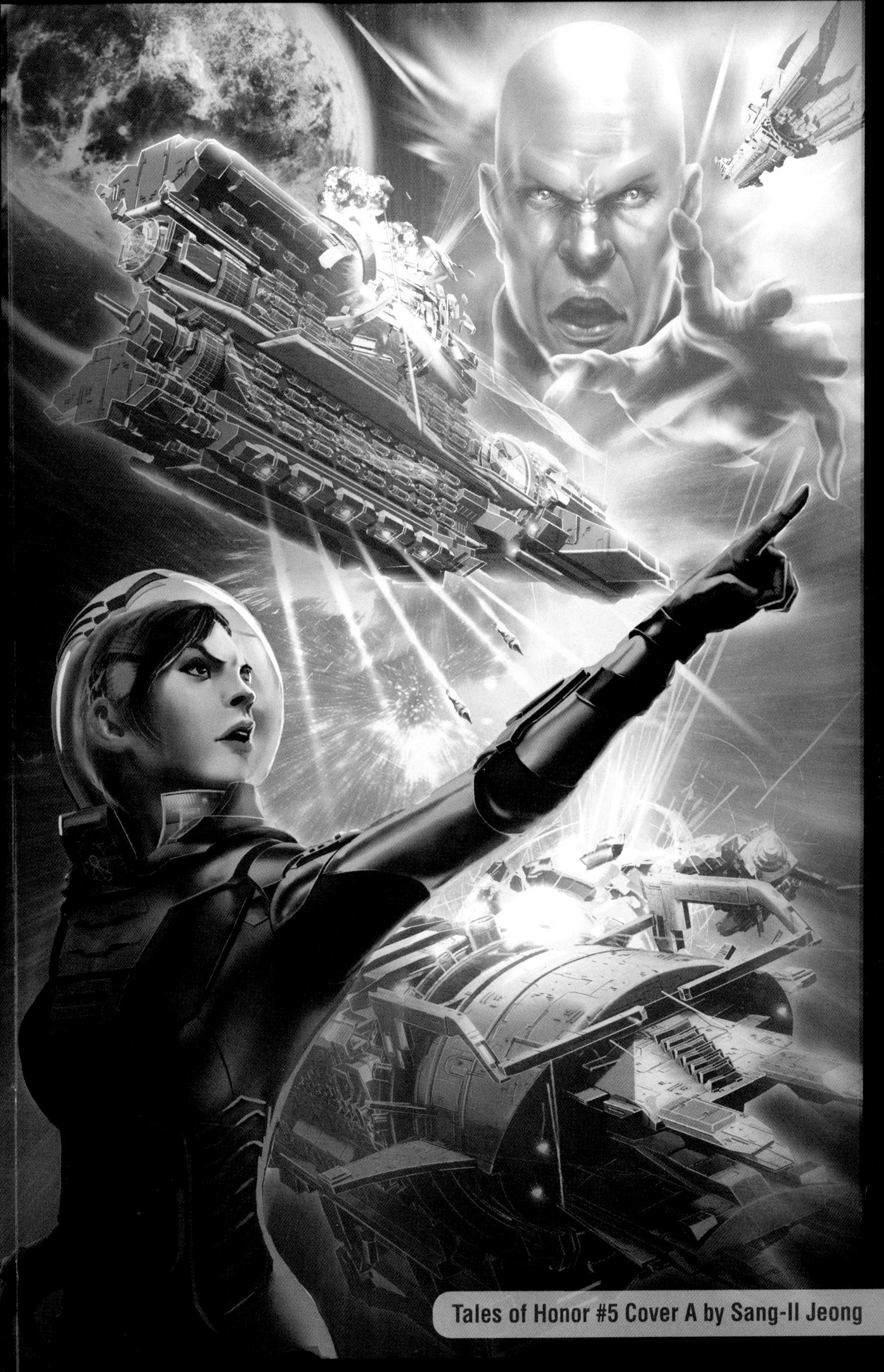

Tales of Honor #5 Cover A by Sang-Il Jeong

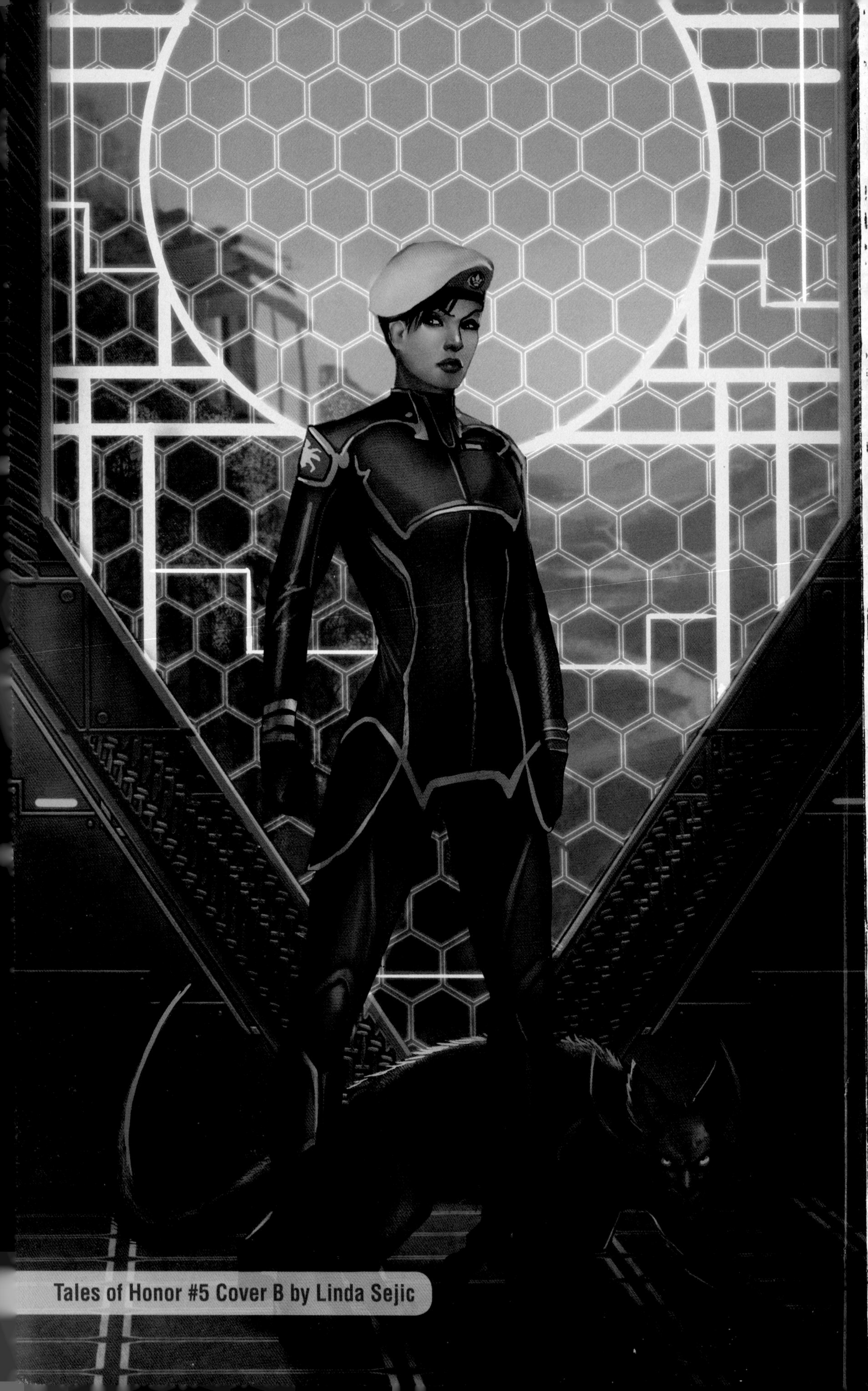

Tales of Honor #5 Cover B by Linda Sejic